# HUMAN NATURE IN POLITICS

NOMOS

# XVII

# N O M O S

# NOMOS XVII

Yearbook of the American Society for Political and Legal Philosophy

# HUMAN NATURE
# IN POLITICS

Edited by

J. ROLAND PENNOCK  *Swarthmore College*

and

JOHN W. CHAPMAN  *University of Pittsburgh*

New York: New York University Press, 1977

JF
2049
. H85

*Human Nature in Politics: Nomos XVII*
J. Roland Pennock and John W. Chapman, editors

Copyright © 1977 by New York University

LCC: 76-23506
ISBN: 0-8147-6568-8
Serial Publication Number: US-ISSN-0078-0979

Manufactured in the United States of America

# PREFACE

The meetings of the American Society for Political and Legal Philosophy held in September 1972 in conjunction with the meetings of the American Political Science Association were devoted to the subject of "Human Nature and Politics." As ancient, and some not so ancient, theorists proposed cyclical theories of the forms of government, so, it might be suggested, the topics that are of especial interest in any particular discipline at a given time exhibit a somewhat cyclical pattern. Arthur O. Lovejoy's *Reflections on Human Nature,* originally delivered as lectures in 1941, was largely a study of the thought of the eighteenth century. In recent times the subject has been out of fashion—until the very *most* recent times, that is. Today, it appears to be staging a comeback.

As is generally and properly the case, in such instances, the present approach is quite different from that of earlier times. Psychology and genetics have supplied us with mountains of new information bearing on the subject. The armchair philosopher must give way to the speculative theorist who is armed with scientific information.

While customarily *Nomos* volumes comprise the revised papers and comments presented at the annual meetings, supplemented by other papers volunteered by members of the Society or solicited by the editors, this year the shoe is on the other foot. Only one chapter of this book, that by Richard Brandt, was presented at the annual meetings, while two others, those by Bernard Gert and Felix Oppenheim, were prompted by it. A fourth author, James C. Davies, participated in the meetings as a commentator, but accepted the editors' encouragement to elaborate his own theory for the volume rather than to confine himself to the comments on Brandt's paper that he presented at the meetings. The other major papers, and with them the comments based upon them, for various reasons fell by the wayside. One of them, for instance, while in the process of being revised and "condensed," grew to book length!

To these authors, to the others who have contributed to the volume, and doubly to George Armstrong Kelly, who both served as program chairman for the meetings and contributed a chapter to the volume, the editors express their gratitude.

This year, as every year since the present editors took over, Eleanor Greitzer has performed invaluable service as editorial assistant. We are deeply indebted to her for her combination of overall comprehension with sharp-eyed attention to detail.

Members of the Society and other regular readers of *Nomos* will note that Charles Lieber, who has for twelve years provided a comfortable publishing home for these volumes, has now relinquished that responsibility. His friendly help and counsel have been a constant source of pleasure and satisfaction to the editors. Happily, the series will henceforth appear under the imprint of New York University Press.

J.R.P.
J.W.C.

# CONTENTS

# CONTRIBUTORS

RICHARD BRANDT
*Philosophy, University of Michigan*

JOHN W. CHAPMAN
*Political Science, University of Pittsburgh*

PETER A. CORNING
*Political Science, Stanford University*

JAMES CHOWNING DAVIES
*Political Science, University of Oregon*

BERNARD GERT
*Philosophy, Dartmouth College*

DONALD W. KEIM
*Formerly Political Science, Baldwin-Wallace College*

GEORGE ARMSTRONG KELLY
*Political Science, Brandeis University*

ROGER D. MASTERS
*Political Science, Dartmouth College*

LISA H. NEWTON
*Philosophy, Fairfield University*

FELIX E. OPPENHEIM
*Philosophy and Political Science, University of Massachusetts*

J. ROLAND PENNOCK
*Political Science, Swarthmore College*

LYMAN TOWER SARGENT
*Political Science, University of Missouri–St.Louis*

MARVIN ZETTERBAUM
*Political Science, University of California, Davis*

# 1

# INTRODUCTION

## J. ROLAND PENNOCK

### "HUMAN NATURE" IN THE HISTORY
### OF POLITICAL THEORY

As long as men have speculated about the nature of politics, it has been common to relate it to the nature of man. Most of the speculators have had no doubt that man had a "nature" and therefore have believed certain generalizations could be made about the way men tended to behave under certain conditions. Some to be sure focused upon the differences among kinds of human nature, whether of gold, of silver, or of bronze; but even Plato and Nietzsche (if the juxtaposition may be forgiven) assumed a common substratum. Most have thought with Aristotle that man was a "political" animal, that is, that something about his nature demanded

1

a life of organized and fixed interaction—"fixed" meaning here
that most people would remain part of a particular organized system larger than the family throughout their lives. It was also believed that this organization would need to have coercive power,
including power over life and liberty, a power not usually acknowledged as being rightly exercised by any other organization.

Typically, theories of human nature have played several roles
in political theorizing. First, they frequently figure in the justification of the state, in particular of the obligation, other things being
equal, to obey governments. The contractualists have assumed that
men's natural needs and demands are such as to bring them ultimately into competition with one another, and that men will tend
to be partial to themselves and those near and dear to them as
opposed to those beyond the pale—wherever that pale might be
located. In short, they have held that conceptions of justice, whether
natural or conventional, would be insufficient in themselves to
counter man's self-partiality. This much at least they have held in
common: men's requirements come into competition with one
another. Some, with Hobbes, would stress their need for respect,
indeed for "glory" (precedence over others); others, like Locke,
were concerned that in the distribution of rights (whether of life,
liberty, or estate) man's partiality to himself would lead to continual "states of war," as men sought justice to all, and especially
to themselves, where their claims came into conflict with those of
others. Even Rousseau was firmly convinced that, once men
reached that state of relative plenty beyond the most primitive
self-sufficiency, competition would lead to the breakdown of peaceable societies and to the establishment of government as the necessary means for the protection of man's natural rights. Even that
sympathy on which Rousseau so greatly relied, once society gave
it occasion to develop, served only to moderate the "impetuosity
of egoism."[1]

If we turn from the contractualists to those who held that the
state was "natural," how different was the situation? Take Aristotle, perhaps the prime exemplar of this school of thought. For
him of course the state was natural, as was the obligation to obey
its laws, because through it alone could man achieve his end, his
"natural destination," in Bradley's phrase. Virtue, which it is man's
end to achieve, calls for laws to regulate behavior, for "to live a
hard and sober life is not an attractive prospect for most"; and

"people are by and large readier to submit to punishment and compulsion than moved by arguments and ideals."[2] The emphasis here is less on the protection of the individual from others than on the development of the best self. Yet the latter cannot be counted on to proceed without political (legal) support. "Man, when perfected, is the best of animals"; Aristotle declared, "but if he be isolated from law and justice he is the worst of all.[3] For the contractualists as well as for Aristotle it is the weakness of man's natural inclination to be virtuous and to act justly that calls for the establishment of the state.[4]

Those who oppose the coercive state—anarchists and Marxists —likewise ground their arguments, explicitly or implicitly, on theories of human nature. Thus Godwin declared that "No man who has ever produced or contemplated the happiness of others with a liberal mind will deny that this exercise is infinitely the most pleasurable of sensations."[5] This naive Utilitarian view was quite different from that of Marx. Like Aristotle and John Stuart Mill, Marx held a developmental theory of human nature. But his theory differed from theirs not only as to the conditions necessary for full development but also with respect to the nature of that development. For Marx, once man rises to the level of species-being, all tension between individual and society vanishes. "The individual *is* the *social being*."[6] Man's true nature, once it is free from all the encumbrances and distorting, even destructive, influences of bourgeois society, reveals itself as devoid of the evils of competitiveness and self-partiality, fully capable of participating in a cooperative commonwealth, in which each would give according to his means and receive according to his needs.

Theories of human nature have also frequently—one is tempted to say "always"—been used to justify particular institutions of government. Thus for Hobbes it was again man's competitiveness-aggressiveness that made absolute monarchy appear to be the best solution to the human predicament. For Rousseau and for the early Utilitarians it was, in somewhat varying proportions, man's rational self-interest and his sympathy or benevolence that made democracy at once possible and desirable. Without abandoning his father's position, John Stuart Mill added an Aristotelian twist to the theory by stressing the development of man's moral and intellectual capacities. In his view experience broadens and deepens men's sympathies with their fellow men, leading them to act increasingly in ways that advance the interests of others.

While democracy thus found support from a theory of human nature that simply moderated the excessive egoism (and pridefulness!) of Hobbes's man, at the same time adding a pinch of sympathy or benevolence, aristocracy relied upon a rather different approach to human nature. Like other aristocrats, Plato gave less attention to certain alleged universal qualities of man than to the distribution of differential qualities. Without necessarily following to the letter Plato's assumption of the hierarchical distribution of the rational, courageous, and appetitive elements of man's nature throughout society, aristocrats generally rest their preference among governmental forms upon the belief that the distribution of ability and morality is steeply pyramidal and tends to perpetuate itself by heredity. General altruism cannot be relied upon to check man's self-seeking proclivities; but a relatively small and intelligent part of the whole, just because it *is* privileged, can be counted on to develop qualities of leadership and a sense of *noblesse oblige* that make good government possible in spite of the ignorance, apathy, shortsightedness, and self-interestedness of the masses. In modified degree, democratic elitists such as John Stuart Mill, Walter Lippmann, and Joseph A. Schumpeter adopt the same line of reasoning, the same assumptions about human nature.

The theory of separation of powers, as expounded by Montesquieu and others, and generally theories of mixed government, to which it is closely allied, all rely on the assumption that persons to whom political power is committed will tend to abuse it: they will be partial to themselves and to the group or class to which they belong.

Finally, theorists regularly rely upon theories of human nature to justify particular policies and more general policy stances. For instance, Machiavelli, making use of the distinction between political and nonpolitical men, or activists and apathetics as we might say today, assumes (argues from history) that it is better to be feared than to be loved, that most men are untrustworthy, indeed venal.[7] In a somewhat different vein, Burke found justification for a conservative stance in man's limited rationality, making it the part of wisdom to rely heavily upon tradition, "the capital of the ages." Mill, with a more optimistic view of man's rationality (or at least of his inclination to be deferential to those who *are* rational), arrived at a more liberal position in terms of policy as well as with respect to forms of government. And Marx, taking the most optimistic view possible, assumed that human nature is potentially cooperative and communal to the exclusion of any but the most benign competitiveness. Consequently an economic system based upon the principle "from each according to his ability, to each according to his needs" would be feasible, as well as desirable.

It is normative theory, justifications, to which these various assumptions about human nature have contributed. The link between empirical premise (about human nature) and normative conclusion (justification) is in each case further, in this case normative, assumptions. These normative assumptions—the value of security of life, of nonarbitrariness, of the opportunity for free personal development, for the satisfaction of desire, and for rational choice—however, are hardly controversial.

It is not contended that the assumptions about human nature discussed above are the only ones that political theorists have made, much less that the applications mentioned are exhaustive. But by all odds these are the most frequently recurring, the most important of such assumptions and applications. What is striking about them is how restricted—yet how significant—is the area of differences of opinion. By far the most weighty is the question of the extent to which man is partial to himself, competitive, and aggressive, as contrasted with being cooperative and devoted to common interests. To be sure not all thinkers take one side or the other in this controversy. Some, with Hume, while maintaining that human nature is uniform in all nations and ages, stress the variety of human motivation.[8]

Only slightly less important than man's assumed motivations, for their implications for political theory, are differing assumptions as to the extent to which man can be counted upon to pursue his goals rationally and the question of whether differences among identifiable classes of people overshadow their likenesses, both judged essentially by the standards implicit in the first question.

All of this is based upon the assumption that man's nature, at least in these fundamentals, is relatively fixed. For those who believe in its indefinite malleability the question is largely irrelevant.

Throughout most of the history of Western civilization, as perhaps the names that have appeared in the discussion above would suggest, differences of opinion with respect to these central issues have not been great. With minor exceptions, it has been held that man's nature called for coercive government by the few. As Plato believed in a hierarchical distribution of virtues rightly reflected in a pyramidal arrangement of political power, so the dominant tradition throughout the Christian and pre-Reformation era supported hierarchical organization in Church and state by belief in Original Sin or, in its secular version, human depravity. Thus the inevitability and therefore the propriety both of coercive political organization and, in general terms, of the monarchical form of that organization found justification in the prevalent theory of human nature.

## THE DECLINE OF HUMAN NATURE THEORIZING

More recent times, however, have seen a change. By the middle decades of the present century, to speak of human nature required temerity. As Peter Corning notes in this volume, empiricists either thought we did not know enough about it to speak of it or to use the concept, or they were convinced that no such thing existed. Normative theorists, on the other hand, tended to reject it because of what were presumed to be conservative implications.

Why the change? Doubtless the empiricists' demand for precision and the normativists' demand for change provide part of the explanation. More generally, the prevailing relativism of the age encouraged a similar conclusion. Einstein gave popularity and the imprimatur of scientific approval to an idea whose time had come. The confidence of the Age of Reason in its ability to propound propositions of universal and eternal validity gave way first to evolutionary theories of human development, of history, and, in some cases, of ethics. Later, as great theoretical systems, especially in the realm of philosophy, political and otherwise, fell into disrepute, a more general skepticism took over. Political theorists, both normative and descriptive, eschewed propositions about human nature and theories derived therefrom.

In addition to the atmosphere of skepticism and positivism, more specific causal factors doubtless contributed to the decline of human nature theorizing. In the early years of the post-Reformation era, reasoning from theories of human nature was exceedingly popular. Theories of human nature, along with secular theories of Natural Law often closely related to them, tended to displace Natural Law theories dependent upon or at least more closely related to ideas of Divine Law. But it soon became apparent that the assumptions about human nature upon which these theories were founded varied significantly one from another. To be sure, it was no new thing for some thinkers to take a more optimistic view of the nature of man than others. But during the Christian era these differences were muted, while among the ancient Greeks the stress had been more upon the distribution of virtue among men than upon a degree of virtue assumed to be characteristic of all. Christian writers pursued the general theme that, while man was naturally sociable and in his primitive state essentially good, he had become depraved and could approximate to goodness only when he was held subject to institutions of authority. Although Thomas Aquinas, following Aristotle, held a less pessimistic view of human nature than had prevailed, no radically changed implications for political theory were drawn from it. It remained for the seventeenth and eighteenth centuries to develop theories in which opposing assumptions about human nature led to opposing theories about desirable forms of government. Hobbes predicated his defense of absolute monarchy partly upon the assumption that the vast generality of men were—at last in the absence of a power to overawe them—so concerned for their own precedence over others that naught but absolute monarchy could hold them in check. Rousseau, despite his ultimate pessimism, held a romantic view of man's potential goodness that could be developed, in civilized society, only in the most fully democratic state. Other thinkers arrayed themselves between these extremes, perhaps as suited their personal political preferences. Herein certainly lay seeds for skepticism regarding human nature as the foundation for political theory. Even a slight variation in the initial assumptions—witness Hobbes and Locke—could produce a striking difference in the political conclusion. Naturally, thinkers were suspect of fitting their assumptions to their political propensities. Thus John Dewey was led to declare that "It would . . . appear that during the greater part of the history of European thought conceptions of human nature have been framed not with scientific objectiveness but on the basis of what was needed to give intellectual formulation and support to practical social movements."[9] Perhaps even more basic than the problem of scientific objectivity, however, was the fact that such relatively small variations in assumptions could lead to great variations in conclusions. Could *the* correct assumptions ever be ascertained with sufficient precision?

To the variations among theorists differences among peoples added to the grounds for skepticism about theories of human nature. Montesquieu provides an early example of a philosopher who took ample note of the great variety of laws, customs, cultures, and forms of government and of their mutual interdependence. To be sure he by no means abandoned a theory of human nature. Whence else did his theory of the separation of powers derive if not from the belief that men in positions of power tend to expand and abuse it if not checked by countervailing power? Nevertheless, in Montesquieu's somewhat ordered speculations on assorted travelers' tales, we have a recognition that diversity in human affairs is at least as important a phenomenon as is uniformity. Since that time anthropologists have provided abundant evidence of human variety, feeding the hungry mouths of both ethical and political relativism. The example of which we have heard most recently is that of the Iks.[10] This miserable north Ugandan tribe has been reduced to a condition in which it manifests none of the characteristics we are proud to call "human." Sociality, love, care for the group, even the family seem to have been reduced to the zero point. Compared to them, Hobbes's natural man was practically benevolent. While they present an extreme case, and the proper interpretation of the evidence is open to dispute, it must not be thought that wide group variations in what have been thought by some to be basic human characteristics do not exist elsewhere. Some tribes are warlike and some are peaceful. Cooperation is the rule among some, while others manifest a degree of individualism that would put Locke to shame.

Anthropology has been joined by psychology in the process of undermining belief in the existence of such a thing as human nature. It is true that this statement by no means applied to all psychologists, even at any particular period. But it has provided the dominant theme for American psychology during much of the present century. From Watson to Skinner, "human nature" has been relegated to the "black box," and nurture has taken over. Thus the central thrust of "hard" behaviorism has been against almost any notion of human nature, whether for use by political theorists or otherwise; but it should be noted that many who have been influenced by this current of thought without adopting it lock, stock, and barrel have been more concerned to deny that human nature is, essentially, self-seeking, competitive, and aggressive, than that any such thing exists.

Finally, and closely related to the last point, the life sciences generally have of late been concerned to stress man's great adaptability. Animals have instincts; to a large extent they live by them. These programmed patterns of dealing with the exigencies of life provide, for the lower forms particularly, the very basis for their survival, and sometimes the basis for their extinction when conditions change; at the least they fail to provide the means for coping with radical change. Here is where the higher forms of life, and especially man, with his relatively enormous brain possess a tremendous advantage. His nature is to be able to adapt to circumstances. Perhaps that is the whole of his nature. That at least would be the extreme view. As Berelson and Steiner have put it, "Once we get much beyond the physiological and neurological base of behavior human nature spreads out as far as we can see."[11]

## THE RECENT RETURN TO FAVOR OF HUMAN NATURE THEORIZING

So, it is not strange that political theorists talk less than was once their wont about human nature. But they have never entirely ceased to do so. At least many of them have not. Nor have those who still make use of the concept always relegated it to a minor role in their theory. One of the leaders of our profession, Harold Lasswell, does not hesitate to list the "chief goals of man" and to rest important conclusions upon the existence of these goals as effective forces.[12] Included in his list, incidentally, are "safety," "income," and "deference," which invite comparison, not to say identification, with Hobbes's "safety," "gain," and "reputation." And today the subject of biopolitics[13] regularly commands attention at conventions of political scientists as well as among more specialized groups of political theorists such as those who selected the topic of this volume for the subject of an annual meeting. In short, the subject of human nature seems to be staging a comeback.

For one thing, it was never entirely dead. If a name is needed to make this point, that of Sigmund Freud should suffice. His

*Civilization and its Discontents* spelled out the pessimistic conclusions for politics which he himself drew from his psychological
theory.[14] Harold Lasswell's *World Politics and Personal Insecurity*
represents an application of this general cast of thought by a political scientist.[15] On the other hand, the works of such neo-Freud-
ians as Erich Fromm and Karen Horney, for instance, not only
underline the continuing concern of psychologists for applying a
theory of human nature to political theory in mid-twentieth-century
America but also make it clear that those who theorize about
human nature fail to agree as to their assumptions with consequent
differences among their political conclusions.

Moreover, the general relativistic atmosphere that characterized
so much of the first half of the century, and which was so unfa-
vorable to theories of a constant and universal human nature, has
largely given way to a greater willingness to postulate some constants in human affairs. Even John Dewey, quoted above as a
skeptic about human nature, limited his skepticism. "Human nature, like other forms of life," he declared, "tends to differentiation, and this moves in the direction of the distinctively individual,
and . . . it also tends toward combination, association."[16] At a
slightly later date, Abraham Maslow gave a new twist to psychological theorizing that helps human nature theorists by combining
fixity with development.[17] Men have basic needs. Some are more
basic than others. Until the most basic are satisfied up to a certain point the others do not manifest themselves; and, if those
basic needs cease to be minimally satisfied, the "higher" aspects
of man's nature, such as his desire for liberty, cooperation, and
self-actualization will deteriorate or even disappear altogether.[18]
In modified form, Maslow's theory has provided the foundation
for James C. Davies's theorizing, as exemplified in his chapter in
this volume.[19]

The final point that I would make by way of explaining the
turnabout that has characterized the standing (as well as the nature) of the human nature approach to political theory is really an
extension of what has just been said. A new movement is sweeping
through several of the studies of man and his culture. I refer to
"structuralism."[20] Structuralists in various disciplines, and perhaps
even in the same discipline, follow different paths. Maslow was
perhaps not a structuralist. At least he developed his theory before
the term was invented. But his idea of a step-by-step unfolding of

basic human needs closely parallels the work of Piaget, Kohlberg, and others in the field of child psychology. Lévi-Strauss's work in anthropology and Chomsky's ideas about linguistics are perhaps (although not surely) less directly related to politics than are the ideas of some of the developmental psychologists. But, as Peter Corning remarks, they are all alike in seeking a deep structure in matters human, one that transcends all societies and all aspects of life, the real human nature. If they succeed, if their intuitions and partial findings are borne out by further research and theory development, "human nature" will indeed have a solid base in the center of things. Meanwhile, the development of this newcomer in our midst, structuralism, has given encouragement to (and perhaps changed the sights of) those political theorists who are inclined to make use of the old-fashioned term, "human nature."

One further point along this line. Structuralists and their forerunners have done more than provide encouragement and a favorable atmosphere for political theorists who would cast assumptions about human nature in an important role. They have also supplied them with possible explanations for the otherwise embarrassing degree of variety in the political forms and practices, past and present, that history and observation bring to our attention. One of these, not new but newly reinforced, is the concept of stages of development related to need satisfaction with its reverse, stages of retrogression related to need frustration. If the Iks, as Turnbull hypothesizes, have been transformed from "cooperative, egalitarian, essentially democratic, and devout believers in their world as a benevolent one"[21] to the brutal almost subhuman society of egoists that they now are by a change in the environment that has brought them to the brink of starvation, what differences and what changes in human behavior might not yield to a similar type of explanation?

The other explanatory device derives both from the findings of students of animal learning and from the linguistic and other learning behavior of children. If, as it is beginning to appear, the kinds of things man can learn, the forms of ideas and of behavioral orientation that given (and common) experiences will impress upon him is programmed into his brain, then his nature sets limits on his plasticity and, given certain types of common experience, determines the content of his consciousness.

## CONTENT AND IMPLICATIONS

Up to this point the discussion has been about theories
of human nature, especially as they relate to politics, in a most
general way. What new light has been cast on the subject by recent
endeavors? The fact is that thus far the new interest in the subject
of human nature has not led to new insights as to what human
nature is; or least has not produced agreement as to what it is.
Areas of agreement go little beyond the traditional wisdom of
political theorists. Human nature is various. Individual men tend
to be ambivalent; that is to say they seek, sometimes at the same
time, mutually opposing or incompatible ends: privacy and sociability; safety and excitement and love of adventure; liberty and
security, and so on.

Probably the most generally accepted proposition remains the
old insight that men tend to be partial to themselves, at least outside of the nuclear family or very small and close face-to-face
groups. What they desire varies from person to person and from
time to time; but they want what they want; and what they want
is generally in limited supply leading to competitiveness and aggressiveness. Often, too, their wants lead them into conflict for
other reasons, as when environmental concerns cannot be met
without limiting the material well-being of others. Frequently,
too, even where ultimate goals are in agreement, men are in conflict because they have different information or they disagree as
to very complicated lines of causation. Thus if the polluter fully
realized the results of his polluting and the environmentalist fully
realized the costs of securing his goals, they might reach agreement.
This point derives from human nature only to the extent that it is
a consequence of the limits of human intelligence; but that is an
important limitation. Another, and very intractable, form of self-
partiality takes the form of the desire for precedence. One does
not have to be a Hobbesian to appreciate the ways in which this
human characteristic leads to strife.

Fortunately, these characteristics of man are accompanied by
certain countervailing tendencies. Man tends to be sociable, to like
the society of others and to seek their affection and approval. His
approbativeness and also, certainly in some measure, his sense of
justice, constitute checks upon his competitive tendencies. He finds

enjoyment in cooperating with others, although sometimes this is spiced by rivalry among groups, and public spirit may become a potent force.

The point, however, is that evidence to date supports the view that these checks are insufficient to negate the need for government. (Even when environmentalist and polluter agree on a common interest, self-interest will not lead them to pursue that interest unless some authority is in a position to assure each that the other will do likewise.) Moreover, the fact that governors are also men establishes the need for constitutional devices to protect against abuse of power as well as to assure that each will bear his fair share of the costs of government—whether those costs be in the form of revenues for the public domain or in the form of constraint to keep his end of the bargain (as in the example of the environmentalist and the polluter).

Beyond this point, agreement as to what form of polity human nature calls for is harder to secure. Many argue that it points to liberal democracy. They contend that both protection against tyranny and the fullest development of human potentiality can best be secured by a democratic regime: and that these facts, as-suming they are facts, provide not only reasons why democracy is desirable but also reasons why men, as they become aware of their interests, will desire it and strive for it. Another argument to the same effect is based upon the findings of those psychologists who study the stages of human development. Thus Kohlberg and Gilligan present evidence in support of the proposition that ado-lescents go through moral as well as cognitive stages of develop-ment. One finding, of particular significance for democratic theory, is that, with respect to the value placed upon human life, ado-lescents progress through six stages, ranging from a complete con-fusion of the value of human life with the value of physical objects to a belief in the sacredness of human life demanding universal respect for the individual.[22]

To be sure, both the individual development and the political evolution toward which it points depend upon favorable circum-stances, which may or may not prevail. Obviously most of the world's population have not attained to the conditions essential for the successful operating of liberal democracy.

Today many of those who believe that some form of democracy is the wave of the future pin their hopes on the possibility of transforming human nature. Or, like Marx, they believe that man is essentially a friendly, cooperative, noncompetitive, community-loving creature whose "species being," up to this time has been obscured and perverted or prevented from developing by unfortunate circumstances. Thus far the attempts, in turn, of the Soviet Union and its Eastern European neighbors, of China, and of Cuba to bring about the hoped-for transformation do not appear to have been highly sucessful; apart, that is, from the splurges of energy and idealism that generally accompany a great revolution that breaks down the obstacles created by the ossification of outmoded traditions and institutions. It is not clear that human nature can either be changed or released in benign form.

It has become increasingly evident that the problem of changing human nature runs much deeper than the old nature-nurture controversy. Students of the subject today are generally agreed that that way of stating the problem was a vast oversimplification. Nature and nurture cannot be so sharply separated. The key word now is "interaction." That fact in itself suggests the complexity of the problem. Also, it is recognized that even if environmental rather than genetic factors were dominant the problem of directed change would remain extremely intractable. The difficulty is that it appears to be very early experience that is fundamental to the development of character, i.e., "nature." How then escape the influence of the older generation, of the family, or of other members of the same generation who train and serve as models for the young?

What then can we hope for from the new interest in the study of human nature? Possibly a way will yet be discovered to bring about significant and enduring shifts in man's less lovely characteristics. Perhaps, far short of Utopian dreams, "piecemeal engineering" of human nature, whether by genetic, educational, or other methods, may accomplish significant changes. Or possibly a fuller and more detailed understanding of human nature as it now is will enable men to fashion institutions that better tame its less civilized aspects, while taking advantage of its more favorable features. Thus John Rawls argues, on the basis of certain psychological propositions, that as social justice is progressively attained envy will become a less significant force.[23]

Meanwhile, the essays in this volume, approaching the subject from a variety of points of view, add some perspectives and provide some insights that may be of assistance to the continuing study of what many believe to be the most difficult *and* the most important problem of political theory.

## NOTES AND REFERENCES

1. For Rousseau in the "true," i.e., most primitive, state of nature, egoism did not exist. But this is only because egoism is a "relative" trait, that has no role in the pre-social condition. Once men develop social relations, their self-respect, that is to say their desire for self-preservation (which *is* natural in the fullest sense of the word), develops, naturally, into that egoism that "leads each individual to make more of himself than of any other." "A Discourse on the Origin of Inequality," *The Social Contract and Discourses,* Everyman edition (London: J. M. Dent & Sons, Ltd., 1923), p. 197, n. 2.
2. *The Ethics of Aristotle,* trans. by J. K. Thompson (The Penguin Classics, 1959), 311 (Bk. X, Ch. 9).
3. *The Politics of Aristotle,* Barker edition (Oxford: Clarendon Press, 1946, I, ii, § 15 (1253a).
4. The contrast between those who hold the state to be "natural" and those who hold it to be "artificial" has been greatly overdone. Aristotle did not believe that the state grew without human volition. In fact, he declared that "the man who first *constructed* such an association was the greatest of benefactors." *Ibid.*
5. William Godwin, *An Enquiry Concerning Political Justice and its Influence on General Virtue and Happiness* (New York: Alfred A. Knopf, 1926), 259.
6. "Economic and Philosophical Manuscripts," in Erich Fromm, *Marx's Concept of Man* (New York: Frederick Ungar Publishing Co., 1961), 130.
7. It is well to remember that even in the *Discourses,* where Machiavelli dealt with a people whose public spirit was of a higher order than that which he thought prevailed in his own day, he held that those who established governments must assume that "all men are bad and are ready to show their vicious nature, whenever they may find occasion for it." (I, 3) and that "human desires are insatiable" (II, Preface). (The quotations are from the Modern Library edition of *The Prince and the Discourses,* 1940, at pages 117 and 275.)
8. Thus Hume writes: "The same motives always produce the same actions; the same events follow the same causes. Ambition, avarice, self-love, vanity, friendship, generosity, public spirit—these passions mixed in various degrees and distributed through society, have been, from the beginning of the world, and still are, the source of all the actions and enterprises which have ever been observed among mankind." David Hume, *Enquiries Concerning the Human Understanding* edited by L. A. Selby-Bigge, second edition (Oxford: Clarendon Press, 1902), Sec. VIII, Part 1, 83.
9. *Encyclopedia of the Social Sciences,* IV, 535.

10. Colin M. Turnbull, *The Mountain People* (New York: Simon & Schuster, 1972).
11. Bernard Berelson and Gary A. Steiner, *Human Behavior—an Inventory of Scientific Findings* (New York: Harcourt, Brace & World, 1964), 667.
12. See, for instance,*The Political Writings of Harold D. Lasswell* (Glencoe, Ill.: The Free Press, 1951), p. 475, n. 20.
13. The title of a volume by Thomas Landon Thorson (New York: Holt, Rinehart & Winston, 1970).
14. Trans. Joan Riviere, 3rd ed., (New York: Jonathan Cape and Harrison Smith, 1930).
15. New York: McGraw-Hill Book Co., 1935.
16. *Freedom and Culture* (New York: G. P. Putnam's Sons, 1939), p. 21.
17. *Motivation and Personality* (New York: Harper & Row, 1954).
18. It will be readily apparent how a theory of this kind might be used to explain what has apparently been the history of the Iks, referred to above. See C. M. Turnbull, "Human Nature and Primal Man," *Social Research*, 40 (Autumn, 1973), 511-530, esp. 518. (Turnbull's own conclusion does not follow this line of reasoning.)
19. See also his *Human Nature and Politics, the Dynamics of Human Behavior* (New York: John Wiley & Sons, 1963). Maslow's theory has been further applied to political theory and supported by extensive empirical research in Jeanne N. Knutson, *The Human Basis of the Polity* (Chicago, Ill.: Aldine-Atherton, 1972). This theory, and especially the concept of self-actualization, are subject to criticism without being completely discounted by Peter Corning in his chapter in the present volume.
20. Lévi-Strauss is doubtless its best-known proponent but the best general exposition of it, in all its applications, is Jean Piaget, *Structuralism*, translated and edited by Chananinhah Maschler (New York: Basic Books, 1970).
21. Turnbull, *loc. cit.*, 518.
22. Lawrence Kohlberg and Carol Gilligan, "The Adolescent as a Philosopher: the Discovery of the Self in a Post-Conventional World," *Daedalus*, Fall 1971, 1051-1086.
23. Rawls does not actually put it this way. He does not speak of the "progressive" (i.e., gradual) attainment of justice but deals rather with the likelihood that a just society, once attained, would be stable. His reasoning, however, would appear to support the suggestion advanced above.

# PERSPECTIVES ON
# HUMAN NATURE

In this first Part of the volume, the reader will find a *potpourri* of vantage points from which to consider the subject of "human nature and politics." Adopting an evolutionary and survival-of-the-fittest perspective, Peter Corning opens the discussion with a sketch of a model of social development, based upon four sets of human needs that are basic, yet constitute levels above the more familiar subgoals of nutrition, sleep, and sex. He argues, provocatively, that "the higher we go among these levels, the more we go from those that are subject to learning and feedback control to those that are more encompassing yet more biologically pre-programmed." After completing his own "model," he examines and criticizes various other possibilities, especially those derived, respectively, from Skinner, Freud, and Maslow.

17

In the following essay, Roger Masters uses theories as to man's nature and theories as to man's control over nature (which themselves derive from theories of human nature) to construct four modal types of political theory. His suggestion—yet to be pursued in depth—is that this typology lays bare the latent structure of human thought about matters political. This application of the structuralist approach to political theory is most intriguing.

Sandwiched in the center of this Part is George Kelly's outright attack upon "psychologism," and, therefore, upon the whole idea of using assumptions about human nature as the fundamental basis for political theorizing. This general argument is set forth in the specific context of a discussion of theories of violence.

Although not written in reply to Kelly, Lisa Newton's paper takes sharp issue with its message. To the question "Can human institutions ever be pronounced good, as tending to fulfill human nature, or bad, as tending to warp or injure it?" she argues a strongly affirmative answer. But human nature must be allowed to develop, particularly to develop rationality and the potentiality for free action. Only government, and particularly government at the local and regional levels, can provide the conditions and opportunities for this kind of development, without which life "is not a fully human life."

In the concluding chapter of this Part, James Davies applies his modified version of Maslow's stages of human development to the subject of political development. (Maslow's theory is criticized by Corning in Chapter 2.) Davies's developmental theory of human nature provides him with a more optimistic outlook on the prospects for the development of the polity than was adumbrated in the Introduction to this volume. Polities develop from oligarchy (which secure the bases of physical survival), to democracy (which provides for group survival), to "the metapolitical condition: civilized anarchy."

We must reflect together about the meaning
of life; we must strive together to attain
to a theory of the universe affirmative of
the world and of life, in which the impulse to
action which we experience as a necessary
and valuable element of our being may
find justification, orientation, clarity and
depth, may receive access to moral strength,
and be re-tempered . . .
Albert Schweitzer

# 2

# HUMAN NATURE *REDIVIVUS*

## PETER A. CORNING

It was never really dead—human nature. But we can
learn something about human nature from the fact that for two
generations the very concept was officiously, if not officially, pronounced dead by many social scientists—with significant consequences for our social practices, and for the practice of social
science. For, as Leon Eisenberg has noted, "the behavior of men
is not independent of the theories of human behavior that men
adopt." [1] Because we did not search for the influence of biological factors in social life, of course we did not find it. And because
we assumed that the basic problem of survival had somehow been
"solved," we acted accordingly.

19

Even now, the mere mention of the term "human nature" evokes deep suspicion in some circles. To many empirically oriented social scientists it suggests simplistic generalizations and premature closure on a subject that should properly be open to scientific investigation, while among some normatively oriented scholars it raises the specter of arch political conservatism—and possibly latent racism. Neither set of fears is necessarily justified, but I will admit at the outset to more than a few anxieties about the hazards involved in resurrecting this venerable term. It is all too easy to draw facile and ill-founded conclusions about what is by all odds the most complex subject known to man—man himself. And the temptations to do so are obviously very great.

Thus, in recent years man's behavior has been likened to that of the Uganda kob, and we have been told that we possess a territorial instinct (Robert Ardrey, *The Territorial Imperative*); Konrad Lorenz, whose pioneering studies of animal behavior recently won him a Nobel Prize, tells us (in *On Aggression*) that we have an instinctual "appetite" for aggression; on the other hand, zoologist Desmond Morris (*The Naked Ape, The Human Zoo*) compares us to neurotic baboons in the London zoo. Perhaps most provocative for political scientists is the assertion by Lionel Tiger and Robin Fox *(The Imperial Animal)* that human politics is merely a refinement of male dominance competition; since dominance rivalry is commonly associated in other species with breeding functions (with competition for mates, nesting sites, etc.), "the political system is a breeding system." [2]

For many social scientists, these and other biologically oriented works have, regardless of their faults, opened a door to new ways of looking at human social and political behavior. But for many others, regrettably, these writings have had the effect of reviving the stereotypes of social Darwinism and biological determinism. The hoary and outmoded nature–nurture controversy has once more reared its head (most distressingly, in the angry debate over race and intelligence) and ancient prejudices have been revived and reinforced.

Yet, despite the risk of abuse and misunderstanding, we cannot turn the clock back. The problem of survival looms larger and becomes more pressing as time goes on; it is increasingly obvious that the biological imperatives are the immediate problem for advanced Western societies, just as they have always been for most societies through most of our evolutionary history. Further, as empirical research on the biological bases of social behavior continues to mount, the evidence is becoming irresistible that biological factors permeate and interact with social variables in many and complex ways.

Human nature—in the sense of certain biological needs and givens that play a significant causal role in human social life—is a fact, even though we may choose to close our eyes to it. Having said this, however, I must add that human nature is proving to be far more complicated and subtle, and hard knowledge of the subject far less certain in many specific details, than has ever been dreamt of in our philosphy. As a scientific concept, we would do well at this juncture to treat human nature not as a set of dogmatic conclusions, but rather as a legitimate object of empirical research. It should only be at the conclusion of research and not at this intermediate stage that we might hope for a fully satisfactory understanding of the subject.

Of what use to us, then, can the concept of human nature be in the interim? Does the term have sufficient definition, and do we know enough about the subject, for it to have value either as a tool for research or as a guide for social ethics? On both counts the answers are affirmative, I believe, and I would like to undertake here a brief review and synthesis to support this conclusion. I will try to show that, at the minimum, the concept of human nature can help us to delineate the most relevant parameters of the human condition; it can help us establish a framework, or paradigm, for research and suggest appropriate modes of analysis. Specifically, it can be utilized to generate a number of important propositions about man and society, and it can help us formulate testable hypotheses of a sort that should enable us to cast new light on the causes and the consequences of human behavior.

In addition, I believe that a number of significant partial conclusions may be drawn. Some of these are quite firmly established or can logically be inferred from what we do know about the nature of man, while others—though consistent with what we know —are more tentative and speculative. However, it is my conviction that, taken as a whole, the concept of human nature can provide us with a coherent frame of reference with respect to normative and empirical issues, and that we are now in a position to move beyond the stale and outdated arguments of an earlier era.

## THE EVOLUTIONARY SYNTHESIS

The primal fact of human existence, from which all else follows, is that man is the product of a continuous line of descent that is perhaps three billion years old. As an evolved species, *Homo sapiens* represents a cumulative legacy of genetic material and biological characteristics (as well as cultural accretions) that reaches back beyond our capacity to imagine. Indeed, modern anthropologists despair of trying to demarcate some critical threshold, or Rubicon, for the emergence of man. At least two million years before the appearance of *Homo sapiens,* the African savanna was inhabited by group-living, bipedal, tool-using hunters who, though small-brained and lacking in sophisticated language skills, had much in common with our more immediate forebears of the Paleolithic. In protohominid nature, in other words, we can discern much of the biological substrate from which human nature evolved. (In fact, we share with all living primates many distinctive characteristics that can be traced to a common ancestor some tens of millions of years ago—including our manual grasping abilities, omnivorous digestive systems, visual acuity, elaborated cerebral cortex and, not least, our sociability.)[3]

Furthermore, through all the many eons during which man's biological inheritance was accumulating, it was being molded, tested, and retested by the "Grand Constructor" (as Lorenz puts it)—natural selection. This is no less true today than it has been in the past: the most fundamental and pervasive human problem, from which we can never escape (this side of our extinction as a species), is survival and reproduction.[4] The ongoing problem of survival is the great common denominator that all species share— the Natural Law to which all species are subject—and it is to the exigencies of this problem that the "value-preferences" of natural selection are addressed.

To be sure, the parameters of the survival problem vary from one species to another and from one habitat to another. For instance, temperature maintenance for the equatorial Batutsi requires the dissipation of excess body heat (thus the evolutionary "rationale" for a tall, lean body build, which maximizes the amount of exposed surface area), whereas the Eskimo must conserve body heat in order to survive (a need well served by the Eskimo's characteristically short, chunky build). Conversely, different societies (or species) may have very different ways of dealing with such commonly shared aspects of the survival problem as, say, reproduction, even when they occupy similar niches. Thus a placental marine mammal like the bottlenose dolphin gives birth to live young and suckles them at the breast; whereas, among the egg-bearing sharks, some species lay their eggs unhatched and others develop and hatch the young internally.

Yet all of the many comparisons and contrasts that can be drawn between species, or between *Homo sapiens* and other species for that matter, can best be understood in relation to how each species has been "tailored" by natural selection to cope with the survival imperatives in its own particular ecological niche. That is to say, functional design in nature is a consequence of the workings of natural selection through time upon the variations that naturally occur in biological processes, and the functional significance of any trait—at least from an evolutionary perspective—lies in its consequences for one or another aspect of the survival problem.

Indeed, this utilitarian feature of evolution is the theoretical foundation upon which rests the science of ethology; the ethologist's explanation of how a particular behavioral character has come to be "fixed" in any species hinges upon a close analysis of its contribution to survival and reproduction. A classic example is Niko Tinbergen's study of the black-headed gull's practice of removing the eggshells from the nest soon after the young are hatched. Tinbergen showed experimentally that the light-colored shells attract avian predators and that shell removal increases significantly the survival chances of the newborn.[5]

It should also be noted that ethological functionalism, or what I have taken to calling "evolutionary functionalism," applies both to the continuities and the changes that occur in a species over time. Both are a reflection, primarily, of the effects of various traits in relation to the ongoing survival problem. (Some modification of these statements is obviously necessary with reference to rapidly changing human cultures, but the basic arguments remain valid—as I hope to show.)

The explanation for this close association between function and causation is that, in biological evolution, causation is circular and feedback-dependent. Natural selection—the most important agent of transgenerational change—is not something external to the relationship between organisms and their environments. It is in reality a way of describing the outcomes of organism-environment interactions, and these outcomes, or "effects," are the "causes" of the more systematic continuities and changes *between* generations that Darwin characterized as "descent with modification." (I shall argue that an analogous kind of relational process lies at the heart of cultural evolution as well.)

The textbook example is "industrial melanism." Until the industrial revolution, light strains of the peppered moth *(Biston betularia)* predominated in numbers in the English countryside over darker, melanic forms of the species. The latter were relatively rare. The reason was that, when the moths were resting on tree trunks, the light forms were all but invisible against the lichen-encrusted trees, while the darker forms stood out. As a result, the light forms were far less subject to predation from insect-eating birds. They survived and reproduced in greater numbers. However, as industrial soot progressively blackened the tree trunks near factory areas, the effect was to alter the relative visibility of light and dark forms, and in time this change in the organism-environment relationship brought about a reversal in the relative frequencies of the two forms.

As the foregoing implies, the basic vocation, or "purpose," of all life forms involves the business of earning a living in the environment. However, purposiveness in the biological realm is not the result of any preordained plan; it does not suggest a teleological or vitalistic view of life. To the contrary, evolution is an open, opportunistic, and contingent historical process. Biological purposiveness relates only to what F. J. Ayala calls "internal teleology"—the design characteristics of complex organic systems, inclusive of their behavior. Thus entelechy, or ends-directedness, exists only in the limited sense that the genotype (the array of genes or genetic blueprint) of each species (and each individual within a species) controls and directs the organization, ontogeny and, indeed, the entire life-cycle of different organisms in characteristic ways. In other words, though Aristotle's famous acorn-oak tree metaphor does not apply to the evolutionary process as a whole, it is an appropriate "model" for the products of evolution. (The question of how, specifically, this purposiveness expresses itself in different species will be taken up below.)

As suggested above, the functional, or purposive character of biological organization applies not only at the organic level but at the behavioral and social levels as well. Behavioral traits are just as much a product of evolution as are organic processes, and the biological substrate upon which behavior depends is subject also to the workings of natural selection. Indeed, we now appreciate that behavior and morphology evolve together in an interactive and mutually supportive manner, with behavioral adaptations often preceding and precipitating changes in morphology. An example in humans is the adoption of milk by some populations as a regular part of the postweaning diet. Over time this has resulted in positive selection for a genetically based lactose tolerance that does not exist in nonmilk-drinking populations. Another example may be human skin pigmentation, which correlates well with variations in latitude and climate.

Of course, cultural evolution has proceeded far more rapidly, at least in recent millennia, than evolution at the genic level. Yet cultural evolution could not have occurred without the benefit of evolved, biologically based human capacities and behavioral "building blocks" (about which more will be said below). Nor have human cultures been liberated, somehow, from the rigors of the survival problem. There is good reason to believe that cultural systems remain subject at all times to feedback from the biological level—that human cultures continue to be tested in terms of their ability to meet the ongoing survival needs of different human populations in different habitats.

Furthermore, the conventional wisdom of an earlier generation to the effect that human evolution had somehow been arrested with the emergence of culture is no longer tenable. Not only have significant changes occurred in recent times in the relative numbers of different human stock, but within any given human population the gene pool continues to "track" cultural changes; microevolutionary changes in gene frequencies are still occurring. In addition, there remains even in Western societies a significant degree of assortative mating and marked fertility differentials. It has been estimated that two-thirds of the genes in the human gene pool two generations hence will be drawn from one-third of the present generation. Needless to say, these changes in the human gene pool are greatly affected by cultural practices and historical processes, although we still do not have a very good fix on this relationship—or its evolutionary implications.

These reproductive biases would be immaterial were it not for two additional properties of our species which should be noted here. As zoologist Ernst Mayr put it, ". . . anyone dealing with human individuals is bound to make grave mistakes if he ignores these two great truths of population zoology: (1) no two individuals are alike, and (2) both environmental and genetic endowment make a contribution to nearly every trait."[6] Since both of these "truths" are fundamental to the understanding of "human nature," let us consider each in turn.

Biological diversity, in the first place, is not simply "noise" that may be relegated to the error term in our models of human behavior. The "genotype" (the genetic "program" for a trait—or an organism) is an independent variable whose contribution to the traits that we actually observe *in situ* (the "phenotype") is exceedingly subtle and complex. It varies from one trait to another, one individual to another, one population to another, one environment to another, and even from one era to another.

To illustrate, one of the many factors that affect genetic diversity is the "fitness value" (or adaptive value) of a trait. Those metric, or continuously distributed, traits that are most vital to survival and reproductive success—where the fitness value is high—often exhibit very little interindividual variation because natural selection operates through time to flatten out genetic variation. However, the adaptive significance of a trait is always a function of the environment. If the environment changes, so might the fitness value, which in turn may result in a relaxation of selection pressures. A good example in humans may be myopia. In Western cultures, short-sightedness is no longer a serious handicap and is thus more common than in the past.

In short, the biological contribution to behavior cannot be couched in terms of universal laws that are applicable "anywhere and anywhen," in J. J. C. Smart's phrase. To quote Mayr again:

All organisms and organic phenomena are composed of unique features and can be described collectively only in statistical terms. Individuals, or any kind of organic entities, form populations of which we can determine the arithmetic mean and the statistics of variation. Averages are merely statistical abstractions; only the individuals of which the populations are composed have reality. The ultimate conclusions of the population thinker and of the typologist are precisely the opposite. For the typologist, the type (*eidos*) is real and the variation an illusion, while for the populationist the type (average) is an abstraction and only the variation is real. No two ways of looking at nature could be more different.[7]

This does not mean, of course, that measurement is a fruitless exercise, or that regularities and measures of central tendency are irrelevant. The populational emphasis in the quotation above is a useful antidote to the prevailing view of an earlier generation that science should properly concern itself only with repetitive phenomena, and that scientists may disregard or exclude the unique. However, it is also true that the biological realm is characterized by *both* continuity and change—both regularity and diversity—through time *and* space. It has been estimated, to use man as an example, that about 95 percent of our genes are a common heritage; they are held in common descent. If this were not so, we could not be classified *Homo sapiens* and could not interbreed with one another. But perhaps 5 percent of each individual's genetic endowment is shared by no other living organism. And, from an evolutionary perspective, neither the 95 percent that is alike nor the 5 percent that is different is inherently more important; both are fundamental to the evolutionary process. Thus a social science that is properly attuned to the basic properties of the phenomena with which it is dealing must concern itself with *both* uniformity and diversity. Furthermore, these properties must be viewed from a perspective that is sensitive to the historical and context-specific nature of evolution. As geneticist Theodosius Dobzhansky has expressed it: "Culture is built on a shifting genetic foundation."[8]

As for the relationship between nature and nurture, or heredity and environment, the Mayr quote above reflects the fact that the older dichotomy between mutually incompatible explanations of behavior has been superseded by a more sophisticated "interactional" model. At the minimum, it is now appreciated that all behavior is biologically based at some level of analysis. Even learned behaviors depend upon evolved biological capacities, including the capacities for being "rewarded" and "punished" in learning situations. Nor are these capacities unique to man. They are found in lowly flatworms and mollusks, as well as in fish, birds, reptiles and mammals. These learning abilities are quite clearly a set of biological adaptations.

Furthermore, the particular repertoire of learning abilities is tailored in each species to its survival needs and strategies. Rats, for instance, are superior maze learners, an aptitude of particular value to a tunnel-dwelling species, whereas, horses, which are adapted for life in open terrain, are "maze stupid." Even when different species are raised in identical environments, they will learn different things; animal trainers in circuses find they can reinforce only those behaviors that come to the animals "naturally" and that they can use as reinforcements only what each animal "naturally" finds desirable or aversive.

The role of biological factors in learning extends not only to learning aptitudes, but also to learning *preferences*. Different species are endowed with different prepotencies for learning certain kinds of things, so that an animal in effect "wants" to learn what it needs to learn in order to survive. This may manifest itself in terms of stimulus preferences, or the kind of phenomena upon which an animal will focus its attention. Among the many examples from recent experiments with humans, one of the more significant is the series demonstrating that infants have an innate preference for visual schema resembling the human face.

Biological influences may also affect the relative ease with which different behaviors are learned. A rather dramatic example is the one-trial, long-term food avoidance conditioning that results from ingesting a food substance that is subsequently associated with gastrointestinal illness.[9]

In the same vein, biological processes may control learning sequences and establish sensitive periods during which the learning of particular behaviors is greatly facilitated. Language development in humans is an excellent example. There is a powerful predisposition for language development in human children, but it appears to peak before puberty; though there are, as always, individual differences, after about 12 years of age children become less proficient at learning a second language, or at relearning language after suffering brain damage in Wernicke's area of the dominant hemisphere (the brain area most centrally involved in linguistic skills).

Conversely, just as heredity potentiates and canalizes the learning process, so environmental factors are generally involved in even the most rigidly instinctual, or "precoded" animal behaviors. At very least, environmental "releasers," or cues may be necessary to trigger a stereotyped and unlearned response. But, in addition, instinctual behaviors are often subject to practice effects: with repeated trials, an animal may increase its proficiency or perhaps lower its response threshold. In many other cases, an animal may be only partially preprogrammed or predisposed to perform a particular behavior, so that environmental influences may be required to fill in the interstices. Thus, biological factors may define the degree of developmental flexibility for a particular trait, as well as establishing norms and limits of reaction to environmental influences (phenotypic plasticity).

Bird vocalizations in several closely related species provide examples of almost every kind of heredity-environmental interaction. Song sparrows, even if they are isolated from their own species, will be able at maturity to reproduce their characteristic song without a flaw (of course, only if their ontogeny has been relatively "normal" in other respects). At the other extreme, isolated meadowlarks can learn the songs of a number of "foster parent" species; they are preprogrammed to sing but the specific song is not preprogrammed. In between these two extremes is the pattern of the white-crowned sparrows. They must hear the adult model of their own particular species' song during a limited sensitive period if they are to perform successfully. Still other species have the ability to learn an entirely new song later in life, or can learn any number of "dialects" of their own species' song but not the song of any other species.

In short, there is no general pattern of behavioral causation that would enable us to predict beforehand the precise relationship between nature and nurture. Even among closely related species, behaviors that appear on the surface to be quite similar may in fact be organized and developed in different ways. Hence, each species, and each trait, must be analyzed in its own terms.[10]

One widely employed method for estimating (at least in global terms) the relationship between nature and nurture in the expression of a particular trait involves the concept of heritability. Heritability ($h^2$) refers not to the total biological contribution to a trait but only to the *proportion* of the total phenotypic variation that can be attributed to genotypic differences among individuals.[11] Researchers in behavior genetics utilize several different research paradigms and, over the years, heritability estimates have been made under experimental conditions for everything from extraversion to schizophrenia—though of course the best-known and most controversial studies involve the heritability of "intelligence."

Although heritability estimates may provide some useful information, under even the best of circumstances they can provide only a limited insight into the precise relationship between nature and nurture. One problem is that a heritability estimate is a very plastic sort of statistic. Because it is calculated as a percentage of the total observed (phenotypic) variation, it is always a function of the amount of environmental variation, which may differ considerably from one population to another.[12] For a population in a uniform environment, most of the observed variation might be genetical, whereas in a population sample drawn from a highly varied environment, the converse might be true. Hence, heritability estimates are specific to the particular population and environment at the particular time the population is sampled; they cannot be generalized to other populations in other environments, nor—since they are population statistics—can they properly be used to deal with individual cases. The most serious pitfall, though, is that heritability estimates reveal nothing about the specific biological mechanisms and environmental factors involved in producing a particular trait—or how these mechanisms may interact with one another. In sum, we cannot equate heritability with human nature. Heritability estimates can help us account for the variations that we observe in human behavior; they do give us some overall indication of the biological contribution to human variability, but nothing more.

What can we conclude from this very brief discussion of man as an evolved species? First, an evolutionary perspective enables us to posit that an intelligible organizing principle underlies the emergence and historical development of man. Human evolution, both at the biological and at the cultural level, has been a relational process oriented to coping with the ongoing survival problem, with all of its many facets and ramifications (see below). However, the biological foundation of human behavior, what anthropologist Earl Count several years ago aptly termed the human "biogram," is not forever fixed and cannot properly be conceived of in terms of some sort of ideal type. Human nature is biologically diversified, developmentally flexible and emergent, and, most important, inextricably enmeshed in a great variety of natural and cultural environments. In each generation, human nature is re-created anew; from the moment of conception on, unique genotypes interact with their unique environments in such a way as to produce diverse phenotypes. These phenotypes are not only capable of reproducing themselves, they are capable also of diverse purposive behaviors, both as individuals and as members of organized human groups, and it is to the purposive nature of man and society that we now turn.

## THE EVOLUTIONARY MODEL
## OF HUMAN NATURE

As biologist Alexander Fraser has observed, purposive behavior of all kinds, and at all phylogenetic levels, has two basic properties: (1) the capacity for specifying an intrinsic or self-determined goal-state, and (2) the ability to initiate and maintain a pattern of behavior directed toward the attainment of that goal.[13]

Any number of examples can be adduced: the process by which, under proper conditions of temperature and moisture, plant seeds germinate, orient themselves to gravity, respond to pressure, grow toward sunlight, differentiate, and, in time, produce new seeds; or animal morphogenesis, the process by which gametes, after combining into zygotes, are transformed and elaborated into fully developed, self-reproducing organisms. Purposiveness is evident too in the reproductive behavior of anadromous fish, which return from the open sea to fresh-water spawning grounds when the breeding season arrives; it is manifest in the sometimes incredible nest-building feats of birds, in the pack-hunting organization of hyenas, and in the tool-using (and in some cases tool-making) behavior of Galapagos woodpecker finches, Egyptian vultures, satin bower birds, common blue jays, California sea otters, hamadryas baboons, chimpanzees and, of course, man.

In *Homo sapiens,* needless to say, purposive behavior very often has an "intentional" or "deliberate" quality, and though conscious intentionality may not be entirely unknown in other species, humans are certainly without peer in being able to orient behavior to perceived relationships between means and ends, and to anticipated outcomes. Yet there remains an important dimension of purposive behavior in humans which involves *un*intentional acts. We call some of them habitual (or "second nature"); others are reflexive in character and involve behaviors that appear, at least, to exclude conscious intervention. A commonplace example is the act of turning a bicycle. A cyclist's decision to make a turn may or may not involve premeditation, but there is very seldom premeditation, or even awareness, about the necessity for first turning the front wheel in the direction opposite to the turn to prevent being thrown outward by centrifugal force. Most cyclists make this movement automatically and unknowingly.

Although there is an almost endless diversity of goal-directed behaviors in the biological realm, they share the common ground of being instrumental, normally, to biological ends. Of course, in complex human societies, the relationship among "motivation," behavior, and survival-related functions is often more indirect. Because of the partial autonomy of human purposiveness, furthermore, maladaptive behaviors are not uncommon. (These are points we shall pursue further below.)

Nonetheless, in a broad sense the functioning of complex organisms can be said to be under the control of endogenous "goal-structures" whose organizing principles reflect the cumulative legacy of each species' evolutionary history. As should become clear presently, this assertion is not a throwback to simplistic notions of biological determinism or free will. Though intrinsic purposiveness and self-regulation in the biological realm is deterministic in nature, it very often includes mechanisms that enable an animal to fabricate instrumental subgoals and to carry out learned behaviors, or behaviors that are feedback-sensitive and modifiable while in progress. Indeed, most behavior is subject to at least some environmental and experiential influence; at one level of analysis, an organism and its environment may be viewed as forming a closed loop in which there are mutual interactions and reciprocal feedback. Thus, it is more accurate to say that both the organism and the environment "determine" behavior. The two dimensions cannot in practice be separated from each other.

To those who are familiar with cybernetics and systems theory, the foregoing will doubtless be suggestive, if not commonplace.[14] The discussion above implies that complex organisms (inclusive of their behavior) may be described, or modeled, as cybernetic systems—that is, as dynamic, goal-oriented, self-regulating, feed-back-dependent organizations of matter and energy. This is indeed the case, although the particular model and underlying theory that I would like to sketch briefly here go beyond the analytic formulations with which social scientists have become familiar in recent years. Even though the explorations and heuristic models of scholars like Talcott Parsons, Karl Deutsch, David Easton, and others represented an important step forward in terms of our ability to identify and describe the "skeletal structure" of social and political organization, unfortunately some social scientists have become disaffected because these efforts did not, in and of themselves, explain "real" systems.

In retrospect, these explorations could have benefited from a broader, multidimensional frame of reference. From an evolutionary and biological vantage point, social systems—in *any* social species—represent, quite simply, one level of biological organization; they are a common outcome of the evolutionary process. Cybernetic models cannot "explain" biological organization (although they may be useful in helping us understand the structure and behavior of a system and its components). Rather it is the theory of evolution that can explain the origins and development of the phenomena encompassed by cybernetic models; in an important sense, the evolutionary process as a whole may be characterized as a series of explorations, or experiments with hierarchical, purposive organization.

What is required to bring cybernetic models of social and political life into proper focus is to meld the theory of evolution (including a formally analogous theory of *cultural* evolution, which I shall describe) to a hierarchical, multilevel cybernetic model of biological organization that embraces "molecular," organismic, behavioral, social, and political levels. Not only is it my contention that such a model best fits the basic architecture of human nature but that it is an appropriate model for other species as well, even those that do not exhibit social or political "levels" of organization. (Indeed, hierarchical, cybernetic organization is probably one of the most important of commonalities among different species.) The concepts that I shall be discussing are not in most cases new, but perhaps my synthesis is.

First, what are some of the more important properties of a cybernetic system? They include: (1) systemic goal-orientation (including possibly many instrumental subgoals); (2) interaction among functionally specialized components, or "subsystems"; (3) hierarchical organization (with higher levels being more encompassing and integrative); (4) synergism (collective properties that cannot be predicted from an understanding of the components); (5) interactions with the external environment across system boundaries (usually referred to as "inputs" and "outputs"); (6) internal control, or self-regulation, in relation to systemic goals and subgoals; (7) communications processes (within the system and between the system and its environment); (8) feedback (information inputs relating specifically to the behavior of the system); (9) historicity (cybernetic systems are irreversible processes taking place through time); and (10) negentropy (cybernetic systems appear to resist the second law of thermodynamics because their processes do not lead inherently to a state of maximum disorder and energy dispersal but to exactly the reverse).

The key to understanding how such a system operates is to envision it as being positioned so that it is an integral part of a closed loop (see Figure 1) that includes: (a) the system; (b) the system's environment; (c) inputs from the environment (including feedback from the system's own behavior); and (d) the system's "outputs" into the environment. In contrast to other models of behavior, the cybernetic model posits that the behavior of the system involves a *relationship* between internal goals (or "reference signals" in systems theorists' parlance) and various environmental inputs (or "sensor signals"). Cybernetic systems are so constructed that they act to achieve and maintain a *dynamic* stability (or a "zero error signal") in relation to their environments.

In other words, behavior is "caused" in a cybernetic system by *both* the internal goal structure of the system and the status of the system in relation to these goals. The desired relationship between the system and its environment is defined by a set of internal referents, and these are "compared" to the actual relationship as indicated by various external inputs.

As Powers has shown,[15] the behavior of such a system can be described mathematically in terms of its tendency to oppose an environmental disturbance of an internally controlled quantity. The derivation of this relationship is, briefly, as follows. Let us suppose that a controlled quantity $q_c$ represents some function (or analog) of certain environmental variables $f(v_1, v_2 \ldots v_n)$,

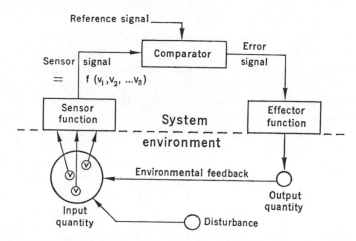

Figure 1. The basic unit of organization in a cybernetic control system. (After William T. Powers, "Feedback: Beyond Behaviorism," *Science*, 179: 4071, 1973. Copyright © 1973, American Association for the Advancement of Science.)

such that $q_c$ will equal zero when the system is in equilibrium. Disregarding signs, if a change in this controlled quantity $\triangle q_c$ is equal to $g(d)$, where d is a quantitatively measurable disturbance affecting at least some of the variables and g is a function describing the relationship between the disturbance and the controlled quantity; and if, further, h represents a function of the environmental relationship between the controlled quantity and the system's output o such that $\triangle q_c = h(o)$; then, assuming control is good, when $g(d) \approx -h(o)$, $\triangle q_c \approx 0$. That is to say, the system will operate in such a way that some function of its output quantities will be nearly equal and opposite to some function of a disturbance in some or all of those environmental variables that affect the controlled quantity, with the result that the controlled quantity will remain nearly at its zero point.

It should be emphasized, however, that the above derivation is greatly simplified and describes only the most rudimentary model. For one thing, more complex cybernetic systems are not limited to maintaining any sort of simple and eternally fixed steady state. In a complex system overarching goals may be maintained by means of an array of hierarchically organized subgoals that may be pursued contemporaneously, cyclically, or even seriatim; certain subgoals may be recurrent or else emergent as a system develops through time or as the system's environment changes. On occasion, in fact, the destabilizing and reorganizing of lower level goals may serve to enhance higher level stability or viability. In other words, reference signals within a complex system may themselves vary in a purposeful way. Some of these subgoals may be preprogrammed, while others may be "learned," or unlearned, as appropriate (an example in human behavior is the many culturally conditioned ways of satisfying basic nutritional needs). Indeed, an appreciation of the hierarchical and flexible organization of goals in complex systems is essential to understanding how the cybernetic model can be applied to the immense variety of learned human behavior patterns, including—significantly—novel behaviors and problem-solving behaviors (see below).

Another important exclusion from the simplified model above is the situation, common in the biological realm, in which a particular cybernetic system may be located within a hierarchy of systems; it is frequently the case that a cybernetic system is composed of subsystems that are themselves cybernetic systems, or that the system's environment largely or wholly consists of a more encompassing cybernetic system. In point of fact, it is coming to be appreciated that hierarchical organization is one of the most important properties of biological systems. As Pattee has observed:

> It is a central lesson of biological evolution that increasing complexity of organization is always accompanied by new levels of hierarchical controls. The loss of these controls at any level is usually malignant for the organization under that level. Furthermore, our experience with many different types of complex systems, both natural and artificial, warns us that loss of hierarchical controls often results in sudden and catastrophic failure. Simple tools may wear out slowly and predictably, but as systems grow in size and complexity they reach a limit where a new level of hierarchical control is necessary if the system is to function reliably.[16]

Because the significance of hierarchical organization is often unappreciated (and equally often misunderstood), let us consider the concept briefly. In the first place, hierarchy involves a partial ordering of phenomena in two dimensions—horizontally among components or subsystems and vertically between sequential levels (or between sets and supersets). The simile most often invoked is a set of Chinese boxes. Grobstein also employs a figure involving subdivided triangles (see Figure 2).

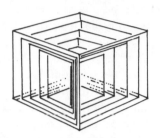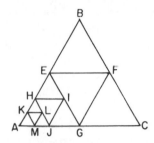

Figure 2. Hierarchical order in Chinese boxes and subdivided triangles. Note that successively larger triangles are in each case composed of several smaller ones. (From *The Strategy of Life*, second edition, by Clifford Grobstein. W. H. Freeman and Company. Copyright © 1974.)

There are, as Grobstein has noted, two distinct kinds of hierarchies, those that are "facultative" or reversible (they can be dispersed and reconstituted) and those that are "obligative" or nonreversible (when the component elements lose their autonomy). In human organizations, both kinds are manifest, often within the same organization—for example, unskilled laborers versus highly specialized technical personnel who cannot readily transfer their skills to other jobs or learn new jobs.

The existence of a hierarchy can be verified empirically in terms of patterns of interaction. For instance, component parts of a hierarchy may or may not interact with one another, but they will generally interact with higher levels. Nonetheless, the total number of horizontal interactions will always be far greater than the number of vertical interactions.

Another important characteristic of hierarchical systems has to do with the paradox that their behavior must be viewed and interpreted differently, depending upon one's level of analysis. A particular phenomenon may have quite different properties at different levels of organization, or it may have consequences at some levels and not at others. James S. Coleman offers the following illustration:

> Once when I was sitting on the edge of a cliff, a bundle of gnats hovered in front of me, and offered a strange sight. Each gnat was flying at high speed, yet the bundle was motionless. Each gnat sped in a ellipse, spanning the diameter of the bundle, and by his frenetic flight, maintaining the bundle motionless. Suddenly, the bundle itself darted—and then hovered again. It expanded and its boundaries became diffuse; then it contracted into a tight, hard knot and darted again—all the while composed of nothing other than gnats flying their endless ellipses. It finally moved off and disappeared. Perhaps also it dissipated and ceased to exist, each gnat going his own way.
>
> Such a phenomenon offers enormous intellectual problems: how is each gnat's flight guided, when its direction bears almost no relation to the direction of the bundle? How does he maintain the path of his endless ellipse? And how does he come to change it, when the bundle moves? What is the structure of control, and what are the signals by which control is transmitted?[17]

As a biological phenomenon, hierarchical organization is not always and everywhere adaptive; its adaptiveness very much depends upon the particular context. Moreover, there are always costs involved, at least from the viewpoint of the components or subsystems. Yet the fact that hierarchical organization is widespread in nature suggests that it is very often advantageous. For example, hierarchical organization produces a significant simplifying and economizing of interactions among the components of a complex system, a phenomenon that can be demonstrated mathematically. Component parts may be freed of many constraints even as the establishment of hierarchical control imposes partial constraints (a point with which Plato was quite familiar).[18] Indeed, hierarchical constraints are always highly selective; "irrelevant" aspects of component behavior are usually "ignored." It can also be demonstrated mathematically that a system will evolve more rapidly when its component parts are organized into stable subsystems. Hierarchical organization may therefore facilitate evolutionary change.

However, the most important advantage of hierarchical organization is that it may facilitate the achievement by the component parts of either shared or complementary goals; hierarchy may lead to synergy. To an evolutionary biologist this means synergy with respect to the problem of survival and reproduction. The basic postulate of the evolutionist is that confusion evolves into order through the workings of natural selection, and insofar (but only insofar) as complexity and its concomitant, hierarchical ordering, enhance the chances of survival and reproductive success, such patterns will also be favored by natural selection, whether it be at the organsimic or the social level of organization. In other words, though in *Homo sapiens* hierarchical, cybernetic organization has reached its fullest expression, it is not a human invention but is instead a common evolutionary strategy.

How, then, do we apply the above model specifically to man? At the level with which we are primarily concerned here, that of the individual organism, we can posit something very like the more complex version that we have described. Because man is normally group-living, each individual represents an intermediate level of organization, below which are several levels that both serve and must be served, and above which is at least one and frequently several levels of social and political organization, beginning with simple "dyadic" relationships (insofar as they involve collaborative, goal-oriented behaviors).

We are not accustomed to treating more encompassing, social levels of organization as an integral part of human nature. We have been taught to think of culture as an artifact or superstructure. Yet, from an evolutionary perspective, social organization is a functionally important dimension of biological organization. Because man is a social animal with a very long history of "togetherness," social organization is, quite simply, an actualization of behaviors that are potentiated by human nature. In an evolutionary model of human nature, therefore, various social levels of organization represent partial orderings at a more encompassing level than that of the individual organism; social organization is a natural extension of human purposiveness. And like any other hierarchically organized cybernetic system, social systems have no existence apart from their constituent individuals and yet may have

40 PETER A. CORNING

collective properties that transcend any given individual. (We shall return to the matter of social organization and its utility below.)

Accordingly, as an integral part of a hierarchical system, each individual is at one and the same time a servant of basic physiological needs, a pursuer of his own personal "psychological" and social needs (and purposes) and a contributor to the functioning of various social, economic, and political organizations. Not only do all of these levels interact with and affect one another, but all are integrally related to the enterprise of earning a living in the environment. As I have argued in detail elsewhere,[19] a human society is in essence a collective survival enterprise in which various aspects of the survival problem are dealt with collaboratively.

The particular organizational patterns vary widely, of course. In every society we know of, there is some division of labor. But most societies also deal collaboratively with certain overriding survival problems (for instance, group defense or food procurement, or a division of water rights). More complex societies divide and subdivide the problem into a myriad of specific functional tasks which are dealt with by the various intermediate-level organizations (beginning with the nuclear family), while a number of coping and integrative functions may also be performed at the most inclusive level.

Not all the purposive social activities in modern societies are adaptively significant, of course. Some are nonessential activities that may perhaps have latent social functions (this is a much-analyzed subject). Others may simply fulfill otherwise unmet social or "psychological" needs, using a society's "margin of profit," so to speak. Others are maladaptive—in the strict Darwinian sense of the term.

The evolutionary significance of human organizations is, needless to say, an exceedingly complex subject and deserves more extended treatment. For our present purpose, though, it is sufficient only to underscore the point that in any social species, including man, social organization evolves in the context of its instrumental relationship to the problem of survival and reproduction (see below).

Consonant with this model of human nature, we would expect the behavioral substrate of the species to have an intelligible pattern of organization. It should be hierarchically organized, with the highest-level goals, those relating to survival and reproduction as a member of a social species, encompassing and integrating an array of subgoals (and subsubgoals) that relate to the many concrete aspects of the survival problem. At one end of the spectrum there are such individual life-support needs as food, water, shelter, physical safety, sleep, etc. At the other end are the transcendent "social" problems associated with maintaining a viable economy, society, and polity. And in between are the problems associated with the reproduction and nurture of the young and with caring for those to whom we are personally "bonded." Indeed, for each individual in a social species like man, the survival problem can be broken down into four distinct sets of needs, each of which relates to the larger problem of sustaining a viable species—but which must also be integrated and reconciled with one another if a society is to remain viable.[20] There are: (1) the needs related to the ontogeny and development of the individual; (2) the needs related to the maintenance and self-fulfillment of mature individuals; (3) the needs of the individuals to whom we are closely "bonded" and who are dependent upon us, particularly mates, progeny, and close relatives; and (4) the needs of the more inclusive social order upon which we and our "loved ones" are in varying degrees dependent for the fulfillment of the needs in 1, 2 and 3.[21]

From an evolutionary perspective, the highest-level goal has to do with maintaining the unbroken chain of life. It involves the survival of the species. Immediately below this come the goals listed above. We may or may not be aware of the fact that we are endowed with such superordinate goals, but I am positing that these goals do transcend and integrate the subservient level of subgoals with which we are more familiar (i.e., nutrition, sleep, sex, etc.) This third level of goals is in turn subserved by the specific behavioral repertoire of the individual—which itself may constitute several levels of instrumental subgoals, subsubgoals and so on (see Figure 3). However, goals at each subservient level, even if they may be pursued as ends in themselves by the individual, can be understood only in terms of their instrumental relationship to higher-level goals. As we *ascend* the hierarchy, moreover, we go from goals that are more specific yet (especially in man) more subject to learning and feedback control to goals that

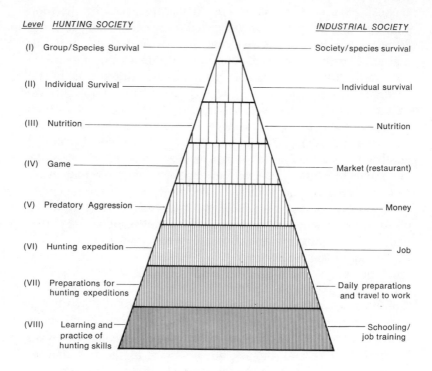

Figure 3. The proposed goal-hierarchy as applied to hypothetical examples in two different cultural contexts.

are at once more encompassing yet more biologically preprogrammed.

What must the motivational substrate and neural organization
of the human brain be like in order to conform to this model?
Obviously, it must organize and integrate the behavior system in
such a way that the diverse and sometimes conflicting survival
needs can in general be harmonized (though the psychic condition
of the individual may be anything but tranquil). To cite one example, the individual should ordinarily be strongly motivated to
engage in behaviors oriented to the meeting of pressing physiological needs. Yet these usually urgent needs might under some circumstances have to be completely suppressed for varying lengths
of time in order to cope with an even more pressing threat to survival—say in a situation in which the individual's life is in immediate danger. In such cases, an elaborate and well–documented
sequence of autonomic responses does in fact suppress many normal bodily functions (fatigue, hunger, digestion, peristalsis, etc.)
and, at the same time, mobilizes the individual for emergency action (increased heart rate, increased respiration, the transfer of
blood from skin and viscera to muscles and brain, release of
stored carbohydrates into the bloodstream, and so forth).

Let us be candid, however. Although we have many partial
insights, human behavior is organized and integrated within each
individual in ways that are still imperfectly understood. Some of
the needs described above express themselves at the individual
level in the form of motivational mechanisms that have been
reasonably well pinpointed—for instance, the so-called deficiency
motivations (such as hunger, thirst, etc.) that create internal
distress and stimulate "coping" responses. In effect, such mechanisms involve a substrate of *psychic* punishments and rewards—
punishments for *not* performing biologically necessary behaviors
and rewards for doing so. Conversely, many maladaptive behaviors are discouraged, so to speak, by well-defined internal mechanisms that are designed to make such behaviors unpleasant, or
"aversive" (for example the subjective experience of pain, various
forms of discomfort, or fear of the strange). Other needs, particularly those involving social, affiliative, and affectional behaviors,
appear to have similar properties, but their biological substrates
are less well understood at the present time.

There is also the class of emotional reactions that amount to a set of innate "reference signals" which, in effect, remain at zero in a psychologically optimal environment. For instance, the "fear-fight, fear-flight" mechanism imposes on the organism a need for an unthreatening environment, and the neural substrate is so organized that it permits alternative coping responses depending upon the particular environmental context. Major elements of this substrate have in fact been identified in the limbic system of the paleocortex. In a similar vein, "boredom" and frustration are a normal response to an environment lacking in stimulation and the opportunity for purposeful activity, and, in this case, the ascending reticular activating system (ARAS) in the upper brain stem is implicated as being of particular importance.

By the same token, the particular repertoire of learning capacities and learning biases exhibited by *Homo sapiens* can better be understood if learning processes are subsumed as instrumental to higher level goals as pursued by different individuals and groups in different ways and in different environments. The objective of learning is not merely to link responses to stimuli in accordance with the "laws" of learning, but to cope with the environment in order to satisfy internal needs.

In sum, what we know about the neural organization of the human brain is consistent with the model I have described. Our knowledge is still so full of gaps that major refinements in current thinking are bound to occur, but I hope that the model will prove to be correct in essentials and will, in any event, improve our understanding of human nature. And this brings us to a consideration of how the model proposed here relates to some of the major alternatives that have been advanced in recent decades.

## ALTERNATIVE MODELS OF HUMAN NATURE

Three more or less systematic models of human nature have been proposed by various behavioral scientists. There is, first, the model of the behaviorist psychologists. In the classical "stimulus-response" (S-R) paradigm postulated by John B. Watson and others in the 1920s, man was characterized as being rather like a switchboard; behavioral outputs were posited to be a simple function of "environmental" inputs, and the organism itself was presumed to impose no order or intrinsic purposes on the input-output transactions. In recent years, of course, the be-

haviorist model has been greatly refined in response to the growing recognition that the organism—the "black box"—is not an
entirely empty receptacle but represents an intervening variable.
It has also become apparent to learning theorists that the reinforcing properties of environmental "stimuli" are somehow hierarchically organized.

Yet "radical" behaviorists, most notably B. F. Skinner, still
deny the concept of endogenous "goals."[22] According to Skinner,
purposes can no more be attributed to a biological entity than
can anthropomorphic properties be assigned to nonliving matter;
we can no more speak of "goals" in behavior than we can speak
of the "exuberance" of a falling stone. Both attributes are to
Skinner metaphysical nonsense. Of course, Skinner's "analogy"
is in fact a non sequitur. Skinner seems unaware of the profound
*dis*analogy between the organized complexity of the biological
realm and the unorganized complexity of nonliving matter; evolved
biological "systems" are and must be goal-oriented, but "weather
systems" are not.

Of all the many questions that have been begged over the
years by the behaviorist model of man, the most telling arises
from our revitalized appreciation of man as an evolved and evolving species. How is it possible that the behavior system of our
species could have emerged without reference to the rigors of the
survival problem? How can it be, in view of the precariousness
of the life process, that natural selection imposed no order upon
the relationship between man and his environment? To so argue
flies in the face of everything we know about the evolutionary
process. It reflects an extraordinary naïveté about the biological
realm.

Consider this problem. When a rat is taught to obtain a food
reward by pressing a lever in response to a light signal, the animal
not only learns the instrumental lever-pressing behavior but learns
also to vary his behavior patterns in accordance with where he
is in the cage at the moment the light signal is emitted, so that,
no matter what the animal's starting position, the outcome is always the same. How is it that the rat is able to vary his behavior
in precise, purposeful ways so as to produce a constant result?
Some behaviorists have postulated environmental "cues" that modify the properties of the main stimulus acting upon the animal
and so modify the animal's behavior. But this argument is implau-

sible. As Powers has pointed out, it requires the modifying cues to work with quantitative precision upon the animal's nervous system; also, these cues are hypothetical and have never been satisfactorily elucidated; but most important, these cues cannot deal with novel situations in which the animal would have had no prior opportunity to learn any modifying "cues." A far more parsimonious explanation is that the animal's behavior is purposive; the rat varies its behavior in response to immediate environmental feedback, so as to achieve an endogenous subgoal (food) which in this case also involves a learned third order goal (pressing the lever).

The second "psychological" model of man involves the postulate of an array of internal drives, or "instinctual appetites." It has had a many-sided career. It can be found in the pessimistic writings of Thomas Hobbes; it was elaborated into a veritable laundry list by William James; Clark Hull gave it scientific respectability through carefully documented exposition; but it was in the hands of Freud that it achieved its apotheosis. In the Freudian schema, there is a sharp trichotomy between: (a) our primitive, uncivilized animal nature (the *id*) which Freud characterized as "a cauldron full of seething excitations";[23] (b) the instrumental, calculating *ego*, which serves the instinctual drives of the *id*; and (c) the *superego*—the internal repository for the constraining and civilizing forces of society. According to Freud, whereas the behavior of early man and contemporary primitives was dominated by instincts (read "nature"), civilized societies have gradually superimposed cultural controls (read "nurture"). But because the instinctual forces in man have not been eliminated, an unavoidable tension exists between instinct and civilization, nature and nurture, *id* and *superego*. Thus, man is doomed to an inner struggle between the dark and even self-destructive forces of his animal nature and the repressive, but also progressive, forces of society.

Though Freud's work contains many important and durable insights (most importantly, his elucidation of the unconscious mind), the model as a whole has not weathered well. First, it is simply not correct to portray our ancestors or contemporary primitives as being governed by instincts, any more than "civilized" man is governed by "rational" (or external) forces. Both aspects are equally "natural" and very ancient. Nor is it correct to assert that egoistic motivations are instinctual, whereas "social" impulses are not; indeed, the tension between self-serving and "altruistic" motivations is typical of any social species. Rather than being the reflection of a meaningless inner turmoil that is unique to civilized man, it reflects a functional, though not always harmonious or successful, balancing act between complementary survival needs; it is an unavoidable concomitant of pursuing a collective survival strategy. Because both the needs of individuals and of the group upon which the individual and his progeny are dependent have relevance to the continued viability of group-living species, natural selection will tend to optimize for both egoistic and altruistic "values"—although what is "optimal" in evolutionary terms is generally context-specific. (We shall have more to say on this point later on.)[24]

Finally, it should be noted that the Freudian model does not conform in important respects with our developing understanding of the neural and endocrine organization of the human brain. For example, it is becoming evident that anger-induced aggression is under the control of both facilitative and inhibitory mechanisms in the limbic system of the "old brain," and that both mechanisms are susceptible to some experiential "programming." Any given instance of anger-induced violence may thus involve a dynamic interplay between inhibitory and facilitative mechanisms, as modified also by immediate perceptual feedback and "real-time" cognitive and evaluative processes.

The most recent, most elaborate, and currently most popular model of man is that of the late Abraham Maslow. Maslow's brand of "humanistic psychology" has had a powerful appeal because it is at once optimistic in tone and very flattering to intellectual and creative people. According to Maslow, man is neither a behavioral sponge (as the behaviorists would have it) nor a tormented neurotic (as the Freudians hold), but a natural innocent (shades of Rousseau) who is endowed with an array of biologically based needs that ascend hierarchically through five categories from "deficiency motivations" (which derive from such physiological needs as food, water, shelter, sleep, sex, etc.) to "being motivations" (at the apex of which is "self-actualization" —or the full use of one's talents and potentialities).[25]

"Evil," by which Maslow means particularly human destructiveness, is *not* innate in man, as Freud postulated, but "reactive" (that is, a response to frustrations). On the other hand, the more complex and constructive human motivations *are* authentic and innate. Only when these "higher" motivations are satisfied is the true potential for human fulfillment realized, but this cannot occur unless the "lower," more basic (and more urgent) needs are satisfied first. Not all men may be capable of self-actualization, but the satisfaction of basic needs will at least make such a flowering possible.

There are many merits to Maslow's model. It involves a more complex and multifaceted view of human motivation, one in which psychological needs are treated as primary rather than merely derivative or artifactual. Also, man is viewed as basically healthy and positive in his relationship to life. Maslow also recognizes, as Freudians and "classical" behaviorists do not, that the motivational substrate of man must be hierarchically organized—that certain basic biological needs must take priority.

It is a noble vision; man has the innate capability of transcending the basic problem of personal survival and has the power to realize the sort of cultural and artistic values to which civilized human societies have always aspired. Indeed, one detects in Maslow an echo of the "good life" that Aristotle posited in *The Politics*. Yet despite the many positive aspects of Maslow's model, it conflicts in some important respects with a rigorously evolutionary perspective and, on closer inspection, involves some normative biases that may be questionable.

A major difficulty is precisely the sort of partiality Maslow shows toward his "metamotivations." Even if we accept that such motivations do exist and that they are innate, the fact that they may seem to be ends in themselves to different individuals does not mean that they are not functionally significant (either adaptive or maladaptive) in relation to more basic survival *and* reproductive needs. In Maslow's hierarchy, there is no inner logic, no organizing principle. Only the "deficiency needs" relate to the problem of survival; the higher needs, though equally biological in origin, are quite distinct and, presumably, frosting on the cake. But from the standpoint of the priorities and value preferences of natural selection, man's social and psychological needs (like those of any other group-living species) must be subsumed as instrumental to the continued viability of the species; it is unlikely that they would have evolved in any other way. From an evolutionary perspective, in other words, Maslow may have his hierarchy upside down. As Marx did to Hegel, it may be necessary to turn Maslow upside down—or rather, right side up.[26]

Another possible problem arises from the concept of self-actualization. Not everyone is capable of achieving this exalted state, it seems, and those who do exhibit a puzzling ambiguity in their relationship to society. On the one hand, we are assured that self-actualized people manifest a transcending commitment to the species. Yet the emphasis is on *self*-fulfillment, while the needs and obligations to the community, one's children, and future generations are de-emphasized. There seems, indeed, to be a possible contradiction between lower-level needs for love and the esteem of others and the detachment and *des*ocialization that are said to accompany self-actualization.

But more to the point, Maslow's self-actualized people are committed to human betterment, yet at the same time they need not deny any of their own needs. Self-actualized people are at once hedonistic and altruistic; they can have their cake and eat it too. But are not some of our most difficult moral dilemmas compounded out of conflicts between the individual's urge to self-gratification and the pressing needs of others? Only if there were no scarcity of the resources needed for survival (and no great inequities in their distribution) could unbridled self-gratification occur without depriving others.[27] But this is the nub of the present political conundrum—we are confronted with an ever-increasing number of people, a limited, if not shrinking, resource base, and gross inequities in the patterns of consumption.

It must also be emphasized that Maslow's hierarchy of needs is only a first approximation. One obvious omission is the need for stimulation and goal-directed activity—a need for which we now have empirical evidence.[28] A satisfactory formulation of human needs must also account for the tension, or dynamic interplay that exists among human motivations.[29] For instance, Maslow's "safety needs" are very often put in jeopardy by human competitiveness and by our propensity to seek out challenges to our capacities.

To summarize, then, in none of the major alternatives to the evolutionary model is the *raison d'être* for human motivations, capacities, and needs made clear; human nature is not related to biological ends in a coherent way. With the possible exception of Maslow's formulation, these views of human nature treat the biological realm either as irrelevant or as a necessary evil which, it is to be hoped, we can rise above. Culture is viewed as something which enables us to transcend our basic nature, rather than as something which is, for the most part, the *servant* of human nature.

Finally, these models lack a sense of perspective. They lack a proper understanding of man's place in nature and of man's unavoidable subjugation to the problem of survival. Equally important, they lack a proper understanding of the time dimension. Neither the legacies of past generations nor the needs of future generations are appreciated or accounted for, whereas in an evolutionary model each individual is, first and foremost, part of a collectivity and a potential link between the past and the future. Both the causes and the consequences of man's behavior must be viewed in that light.

## CULTURE, POLITICS, AND HUMAN NATURE

Although space does not permit an extended treatment here, two other aspects of the evolutionary model of human nature should be brought into focus: namely, how are culture (including cultural evolution) and politics to be comprehended and accounted for?[30]

First, regarding culture, it has been fashionable in recent years to define culture in linguistic terms—to speak of the "symbol pool" of a society as being a cultural analogue of the gene pool and to identify cultural evolution with the accumulation and transmission of new symbols (new "cultural DNA"). Like so many other partial truths, such a view of culture and cultural change can be at once enlightening and misleading—if it is accepted without qualification. For language is only a means, albeit an important and marvelously efficient one. It facilitates culture and cultural change, but it is not the only mechanism by which cultural accretions are stored and transmitted. Nonverbal communications are often underrated. But more to the point, to a considerable extent each succeeding generation *rediscovers* culture, or models *selectively* the behavior of the older generation, rather than simply absorbing culture indiscriminately. Children are not sponges; they take an active (and often quite critical) role in their own learning process.

Thus, the transmission of culture from one generation to the next takes place within the context of the purposeful efforts of children to acquire adaptive adult roles. (Of course, it is also true that the relative adaptiveness of different roles is partly a function of their intrinsic properties and partly also a reflection of the differential rewards and punishments imposed on them by society.) Language is certainly an important enabler in this process, but the structural elements of culture also include knowledge, tools and material artifacts, and, most important, organization.

From an evolutionary perspective, what is most significant is the way in which man puts language and knowledge and tools to use in goal-oriented social contexts—in order to satisfy his needs and wants. Just as, at the morphological level, individual traits take on significance only as functioning parts of the total phenotype, so man's purposive behavioral systems—the systems by which means are fitted to ends—represent the cultural payoffs.

Furthermore, man is the quintessential cybernetic animal, solving problems and pursuing goals in collaboration with his fellows. Man excels at devising and playing roles in "social systems"—systems designed to achieve through collective efforts whatever ends he sets for himself. And because politics (in the broad, Aristotelian sense) is the process by which man goes about cybernating his behavior—that is, solving "public" problems, making authoritative decisions, and organizing and coordinating the behavior of his fellows—man is distinctively a political animal.

In these terms, political behavior is not confined to specialized governmental institutions. It is a facet of any organized, interpersonal activity, insofar as that activity manifests the properties of a cybernetic social system (insofar, that is, as it is goal-oriented, self-regulating, and has internal processes of communication and control among the constituent individuals).

Accordingly, most complex human organizations may be said to have a political aspect, and, for analytical purposes, we could abstract the "political system" out of the stream of social activity and treat it as a "subsystem" of the total process. By the same token, other species too can be said to exhibit political behaviors. However, the repertoire of such behaviors in other species is quite limited and stereotyped by our standards. Other species cannot readily adapt their social behaviors to new goals. What sets man apart and makes him a distinctively political animal is the fact that he has learned how to elaborate upon and adapt the basic principles of cybernetic behavioral organization—the basic social building blocks—to encompass an extraordinary variety of goals. Man alone is able to invent new and more intricate forms of organization, and the increasingly complex cybernation of human societies has been one of the most significant trends in cultural evolution.

How, then, have social systems (and macrolevel governmental systems) evolved? What is the mechanism of cultural evolution? Above I suggested that natural selection involves the relationship (or the "fit") between purposive organisms and their environments. My argument is that precisely the same sort of relationship is involved in cultural and political evolution. The causes of continuity and change in cultural processes are to be found neither in environmental factors nor in human mentation and action but in both—that is, in the interactions between human organisms and their various environments (cultural and natural). Changes either in the behavior of the human organism (or the collective behavior of a group of organisms) or in any of the environments in which the human organism is embedded (or changes in both, for that matter) become selectively relevant only insofar as the organism-environment *relationship* is significantly altered, and it is those alterations (or "variations") that are subjected to cultural "selection."

Of course, natural selection has been responsible in the first instance for the emergence of the motivational and behavioral propensities of the human species and for shaping the biosphere within which man must earn his living. In addition, natural selection continues to pass final judgment on the various ways in which these propensities are expressed, as indicated above. But the *immediate* source of cultural selection is a more proximate, intermediate mechanism that I have taken to calling "human selection."[31] By human selection, I am referring to the processes by which human needs and wants, what Donald T. Campbell[32] refers to as "internal selection criteria," "select" from ongoing behavior-environment interactions. Just as natural selection refers not to the *initial* sources of change (say a new mutation) but to the *consequences* of that change, so human selection refers, not to human inventions or behavioral adaptations *per se,* but to selection based on the *effects* of those changes in relation to the satisfaction of human needs and wants. It is the perceived or actualized utility—the rewarding or reinforcing properties of the change—that counts. Artifacts and behaviors that contribute to the satisfaction of human needs and wants (needs and wants whose origins are biological and a product of the evolutionary process) will be selectively favored (though, for a variety of reasons, favorable "variations" may sometimes fail to be incorporated into the cultural system), and those that are nonrewarding, or negatively reinforcing, will be disfavored.

The proposition, then, is that the variations (or pressures) that initiate cultural changes may arise from many sources: population increases, depletion of an essential resource, a climatic change, a human invention, or perhaps a new survival strategy developed and organized at the group level through the political process. However, it is the differential effects (or functions) of these changes in relation to the matrix of human needs that determines which cultural modifications will persist and contribute to the ongoing evolution of a society. Thus, "human selection," like natural selection, is a global abstraction that applies to a very wide array of phenomena. The reason why such phenomena may be classed together is that they have a *functional equivalence* in terms of the problem of human survival as manifested in specific human needs.

There are, of course, many problems and complexities relating to the theory of cultural evolution that I have described, and I can allude to only a few of the more important issues here.

1. For one thing, there is the problem of specifying in greater detail precisely what the postulated substrate of human needs consists of and how these needs are integrated with one another. What the problem comes down to is the fact that our understanding of the mechanisms of human selection is limited at this juncture by the limits of our knowledge about the biopsychological bases of human motivation and learning. Of course, our understanding of the workings of natural selection is similarly limited; we are not therefore required to understand human selection completely in order to recognize its existence. Furthermore, as behavioral scientists increase our understanding of the substrate of human behavior, we will, at the same time, be illuminating the mechanisms of cultural evolution.

2. Where, precisely, is the locus of human selection? Who does

the selecting? Presumably, when one is given the opportunity to do so, the locus of selection is the individual. But, as Campbell suggested, individuals do not always choose for themselves. Much human selection may be imposed on an individual by parents, teachers, coaches, employers and government officials. On the other hand, the authorities may have considerable difficulty enforcing their choices. Many individuals may resist what they perceive or experience as aversive choices made by others on their behalf.

3. How, specifically, are cultural changes diffused and retained in the cultural system? Although data bearing on these questions are available, no one has done any systematic analysis, as far as I know.

4. The human selection model must take into account the existence of feedback loops, which affect the ongoing organism-environment relationship. Especially important is the problem of feedback lag. Though man's behavior may have immediately rewarding properties, it may also alter the natural environment in such a way as to precipitate unanticipated and possible aversive later consequences. Thus, what is adaptive in terms of the human selection model may not be adaptive in Darwinian terms—in terms of the longer–range problems of survival and reproduction.

5. Finally, there is the complicated question of how macrolevel politics and government fit into the human selection model. As I have defined the term here, political systems at the macrolevel are viewed as having primary responsibility for the collective survival strategies of human societies; they are major contributors to the process of human selection at the collective level. Accordingly, the evolution of "government" may be viewed as the progressive elaboration of specialized and routinized structures for the performance of these functions. And, like other cultural accretions, the emergence of formalized governmental institutions has involved a cumulative (though by no means linear) process of invention, testing for cultural "fitness" and subsequent modification.

This view of politics is not new, of course. The idea that steering and control functions are an "organic" and indispensable property of self-sufficient societies—whether among army ants, baboons, wolves, or men—can be traced back at least to the Greeks. Although it has not usually been expressed in precisely these terms, the notion has also been commonplace that, at least in human societies, these steering functions may be performed badly or not at all; for lack of adaptive government, the collective behavior of a society might become quite detrimental to the longer–run objective of corporate survival. How one should go about making such value judgments about particular political systems is, of course, another matter. But such evaluations are not in principle impossible to make, and this leads us to some implications of the perspective that we have been advancing here.

## SOME IMPLICATIONS FOR SOCIAL SCIENCE RESEARCH

We have posited here a model of human nature whose basic properties are functionally related to the fundamental problem of human existence. Far from being either a *tabula rasa* or a social artifact, human nature is basically purposive and basically oriented to biological ends (even though we are often unconscious of these ends). Human needs, human motivations, and even human capacities for creating and learning culture can best be understood as the concrete manifestations of man's nature as a hierarchically organized, self-regulating, partially autonomous (but also partially externally controlled) cybernetic system.

Many of the precise properties and characteristics of this system remain to be explored. What was described above was no more than an outline—a progress report on an area of behavioral science research that is being very intensively investigated at the present time. Even so, this outline does point the way to a certain kind of research orientation with respect to the causes and consequences of social and political behavior.

First, for those who are concerned particularly with causal analyses, this model suggests that social causation involves interactions between the substrate of basic human needs (as mediated and filtered by cultures) and an array of critical environmental variables. These "master" variables include population, resources (food, water, energy, hard minerals, and so forth), various properties of the natural environment, technology and social organization. Furthermore, these variables act (and interact) in complex and configural ways, with many nonlinear aspects. In other words, Malthus (who identified the population-resource nexus), Marx (who concentrated on changes in the "mode of production of material life") and Aristotle (who viewed politics as an independent variable) were each partially correct about the locus of social causation. But these several variables are causally significant only insofar as they affect (and in turn are affected by) human efforts to satisfy human needs (and wants). The problem for social science research is thus twofold. Not only must we attempt a more precise specification of the configuration of human needs (the "reference signals") but we must get a much better fix than we have obtained heretofore on the relevant "exogenous" variables. We need to enlarge our view of what constitutes the relevant human environment and to learn more about the specific parameters of the survival problem for man and how these survival imperatives shape our survival strategies.

A second major research implication that may be drawn from the model above has to do with the role of biological "forces" in behavioral causation. The model suggests that we should not rule out such influences in principle, but neither should we jump to any conclusions. We have only just begun to explore the biology of human behavior—the extent to which biological characteristics may create behavioral "imperatives," bias learning processes, predetermine which kinds of environmental experiences will be reinforcing, set boundaries and limits on cultural manipulations, and contribute significantly to the many individual differences we observe in behavior. If we can as yet draw only a limited number of firm conclusions, nonetheless we may legitimately anticipate that more will be forthcoming.

For those who are concerned with functional analyses, and with policy issues, on the other hand, the basic problem is how to measure adaptation. Is it possible to develop some sort of profile of what constitutes adaptiveness in human societies which could be used as a baseline for evaluating specific cases? It is indeed strange (and a token of our theoretical confusion) that we do not have available even a consensually acceptable first approximation; we have no systematic way of measuring adaptation. In fact, we are not even agreed upon what unit (or level) of analysis we should be employing. Should we be concerned with each individual member of a society or with certain collective properties? And, if the latter, which of the many different kinds of human collectivities should we focus upon?

For more than two centuries, Western societies have, in effect, relied on narrowly economic measures of adaptiveness. To the classical economists, the relevant unit of analysis was the individual, and the most important criterion of "success" was the individual's return on his invested capital or his labor. The presumption was that the sum of all the individual "goods" would automatically produce the collective welfare. We have learned that this is not necessarily so. For instance, the sum of many individual choices to have more children could be a collective "bad"—a Malthusian disaster, in fact.

Modern industrial societies have come to rely on various aggregate economic measures—gross national product, income per capita, and so forth. And yet, these measures have proved to be equally deficient if not, to some extent, actually misleading. For one thing, a statistic like GNP is so constructed that it treats as a "good' the wasteful squandering of resources on conspicuous consumption; it tells us nothing about how sensibly we are using nonrenewable resources. Indeed, husbanding resources and reducing unnecessary consumption would reflect negatively upon the GNP. Nor, as we have learned in recent years, does GNP tell us anything about how well we are doing with respect to noneconomic aspects of the problem of adaptation—aspects that economists have traditionally treated as "externalities." In some instances, these adaptively significant externalities seem to have been adversely affected in an almost perfectly inverse relationship to improvements in the GNP. Economic "goods," in short, may produce adaptive "bads." By the same token, a measure such as average income per capita can obscure the maladaptive consequences of a highly skewed distribution of income within a society: while there may be a few members who are very rich, many more may be ill-fed, ill-clothed, and ill-housed.

In recent years, some anthropologists have sought more subtle ways of measuring adaptiveness, such as energy flows, or various criteria of environmental "mastery" (for instance, the proportion of the population engaged in the food quest, relative freedom from environmental variation, more substitutions and alternatives for meeting needs, greater knowledge of cause and effect, etc.). Criteria of this kind are, in reality, derived from major properties of Western societies, but such ethnocentrism begs the question. Are Western industrial societies better adapted? Do we indeed have greater mastery over the problem of survival, or are past and present adaptive successes unstable? Over the longer run, it is possible that the survival strategies we have been pursuing will lead us into a *cul de sac,* or at very least may have to be modified significantly. Furthermore, we remain unenlightened about the relationship between populations and their resource bases. Is a proper balance being maintained? And are goods and services being distributed in such a way that *individual* needs are being satisfied? There may be, in sum, a significant difference between what we *are* doing and what we need to do in order to ensure continued survival.

In reality, there are two problems, or rather two levels upon which adaptiveness can be measured. Because reproducing populations, or "demes", are the most important unit of biological adaptation over the long haul—and because demes have many collective properties that can only be adequately evaluated at the collective level, some measure or measures of collective adaptiveness is an important desideratum. Aggregate economic measures or measures that use industrial societies as a baseline may not be satisfactory, but the search for better holistic measures should be encouraged. At the same time, since adaptation is also a problem for each individual, finer-grained measures of adaptation—ones that would enable us to tell how well any given individual is doing—are also relevant.

Accordingly, a first step might be further efforts to develop a set of criteria for determining what is the "optimum" human population size for a given environment. Such an estimate would necessarily involve a synthesis of several different criteria of optimality, and each estimate would be specific to a particular environment. It might also change through time, as conditions change. It would thus be a very dynamic and multidimensional measuring rod.

In addition, an array of "indicators" might be developed that would reflect several specific dimensions of the total process of human adaptation. These could include economic indicators, social indicators, ecological indicators, health indicators, and even genetic indicators.

The matter of what constitutes the most appropriate population "boundary" might also be handled in a flexible way. In theory, the relevant population should be that unit which, in a given instance, is essentially autonomous and self-sufficient with respect to all of the major dimensions of the survival problem. In practice, it is often very difficult to make such a determination unambiguously. To an increasing degree, the autonomous unit varies with different dimensions of the survival problem. Also, the patterns of autonomy and interdependence are rapidly changing.

In order to measure adaptation at the individual level, on the other hand, an effort might be made to develop at least a crude profile of individual needs (both biological and "psychological"). Rather than using a single, standardized profile, though, one might anticipate a "set" of profiles that would accommodate, within some maximum range of variation, the many individual and cultural differences that exist. Such an enterprise would be enormously ambitious and fraught with uncertainties and subjectivity. However, we would at least be focusing on the right questions— and on the "right" model of human nature.

## SOME NORMATIVE IMPLICATIONS

Is there a general welfare—a *summum bonum?* And, equally important, does an evolutionary view of man provide an answer to Albert Schweitzer's challenge at the start of this essay? Can we discern a transcendent social purpose for human strivings and accomplishments?

It all depends upon how one views the evolutionary process and man's place in it. Schweitzer's anguished search for meaning has been shared by many modern thinkers, particularly those who have felt compelled by the victory of Darwinism to reject notions of a divine purpose or "Natural Law." Some have been led by the evidence of evolution to conclude that man must therefore be the product of a meaningless and even capricious process. Molecular biologist (and Nobel Laureate) Jacques Monod echoes this sentiment in his recent book, *Chance and Necessity:* "Pure chance, absolutely free but blind, [is] at the very root of the stupendous edifice of evolution."[33]

However, such an extreme view overlooks an important dimension of the process. Chance, or nonpurposive changes (such as genetic mutations), may produce the raw material of evolution, but it is natural selection that steers the ultimate course. And natural selection is basically utilitarian. As Dobzhansky observes, "natural selection is an anti-chance agency."[34] Furthermore, nat-

ural selection has through time produced in *Homo sapiens* a
creature that is not only purposive but self-aware and creative—
a creature that is increasingly capable of understanding and exert-
ing influence (for better or worse) over the evolutionary process
itself. Only if we were to assume that man is helpless to guide his
own fate could self-pity and inaction be countenanced. And only
if we were to assume that the survival problem has somehow been
"solved" could we feel complacent about man's fate. But neither
assumption is warranted by the evidence.

The most compelling lesson of the multiple crises we have been
experiencing these past few years is that the survival of the species
as a corporate entity is at very least a continuing adventure, if not
a relentless and inescapable challenge. (There is, indeed, considerable irony in the fact that, for as far into the future as we
can peer at this point, the greatest threat to mankind is man.)
Not only is the outcome of the human adventure not predeter-
mined, but human choices and actions must be counted among the
many *partial determinants* of the ongoing process. (In fact, it is
well to keep in mind that even our assumptions about the very
long run—our assumptions about the finite life of the solar system—are based on something less than perfect human knowledge
of the cosmos.) Not until the evolutionary adventure has actually
been played out will we or our descendants know the ultimate
fate of the human species. In short, the future is not vouchsafed
by any law of nature (much less any law of history), but it may
be striven for; it is within our power to further this adventure, if
we so choose. Dobzhansky notes:

> Man and his place in nature can be seen in a different light if
> mankind is evolving, or can be made to evolve, towards some-
> thing better than it is at present. The fundamental fact is that
> when mankind discovered that it had evolved, it ceased to be
> a flotsam carried helplessly on the evolutionary current. It can
> now aspire to steer for directions man himself chooses, if need
> be against the current.[35]

Because of the very nature of human nature, each of us is,
whether we like it or not, a steward of the human species. Each
of us represents a link in a long biological (and cultural) chain
and each is in a sense a vessel—a bearer (with modifications) of

legacies passed down to us against very long odds by ancestors who fought the good fight and managed to endure.

Of course, the fact of this inheritance cannot logically bind us to any normative imperatives. There is no Natural Law that compels us to accept a fiduciary responsibility for future generations. And yet, we cannot escape the fact that many of our actions, individually and collectively, do affect the future of the species. In other words, whether or not we choose to accept a conscious obligation for the future, we cannot avoid the blame for it.

The philosophers tell us that we cannot infer moral obligations, or "oughts," from any fact in the empirical world, from what "is." Science may be able to explain how things work, but it cannot tell us how we should live our lives. In practice, though, this logical gulf between facts and values (the so-called "Is-Ought" dichotomy)[36] has been bridged for many of us by the psychological realities—by the fact that we are endowed with a strong compulsion to survive (and survival is a prerequisite for any other value choices), and by the subjective sense of obligation that we normally feel at least to our immediate forebears and to our immediate progeny. In a passage reminiscent of Edmund Burke, Walter Lippmann several years ago captured this sentiment with great poignancy:

> Besides the happiness and the security of the individuals of whom a community is at any moment composed, there are also the happiness and security of the individuals of whom generation after generation it will be composed. . . . That is why young men die in battle for their country's sake and why old men plant trees they will never sit under.[37]

Accordingly, the general welfare is not a figment of our imagination, nor a product of a naive idealism, nor yet the cunning ploy of a self-serving political or economic elite. If we include all of the potential members of future generations among those whose interests may be affected by our actions in this generation, then the aggregated interests of those who are yet to be born outweigh by a very wide margin either the interests of any living individual, or even the "collective goods," as political economists use the term,[38] of all living souls. And it is those aggregated future interests that constitute the general welfare. To the extent that we so tailor our value choices and actions that we are striving, to the very limit of our capacity for intelligent planning and foresight, to maximize the long-run survival chances of the species, only then can it be said that we are acting in accordance with the general welfare.

Yet even if we are ready and willing to accept the ukase that we must subordinate our interests to the future interests of the species, how do we translate our very uncertain notions about what the needs of subsequent generations will be into a concrete framework of social and political values? On the one hand, we face the problem of specifying individual "rights" and "duties" in a way that will best serve the welfare of those who may come after us, and, on the other hand, we need to develop criteria and objectives to guide collective (or political) decision-making. Although a full discussion of these issues is not possible here, certain basic guideposts may be set forth.

I suggested above that survival is at once an individual and a collective affair—the two levels of adaptation are neither wholly distinct nor wholly concordant. To a considerable extent, the satisfaction of individual needs also furthers the interests of the collective survival enterprise. At the same time, transcendent "species needs" may directly conflict with individual self-gratification. The most conclusive example relates to resource consumption. If a critical nonrenewable resource is consumed without being recycled (or else replaced by a suitable substitute), a direct cost is imposed on subsequent generations. Such actions amount to the payoffs in a zero-sum game in which our descendants lose whatever "goods" we gain. Only the recycling or replacement of resources (or sustained yield exploitation of renewable resources) can be considered adaptive—that is, in harmony with the general welfare.

From an evolutionary perspective, both our "rights" and our "duties" derive from our status as bearers of our evolutionary heritage and as potential contributors (biologically and/or culturally, since cultural legacies are also important for man) to the future of the species, to the general welfare. Insofar as both personal freedom and social constraints (or, more broadly, self-serving as well as altruistic behaviors) may advance the general welfare, both are justified. As I noted elsewhere:

there is no clearcut ethical dichotomy between the individual and the group. Rather, the problem is one of maintaining a dynamic balance between the two, a balance that may have to be adjusted frequently in order to sustain the adaptiveness of a society. The proper balance is not something that can be determined *a priori* in all cases. Each problem, or type of problem, may have to be weighed separately. But in theory, at least, there would appear to be three possible forms of self-serving behavior: 1) that which also contributes to the welfare of the group; 2) that which is neutral in its effects on the group; and 3) that which is maladaptive, or detrimental to the long-run survival potential of the group.[39]

But how do we go about finding the proper balance? The general welfare, as we have defined it here, is not necessarily associated with any particular economic or political system. Nor does it necessarily have either "conservative" or "radical" political implications. Depending upon the context, either continuities or changes in a society might be adaptive, and both should be judged by the same yardstick—their contribution to the collective survival enterprise; the goal in either event should be to maximize our ability to meet the basic needs of present and future generations.

However, given our very imperfect knowledge of what will best serve the needs of our remote descendants, George Wald has suggested that we use as a seat-of-the-pants criterion for social choice whatever is perceived to be best for the *children* of a society. He asks, are nuclear weapons good for children? Or is pollution? Or the wanton and wasteful squandering of resources? Or a value system that permits a society to pay entertainers vastly more than it pays educators?

What, more specifically, should be the "ideal" goals of a society that aspires to act in accordance with the general welfare? First, there should be a stable relationship with the basic life-support system upon which we are dependent. Second, the economy should be reorganized for long-term stability rather than growth; the emphasis should be upon maintaining our capital stock, rather than upon maximizing throughputs (as the economists would say). Third, there should be an approximation of the Marxian dictum "From each according to his ability, to each according to his needs!" And fourth, there should be a harmonious social and political order. Indeed, we might strive to approximate (insofar as we are able) the Platonic ideal—a society in which a mesh is achieved between the needs and abilities of individual citizens and the needs of society. The leadership of such a society would also be required to have an unwavering commitment to the general welfare—and the requisite ability to act upon it.

For a society such as ours, this prescription, even if only partially realized, would require fundamental changes in our values, our economic system, and our politics. It would mean, at least for the upper strata in our society, considerably less freedom to pursue self-gratifications and considerably more personal constraint and social discipline. Because our society has generally permitted its political leaders to act as if the political realm were analogous to a capitalist market—as if the functions of leadership amounted to serving as a kind of broker between contending interest groups —it would mean that we would have to accept considerably more political "steering," or political "cybernation," than we have been accustomed to. There would be more planning and political control, not less. Such a prescription would, in short, be incompatible with "radical" freedom and infantile utopianism.

Is even an approximation of such a political vision practicable? Is it realistic to think that people in our society would ever be willing to make such fundamental changes in their way of life and their public philosophy? Is it not naïve to think that people would ever accept a heavy new burden of social duties and constraints? Who is to do the political steering? And who will guard the guardians? In the wake of Watergate, would anyone argue that we have solved the classic problems of political engineering, the rock upon which Plato himself foundered? How does one design an economic and political system that can compensate for human frailties and ensure political "outputs" that accord with the general welfare?

There is no ready answer. And yet, we confront increasingly urgent ecological imperatives (the population-resource-environment nexus), and they are forcing us to the wall. The time is rapidly approaching when we (and other Western societies as well) will be compelled to make drastic changes. The real issue is not whether radical changes are desirable or possible. The choice we confront is between radical changes by incremental means and radical changes by radical means. We can make the transition to "Spaceship Earth," in Kenneth Boulding's phrase, in such a way as to minimize hardships and preserve, as far as possible, the best values of Western civilization. Or, we can be overwhelmed with convulsive events that will surely exact a fearful toll in human suffering and evoke Draconian, or even totalitarian, responses. As Mort Sahl would say, the future lies ahead. Will we get there under the guidance of clear objectives and intelligent planning, or will we find ourselves blindly groping, with increasing desperation, for a way out of a situation that is out of control?

In place of either the dogma of self-sustained progress or utopian fantasies based on Enlightenment or nineteenth–century optimism, what we need at this point are hard and disciplined efforts to model a realizable and adaptive future—and a set of strategies for implementing it. (In the truest sense, what we require is "neogenesis"—new forms of biological organization.) This must be based on a sensitive understanding of the natural environment, a balanced "best guess" assessment of human nature and human needs, and a sophisticated understanding of economic and political realities.

If there is to be controlled, adaptive change, we will need, above all, extraordinarily gifted and dedicated leadership. This has been the indispensable element in all of the great "revitalization movements" of the modern era, and we have no reason to believe that we will be able to do without it in the period of transition that lies ahead. Whether we will be fortunate enough to have it when we need it remains to be seen. But one thing is certain, we will have to organize ourselves if we hope to save ourselves.

## NOTES AND REFERENCES

1. Leon Eisenberg, "The Human Nature of Human Nature," *Science* 176 (April 1972), p. 123.
2. Lionel Tiger and Robin Fox, *The Imperial Animal* (New York: Holt, Rinehart and Winston, 1972), p. 25.
3. Indeed, solutions to many of the most fundamental problems of biological organization, from which *Homo sapiens* also benefits, were worked out in the evolutionary process long before the emergence even of the primate line.

4. For fuller discussions of this point, see Peter A. Corning, "The Biological Bases of Behavior and Some Implications for Political Science," *World Politics* 23 (April 1971); also "Comparative Survival Strategies: An Approach to Social and Political Analysis," prepared for delivery at the 1973 Annual Meeting of the American Political Science Association, New Orleans, Sept. 4-8, 1973.

5. Described in R. A. Hinde, *Animal Behavior* (New York: McGraw-Hill, 1966), p. 436.

6. Ernst Mayr, *Populations, Species and Evolution* (Cambridge, Mass.: Harvard, 1971), p. 402.

7. *Ibid.,* pp. 4-5.

8. Theodosius Dobzhansky, *Mankind Evolving* (New Haven: Yale, 1962), p. 287.

9. For an extensive review of research on biological dimensions of learning, see Martin E. P. Seligman and Joanne L. Hager, eds., *Biological Boundaries of Learning* (New York: Appleton-Century-Crofts, 1972).

10. On the other hand, as David A. Hamburg has argued: "Why should one study other animals if one is primarily interested in understanding man? Principally to obtain an evolutionary perspective in which we attempt to reconstruct how man came to be the way he is, and to search for subtle legacies of his ancient past that may have been transmitted both through biological and social channels. Such studies should attempt to delineate broad *trends* in evolution, asking whether certain characteristics of vertebrate, mammalian, and primate organisms are maintained as we draw closer to man. Building on these broad evolutionary trends, we pay special attention to the behavior patterns of man's closest relatives, such as the chimpanzee. If a behavioral trend of primate evolution is strengthened in these closely related species, it should orient us to investigate these characteristics as possible underlying components of human behavior." "An Evolutionary and Developmental Approach to Human Aggressiveness," *The Psychoanalytic Quarterly* 42 (April 1973), p. 185.

11. For the present discussion, one complication involving the prenatal "environment" will not be considered.

12. The simplified formula for heritability is: $h^2 = \dfrac{V_g}{V_p}$ Let us consider a hypothetical study in which two different populations are sampled. In each sample, the actual amount of biological variation is quite large. But in one case the environmental variation is even larger, so that the biological variation turns out to be a relatively small proportion of the *total* variation. For the second sample, though, the environment is quite uniform, so that most of the observed phenotypic variation is biologically based. Accordingly, the heritabilities for these two biologically similar samples might be, say, .3 and .8 respectively. Since heritabilities can neve be greater than unity (or 1.0), this is a substantial difference— 50% to be precise. Conversely, two samples that are quite different from each other biologically might yield identical heritability estimates if the environments were sufficiently different from each other to make biological differences proportionately the same.

13. Alexander Fraser, "The Evolution of Purposive Behavior," in Heinz Von Foerster *et al.,* eds., *Purposive Systems* (New York: Spartan Books, 1968), p. 15.

14. The literature on purposive, or goal-oriented, control systems is exten-

sive. In particular, see Norbert Wiener, *The Human Use of Human Beings: Cybernetics and Society* (Boston: Houghton Mifflin, 1950); H. Ross Ashby, *Design for a Brain* (London: Chapman and Hall, 1960); Walter Buckley, ed., *Modern Systems Research for the Behavioral Scientist* (Chicago: Aldine, 1968); Ludwig von Bertalanffy, *General Systems Theory* (New York: George Braziller, 1968); and Karl Deutsch, *The Nerves of Government* (New York: The Free Press, 1966).

15. William T. Powers, "Feedback: Beyond Behaviorism," *Science* 179 (26 January, 1973), pp. 351-356.

16. Edward H. Pattee, ed., *Hierarchy Theory* (New York: George Braziller, 1973), p. xi.

17. James S. Coleman, "Social Systems," in Paul A. Weiss, ed., *Hierarchically Organized Systems in Theory and Practice* (New York: Hafner, 1971), p. 69.

18. I hasten to emphasize that this is not a veiled argument in favor of social or economic exploitation and injustice. Hierarchy here refers to task-specific organizational functions, or "roles." Hierarchy is not, in the natural world, an end in itself, nor is it necessarily related to individual advantage.

19. See Corning, "The Biological Bases of Behavior and Some Implications for Political Science," *op. cit.,* and "Comparative Survival Strategies," *op. cit.* See note 4 above.

20. The concept of "adaptiveness" is explored at length in Corning, "Comparative Survival Strategies," *op. cit.*

21. Since the "fit" between what is adaptive for the individual and what is adaptive for the collectivity is often imperfect, this creates a difficult optimization problem for social species in general and for human societies in particular. This issue will be discussed further below.

22. For the most up-to-date exposition of Skinner's views, see *Beyond Freedom and Dignity* (New York: Knopf, 1971); also *Science and Human Behavior* (New York: Macmillan, 1953).

23. Sigmund Freud, *New Introductory Lectures on Psychoanalysis* (1933), translated by James Strachey (New York: W. W. Norton, 1965), p. 73.

24. Though it is not pertinent here, it is worth noting that several different models have been developed to describe the workings of natural selection among various population aggregates.

25. Maslow's five categories consist of the following: (1) physiological needs; (2) safety needs; (3) "belongingness" and love needs; (4) esteem needs; and (5) self-actualization needs. Abraham Maslow, *Motivation and Personality* (New York: Harper & Row, 1954), pp. 80ff.

26. To some, this line of reasoning may seem to threaten Western cultural values, but such is not necessarily the case. An explanation of how our psychological characteristics and abilities evolved does not require a normative judgment about them. Nor does an evolutionary explanation of the origins of these traits imply that they are always adaptive.

27. We will skirt in the present discussion the gloomy postulate that at least some men may be so designed that they can achieve certain kinds of self-gratifications *only* at the expense of others.

28. See especially, Daniel E. Berlyne, *Conflict, Arousal and Curiosity* (New York: McGraw-Hill, 1960); also "Conflict and Arousal," *Scientific American* 217 (August 1966), pp. 82-87.

29. An authoritative and sophisticated review of the subject of human motivation may be found in Harry F. Harlow, *et al., Psychology* (San

Francisco: Albion, 1971), chap. 10. This point is also discussed by Gerald Cory in "The Biopsychological Basis of Political Socialization and Political Culture" (unpublished Ph.D. dissertation, Stanford, 1974).

30. The following is derived from a more lengthy discussion of these matters in Peter A. Corning "Politics and the Evolutionary Process," *Evolutionary Biology* (VII) (New York: Plenum Press, 1974).

31. *Ibid.* The term "customer selection" has also been suggested by Luigi Luca Cavalli-Sforza.

32. Donald T. Campbell, "Variation and Selective Retention in Socio-Cultural Evolution," in H. R. Barringer *et al.*, eds., *Social Change in Developing Areas: A Reinterpretation of Evolutionary Theory* (Cambridge, Mass.: Schenkman, 1965).

33. Jacques Monod, *Chance and Necessity* (New York: Knopf, 1971), p. 112.

34. Theodosius Dobzhansky, "The Ascent of Man," *Social Biology* 19 (December 1972), p. 375. Actually, mutations at the molecular level are not the only source of the variations that fuel evolutionary change. Nor are such mutations strictly speaking random in nature. Compared to the infinity of theoretical possibilities, only a very limited number of nucleotide substitutions are possible in any given gene at a particular moment in time.

35. *Ibid.,* p. 377.

36. For extended discussions of the "Is-Ought" dichotomy, see Arnold Brecht, *Political Theory: The Foundations of Twentieth-Century Political Thought* (Princeton, N.J.: Princeton University Press, 1959); W. D. Hudson, *The Is-Ought Question* (New York: St. Martin's Press, 1969); and Fred M. Frohock, *Normative Political Theory* (Englewood Cliffs, N.J.: Prentice-Hall, 1974).

37. Walter Lippmann, *The Public Philosophy,* Boston: Little, Brown, 1955, p. 35.

38. "Collective goods" involve benefits that are indivisible and that are jointly supplied to all members of the community. No individual can be excluded from such benefits and no individual can appropriate them for himself. The most commonly cited example is national defense. For a sampler of the literature on the theory of collective goods, see Mancur Olson, *The Logic of Collective Action: Public Goods and the Theory of Groups* (New York: Schocken, 1971); Norman Frohlich *et al., Political Leadership and Collective Goods* (Princeton, N.J.: Princeton University Press, 1971); John Gerard Ruggie, "Collective Goods and Future International Collaboration," *American Political Science Review* 66 (September 1972), pp. 874-893; and Peter F. Cowhey *et al.,* "The Theory of Collective Goods and the Future Regime of Ocean Space" (unpublished paper presented at the International Studies Association Convention, 1973).

39. Peter A. Corning, "The Biological Bases of Behavior and Some Implications for Political Science," *World Politics* 23 (April 1971).

# 3

# HUMAN NATURE, NATURE, AND POLITICAL THOUGHT

ROGER D. MASTERS

## THE DIMENSIONS OF SECULAR POLITICAL THEORY

Customarily, political thought is taught as a historical sequence from Plato to modern times (e.g., Ebenstein, 1969). While there are good reasons for this pattern, it leads us to treat individual philosophers or schools of thought as if each were somehow unique. At most, we are tempted to see a historical trend toward the ideas of our own times, without a sense of the structure underlying all political theory.

Surprisingly enough, however, there are relatively few distinct approaches to the study of political life. Every theorist, whatever else he argues, makes fundamental assumptions concerning the nature of man. Some, like Rousseau, assert that "man is naturally good" (*Second Discourse*. Note i, p. 193); others, like Machiavelli, claim that "men are wretched" or naturally selfish (*Prince,* ch. xvii, pp. 138-139.)[1] Such assumptions are usually described as the difference between theorists whose view of "human nature" is "optimistic" or "pessimistic."

Careful reflection, however, indicates that a simplistic dichotomy between "optimists" and "pessimists" is inadequate. For example, Machiavelli's conclusions are very different from those of St. Paul, though both make similar judgments on the tendency of most men to violate standards of "good" behavior. Conversely, both Marx and Plato begin from the denial that man is essentially selfish,[2] yet their conclusions differ so radically that it would be misleading to classify them as similar "optimists."

Clearly, at least one additional element must be considered: "optimism" or "pessimism" concerning human nature is quite different from an "optimistic" or "pessimistic" assessment of the possibility of establishing a just human society, utilizing knowledge or science to solve practical problems. Machiavelli and Marx, for example, consider their theoretical writings as a guide to human action which can make possible a better human society on earth, whereas (albeit for different reasons) St. Paul and Plato cast doubt on the likelihood that their thought can or will be the basis for a lasting solution to *political* problems.

"Optimism" or "pessimism" concerning human *nature* is thus distinct from "optimism" or "pessimism" concerning the effects of human *action* in the future. In the tradition stretching from the Greeks to modern industrial society, therefore, I will argue that secular or nonreligious thought can be arrayed along two fundamental dimensions.[3] By looking at the polar answers to each of these questions, we can set up a fourfold table (Table 1), each cell of which marks the extremity of the "field" of political thought (Figure 1).

Precisely stated, the first dimension or question concerns the relationship between human nature and society. At one extreme is the view that *men are inherently asocial* if not antisocial; society— and hence all politics—is thus seen as a conventional or customary restraint on the natural drives or passions of naturally equal men. From this perspective, political institutions are man-made conveniences or creations, and standards of justice are necessarily rel-

## Table 1

### Relation of Human Nature to Society

| | Man Naturally Asocial<br>("pessimistic" view<br>of Human Nature) | Man Naturally Social<br>("optimistic" view<br>of Human Nature) |
|---|---|---|
| *Relation of*<br>*Human Action*<br>*to Nature* | | |
| *Knowledge permits*<br>*Understanding of*<br>*Nature* | Antiphon the<br>Sophist<br><br>Thrasymachus | Aristotle |
| *Knowledge permits*<br>*Control of Nature* | Hobbes | Marx |

## Figure 1

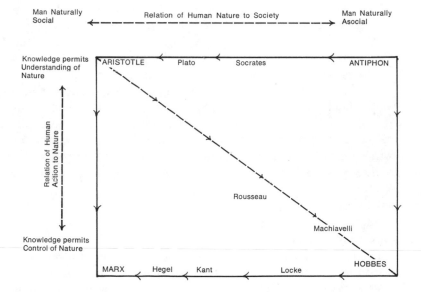

ative to time and place. At the other extreme of this dimension, it is asserted that *man is social by nature*—i.e., that society and political life arise naturally from the needs and historical development of our species. From this perspective, standards concerning the "right" or "just" society are inherent in human nature or history.

The second dimension concerns the role of scientific knowledge and the extent to which human action can create a social order that establishes material abundance and freedom on earth. At one pole is the view, characteristic of pagan antiquity, that *science is limited to an understanding of nature,* and that men cannot freely control natural necessity. At most, some men could profit from knowledge to improve their power or wealth, without thereby changing the fundamental condition of natural scarcity facing mankind. At the other extreme of this dimension lies the modern position that *science can control or master nature* "for the relief of man's estate" (to use Bacon's phrase); by overcoming natural scarcity and increasing social wealth, science, technology, and industry are viewed as mitigating if not resolving the perennial conflict between the rich and the poor. This conception of science permits the *creation* of a political and social order that transcends prior natural or historical limits on human freedom and well-being (cf. Lasswell, 1958: 23-24).

The major variants of secular political thought in the West can be arrayed on a fourfold table, in which the cells are exemplified by Antiphon the Sophist, Aristotle, Hobbes, and Marx. Although Table 1 is subject to the objection that each position is located as if it developed without reference to the others, it can easily be converted into a vector diagram. In Figure 1, therefore, the four typical thinkers are portrayed as extreme points on a plane symbolizing the "field" or domain of political theory; other philosophical positions can then be considered as different weightings of the two basic dimensions. By adding arrows reflecting historical influence, this figure can conveniently illustrate the main trends of Western political thought.[4] This schema thus permits us to suggest both the main influences on the four modal thinkers and the location of the intermediary positions represented by other well-known political theorists.

The primary interest of such a diagram is, of course, not so much historical as analytical. If Western political thinkers can be adequately characterized in terms of their positions on a small number of fundamental dimensions, then perhaps this underlying structure explains not only major trends in the history of political theory but also the articulation of perennial issues by individual theorists. Without denying that every philosopher is to some degree the product of his age and political circumstances, such an approach might reveal the basic elements of which all theoretical systems are recombinations or transformations.[5]

To be sure, each political theorist discusses a wide range of problems—so much so that political thought at first seems to have little or no intrinsic pattern beyond the historical sequence familiar in our textbooks. But primitive kinship systems, myths, and languages also appeared highly idiosyncratic until structural analysis revealed that they constitute myriad transformations of elementary structures; similarly, biological inheritance was difficult to explain beyond the mere observation of similarities and differences until Mendelian genetics paved the way for the discovery of DNA's structure, and chemical analysis was largely limited to descriptive work until Mendeleev's periodic table codified the structural combinations and permutations of the various elements.

Needless to say, the two dimensions defined above cannot pretend to do more than illustrate a mode of analysis, since they are far from specifying the latent structure of all political thought. Figure 1 is presented here merely as a hypothesis which should clarify the recurring themes of human nature and nature in Western political thought. Indeed, as will be shown below, this scheme is incomplete even on a superficial level, since it ignores a third dimension connected with religion, myth, and nonscientific explanation. Before we can hope to understand the relations between scientific thought and religion or myth, however, it is important to see whether a structural approach illuminates secular political theory in the West.

The main task of this essay, therefore, will be an analysis of the four modal political theorists identified in Table 1. Does the thought of Antiphon, Aristotle, Hobbes, and Marx represent four different combinations of the extreme positions on each of the two fundamental dimensions—i.e., the relation of *human nature* to society, and the relation of human knowledge and action to *nature*? If so, the hypothesis that these dimensions have a fundamental status, at least in Western political philosophy, would seem at least plausible. And if not, do the two dimensions proposed at least reveal a complexity in what is usually called "human nature," requiring us to distinguish a theorist's conception of the political implications of human nature from his view of the natural consequences of human politics?

## FOUR MODAL TYPES OF WESTERN POLITICAL THEORY

*The Origins of Political Science*
(*Antiphon the Sophist,* On Truth)

Historically speaking, the notion of natural science that we currently accept can be traced to the pre-Socratic Greeks. The so-called "Sophists" therefore represent one of the earliest and most influential attempts to develop the notion of science and apply it to human behavior. Their views are concisely presented in a famous passage from the Sophist Antiphon's *On Truth*.[6] While only fragments of his treatise are extant, it reflects a widespread view in Greek antiquity, as can be shown by Plato's restatement of the Sophist position—most notably in the *Republic* (the speeches of Thrasymachus in Book I and those of Glaucon and Adeimantus, II, 375a–367e).

Antiphon begins, in Fragment I, from the general view that "justice consists in not transgressing any of the legal rules of the State in which one lives as a citizen"; a just act is one that is legal. As Antiphon immediately observes, however, an individual can maximize his self-interest by gaining all of the benefits of practicing justice in public *and* all the benefits of cheating in private: "A man, therefore, would practice justice in the way most advantageous to himself if, in the presence of witnesses, he held the laws in high esteem, but, in the absence of witnesses, and when he was by himself, he held in high esteem the rules of nature."

This conception of the "rules of nature" as something distinct from the "laws" is not a universal—or even a typical—way of viewing the world. In most primitive societies, no sharp distinction is made between "law" or custom, with its appropriate rituals for varied aspects of human behavior, and the cosmos or (as we say) "nature"; rather, the universe is interpreted in terms of myths and rituals that simultaneously *describe* natural phenomena and *prescribe* legal or appropriate behavior (e.g., Eliade, 1959; Lévi-Strauss, 1962).

Antiphon the Sophist, like other pre-Socratics, breaks sharply from this traditional or mythic view; in place of the perception of the world and of human conduct in terms of overarching myths, he distinguishes between man-made social custom and natural processes:

The rules of the laws are adventitious [man-made], while the rules of nature are inevitable, and again . . . the rules of the laws are created by covenant and not produced by nature, while the rules of nature are exactly the reverse.

The distinction is clearly one of what we call "causality"—a word which, it should be noted in passing, in Greek was derived from the word for "guilt."

Antiphon's demonstration that the "rules of nature," unlike man-made "rules of laws," are not dependent on social custom is extremely simple. A man who violates the laws without being caught "is free from shame and punishment . . . and is subject to shame and punishment only when he is observed." In contrast, the causes of "the rules of nature" do not depend on human agents: "If a man strains any of these rules (which are innate in nature) beyond what it can bear, the evil consequences are none the less, if he is entirely unobserved, and none the greater, if he is seen of all men." If one drinks too much, he has a hangover whether or not others have seen him drinking. Note Antiphon's reasoning here: "This is because the injury which he incurs is not due to men's opinion, but to the facts of the case." [7]

The truth, therefore, must in the first instance be based on the "rules of nature," for only these natural causes operate everywhere in the same manner; science or knowledge consists of going beyond mere "opinions" (which vary from one society to another) to an understanding of nature. Whereas Greeks had different laws and customs from barbarians, "our natural endowment is the same for us all, on all points, whether we are Greeks or barbarians. . . . We all breathe the air through our mouth and nostrils," (Fragment II). In the decisive political respect, all men are naturally equal.

The attempt of early Ionian philosophers to develop a science of nature had tremendous implications because it suggested to the Sophists that, as far as nature is concerned, what the laws define

76

as good or bad, just or unjust, is artificial. As Antiphon puts it: "The things which are established as advantageous in the view of the law are restraints on nature, whereas the things established by nature as advantageous are free." Although the law restrains (or, as Freud put it, represses) natural desires for pleasure and gain, most humans accept it as a necessary evil; society rests on a contract among essentially selfish individuals (cf. *Republic,* II. 358a, 359a–360e).

Such a perspective leads to the quest for natural regularities in all political systems. One example of this early science of politics may be seen in Thrasymachus's analysis of justice in Book I of Plato's *Republic.* By comparing the rules of law in different cities, Thrasymachus is led to define justice as something that has a common basis everywhere. Although "some cities are ruled tyrannically, some democratically, and some aristocratically . . . each ruling group sets down laws, for its own advantage; a democracy sets down democratic laws; a tyranny, tyrannical laws, and the others do the same . . . in every city the same thing is just, the advantage of the established ruling body" (I. 338d–339a).

Without attempting a more complete analysis of Sophists like Antiphon or Thrasymachus, it is important to note that their distinction between convention and nature did not imply that scientific knowledge could radically alter the natural necessities that produce political rivalry and competition. On the contrary, although their rudimentary science of politics treats the substantive concepts of justice or the "common good" as entirely relative or conventional, the Sophists insisted that necessity will determine much human behavior, including conflicts requiring the rule of some men by others.[8] As Muller puts it, "their skepticism involved . . . a clear, honest recognition of the limits of human knowledge" (1962: 190).

Hence the Sophists took it for granted that differences between the powerful and the weak would persist and contented themselves with practical advice to potential or actual rulers and men of wealth (cf. Wheelwright, 1966: Ch. viii, esp. Protagoras, Fragment I and Testimonia 2-4; Gorgias, Fragments 7-10 and Testimonia 1-2; Jaeger, 1945: 323-331). The political theory of Antiphon and the Sophists thus presumes not only that *political organizations are an unnatural restraint on naturally free and equal individuals* but also that *science cannot overcome the natural scarcities confronting civilized societies.* In this case, at least, the two dimensions identified in Figure 1 serve to situate the fundamental characteristics of a major type of political theory in the Western tradition.

### Classic Political Theory: Politics and Justice
### (*Aristotle,* Politics)

Aristotle begins the *Politics* from the "observation" that "every polis [i.e., political community] is a species of association." [9] But, he adds, all human action is connected with intention or purpose: "All men do all their acts with a view to achieving something which is, in their view, a good." Since the common element in a human association must somehow be related to a shared intention or purpose of its members, it follows that "all associations are instituted for the purpose of attaining some good." As the most encompassing or "sovereign" association, the polis will thus be directed to the "most sovereign of all goods"—namely, what is usually called the "common good" or justice (I. 1252a; p. 1). [10]

Aristotle knew the position of Sophists like Antiphon, for whom the "rules of the laws" governing each political community are merely customary or conventional "restraints" on "nature." But he rejects this view by stating—in one of the most famous lines of political thought—"that the polis belongs to the class of things that exist by nature, and that man is by nature an animal intended to live in a polis" (*Politics,* I. 1253a; p. 5). This difference between Antiphon and Aristotle could be stated as the question: Is the basis of the political community really the intention or goal its members claim to share? Or is it possible that the political association is actually a means of achieving individual self-preservation, and that talk about justice or the "common good" is merely propaganda?

Aristotle's answer in the *Politics* is to combine his "normal method of analysis," in which "a compound should be analyzed until we reach its simple and uncompounded elements" (I. 1252a; p.2), with a historical or genetic study that will "begin at the beginning, and consider things in the process of their growth" (I. 1252a; p. 3). This method is *not* the same as Antiphon's; instead of considering the "good" or benefit of an isolated individual, Aristotle looks from the outset at the kinds of groups of individuals ("associations") which are found within a political community and from which it could be said to "grow" or develop historically.

The first element of any human association is the sexual pair, which is necessary for reproduction. Apparently contradicting his own statement that all human action results from intention, Aristotle identifies the minimal social unit as an association that exists "not from deliberate intention," but from a "natural impulse" (1252a; p. 3). Since men do not deny that they "intend" to reproduce when they marry, Aristotle thereby implies that human purpose and natural necessity are inherently related; unlike Antiphon, Aristotle does not treat "natural" causes as by definition distinct from "conventional" motives.

Natural and conventional factors are also combined in the second component of the political community: "Next, there must necessarily be a union of the naturally ruling element with the element which is naturally ruled, for the preservation of both" (1252a; p. 3). Whereas Antiphon treats the restraint or rule of one individual by another as a "convention" or "law," opposed to natural freedom, Aristotle speaks of "natural rule."

Aristotle's point is not absurd, since the newborn infant is "naturally ruled" by his parents for the "preservation of both" (i.e., the family cannot survive if parents do not take care of their infants). But he does not use this evident example to define the "naturally ruling element" (however, cf. I. 1259a-b; pp. 32-33); rather, he apparently refers to adults when saying: "The element which is able, by virtue of its intelligence, to exercise forethought, is naturally a ruling and master element; the element which is able, by virtue of its bodily power, to do what the other element plans, is a ruled element, which is naturally in a state of slavery..." (1252a; p. 3). Although this view is shocking to our way of thinking, some humans do fit this description: retarded or mentally ill individuals, for example, may be physically capable of work without being able to plan ahead.

When Aristotle says that the naturally ruled individual is "naturally in a state of slavery," he goes on to add that "master and slave have accordingly a common interest." The Sophists had argued that this is a silly way of putting it, since the natural ruler is primarily motivated by his own self-interest (cf. *Republic,* I. 343a–344c). Aristotle's answer is that *such* slavery is *not* natural; the natural form of slavery concerns those individuals, though we may debate who they are and why, whose self-interest requires that someone else tell them what to do (1245b; p. 13).

Having analyzed two basic relations, Aristotle then combines them: "The first result of these two elementary associations (of male and female, and of master and slave) is the household or family." (1252b; p. 4).[11] Within the "family," the father is naturally superior to his children, ruling them "like a monarch over subjects" (1259b; pp. 32-33). The husband also is naturally superior to his wife, though his authority is of a more egalitarian nature, "like that of a statesman over fellow citizens" (*ibid.*). Finally, wherever there are domesticated animals or servants who must be told what to do, there is a natural superiority of the master over his servants or slaves.

This household community represents a kind of "common interest"—namely the common interest in a comfortable life; the head of the family does not rule either his wife or his domestic animals with the intention of secretly violating his own rules (as Antiphon describes the "rule of laws"). On the contrary, the family is "the first form of association naturally instituted for the satisfaction of daily recurrent needs" and its members are called "associates of the bread-chest" or "associates of the manger" by earlier thinkers, as if to represent the natural complementarity of their interests (1252b; p. 4. Cf. VII. 1324b; pp. 284-286).

Once we have granted Aristotle the view that the sedentary, agricultural family is "naturally instituted," it is relatively easy to follow the remainder of his argument that the *polis* or Greek city-state "exists by nature, having itself the same quality as the earlier associations from which it grew" (1252b; p. 5). Neither the agricultural family nor the Greek city-state is natural in Antiphon's sense of breathing "air through our mouth and nostrils"; the barbarians lack the form of the city-state, and in some cases even settled homesites and the use of domesticated cattle. But both the agricultural family and the Greek city-state—as well as the intervening stages of the "village"—represent a fulfillment of human potentiality. Thus, in Aristotle's sense, they are natural communities even though (or rather, precisely because) they presuppose education, training, and the restraint of physical impulses and desires.

This way of looking at things is usually called "teleology": the nature of a thing is the fulfillment of its potential, not the necessary and invariant element that is everywhere the same. As Aristotle puts it, "the 'nature' of things consists in their end or consummation; for what each thing is when its growth is completed we call the nature of that thing, whether it be a man or a horse or a family" (1252b; p. 5). This tendency or end of a thing is the best realization of its natural "function" or purpose. "All things derive their essential character from their function and their capacity" (1253a; p. 6).

While living organisms are analyzed in terms of their function or end by many contemporary biologists (Pittendrigh, 1958), teleological reasoning at first looks ridiculous. One is reminded of the argument that the "end" or purpose of the human nose is to hold eyeglasses. But the teleological approach seems more reasonable for domestic animals like the horse, because human intention has selected many of the animal's traits through controlled breeding. And for Aristotle (1254b; p. 13)—as more recently for Konrad Lorenz (1971)—humans are domesticated or tamed animals.

What makes the Greek *polis* or political community the highest form of association for Aristotle is its closer approximation to the end or perfection of human life. "When we come to the final and perfect association, formed from a number of villages, we have already reached the *polis*—an association which may be said to have reached the height of full self-sufficiency; or rather we may say that while it grows for the sake of mere life, it exists for the sake of a good life" (1252b; pp. 4-5). A political community is capable of "self-sufficiency," by which Aristotle means not merely the capacity to provide for the survival of its members, but above all the ability to determine, through human intention, the criteria that will define "the good life."

The connection between the perfection of human capacities and the Greek *polis* is underscored by a passage in Book VII:

The peoples of cold countries generally, and particularly those of Europe, are full of spirit, but deficient in skill and intelligence; and this is why they continue to remain comparatively free, but attain no political development and show no capacity for governing others. The peoples of Asia are endowed with skill and intelligence, but are deficient in spirit; and this is why they continue to be peoples of subjects and slaves. The Greek stock, intermediate in geographical position, unites the qualities of both sets of peoples. It possesses both spirit and intelligence: the one quality makes it continue free; the other enables it to attain the highest political development, and to show a capacity for governing every other people—if only it could once achieve political unity (VII. 1327; p. 296).

While it is perhaps irrelevant that the Romans ultimately demonstrated such a capacity for world government, this passage clarifies the discussion in Book I: barbarian and slave are equally inferior to the Greek because only the latter combine the "spirit" of free men and the "skill and intelligence" of civilized peoples. Neither foresight alone nor freedom alone is adequate to describe human nature. Rather, the natural fulfillment or perfection of human life represents a combination of these traits—and those who combine them can be described as the "naturally ruling element."

Because the analysis of a political community must focus on the notion of a "good life" shared by its members, Aristotle does not distinguish between "fact" and "value" in the manner of many contemporary political scientists (e.g., Brecht, 1959). Instead, Aristotle flatly asserts that there is a scientific definition of the end or goal of politics. "The chief end of man . . . the true end which good law-givers should keep in view, for any state or stock or society with which they may be concerned, is the enjoyment of partnership in a good life and the felicity thereby attainable" (VII. 1325a; p. 286). Unlike the Sophists, Aristotle's teleological method leads to a conclusion concerning the best political institutions, which must rest on the rule of law and a "partnership" among citizens.

Like Antiphon and the Sophists, however, Aristotle's political theory assumes that human knowledge cannot fundamentally overcome natural limits on wealth. Since "it is the business of nature to furnish subsistence for each being brought into the world" (I. 1258a; p. 28), economic activity cannot transcend the natural scarcity that produces the distinction between rich and poor in civilized societies. "The natural form . . . of the art of acquisition is always, and in all cases, acquisition from fruits and animals"— and such a natural art of acquisition has inherent limits *(ibid.).*

To be sure, Aristotle admits that there is also an unnatural art of acquisition, namely, the gain of wealth or "currency without any limit or pause" (I. 1257b; p. 26) in "retail trade" and "usury," with the latter being even more "unnatural" than the former (I. 1258b; p. 29). Moreover, science can be used to increase monetary wealth, as Thales proved by using his "knowledge of meteorology" to establish a monopoly of olive-presses (I. 1259a; p. 31). Indeed, "knowledge of these methods is useful to statesmen" as well as private individuals, since "states—like households, but to an even greater extent—are often in want of financial resources" *(ibid.).*

Aristotle nonetheless denies that science could overcome or master natural necessity as such. At best, scientific knowledge permits some men to increase their power or wealth at the expense of others; the perennial conflicts of interest between rulers and ruled, found in existing regimes, cannot be transcended by the use of science to create wealth and abundance.

> There is only one condition on which we can imagine managers not needing subordinates, and masters not needing slaves. This condition would be that each instrument could do its own work at the word of command or by intelligent anticipation . . . as if a shuttle should weave of itself, and a plectrum should do its own harp-playing (I. 1253b; p. 10).

This "imagined" *reductio ad absurdum,* although apparently achieved by modern industrial technology, was never considered seriously by Aristotle, for whom natural scarcity always served as a limit on human society. For Aristotle, science or knowledge is ultimately "contemplative" rather than manipulative (VII. 1323a-b, 1325b; pp. 280-281, 289).

Hence, Aristotle accepts as inevitable a distinction in power and wealth within highly developed human societies. He seeks standards of political and human excellence that could be derived from human nature and history, providing a notion of justice and law that is neither purely relative nor dependent on force and power for its realization. In this context, Aristotle's thought seems fairly characterized as a combination of the premises that *men are naturally social* (i.e., that some naturally rule others in civilized society) and that *science can at best understand nature* without controlling or transforming its impact on human life.

### The Modern Definition: Politics, Law, and Consent
### (*Hobbes*, Leviathan)

Hobbes's political philosophy can be summarized—at the risk of oversimplification—as an attempt to develop, on the basis of premises like those of Antiphon, a political community like that described in Aristotle (*cf.* Strauss, 1952). Using Galileo's physics as his model of natural regularities,[12] Hobbes begins from men as naturally free and seeks a means of establishing admittedly "conventional" laws that nonetheless produce justice, a "common good," and political virtue.

It was extremely difficult to combine the principles of Antiphon and Aristotle. For Antiphon, after all, man is by nature free— and all political rules are "restraints" on nature which are accepted only as a necessary evil; for Aristotle, in contrast, man is by nature a political being—and one who attempts to escape political restraint must be "either a beast or a God" (I. 1253a; p. 6). Hobbes achieves this combination by reinterpreting Antiphon's view of human nature in the light of the emerging science of physics.

Human beings are essentially bodies which, like all natural bodies, exhibit inertia. Not only do sense impressions and thoughts consist of matter in motion, as the senses are moved by environmental objects and produce motions in the brain (Ch. 1-3), but the human body as such seeks to preserve its own motion through the operation of the natural desires (Ch. 6, 11). These desires, of which the most important is the desire for self-preservation, are fundamentally identical in all men, though differences in education and training will produce different *objects* of desire—or, as we now say, different "values" (Author's Introduction; Ch. 11).

All men are, in this sense, fundamentally equal by nature (as Antiphon had argued). The desires of men conflict, especially because the means to one individual's self-preservation—i.e., the objects of his desires—are often material things desired by others. Since there is no "natural" limit in the things desired by man, "if any two men desire the same thing, which nevertheless they cannot both enjoy, they become enemies" (Ch. 13, p. 81).[13] As a result, when "men live without a common power to keep them all in awe, they are in that condition which is called war; and such a war, as is of every man, against every man" (Ch. 13, p. 82).

This war of all, for Hobbes the "natural condition of man," is ended only by a contract creating the Sovereign. But whereas Antiphon had argued that the conventions establishing political society are unnatural and arbitrary restraints which the real man will violate if he can, Hobbes tries to make such conventions legitimate and rational (see especially the rejection of the Sophist view: Ch. 15, pp. 94-95 and Ch. 27, pp. 192-193). He does so by developing his conception of the "covenant" as a means by which all man can achieve not merely self-preservation but comfortable self-preservation, economic wealth, and social justice.

Whereas Antiphon had distinguished between "rules of nature" and "rules of law," Hobbes draws a distinction between "right of nature" and "law of nature." Hobbes's rights of nature, like Antiphon's rules of nature, are inevitable: they consist of "the liberty each man hath, to use his own power, as he will himself, for the preservation of his own nature; that is to say, of his own life; and consequently, of doing any thing, which in his own judgment, and reason, he shall conceive to be the aptest means thereunto" (Ch. 14, p. 84).

Hobbes does not conclude, however, that the best human life is that of the tyrant (as did Sophists like Thrasymachus). Rather, Hobbes argues that there are also "laws of nature," which he defines as "a precept or general rule, found out by reason, by which a man is forbidden to do that, which is destructive of his life, or taketh away the means of preserving the same; and to omit that, by which he thinketh it may be best preserved" (Ch. 14, p. 84). If humans reason about nature, they discover "laws of nature" defining the obligations which—if freely accepted by men —will permit them to escape from the war of all against all.

These obligations, which Antiphon had treated as conventions or agreements (the laws), are based on what Hobbes calls the "covenant" or social contract. A contract is "the mutual transferring of right" (Ch. 14, p. 87): by mutually transferring or giving up their natural rights, men create a civilized society with a government. This government can then punish men should they violate their contracts with one another.

Without such a "common power," the life of man is "solitary, poor, nasty, brutish, and short"—no industry, commerce, or science is possible, because the precondition of civilization is an arbiter who can judge between the conflicting desires of naturally free and equal men (Ch. 13, p. 82). Once the social contract has been established, it is possible to develop industry, agriculture, navigation and trade, and, above all, science. But to achieve these ends, any form of government consistent with the laws of nature will produce a lasting and prosperous society; like Thrasymachus (and unlike Aristotle), Hobbes views the conventional distinction of forms of government as secondary in importance (Ch. 18, p. 120; Ch. 19, pp. 121-122; Ch. 30, p. 221-222).

At this point, however, Hobbes diverges from Antiphon and the Sophists, for whom every society was equally "conventional" (and therefore equally restraining on the naturally free man, whose inner desire is to be a tyrant over his fellow men). Hobbes substitutes a human control over nature (by means of science and industry) for the Sophists' tyranny of one man over another. He does this by showing that *no* social contract can lead men to abandon their natural right to self-preservation; "a covenant not to defend myself from force, by force, is always void . . . for though a man may covenant thus; *unless I do so, or so, kill me,* he cannot covenant thus, *unless I do so, or so, I will not resist you when you come to kill me"* (Ch. 14, p. 91). This limitation on any conceivable contract could be described as a human drive analogous to the inertia of inanimate bodies, since Hobbes says that the natural desire for life "cannot" be abandoned in advance by any man.

As a result of this inviolable right to self-preservation, the government created by the social contract is in a paradoxical position. As Hobbes makes clear, the "sovereign" or ruler remains in the state of nature and is not himself bound by the social contract. This is necessary, for Hobbes, because if the covenant obligated the sovereign as well as his subjects, they would be without a "common power to keep them all in awe." In principle, the Hobbesian ruler seems to be absolute (e.g., Watkins, 1948:79).

Unlike the tyrant as understood by the Sophists, however, Hobbes's sovereign must realize that his authority is in practice very limited. Since no man can rationally abandon the fundamental natural right "of defending his life, and means of living," any attempt to punish a subject re-establishes the state of nature between the subject and the ruler; while it may be irrational to do so, the subjects can always rebel if they feel that their lives are endangered by the rulers in power (Ch. 14, pp. 90, 91-92; Ch. 18, pp. 114,

116-117; Ch. 21, pp. 142-145). The sovereign is the "representative" of his subjects (Ch. 16, pp. 107-108). Law must rest on consent.[14]

Hobbes's theory thus provides the outlines of a rule of law, in which the sovereign establishes the general principles of social life and allows his subjects the maximum liberty to seek their own selfish ends within these limits (Ch. 21, p. 139; Ch. 30, pp. 225-228). As this notion was ultimately called in the eighteenth century, Hobbes establishes a theory of the "laissez faire" or liberal state, in which political power is reduced to the most limited possible intervention in the private affairs of the citizens (cf. Macpherson, 1962; Strauss, 1953; Coleman, 1974).

While this development of Hobbes's principles becomes particularly clear in the thought of John Locke and the English utilitarians, its broad outlines are already present in the *Leviathan*. The orientation of human activity toward economic enrichment, rather than political conflict, is quite evident, for example, in Hobbes's definition of liberty: "The liberty of a subject, lieth therefore only in those things, which in regulating their actions, the sovereign hath praetermitted: such as is the liberty to buy and sell, and otherwise contract with one another; to choose their own abode, their own diet, their own trade of life, and institute their children as they themselves think fit; and the like" (Ch. 21, p. 139). Similarly, Hobbes's striking criticism of monopolies (Ch. 22, p. 151-152; Ch. 29, p. 217) points to the need for free competition in economic affairs.

To be sure, Hobbes includes "public charity" in the matters appropriate to the "office of the sovereign." As his discussion makes clear, however, this is not an argument for a welfare state; public charity should be reserved for those who "by accident inevitable, become unable to maintain themselves by their labor" and does not extend to "such as have strong bodies" and "are to be forced to work" (Ch. 30, p. 227). Nor is Hobbes speaking here of forced labor camps; rather, he is pointing to the development of science and industry as a solution to the perennial problem of poverty: "To avoid the excuse of not finding employment, there ought to be such laws, as may encourage all manner of arts; as navigation, agriculture, fishing, and all manner of manufacture that requires labor" (*ibid.*).

That Hobbes can be viewed as an early exponent of industrialization—and not merely as a spokesman for traditional modes of commerce—is crucial to a full understanding of his position. Reread the famous description of the state of nature, without the negatives, as an image of the Hobbesian commonwealth: it is a society in which "there is . . . place for industry, because the fruit thereof is . . . certain: and consequently . . . culture of the earth; . . . navigation, . . . use of the commodities that may be imported by sea; . . . commodious building; . . . instruments of moving and removing, such things as require much force; . . . knowledge of the face of the earth; . . . account of time; . . . arts; . . . letters . . ." (Ch. 13, p. 82.). Although the sciences themselves are "small power" (because they are "not eminent"), they are "the true mother" of "instruments" of power—and such "instrumental power" is capable of "increasing as it proceeds" (Ch. 10, pp. 56-58), fundamentally transcending the scarcity and conflict of the "natural condition of mankind."

The emphatic view that science and technology will permit a solution to the problem of poverty which had previously dominated human life explains a little noted characteristic of the "table" of the sciences in Chapter 9. While the "science of just and unjust" as well as logic, rhetoric, poetry, ethics, and what we today call psychology (i.e., broadly the social sciences and humanities as scholarly disciplines) are described as branches of "physics," the "science of engineers, architecture, navigation and geography" are derived from a different branch of natural philosophy (Ch. 9, pp. 54-55). That is, engineering, architecture, navigation, and geography—which seem essential to the healthy commonwealth (see again Ch. 13, p. 82)—are "consequences from . . . *quantity* and *motion*," the "accidents common to all bodies natural"; while we would tend to call these applied sciences, Hobbes classifies them along with Philosophia prima, geometry, arithmetic, and astronomy as more exact than the branches of "physics," supposedly devoted to "consequences from *qualities*."

In other words, those sciences that can give rise to "industry" and thereby plenty have a privileged status in Hobbes's table of the sciences. Indeed, Hobbes later uses architecture as a metaphor for the construction of his commonwealth, implying that the conjunction of knowledge and industry will make possible a radically new and durable answer to the traditional questions of political theory. As Hobbes puts it, those who deny his principles argue as ill, as if the savage people of America, should deny there were any grounds, or principles of reason, so to build a house, as to last as long as the materials, because they never yet saw any so well built. Time, and industry, produce every day new knowledge. And as the art of well building is derived from principles of reason, observed by industrious men, that had long studied the nature of materials, and the divers effects of figure, and proportion, long after mankind began, though poorly, to build: so, long time after men have begun to constitute commonwealths, imperfect, and apt to relapse into disorder, there may principles of reason be found out, by industrious meditation, to make their constitution, excepting by external violence, everlasting. (Ch. 30, p. 220).

It is therefore quite evident that, for Hobbes, human science is capable of the *mastery* or *control* of physical nature. To be sure, he was aware of an ultimate natural limit on human life: "as for the plenty of matter, it is a thing limited by nature" (Ch. 24, p. 160). But given the resources of the planet, "consisting in animals, vegetables, and minerals" which "God hath freely laid . . . before us, in or near to the face of the earth," human action can transcend scarcities which had previously been attributed to natural necessity. "Plenty dependeth, next to God's favour, merely on the labour and industry of men" (Ch. 24, pp. 160-161).

Hobbes seems to feel that just as modern industry can be based on the invention of useful machines that conform to the physical properties of matter in motion, so modern politics can be based on the invention of useful laws that conform to the properties of human nature (cf. Ch. 20, p. 136; Ch. 30, p. 220). The guarantee of Hobbesian justice is no longer the good will or piety of the Prince, as in the Middle Ages; rather, justice will be insured by training all men to claim rationally their natural rights whenever they are infringed upon. The sovereign has an obligation to enlighten his subjects by the public teaching of Hobbes's scientific truths (Ch. 30, p. 219-225; Ch. 31, p. 241; "A Review and Conclusion," p. 467).

Ultimately, Hobbes views the political community as a product of human art (like Antiphon), but one that imitates nature (like Aristotle). The science on which Hobbes bases his "constructive" theory of the state is a modern science, however. It rests upon the assertion that the motions of human bodies—and particularly, the desires of men—exhibit regularities which can be discovered by a science that is ultimately derived from physics (Ch. 9, pp. 54-55). Like any other science, Hobbes's "Science of the just and unjust" (*ibid.*) is subject to empirical verification. Hence the truth of his theory of the state of nature can be "demonstrated" by consulting one's own desires and passions ("Introduction," p. 6): deductive propositions ("inference made from the passions") are confirmed by the experience of each reader ("let him therefore consider with himself"—Ch. 13, p. 82) as well as from the behavior of primitive societies, sovereigns in international relations, and men during a civil war (Ch. 13, p. 83).

Hobbes's use of modern physics as a model (cf. Collingwood, 1945: 102-103) leads him to distinguish sharply between the desires and the objects of desire—or, to use the modern distinction, between "facts" and "values." For Hobbes, it is a "fact" that men desire things, whereas *what* they desire varies according to "the constitution individual, and particular education" ("Introduction," p. 6). Having explicitly rejected the notion of *"finis ultimus,* utmost aim, or *summum bonum,* greatest good, such as is spoken of in the books of the old moral philosophers" like Aristotle (Ch. 11, p. 63), Hobbes can thus describe how men can agree to pursue what each individual should rationally view as the greatest good, viz., his own self-preservation and prosperity, without producing the war of all against all.

Antiphon's teaching is radically defective, because it gives men no reason to accept the laws as legitimate once they come to study the truth; for Antiphon, therefore, it would be dangerous for all men to study the "rules of nature." For Hobbes, in contrast, the universal study of the laws of nature can only improve the political condition of men, since they will learn that the combination of political obedience and private interest can redound to the common benefit of all (Ch. 15, pp. 94-96). "For such truth, as opposeth no man's profit, nor pleasure, is to all men welcome" ("A Review and Conclusion," p. 468).

Aristotle's teaching is also defective, because it begins from the premise that man is a political animal for whom the highest end is goodness or felicity. But once Hobbes has replaced Aristotelian teleology with a modern science of the passions, he can propose a political solution in which justice is both possible and legitimate.

And while Hobbes views "communicative justice"—the justice of "buying and selling" in contractual relations—as a more solid standard than Aristotle's "distributive justice" (Ch. 15, p. 98), the Hobbesian commonwealth, like Aristotle's best *polis,* is a rule of law which the rational man should respect.

Hobbes thus combines the premises that *society is unnatural* (i.e., that all men are equal in the decisive political respects) and that *scientific knowledge and industry can overcome the natural limits on wealth* that had hitherto produced social conflict. Once again, the two dimensions specified in Figure 1 seem essential to an understanding of Hobbes's political thought.

### The Marxist Definition: Politics as Superstructure (Marx & Engels, German Ideology; Marx, 1844 Manuscripts and Contribution to the Critique of Political Economy)

If Hobbes can be said to have combined the premises of Antiphon with the conclusions of Aristotle, Marx could be described as a combination of Aristotle's premises and Hobbes's conclusions. Like Aristotle, Marx rejects the Sophist distinction between nature and convention; instead Marx shares Aristotle's emphasis on a "genetic" or historical method.[15] But whereas Aristotle conceived of society as ultimately limited by nature and natural necessity, Marx—like Hobbes—considers mankind capable of using a science of man and nature to create a society of material abundance and freedom.

At first, it might appear that Marx is simply a relativist who starts from the Sophist assumption that might makes right. Just as Thrasymachus says "each ruling group sets down laws for its own advantage" (*Republic,* I. 338e), Marx asserts that "the ruling ideas are nothing more than the ideal expression . . . of the relationships which make the one class the ruling one . . ." (*GI,* p. 438).[16] But from Marx's point of view, the Sophists Antiphon and Thrasymachus made the same mistake as the German philosopher Feuerbach by speaking "of 'Man' instead of 'real historical men' " (*GI,* p. 416). A science of politics must begin with a *historical* analysis of *society,* on the assumption that men need to cooperate with one another in order to survive.

Marx says of his own approach that it starts from the premises of "men, not in any fantastic isolation and fixation, but in their real, empirically perceptible process of development under certain conditions" (*GI*, p. 415). Hobbes's state of nature—the "war of all against all"—is as unempirical as the Sophist theory of the conventional origin of law and government. "Do not let us go back to a fictitious primordial condition. . . . Such a primordial condition explains nothing" (*1844 MS*, p. 107).

Just as Aristotle begins with the natural development of the family, village, and city as means of satisfying human needs, Marx begins from the moment man "begins to *produce* his means of subsistence" (*GI*, p. 409). And like Aristotle (cf. *Politics*, 1256a-b, pp. 19-20), Marx assumes that "the mode of production" is "a definite *mode of life*" which "begins with *population growth*" which in turn presupposes *interaction* among individuals" (*GI*, p. 409). "The individual *is the social being*" (*1844 MS*, p. 138). Both Aristotle and Marx represent the pole of political thought which assumes that man is naturally social.

Marx's conception of both nature and society is, however, radically different from that of any pagan thinker. When Aristotle speaks of growth and development, he thinks of biological growth —e.g., the development of a horse—as a model. Hence, for Aristotle, there is a natural limit or end to production (as is revealed by his hostility to large-scale commerce, banking, or industry). In contrast, Marx thinks of nature and society as historical processes of development, passing through stages that definitively overcome or surpass each other as the human species moves toward a stage of greater power over nature and of radical human freedom (cf. *1844 MS*, p. 143).

Although Marx is often called an economic determinist, his thought is best described by his insistence on the *historical* character of all social life. "The entire internal structure of the nation itself depends on the stage of development achieved by its production and its domestic and international commerce" (*GI*, p. 110). Each stage of economic development or "mode of production" establishes a characteristic "division of labor" (i.e., structure of social classes) and characteristic "forms of ownership" (i.e., kinds of property.)[17]

While Marx insist that all consciousness and thought is a product of these economic stages, this frequently cited position does not explain the dynamics of historical *change*.[18] For Marx, contradictions arise necessarily between "the stage of development of man's material powers of production" and the "relations of production" (i.e., "the economic structure of society" or "property relations"): "At a certain stage of their development, the material forces of production in society come into conflict with the existing relations of production. . . . From forms of development of the forces of production these relations turn into their fetters. Then comes the period of social revolution" (Preface, *CPE,* pp. 43-44).

While politics is thus an element of "superstructure" according to Marx, it is an essential component in all historical epochs prior to the emergence of communism. Through the State, the dominant classes enforce their economic and social interests by preserving their concept of property (the "relations of production") in the face of new "forces of production." Since these new "material forces" create new classes—such as the industrial proletariat—which challenge the outmoded relations of production (or laws), the decisive battles are fought in the political arena. Even though the determining factors in history are ultimately economic, "men become conscious of this conflict and fight it out" in terms of "legal, political, religious, aesthetic, or philosophic—in short, ideological—forms" (Preface, *CPE,* p. 44). Political conflict is thus, in certain crucial epochs of history, absolutely decisive.

Marx saw his own era as the precursor of a revolutionary change in which all civilized men would ultimately be freed from estrangement or alienated labor. While communism, as the "annulment of private property," is a necessary movement toward this end, "communism as such is not the goal of human development" (*1844 MS,* p. 146); rather, "the transcendence of private property is . . . the complete *emancipation* of all human senses and qualities, but it is this emancipation precisely because these senses and attributes have become, subjectively and objectively, human" (*1844 MS,* p. 139).

This radical freedom, in which the traditional dichotomies between "subjectivism and objectivism, spiritualism and materialism, activity and suffering . . . lose their antithetical character" (*1844 MS,* p. 141), is made possible by the unification of the theoretical and practical implications of science. Theoretical natural science has hitherto been "abstractly material" or "idealistic," cut off from "man's essential being" as an active, social, producing species. "But natural science has invaded and transformed human life all the more *practically* through the medium of industry, and has prepared human emancipation, although its immediate effect had to be the furthering of the dehumanization of man" (*1844* MS, p. 142).

Whatever its defects, bourgeois society represents unparalleled technological progress. It is often forgotten, for example, that the *Communist Manifesto* praises the bourgeoisie as the class that "has been the first to show what man's activity can bring about"; "the bourgeoisie, during its rule of scarce one hundred years, has created more massive and more colossal productive forces than have all preceding generations together" (Marx and Engels, 1971:92, 94). The root of this "constant revolutionizing of production" is the "subjection of nature's forces to man"—i.e., the use of modern science to control nature, as in "the application of chemistry to industry and agriculture" (*ibid.*, p. 94).

The basis of the potential transformation of the human condition is thus a change in the productive process itself:

The worker no longer inserts transcendental natural objects as intermediaries between the material and himself; he now inserts the natural process that he has transformed into an industrial one between himself and inorganic nature, *over which he has achieved mastery.* He is no longer the principal agent of the productive process: he exists alongside it. In this transformation, what appears as the mainstay of production and wealth is neither the immediate labor performed by the worker, nor the time that he works—*but the appropriation by man of his own general productive force, his understanding of nature and mastery of it;* in a word, the development of the social individual (*Grundrisse,* p. 142).

Foreseeing the impact of automation, Marx saw that in industrial society "the human factor is restricted to watching and supervising the production process" not only with respect to "machinery," but also in "the combination of human activities and the development of human commerce" (*ibid.*).[19] Given these developments, Marx claims, "the surplus labor of the masses has ceased to be a condition for the development of wealth in general"; for the first time in human history, "individuals [will be] in a position to develop freely" (*ibid.*).

While industry based on natural science makes possible the emancipation of humans, the realization of such social freedom entails a transcendence of the gap between the natural and social sciences: "Natural science will in time incorporate into itself the science of man, just as the science of man will incorporate into itself natural science: there will be *one science*" (*1844 MS,* p. 143).

Marx's science of human history is thus not only an explanation of change but also a guide to action in the political conflicts of the present and future. Just as Hobbes sought to teach men how to create an immortal commonwealth on the basis of scientific "laws of nature," Marx seeks the laws of history that will permit men to end, once and for all, "the last antagonistic form of the social relations of production" (Preface, *CPE,* p. 44). Moreover, Marx's science is not intended as a passive attitude, awaiting the "Second Coming" so to speak; rather, Marx's work is intended as a guide to action. As he put it in the *Eleventh Thesis on Feuerbach:* "The philosophers have only *interpreted the world,* in various ways; the point, however, is to *change* it" (Feuer, 1959:245).

Marx thus combines the promises that *man is by nature social* and that *scientific knowledge can overcome the natural limits on wealth* that had hitherto produced social conflict. Like Aristotle, Marx refuses to accept the view that society can be analyzed from the perspective of the isolated individual; like Hobbes, Marx believes that modern science can increase the "productive forces" of man so that wealth "will flow more abundantly" (*Critique of the Gotha Programme,* p. 10). As for the other theorists discussed, the two dimensions of Figure 1 seem adequate to indicate the fundamental orientation of Marx's thought.


## THE CHARACTER OF WESTERN
## POLITICAL THEORY

Four modal approaches to political theory in the West, represented by Antiphon the Sophist, Aristotle, Hobbes, and Marx, have been briefly restated. Other traditional theorists as well as more recent approaches to political (or social) science can be usefully conceptualized as variants of these basic types, and situated on the field diagram presented as Figure 1. For example, the political theory implicit in B. F. Skinner's behaviorism appears to be a contemporary version of the Hobbesian mode of thought: for Skinner, political institutions and values are "contingencies" (i.e., conventions) established by conditioning and subject to scientific manipulation. Man is thus assumed to be asocial by nature (since the origin of political society is a human habit, not a natural tendency, Skinner focuses on *individual behavior*) and scientific knowledge is assumed to permit human mastery of nature (cf. Skinner, 1972).[20]

While the four basic types of political inquiry have been defined in terms of two axes, they can be fruitfully compared on other dimensions as well. Each type of thought has characteristic implications for the science taken as the model of political knowledge, for the concept of the political community, for the end or goal of politics, for the best form of government, and for the role of human freedom. (For a suggestive but highly compressed comparison, see Table 2.)[21]

Whatever these differences, however, all four types of thought have been developed in what is conventionally described as the "Western" or "European" historical tradition. It is all too easy to equate this tradition with the entire range of human thought and politics: our educational curriculum frequently begins surveys of philosophy, music, art, or history—as well as political thought—with ancient Greece and Rome; only rarely is this tradition viewed in the broader context of other forms of culture, either prior to or outside our own Western civilization.

There is, however, a reason for this tendency. The notion of "science" that serves as the foundation for our educational system is a peculiarly Western one (cf. Watkins, 1948:10-14). To be sure, other civilizations have developed a form of "science." But our notion of scientific knowledge—and, perhaps more important, the use of this knowledge as the basis of an apparently self-generating industrial technology—did not arise in similar form in earlier civilizations or other cultures. No other cultural tradition produced either a technology or a science capable of dominating the entire planet as Western technology and science have done in the last three centuries. The industrial mode of production, whether understood in strictly Marxian terms or from other sociological perspectives, distinguishes our culture from all others known to have existed.

It can be suggested that one of the underlying grounds of this unique dynamism of Western science and technology—though not the only one—is the peculiar notion of "nature" discovered by the ancient Greeks and developed most notably since the Renaissance

### Table 2.
### Nature distinguished from Convention or Law

| | Convention or law is Unnatural ("relativism") | | Convention or law has natural basis ("naturalism" or "realism") | |
|---|---|---|---|---|
| | Facts distinct from Values | | Facts and Values Interrelated | |
| | Analytical | | Genetic or Historical | |
| | Science as Understanding (Antiphon) | Science as Control (Hobbes) | Science as Understanding (Aristotle) | Science as Control (Marx) |
| Epistemology: | Facts distinct from Values | | Facts and Values Interrelated | |
| Method: | Analytical | | Genetic or Historical | |
| Model Science: | Rhetoric | Physics | Biology | History |
| Concept of Political Community: | Accidental group | Created imitation of natural body | Natural association | Historical form |
| End of Politics: | Pleasure for individual | Pleasure for many individuals | Good life for community | Good life for species |
| Best form of Government: | Tyranny (law satisfying interest of ruler) | Government by consent (law satisfying interest of all citizens) | Natural aristocracy, **Rule** & be ruled in turn (law according to natural perfection of citizens) | Communist society, revolutionary praxis (freedom transcending law of formal state) |
| Role of Freedom: | Maximize individual freedom | Maximize freedom for all members of society | Combine freedom with intelligence or knowledge = maximize virtue | Maximize freedom and knowledge |
| Concept of Virtue: | Acquired skill of successful individual | Standard of praise relative to society and individual concerned | Natural perfection of man | Historically determined ideology |
| Function of Knowledge: | Train individuals in useful skills | Construct lasting commonwealth based on science | Perfect virtue by training intelligence and limiting excess desires | Destroy obstacles to freedom (overcome alienation) |

(Collingwood, 1945). The four types of political thought discussed above all *share* one crucial element: each assumes regularities in the physical universe can be discovered and understood by human reason. Although Aristotle and Marx denied that the distinction between nature and convention was as absolute as Antiphon and Hobbes imply, all four assume that the motions of the heavenly bodies, the growth of organisms, or the structure of physical matter cannot be explained by the religious, poetic, or mythical beliefs that vary from society to society. In this sense, all four of the Western thinkers can be contrasted to the thought of other religious or mythical traditions which lack the concept of "nature" and natural regularities discoverable by human reason.

This view of "nature," moreover, accounts for the particular form of the questions that have dominated Western political thought. The two dimensions underlying Figure 1 flow from the assumption that a secular or nonmythical knowledge of the world is accessible to human reason. If all things have a "nature," a scientific study of politics leads necessarily to the analysis of *human* nature, and hence to the question of whether man is by nature social. Similarly, if a rational science of nature is deemed possible, one can question the extent to which such knowledge permits control over the natural conditions hitherto constraining social and political life.

Both dimensions identified in this survey thus presuppose the concept of "nature." Indeed, this idea is so deeply ingrained in Western thought that we can conceive only with difficulty of the effort required to discover it. Yet both historical research into early civilizations and contemporary anthropology confirm the striking fact that most human cultures have not conceived of the world around them as "nature."

## MYTHICO-RELIGIOUS BELIEF AND THE DISCOVERY OF NATURE

In general, primitive thought is based on myth—tales and rituals that explain the cosmos in terms of the actions of personified forces. For example, consider the following passage of the Mesopotamian Creation Epic, the so-called *Enuma Elis,* in which the origin of the cosmos was attributed to a God, Marduk, who rebelled against previous gods:

Marduk, the king of the gods, divided
All the Anunnaki above and below.
He assigned (them) to Anu to guard his instructions.
Three hundred in the heavens he stationed as a guard.
In like manner the ways of the earth he defined.
In heaven and on earth six hundred (thus) he settled.
                              VI. 39-44 (Pritchard, 1958:37)

The Anunnaki—the gods of the heavens and earth—were thus
created by a single divine figure, who arranged the visible universe
now seen by men.

Two aspects of this myth are important for our purposes. First,
the epic poem cited above was not merely a story; it was part of
a religious ritual repeated yearly at the New Year's festival. The
primitive account of the origin of the heavens and "the ways of the
earth" was simultaneously part of the rituals without which the
gods will be angry and human life impossible. The *description* of
what we call "nature" was thus intrinsically related to the religious
*prescription* of acceptable human behavior.

Second, and perhaps most relevant to our study, was the symbolic connection between Marduk and the city of Babylon. In earlier versions of this same myth, the role attributed to Marduk had
been fulfilled by another Mesopotamian god—Enlil, associated with
the city of Nippur (Frankfort, et al., 1949:183). The gods defined
in ancient myth were not merely religious: they also symbolized
the political order of the society concerned. Hence the myths, describing the "way" of all natural and human things, were simultaneously religious rituals and mechanisms of political control. (On
the relationship between social structure and religion in primitive
society, see Swanson, 1960).

In its original form, therefore, human thought did not distinguish between "the realm of nature and the realm of man": "The
ancients, like the modern savages, saw man always as part of society, and society as imbedded in nature and dependent on cosmic
forces . . . natural phenomena were regularly conceived in terms
of human experience and . . . human experience was conceived in
terms of cosmic events." (Frankfort et al., 1949:12). In such a
world view, obviously, it is difficult to speak of a science of politics—if only because the very possibility of science as we know it
does not exist.[22]

To be sure, some form of knowledge concerning what we call natural phenomena is very old. Recent analysis of notations on a Magdalenian bone fragment in the Musée de l'Homme in Paris indicates the likelihood of a ritual calendar of lunar cycles approximately 13,000 years ago (Marshack, 1972). Egyptian and Mesopotamian civilizations, while describing the cosmos in terms of myths like the Creation Epic cited above, developed calendars, arithmetic, geometry, and considerable knowledge of astronomic and physical phenomena. But as long as such knowledge remained embedded in myth, scientific inquiry could never fully transcend the religious framework which organized social behavior.

The discovery of "nature" as a realm distinct from social custom was therefore a crucial step in the history of human thought. This discovery is usually associated with the Ionian philosophers in early Greece. In the sixth century B.C., a series of thinkers—conventionally said to begin with Thales's assertion that "water is best"—sought to understand the underlying principles of the world in general, nonmythical terms (Jaeger, 1945: Ch. 9; Russell, 1945; Ch. 11). These thinkers, often classified as the pre-Socratics, developed numerous, apparently crude, theories, ranging from Thales's identification of water as the fundamental element to Democritus's atomic theory.

We need not stress these theories here save for one point: the Ionians created Western philosophy or science—the concepts were originally synonymous—by thinking in terms of "nature" (in Greek, *physis,* the root of our word "physics") as a universal set of principles or processes that is radically independent of myth, religion, and social custom (cf. Collingwood, 1945:43-48). Only on this basis was it possible for other pre-Socratic thinkers, the Sophists, to attempt to develop a similar science of politics, based on the elemental distinction between nature and society which constitutes the first dimension in Table 1.

Although one representative of this original conception of political science—Antiphon the Sophist—has already been discussed, a further point should be added. The Sophists represent a sharp break away from traditional myth and religion. Indeed, it appears that many of the Sophists attempted to establish their scientific stature by demonstrating the absurdities contained in the Homeric poems and other myths then dominating Greek society (cf. Wheelright, 1966: esp. Protagoras, Fragment 6; Gorgias, Fragment 7; Thrasy-

machus, Fragment 2). As this historical detail suggests, secular
political thought has always represented a challenge to a religious
or mythical frame of reference.


## THE LATENT STRUCTURE
## OF HUMAN THOUGHT

The dimension of Table 1 or Figure 1 called "Human
Nature and Society" thus contains an implicit historical element,
since it presupposes a challenge to an earlier view according to
which nature and society were not distinguished. This earlier conception, which could be called the mythical or ritualistic approach
to man's place in the cosmos, is thus another pole on a deeper dimension that is, so to speak, at right angles to Table 1 or Figure 1.
To represent such an analysis of human thought, therefore, a three-
dimensional structure is necessary.

Figure 2, a cube in which the four polar positions of Figure 1
occupy one plane surface, is presented here merely as an illustration of the possibility that the latent structure of all human thought
is amenable to analysis. If this hypothesis were to be confirmed by
further study, it would be possible to situate the various forms of
Western political theory more precisely than has hitherto been customary. But even if Figure 2 is merely a crude means of visual-
izing different modes of thought, it would conveniently suggest the
limits of our traditional conceptions of nature and human nature.

Since many of the terms used in Figure 1 cannot, by definition,
apply to mythico-religious thought, the three dimensions set forth
in Figure 2 have been renamed in their most general form. Because
we cannot speak of "nature" as a conscious concept in preliterate
societies or early civilizations, the dimension of natural sociability
versus a conventional origin of society is described as *the relationship between human laws or customs and the cosmos* (or the
"World"). The dimension of science as understanding nature versus
science as controlling nature appears, more generally, as *the relationship of human action* (including not only science and technology, but also ritual, prayer, etc.) *to the cosmos*. And the dimension of reason versus faith can be called *the relationship of
human thought to the cosmos*.

It should be noted that the polar terms on each of these dimensions differ on the plane of mythico-religious thought from the

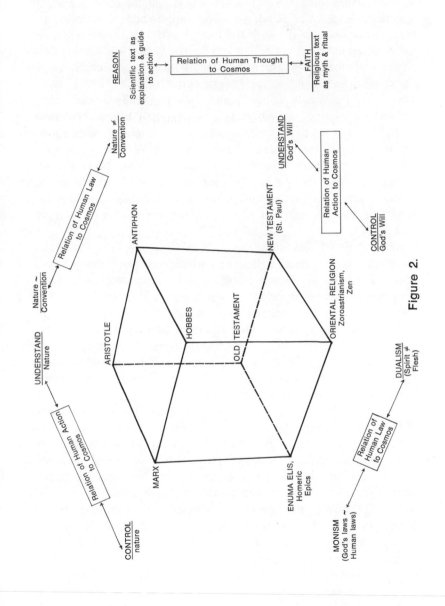

Figure 2.

terms used to describe the field of secular political thought. Whereas the relationship between human action and the cosmos had, in Figure 1, the poles of "Understanding nature" and "Control of nature," in mythico-religious thought these extremes are transformed to "Understand God's will" and "Control God's will" respectively. And whereas in Figure 1 the dimension relating human law to the cosmos had as its poles "Man naturally social" (i.e., convention or law has a natural basis) and "Man naturally asocial" (i.e., convention or law as radically unnatural), in mythico-religious thought these extremes are transformed to "Monism" (God's laws are the basis of human laws) and "Dualism" (spirit is radically different from flesh). The poles of the third dimension—the relation of human thought to the cosmos—are evidently "Reason" (according to which the scientific text is an explanation and guide to action) and "Faith" (for which the religious text serves as myth and ritual).

While I now believe that these three dimensions may form the latent structure of human thought—which individual theories and social beliefs elaborate and manifest in a myriad ways—it is not possible here to go beyond the merest presentation of Figure 2.[23] One observation, however, should indicate that this three-dimensional model taps an underlying structural characteristic of secular political thought. The diagonally opposed poles in Figure 2 have a peculiar status, since in at least three cases the modal political thinker represents a conscious rejection and transformation of the most distant religious type of thought.

That Sophists like Antiphon consciously sought to overturn the Homeric epics and religious myths prevailing in Greek society has been noted. It appears, however, that in so doing the Sophists transform the mythical hero or god into the conscious, rational leader—i.e., into the *politician*. Hence the relation between Greek mythico-religious tradition and Sophist thought takes the form of what Hegel called "transcendence" (*Aufhebung*), namely the transformation of a prior "moment" or position that is simultaneously rejected, preserved, and raised to a new level. In Sartre's terminology, Sophist political theory is a "project" in which the Homeric epics are "surpassed and maintained" (1968:105).

Much the same relation exists between the Old Testament and Hobbes's political theory. Any thoughtful reader of the *Leviathan,* especially if he has studied Parts III and IV, will see it as a radical secularization of the religious teaching of the Old Testament, replacing Yahweh with a human sovereign and converting the Mosaic covenant into a Hobbesian contract. Hence "the kingdom of God is a civil kingdom" (Ch. 35, p. 270); "In the commonwealth of the Jews, God himself was made the sovereign, by pact with the people" ("A Review and Conclusion," p. 463). Indeed, Hobbes's title makes evident his intention to transform Old Testament theology into a science of "the nature of man," for the comparison of a man-made sovereign with the "Leviathan" effectively reverses the biblical teaching he cites while preserving it and raising it to a new level (cf. Ch. 28, p. 209 with *Job*, 38–42 and Hobbes's own discussion in Ch. 31, p. 234–235).

Many commentators have noted a similar relationship between New Testament theology and Marx. The interpretation of Marx's view of history as an atheistic rejection of Christianity which preserves the Pauline notion of time, especially as set forth implicitly in *Romans* and explicitly in Augustine's *City of God,* is hardly novel (e.g., Ebenstein, 1969:692; Sabine, 1961:759-760; Watkins, 1948:232-233); communism itself can be seen as a feature of the early Christian community (e.g., *Acts,* iv. 34-37; v. 1-11) which is "surpassed and mantained" by Marxian thought (cf. *Communist Manifesto,* 1971:114). Again, it appears that a conscious transformation of the diametrically opposed type of religious thought characterizes Marx as a modal political theorist—even though this relationship was not defined at the outset in formulating the structural diagrams in Figures 1 and 2.

Whether Aristotle could similarly be viewed as a transformation and radical secularization of the tenets of oriental religions, which during the fourth century B.C. had made great inroads in Greece, remains to be seen (cf. Wheelwright, 1966:214-215). But not the least of the merits of a structural analysis is the possibility that it reveals the underlying polarities and dynamics of religious doctrine and secular political thought. As in any science, the merits of a new hypothesis are best tested by an unsuspected proposition that can be subjected to empirical analysis.

Even if the latent structure outlined in Figure 2 is entirely imaginary, it should remind us of one truth that is all too easily forgotten. Western science is not a ubiquitous way of looking at the universe, and Western political thought is not the only form of human consciousness about public and political things. In some cultures, "nature" does not exist. Therefore, when studying the role of "human nature" in political thought, we should keep in mind not only the varieties of secular political theory in the West, but above all the existence of mythico-religious traditions in which the claims of science as we know it have been denied.

To be sure, such an awareness of the limits of the Western scientific or rationalist thought need not lead us to reject it entirely—or in part (although many in the United States, particularly among the young, have done so in turning to religious orientations of all types). No attempt can be made here to suggest whether any one form of political or religious thought is intrinsically superior to all others. Indeed, it should be evident that the eight polar positions in Figure 2 are ultimately irreducible in the sense that, from any one perspective, each alternative could be explained as an error that demonstrates the truth of one's own position.

The most that could be hazarded is an assessment of the implications of recent scientific research on the perennial issues underlying the rationalist tradition in the West. That human nature is radically asocial or antisocial, as assumed by Antiphon or Hobbes, seems questionable in the light of recent findings in paleontology, evolutionary anthropology, ethology, neuro-biology, and linguistics; competitive behavior, far from showing that society is unnatural, seems to be characteristic of mammalian social life—and hence fully consistent with the view that society is natural to humans (Montagu, 1968; Lorenz, 1971; Morin, 1973). Although both Antiphon and Hobbes try to deduce social cooperation from the hedonistic calculation of selfish, competing individuals, contemporary biology shows that both competition and cooperation have a similar status in the higher vertebrates (Masters, 1975).

At the same time, it is an open question whether the control over nature made possible by science is as unlimited as the modern followers of Hobbes or Marx assumed. Whether based on the ecology crisis, the inner dynamics of exponential change in industrial society, or the exhaustion of the natural resource base, it is increasingly evident that science does not insure an infinite progress that definitively surmounts the challenge of natural scarcity (Commoner, 1970; Stent, 1973; Meadows, et al., 1972). Could it be, therefore, that within the Western rationalist tradition, the classic mode of thought—represented here by Aristotle—is the closest to a true assessment of human nature?

## NOTES AND REFERENCES

1. Page references are to editions cited in the bibliography. Incidentally, it is probably an error to say, as Sabine does, that for Machiavelli "men are in general bad" (1961: 342). The precise formulation in *The Prince* is "per essere li uomini tristi"—which could be translated "men are wretched" or "miserable" or perhaps even "sad" (*Prince*, Ch. xvii, p. 139). Machiavelli does not use the word "bad" (*malo*) to describe the tendency of men to be "ungrateful, fickle, liars and deceivers, avoiders of danger, greedy for profit," etc. (*ibid.*); rather, he merely says that men are "not good" (e.g., "tanti che non sono buoni"— Ch. xv, pp. 126–127).
2. Cf. *German Ideology* (in Feuer, ed., pp. 410–411, 422) with the description of the "origin of the city" as men living in "peace and health," *Republic*, II. 369c–372d.
3. The reason for specifically excluding religious thought will be made clear below. It should be noted that these dimensions concern cognitive content rather than affect or mood.
4. Note that Aristotle's thought can be seen as a development away from the premises of Antiphon, marking the full elaboration of a trend represented by Socrates and Plato. Hobbes's position can be seen as a recombination of the views of Aristotle and Antiphon, whereas Marx represents the development of a tradition stemming from Hobbes when combined with assumptions derived from Aristotle.
5. Since writing these lines, an article has appeared (Salkever, 1974) which points in this direction and is complementary to the approach adopted here; see note 21 below.
6. Citations are from the translation in Barker (1960: 95–98).
7. The Greek word here translated as "the facts of the case"—*aletheia*—means truth or reality (cf. Collingwood, 1945: 56), as distinct from a mere opinion, custom, or religious belief (*doxa*). While not exactly identical to the modern distinction between "fact" and "value," Antiphon's usage is obviously similar to it.
8. This is perhaps nowhere more obvious than in those speeches in Thucydides's *History of the Peloponnesian War* that seem most clearly to reflect the Sophist view. See the speeches of the Athenians at Sparta (I. 73–78, esp. 76: "for it has always been the law that the weaker should be subject to the stronger"), the Ambassadors at Melos (V. 86–111, esp. 105: "of men we know, that by a necessary law of their nature they rule wherever they can"), and Diodotus (III. 42–48, esp. 45: "it is impossible to prevent . . . human nature doing what it has once set its mind upon, by force of law or by any other deterrent force whatsoever" [1951: 44, 334, 170]). Cf. Antiphon, Fragment I: "it is obvious that legal justice is inadequate. . . ." On the general relation between the political thought of the Sophists and these speeches in Thucydides, see Barker (1960: 84–85) and Jaeger (1945: 286–331; 382–411).
9. The word "association," for Aristotle, distinguishes those groups that are *not* merely an accidental aggregation, like a transitory crowd at an international airport or a school of fish whose membership constantly fluctuates; in contemporary terms, he means a community as distinct from a contractual association or corporation (e.g., MacIver, 1964: 3–8, 474–479, *et passim*).

10. The exposition of Aristotle's position will focus on the *Politics*, Book I, 1252a–1258a; all references are to Barker's edition (1946).

11. At this point, Aristotle adds a deceptively simple reference: "Hesiod spoke truly in the verse, 'First house, and wife, and ox to draw the plough,' for oxen serve the poor in lieu of household slaves" (1252b; p. 4). As on other occasions in\ the *Politics*, Aristotle cites a famous Greek poet as evidence, even though the poetic statement requires some revision of the prior theoretical formulation. Here Aristotle has treated the family as the resultant of two *analytical* relations (male–female and master–slave), whereas Hesiod's verse reminds us that the household, as the first civilized association, presupposed the historical emergence of a sedentary life ("First house") and reliance on agriculture ("ox to draw the plough"). Historically speaking, at the beginning of civilization the function ultimately satisfied by slaves was fulfilled by mere animals, "for oxen serve the poor"—including the relatively poor early agriculturalists—"in lieu of household slaves" (cf. 1254b; p. 13). Unlike Antiphon's analysis, Aristotle's analytical categories are intended to conform with the history of human development.

12. While it is not possible here to analyze the difference between premodern or classical physics and post-Renaissance physics, it should be emphasized that the latter—from its very origins—implied a shift toward the view that science can master or control nature. For example, it has been argued that the Copernican view of the cosmos, "so far from diminishing the scope of man's powers, vastly enlarged it" (Collingwood, 1945: 97). "Both God and man are regarded by Galileo as transcending nature; and rightly, because if nature consists of mere quantity its apparent qualitative aspects must be conferred upon it from outside, namely by the human mind as transcending it . . ." (*ibid.*, p. 103). In contrast, the Ionian philosophers—and the classics generally—used the word "nature" to mean "the internal source of a thing's behavior"; "a thing's 'nature' is the thing in it which makes it behave as it does" (*ibid.*, pp. 45–46). Hence, in premodern physics, nature transcends man, and human action cannot be viewed as controlling or mastering the natural phenomena impinging on social life. It is, of course, not without interest that contemporary natural science has fundamentally called into question the scientific perspective of Galileo and Newton on which political thought has rested since the seventeenth century: "if modern physics is coming closer to Plato as the great mathematician-philosopher of antiquity, modern biology is coming closer to its great biologist-philosopher Aristotle" (*ibid.*, p. 83). Cf. Strauss (1953: 7-8).

13. All page references are to the Oakeshott edition (1960).

14. Lest this seem an extreme formulation, consider "A Review and Conclusion" (p. 461): "the point in time, wherein a man becomes subject to a conqueror, is that point, wherein having liberty to submit to him, he *consenteth*, either by express words, or by other sufficient sign, to be his subject."

15. "We know only one science, the science of history. History can be viewed from two sides: it can be divided into the history of nature and that of man. The two sides, however, are not to be seen as independent entities" *German Ideology* (Easton and Guddat, 1967: 408. Cf. p. 418). Hereafter the *German Ideology* will be abbreviated *GI*, and the Preface to the *Contribution to the Critique of Political Economy, CPE;* refer-

ences to the latter are to Feuer (1959). Marx's *Economic and Philosophic Manuscripts of 1844*, abbreviated as *1844 MS*, will be cited in Struik's edition (1964). On the combination of genetic and analytic methods in Marxian thought, see Sartre (1968: esp. pp. 51–52), and compare pp. 78-80 above.

16. Although the *German Ideology* was written by both Marx and Engels, by Engels's own account, the crucial conception of the historical process underlying their work was due to Marx; for this reason, if no other, I will speak throughout of Marx. On the relationship between Marx and Engels, see Avineri (1968).

17. As human history is summarized in the *German Ideology,* society passes through a sequence of distinct stages: first, "tribal ownership," "the undeveloped stage of production where people live by hunting and fishing, by breeding animals, or, in the highest stage, by agriculture" (*GI,* p. 410–411); second, "ancient communal and state ownership" combined with the rise of "private property," based on the antagonisms "between citizens and slaves," "between town and country," and "between industry and maritime commerce" (*GI,* pp. 411–412); third, "feudal or estate ownership," manifested in agriculture by "landed property with serf labor" and in towns by "individual labor with small capital controlling the labor of journeymen" (*GI,* pp. 412–413). The origins and character of the modern state—"industry," based on private property, large scale, and a radical division of labor—is described later in the *German Ideology* (pp. 442–473) and in Marx's other writings; this contemporary period is viewed as leading necessarily to "communist" society, in which the division of labor and private property will be definitely overcome (e.g., *GI,* pp. 424–428). In the slightly different formulation of the Preface to the *Critique of Political Economy,* Marx speaks of "the Asiatic (i.e., state controlled, as in China), the ancient (i.e., Greece and Rome), the feudal, and the modern bourgeois methods of production as so many epochs in the progress of the economic formation of society" (p. 44).

18. "Consciousness does not determine life, but life determines consciousness" (*GI,* p. 415). "It is not the consciousness of men that determines their existence, but on the contrary, their social existence determines their consciousness" (Preface, *CPE,* p. 43). Cf., however, the Third Thesis on Feuerbach (Feuer, 1959: 244).

19. Cf. Aristotle, *Politics* (I. 1253b) quoted above p. 82.

20. It is, for example, instructive to compare Skinner's view of the plasticity of human behavior with Hobbes's remark that common men are "like clean paper" (*Leviathan,* Ch. 30, p. 221)—a remark that is obviously also the antecedent of Locke's "tabula rasa."

21. Salkever's recent article (1974), published after this manuscript was completed, is an example of further characteristics that seem to be linked to the fundamental dimensions stressed here. His distinction between theories of *virtue* and of political *obligation* is roughly parallel to what has been called the dimension of "the relation of human action to nature" in Table 1 and Figure 1; his distinction between theories of freedom and those of *community* parallels the dimension called "the relation of human nature to society." Salkever ignores the Sophist view, though it would fit easily enough into his categories, but his article shows the utility of a structural approach such as the one used here.

108                                                    ROGER D. MASTERS

22. Compare: "Nature for the Japanese has not traditionally been an object
of man's investigation or of exploitation for human benefit, as it has
been for Westerners. For the Japanese and for other Oriental peoples,
man was considered a part of nature, and the art of living with nature
was their wisdom of life" (Watanabe, 1974: 279).
23. A full elaboration of this possibility would require a careful consideration of such diverse approaches as Charles Osgood's "semantic differential," Claude Lévi-Strauss's "structural anthropology," and Noam
Chomsky's "transformational grammar"—an endeavor that is, needless
to say, out of the question here. It is, however, perhaps not accidental
that a leading American anthropologist has suggested that all human
cultures can be situated on an "$n$-dimensional quality space"—and has
illustrated his approach by a cube not unlike Figure 2 (Fernandez,
1974: esp. 124–125, 127).


# BIBLIOGRAPHY

Aristotle, 1946. *Politics* (E. Barker, ed.). Oxford, Clarendon Press.
Avineri, Shlomo, 1968. *Social and Political Thought of Karl Marx.* N.Y.,
Cambridge University Press.
Barker, Ernest, 1960 (1918). *Greek Political Theory.* N.Y., Barnes and
Noble Books.
Brecht, Arnold, 1969. *Political Theory.* Princeton, Princeton University
Press.
Coleman, Frank M., 1974. "The Hobbesian Basis of American Constitu-
tionalism," *Polity,* VII (Fall), 57–89.
Collingwood, R. G., 1945. *The Idea of Nature.* Oxford, Clarendon Press.
Commoner, Barry, 1970 (1963). *Science and Survival.* N.Y., Ballantine
Books.
Easton, Lloyd D., and Kurt H. Guddat, 1967. *Writings of the Young Marx
on Philosophy and Society.* N.Y., Doubleday, Anchor Books.
Ebenstein, William, 1969. *Great Political Thinkers* (4th ed.). N.Y., Holt,
Rinehart and Winston.
Eliade, Mirca, 1959. *Cosmos and History: The Myth of the Eternal Return.*
N.Y., Harper Torchbooks.
Fernandez, James, 1974. "The Mission of Metaphor in Expressive Culture,"
*Current Anthropology,* 15 (June), 119–46.
Feuer, Lewis, (ed.), 1959. *Marx and Engels: Basic Writings.* N.Y., Double-
day, Anchor Books.
Frankfort, Henri, *et al.,* 1949. *Before Philosophy.* Harmondsworth, Essex,
Penguin Books.
Hobbes, Thomas, 1960 (1651). *Leviathan* (Michael Oakeshott, ed.). Ox-
ford, Basil Blackwell.
Jaeger, Werner, 1945 (1939). *Paideia,* Vol. I. N.Y., Oxford University Press.
Lévi-Strauss, Claude, 1962. *La Pensée Sauvage.* Paris, Plon.
Lorenz, Konrad, 1971. *Studies in Animal and Human Behavior,* Vol. II.
Cambridge, Harvard University Press.
Machiavelli, Niccolò, 1964 (1532). *The Prince* (Mark Musa, ed.). N.Y.,
St. Martin's Press.

MacIver, R. M., 1946 (1926). *The Modern State.* N.Y., Oxford University Press.

Macpherson, C. B., 1962. *The Political Theory of Possessive Individualism.* Oxford, Clarendon Press.

Marshack, Alexander, 1972. "Upper Paleolithic Notation and Symbol," *Science,* 178 (Nov. 24), 817–828.

Marx, Karl, 1938 (1875). *Critique of the Gotha Program.* N.Y., International Publishers.

————, 1964 (1844). *The Economic and Philosophic Manuscripts of 1844* (Dirk J. Struik, ed.). N.Y., International Publishers.

————, 1972 (1857-58). *The Grundrisse* (David McLellan, ed.). N.Y., Harper Torchbooks.

———— and Friedrich Engels, 1971 (1848). *The Communist Manifesto* (Dirk J. Struik, ed.). N.Y., International Publishers.

Masters, Roger D., 1975. "Politics as a Biological Phenomenon." *Social Science Information,* XIV (April), 7-63.

————, In Press. "Of Marmots and Men: Human Altruism and Animal Behavior." In Lauren Wispé, ed., *Positive Forms of Social Behavior.* Cambridge, Harvard University Press.

Meadows, Donella H., *et al.,* 1972. *The Limits of Growth.* N.Y., Potomac Books/Universe Books.

Montagu, M. F. A., ed., 1968. *Culture: Man's Adaptive Dimension.* N.Y., Oxford University Press.

Morin, Edgar, 1973. *Le Paradigme Perdu: La Nature Humaine.* Paris, Le Seuil.

Muller, Herbert J., 1962. *Freedom in the Ancient World.* London, Martin Secker and Warburg.

Pittendrigh, Colin S., 1958. "Adaptation, Natural Selection, and Behavior," in A. Roe and G. Simpson, eds., *Behavior and Evolution,* New Haven, Yale University Press, pp. 390–416.

Plato, 1968. *The Republic* (Allan Bloom, ed.). N.Y., Basic Books.

Pritchard, James B., ed., 1958. *The Ancient Near East.* Princeton, Princeton University Press.

Rousseau, Jean-Jacques, 1964 (1750-55). *First and Second Discourses* (Roger D. Masters, cd.). N.Y., St. Martin's Press.

Russell, Bertrand, 1945. *A History of Western Philosophy.* N.Y., Simon & Schuster.

Sabine, George, 1961. *A History of Political Theory* (3rd ed.). N.Y., Holt, Rinehart and Winston.

Salkever, Stephen, 1974. "Virtue, Obligation and Politics," *American Political Science Review,* LXVIII (March) 78–92.

Sartre, Jean-Paul, 1968 (1960). *Search for a Method.* N.Y., Random House, Vintage Books.

Skinner, B. F., 1972. *Beyond Freedom and Dignity.* N.Y., New American Library, Signet.

Strauss, Leo, 1952. *The Political Philosophy of Hobbes.* Chicago, University of Chicago Press.

————, 1953. *Natural Right and History.* Chicago, University of Chicago Press.

————, 1964. *The City and Man.* Chicago, Rand McNally.

Swanson, Guy, 1960. *The Birth of the Gods.* Ann Arbor, University of Michigan Press.

Thucydides, 1951. *The Peloponnesian War* (John H. Finley, Jr., ed.). N.Y., Random House, Modern Library.

Watanabe, Masao, 1974. "The Conception of Nature in Japanese Culture," *Science* 183 (Jan. 25), 279–282.

Watkins, Frederick M., 1948. *The Political Tradition of the West*. Cambridge, Harvard University Press.

Wheelwright, Philip, ed., 1966. *The Presocratics*. N.Y., Odyssey Press.

# 4

## POLITICS, VIOLENCE, AND HUMAN NATURE

GEORGE ARMSTRONG KELLY

I

In general debate, we are not terribly clear as to what violence is. Although it is a shock word for most people, it has become a plus word for some.[1] It is part of a common—and technical—vocabulary, with connotations that spray out in every direction, even though certain commentators have tried to limit its scope. In emotional situations, the acceptances of the word have become diverse—particularly when it is a conceptual word, but also in practical cases where it has been used to convey blame or approval. Though we cannot properly clarify the meaning of violence without conscientiously attempting to establish what persons engaged in violent acts intend to achieve by those acts—no matter on whose behalf they are performed—the beginning of an analysis of violence should not make an instance of group subjectivity.

In the simplest and crudest renditions of the term, as it applies to human behavior, we are faced with some initial, but not insurmountable, problems. The first of these is: What constitutes violence? Many, perhaps most, commentators acquiesce in defining violence as "behavior to inflict physical injury to people or damage to property."[2] As James C. Davies puts it:

> To understand violence, it is appropriate to establish fairly rigorous limits to its meaning that do not confuse visible, overt acts with their causes. So I will define violence as an act whose intent is to injure a person or damage property. . . . If [a person] pushes [an] old lady or if he throws a stone at [a] window, this is violence. . . .[3]

Violence then is what violence does. Thinking violent thoughts or harboring violent intentions *in fore interno* do not in themselves constitute violence unless they burst to the surface in assignable acts that could presumably be observed, dealt with, or judged. And yet, if the substrate of violence is a particular species of frustration, loss of control, or rancor, it may find equivalent expression in social behavior that irritates or tortures other human beings without recourse to specifically physical means, or that affects the disposition of property without overt damage or destruction. Thus, one is obliged to speak—metaphorically or not— of a "violence of language" or of "violence done to the spirit of an agreement," and so forth. Consequently, it is not strange that a recent writer recurrently argues that, within a certain democracy that he takes as constituting an adequate human society, economic impediments to democratic values may, in some cases, be more obstructive to the realization of human goals than violence.[4] As victims of minority persecution will attest, it is not precisely true that "sticks and stones will break my bones, but words will never hurt me." The fact that verbal controversy passes under the English label of "polemics" reminds us that the Greek word *polemikos* means "of or pertaining to war." The classical example of the transition from mute or inexpressible grievance to physical fury is found in Melville's novella *Billy Budd*.

Although it is convenient, perhaps necessary, to define violence, according to law or by prefigured statistics, in an extremely physicalist way, such a description will not satisfy those whose potential violence convention or the law restrains or those who claim to justify their overt acts of physical violence on the ground that verbal or more subtle kinds of violence have previously injured them or even their kinsmen and forefathers. To such persons (perhaps insufficiently educated to the delicacies of legal abuse), violence hardly begins with a clearly designated species of acts, but is a sensate continuum along which, beginning perhaps with the merest social slight, escalatory retributions or counterretributions are exacted. As one knows, the origins of vengeance or vendetta are often lost in the mists of time. However the aim here is not to censure or ridicule human beings who fail to detect whether certain of their acts are legally determinable as violent or nonviolent, or to help them to a proper understanding of the rule of society. Neither is it to cast in doubt the laws, conventions, or even the social science definitions that establish judgments about permissible and nonpermissible social responses. It is merely to set forth the problem in some of its complexity.

To say that violence is as violence does can be a useful rule of thumb but it does not help us to regress logically to the root causes of human violence. In this instance, the psychological investigator has two options: he may either concern himself with individual frustrations and disturbances that may or may not come to the collective social surface and have political consequences; or he may recreate his insights at a more frankly sociological level. Similarly, the moral philosopher has two choices: he may either enunciate, according to extremely general and yet obviously culture-bound criteria, what he believes to be the conditions under which persons may fight with fists and bullets rather than with their tongues; or he, too, may cultivate a sociological strategy, which, if not completely relativistic, at least proceeds by the most prudent induction across time and space to found hypotheses that are never susceptible to being confused with moral imperatives.

A second, related problem with respect to violence is the matter of intention. Intention is a tricky business, not only because it is involved with the attempted enactment of envisaged outcomes, that is, what Weber would call *zweckrational* action, but also because an intention to commit violence may crystallize with great purity in the violent act itself, becoming almost a case of *la violence pour la violence.* "Violence," according to Arendt, "[is] instrumental in nature."[5] I am not so sure she is right, unless she means no more than that the reduction of intolerable frustration is one of the possible goals that perpetrators of violence may instrumentally pursue. For, as E. V. Walter correctly states: "A violent event . . . may be simply an act of destruction—for vengeance or other reasons, or for no apparent reason. In this case, violence is not an instrument of power, for the violent act is complete and the object destroyed."[6] I do not mean to imply here that violence cannot rationally or intentionally be a means to the destruction of a desired object (e.g., for the sake of denial to others); but it does seem to me clear that we often use the term violence to include a category of actions that are too spontaneous to be called intentional, purposive, or instrumental. For example, as John Spiegel writes:

> Violence lies at the extreme end of a spectrum of aggressive behavior. It is characterized by acts of physical force aimed at the severe injury or destruction of persons, objects or organizations. A second defining feature is concerned with timing or tempo, usually expressed as "explosiveness." Violent behavior, in other words, is aggression released fully and abruptly, usually in a state of high energy arousal. . . . It excludes brutalizing social arrangements not characterized by the use of physical force.[7]

Spiegel's account of violence lays emphasis on its explosive and possibly unpremeditated quality. I believe that this is a seemly emphasis, psychologically understood. Violence is not always, in any strong sense, *intended,* although quite often it is clearly intended. And it goes without saying that intentions do not always translate themselves perfectly into consequences: the most violent thoughts, bottled up, can often produce inoffensive forms of behavior that are scarcely interesting to the social scientist who is looking for damage or injury.

This discussion may seem banal and unrewarding as long as the focus is on violence, *per se.* But when we seek to define what is specifically collective, social, or political about violence, the issues become more interesting. Without anticipating arguments that I will present below in fuller detail, I shall postulate (1) that not all violence is political in impact or scope; (2) that the sphere of political violence can be delimited with somewhat more rigor than certain specialists believe;[8] (3) that important criteria for these forms of violence consist, of course, in the sphere and consequences of their impact, as well as in the character of their intentionality and the way that intentions are translated into impacts; and (4) that much social violence, though only haphazardly political, is interpreted as such because of improper conceptions of what is political, even though *any* act of violence may become political under certain conditions. Additionally, I would assert, without offering proof in this essay, that the violence that is *most* political in thrust is almost surely that which is most premeditated or intentional and most consciously organized through what Walter calls "staffs" or "regimes."

In short, I am defending the autonomy and specificity of the political by asserting a set of conditions that assist us in locating *political* violence, although I concede fully that politics is permeable to violence from other sources and frequently born out of other motives. Indeed, the most complex and cumulative actions of violence in the political sphere resemble a vortex toward which diverse hostilities converge; but only the romantic imagination invests them with those demonic and unreflective attributes, mobilized by the deities of History and Progress, that Proudhon, for example, assigns to them:

> A revolution is a force against which no power, divine or human, can prevail, and whose nature it is to grow by the very resistance it encounters. . . . The more you repress it, the more you increase its rebound and render its action irresistible, so that it is precisely the same for the triumph of an idea whether it is persecuted, harrassed, beaten down from the start, or whether it grows and develops unobstructed. Like the Nemesis of the ancients, whom neither prayers nor threats could move, the revolution advances, with sombre and predestined tread. . . .[9]

Without going overboard in defense of some of its claims, we may be sure that "normal" social science has something more trenchant to offer in the way of causal and compositional analysis than this hymn to the unfathomable. In brief, there is a case for

the concept "political violence," which involves a discussion of
what is properly political and what is not and which, in certain
ways, suggests limits as to what our adequate understanding of
violence, pure and simple, is. Political violence, in true form,
scarcely assumes the contours of mere "explosiveness"; nor can
it develop, in its true form, without cognizable objects of political
attack or defense; nor can it really be said to reside in aggressive
intentions that are not translated into concerted physical action.
Cases for "ritual violence" have been and obviously can be made;[10]
and at least one writer has asserted that, outside of the matter
of political domination, violence can signify and accompany the
mere exercise of social privilege.[11] Politics is of course a symbolic
as well as a literal activity; and status in society and status in the
political order, both of them desirable and both subject to struggle,
may not be totally compatible goals. With these provisos, we can
begin to scrutinize the notion of political violence without the
feeling of embarking on a wild goose chasse.


## II

What is there in certain kinds of violence that is per-
sistently political in form, in intent, and in results? Let us disregard
cases where violent and frankly political intentions achieve no
results: in such instances, we may have suppositions, but no phenomena. However, we cannot pass lightly over cases where ostensibly subpolitical origins of violence are transformed in such a
way as to have unambiguous political consequences.

In general, the violence of a deranged man or of a mother defending her children would have only the most dimly perceivable
political consequences, unless the madman happened to be a Boris
Godunov and the mother a Marie Antoinette. Here, role and office, rather than the individual pathology of the situation, serve
as intervening terms to lead us toward a grasp of our concept.
This, I think, holds no less true in a democratic or revolutionary
age than it does in periods when specifically political activity
belongs, as if by right, only to the few. However, it is evidently
easier, in ages where mass action has the capacity to affect the
performance of society for a variety of subpolitical frustrations to
be released tellingly into the political arena.

A second point is that the more aimless, unreflective, and

"abrupt" acts of violence are, the less political they will seem in their genesis. The word "genesis" saves us from dealing with the problem of premeditation and merely implies that there is a mediating membrane of intentionality and conscientious fixation through which violent frustrations may be channeled, organized, and brought to a point of political thrust. When one stops blaming one's parents, the storekeeper, or even the cop on the block and begins to feel one's aggressions as being directed against public authority in its literal or symbolic manifestations, one is presumably crossing a certain threshold to political violence. To illustrate: on a hot summer's day a diligent fireman turns off a water hydrant in a city ghetto; the children are angrily resentful. A teenager brawls with a policeman and is carted off to jail. The situation in the neighborhood becomes tense through variant communications of the incident; latent hostility is heightened and haphazardly mobilized by an ad hoc leadership. There is retaliation; the same night several stores are looted and set ablaze. This example touches on two ways in which violence *per se* relates to the political process, thereby becoming a political problem and an appropriate subject for political research. In the first place, there is a sequence of accidental or even unpremeditated social events which, even though initially subpolitical in character, is susceptible to awakening politically conscious responses as the hostility crystallizes. Second, carried beyond a certain degree, violence inevitably implicates agencies of control, law-enforcement, coercion, and judgment that are themselves politically founded and may even be politically partisan. Indeed, a third possibility, expressed most forcefully in various studies by Charles Tilly, is that most collective events of violence—at least in modern Western civilization—are explicitly political in nature. For example, as Tilly writes, with regard to a quantitative study he has made of violence in France:

> violent protests seem to grow more directly from the struggle for established places in the structure of power.[12] Even presumably nonpolitical forms of collective violence like the anti-tax revolt are normally directed against the authorities, accompanied by a critique of the authorities' failures to meet their responsibilities, and informed by a sense of justice denied to the participants in the process. . . . Over the long run, the processes most regularly producing collective violence are those by which

groups acquire or lose membership in the political community.[13]

It is interesting to note that his thesis is supported by another writer, T. R. Gurr, with whom Tilly has had certain fundamental disagreements regarding the understanding of political violence:

Political actors are by far the most common objects of verbal and physical attack. Demonstrations are typically directed against the political figures who are held responsible for grievances by their sins of commission or omission; riots usually include attacks on several kinds of political actors, including both officials and the police.[14]

There are perhaps three chief reasons why this attempt to establish the existence of so close a relationship between collective violence and political motivation should not be endorsed uncritically. The first stems from the belief, shared by this writer, that the set of approaches to political science that passes under the label of "behavioralism" encourages a conceptualization of political activity dangerously far removed from the core of political subject matter and constitutes an invitation to treat any topic of potential interest to the political scientist as "political."[15] This might cause analysts to extend the notion "political" indiscriminately to all sorts of acts, including violence. In my view, Tilly takes pains to avoid this trap; but the temptation to make politics—and especially the "study of politics"—coextensive with all social relations is unfortunately great. I shall deal somewhat more closely with this issue later on in this section, since it is basic to much else that will be asserted in this essay.

The second reason is clearly a corollary of the first, although it is specifically involved with intersecting questions of political consciousness, development, and organization. According to this thesis, the achievement of "modernity" (which implies democratization, massification, the extension of social services by the state, and the bureaucratic apparatus of "socialist" or "welfare" states) carries with it an expansion of human concerns affected directly by "politics" that was inconceivable in societies with unsophisticated technology and lesser aspiration and consumption. In other words, according to this argument, there might be a natural tendency for merely "social" violence to become "political" in scope insofar as the gratification of redresses and wants is seen to be linked to the action of public authority. Thus, the allegedly increasing "politicization" of violence in America and other nations may not only be attributable to the heightened consciousness of the objectors, but may also function as a response to the economic and social extensions of modern government. For example, Janowitz attempts to interpret this feature in the United States through the use of the concepts "communal riot" and "commodity riot": "Whereas the [old-style] communal riot involved a confrontation between the white and black community (e.g., the Chicago race riot of 1919), the commodity riot, especially as it entered into the third and destructive phase, represents a confrontation between the black community and law enforcement officials of the larger society."[16] Evidently, beyond a certain point, the state becomes a target of violent grievances which had previously expressed themselves in strife of a more specifically intercommunal character. The violent petitioners gradually or abruptly discover that they are subject to a Leviathan State that has the power to frustrate or gratify their desires.

Yet it might be unwise to leap to such a conclusion without considering some serious objections. In the first place, the incidence of political violence, in the sense that Tilly and some other writers have used the term, seems scarcely to correlate with the advanced development of state power and bureaucratic services, except in the banal sense that if allocations of *desiderata* are to be changed by violent means, this in itself requires some prior concentration of more than casual control over the allocating process, which then becomes a logical target for coercion or conquest by the malcontents.[17] Secondly, in some systems of explanation—such as the Marxist (especially in its "revisionist" and "deterministic" tendencies)—more formally political sequences of change tend to be subsumed into increasingly complex "social" formulations as the productive capacities of the society develop. Though the point cannot be analyzed here in detail, the supposition is not that one can reason from social complexity toward discrete political explanations, but rather that political results are the consequences of a complex, though analyzable, nexus of increasingly conscious and organized social behavior. Finally, if we regard the extension of state services in modern industrial society as an extension of the political function *per se,* we will perhaps be led to conclude that violence, too, because of its associations, has become more politicalized. But if such a society shows no appreciable rise in the measurable scope and incidence of violence from antecedent conditions, we would be led to the curious conclusion that nonpolitical violence had abated. However, the real problem is not the manipulation of a rather arid classification scheme, but a matter of distinctions that must be made between the basic and contingent aspects of political violence, the various aggregative and cumulative patterns or situations in which violence plays a leading role, and the definition of politics that we will observe in drawing our conclusions.

The third reason is of a different sort and has to do with an analytical question that must be reserved for a later part of the essay. Briefly put, however, the criticism involves ideological and partisan hostility. In dealing with the subject, Gurr, the Feierabends, and others imply that political violence (or "civil strife" or "rebellion" or whatever the label may be) comprises a defined set of acts committed by rioters, insurgents, mutineers, or the like against the *de facto* legal power.[18] These scholars do not attempt to defend the status and acts of that power, but merely to set a context. However, in some ways this approach has promoted the view, criticized at great length by Nardin,[19] that such an investigation of violence can or should lead logically to policy science and the development of specific governmental skills of "conflict management." It is all too evident that if we are to have a comprehensive theoretical view of political violence we must take into account the further possibilities that (1) the state is itself a crucible of violence, interacting with or, at the maximum, causing—as anarchists would argue—the phenomena under investigation, or (2) the state, despite its necessary function as a conflict regulator and its dispensations to employ forms of physical coercion that cannot be legally impeached as "violence," frequently exceeds the legal and functional restraints that inhere in its privileged position.[20] Important normative and analytical implications for the theory of political violence flow from this debate. For present purposes of discussion, I shall take the position that any adequate study of the processes of political violence must accept the full implications of the possibility of the state as an agent of violence, but that the state is not simply a primordial reservoir of violence nor should it be theoretically regarded as merely another specialized agency of society interacting in structures that are sometimes violent, sometimes peaceable. In this regard, the traditional distinction between "state" and "government" or "regime" may both clarify and mislead. Indeed, the notion of "state" often entails an ongoingness, a cultural and juridical integrity, that we must deny to actual or even ideal-typical forms of government in which state power may be manifested. For example, we can easily distinguish the "French state" from the forms and practices of the Fourth or Fifth Republics; and we can similarly conceive of a "Chilean state" that is embodied neither in the acts and aims of the Allende regime nor in those of the military dictatorship that overthrew it. It is easier to think of the incarnation of violence (internally) in governments of particular kinds than in states, if only because the notion of the state seems to provide analytically for certain consensual norms for the peaceable conduct of public life. However, even the idea of the state conveys the reality of asymmetrical, if functional, relations of domination and the possibility that legitimate coercion may spill over into violence.

These brief comments about the state recall our attention to the question of how and when violence is "political." It is common today to assert that practically every human relationship has its "politics," which is another way of saying that essentialist definitions are in bad odor and should give way to "processual" or "operational" ones. What does politics mean? Every student of classical political theory is usually pretty certain that he knows what his subject is; but when asked to articulate the content of that subject, he frequently founders. Politics seems then either more an expansive inclusion of all relationships of domination or a selective convergence of diverse human interests than a discrete area of study. Yet I believe that in current usage political theory has operated in essentially two frames of reference: (1) formal and legal human government; and (2) instances of so-called political behavior.

The criticisms of these two conceptions of politics are well known. The first misleads us as to the reality and dynamics of political situations, encouraging false and/or idealistic conclusions. The second sacrifices the specificity of politics, as a practice, profession, art, or skill, to the diverse activities of the social milieu in which politics operates. The study of political behavior and of the structures in which political behavior takes place has provided so many genuine insights that it would be absurd to ignore the merits of the various findings so grouped. However, when viewed as a sacrosanct research dogma, it is infinitely regressive and falsely imperialistic at the same time. It has the propensity to extend political analysis to all areas of human choice. In so doing, it weakens the sense and, indeed, the majesty of the political. Thus such things as apartment-seeking, children's games, or family relations are miraculously transformed into "political subjects," when, in reality, they might at most function as political metaphors. This is unfortunate, because Aristotle himself already knew that even if certain areas of inquiry were potentially interesting to politics, they were not the primary matter of politics. Our current ideologies do not encourage us to separate the business of the polity from its surrounding arrangements in quite the same manner as Aristotle; but this does not invalidate his methodological lesson. Even if one believes—in a neo-Lockean or even a Marxian sense— that the state is or ought to be subordinate to the rights and powers of society, this does not give license to make the sociology of power queen of the political disciplines.

In my judgment, the more classical definition of politics, as modified and illuminated by insights obtained from the behavioral approach, avoids the regressive trap of regarding politics as the sociological investigation of how all power relations come to operate. The thesis asserts simply that politics is concerned with the state, not with persons who behave in part as if they were the subjects or rulers of socially constituted ministates.[21] It is concerned with the relations of states to one another, to their sub-agencies, to societal groups, or to individuals. The relations may be intermittent or serried, hostile or friendly, but they obviously cannot be null. Various combinations of these relationships constitute political systems. It is really only in the recent period of widespread mass participation in various political functions and the restless search for other-disciplinary metaphors in the effort to exalt political studies to a "science" that it was possible to see politics as anything else.

Giovanni Sartori has recently commented, somewhat in the same vein: "The democratization or massification of politics entails not only its diffusion or, if you wish, its dilution, but, above all, the ubiquity of politics."[22] This leads him to the conclusion: "Though the state expands, political processes can no longer be contained within, or brought under, its institutions. Consequently, the concept of the state gives way to the broader and more flexible idea of the political system. . . . This leads to a dilution of the concept of politics which comes very close to vaporizing it out of existence."[23] My line of reasoning is close to this, but, for both theoretical and practical reasons, it reaches a view of politics that is somewhat more restrictive. However, when Sartori maintains, "if . . . decisions are essentially political, it is because they are made by personnel located in *political sites,*"[24] I perceive a flexible version of state-orientedness reemerging, and I have no quarrel. To be in a "political site" and to act is quite different from being in any site whatever and acting "politically."

We have already noted, however—and Sartori's "massification" thesis corroborates—that the nonpolitical is still often the potentially political and that its irruption into situations of political interest to political observers is a mysterious but undeniable fact of the social order. Let us take an illustration of violence to bring out the point more clearly.

Suppose that a given American family practices household democracy. Suppose further that the members of the family, children and adults, are in the habit of voting (voting, *par excellence,* is held to be a political act) on where the vacation will be spent. Johnny, age fourteen, who likes the seashore, is outvoted 4-1 by the others, who prefer inland lakes. He goes to his room angrily, slams the door, sulks, and ends by breaking most of his furniture. Is this an act of political violence? Most assuredly not. It is an act of adolescent rage, just as it would have been in an authoritarian family where father had laid down the law.

Political violence occurs when the violent act (or acts) are of political significance to members of a political community (not when they behaviorally replicate politics in other milieux). Yet even here we run into the problem of unintended consequences. If Johnny's father had been mayor of the town and Johnny had poisoned him instead of breaking furniture, thus leading to a special election and new political realignments, the definition just given would have been fulfilled. We should therefore state that political violence occurs when the violent acts arc of political

significance to members of a political community *and* transacted
in a political setting *(à la* Sartori). There is obviously also a
spectrum of political violence going from the opaque to the perfectly transparent. In purest form, political violence has premeditated collective ends and impugns or threatens the central
exercise of political authority; or, conversely, it may be a species
of *coup d'état* (in the original sense of that phrase)[25] whereby
authority oversteps its constitutional or functional boundaries so
as to deal violently with its challengers.

There are no watertight compartments for messy reality. In
this instance, the general rule is: the farther one gets from the
state, the farther one gets from politics; fundamentally, violence
meted out by or consciously directed against public authority
merits the epithet "political." If greater confusion that this
abounds, it is probably because we have no very clear notion of
the "state" in contemporary political science. H. L. Nieburg, a
behavioralist, writes of political violence as a species of disrup-
tive or destructive acts whose effects *"tend to modify the behavior of others in a bargaining system that has consequences
for the social system"* (author's italics).[26] There is no need to
invoke a definition that is so roundabout or porous. T. Honderich
is more consequent when he writes more simply of *"a considerable
or destroying use of force against persons or things, a use of force
prohibited by law and directed to a change in the policies, personnel, or system of government"* (author's italics).[27] I would only
add to that: "and perceived in its consequences as such."


## III

To ask, in the naked abstract, is my act of political violence (against the state, on behalf of the state) justified? is a matter
of immediate moral concern to me. Whether it is a matter of immediate public concern depends on a number of other qualifications: in what terms I decide to answer the question, what range
of justifications I will give, who I am, with whom I will be acting,
what forces or ideas I think I am representing or symbolizing,
what the probabilities are that I will succeed in or forward a
process believed to be desirable, etc. To make qualifications of
this sort—as opposed to asking the type of question that inquires
merely why I would propose to commit hurtful or destructive

acts in a variety of other social settings—helps to distinguish the cases in which violence may be properly conceived as political. I think we may also grant—though this matter would call for further exposition—that my observations may be applied unproblematically to both political "incumbents" and "insurgents," at least in the cases that are apt to interest us the most. Although there is considerable power in the "moral man, immoral society" type of argument which holds that the statesman's role is tragic because he is doomed to commit moral evils, *nolens volens,* for the sake of some composite political good,[28] the same idea may be extended to actors who challenge a political order violently with the intention of setting another, better one in its place.

So-called scientific analyses of political violence will scarcely reflect the kind of concerns I have been expressing, because their methodological intent is to classify, quantify, and objectivize a certain range of phenomena, reducing the problematic of violence, at the theoretical level, to an interplay of more-or-less accurately posited and measurable variables and, at the practical level, to the responses that an intelligent and purposive (i.e., *zweckrational*) mind or organizational process would be expected to make to the reception of accurate information, appropriately classified, and conceptually linked within a set of models or paradigms that are susceptible to being "operationalized." To the extent that such a strategy of understanding is possible or useful (skeptics should at least be warned that it responds to a deeply ingrained modern technique of problem-solving in wide areas of social management), it appears to leave out some very important details.

Paradoxically, the prescriptive and descriptive aspects of political violence are both separate and linked to each other. This is in part inevitable, given the charged ethical overtones of the subject. But that fact is itself of minor significance: if one wants to treat moral questions in the same manner as tons of coal or quotations on the stock exchange, that is one's methodological prerogative. The trouble really arises elsewhere—in the loop of explanation required by an account of political violence connecting perpetrator and respondent in intention and goal, action and reaction. In effect, modern social science leaves certain gaps in its rendition of a subject that is of passionate human concern.

It not only ultimately fails to explain "why men rebel" or exactly what to do about it; it slights the moral dimension of both rebellion and repression for aggregate explanations of each or either that seem almost enzymal or hormonal; or else it assumes, very broadly, with a whole range of "power theorists" (whose most sophisticated archetype is Hobbes) that "power is simply no more, but the excess of power of one above that of another" and that violence is the most obvious, unfettered, and perhaps measurable (if we except market mechanisms and voting) expression of clashes of power with power. The difference between the contemporary empiricists and Hobbes is, of course, that Hobbes undertook a complex, if one-sided, examination of human psychology before he attemped to use his axioms about power and natural right as the substance of his prescriptions for holding society together (and moreover presented nature and society as antitheses), whereas writers like Kaplan, Lasswell, and Dahl appear to take the psychological presuppositions about power as a given and to hypostatize them as "politics." Political power is in part "power *over* other men" (or countervailing resistances), but, as Arendt points out, its correspondence with violence (the natural property of the less powerful) is quite anomalous,[29] and it is furthermore not only the exercise of domination in some interpersonal, essentially zero-sum game, but also the consolidation and regulation of those other powers for collective ends—that is to say, the state.[30] Conversely, violence cannot just *be about* or be explained in terms of its psychic and somatic origins, because this tells us next to nothing about its social construction and uses. Psychological analysis completes the demolition of the political that sociological behavioralism had begun.

To be more specific, this last assertion seems true on two counts. One, psychologism ignores or plays down much of political analysis that deals explicitly with organized power relations, incomplete in itself but indispensable as a tool of explanation.[31] Two, instead of decomposing political societal analytically for the purpose of rebuilding that edifice in ways prescriptively compatible with certain "natural" traits and "rights" of the constituent members (à la social contract theory), psychologism assumes that the solution to violence is to be found exclusively in the decomposition and what it teaches us about human drives and responses. That there can be no reconstruction on a socio-political scale is evident; for the existent order is taken as a given (with little or no discrimination concerning its theoretical rationale): in the most typical form of the argument, the state or political system assumes importance neither as a commonwealth nor as a multilevel structure of authority relations, but merely as the superior agency that stimulates material expectations and succeeds or fails in fulfilling them. Since theories of this kind frequently aspire to be universalistic or "general," canvassing the human condition across time and space,[32] we are left with an indelible propensity in human nature called the "sense of relative deprivation."[33] Under certain circumstances, this perception channels frustration of *Lebenschancen* into collective and political paths leading to civil strife and violence. Facing this situation is a very vaguely defined state whose functions are apparently both nurturant and therapeutic (since deprivation is a state of mind). The richness and complexity of the political are pretty well abolished in this scenario, as are the ethical quandaries of both resistance and statesmanship.

At this point I should like to leave the reader with as few doubts as possible regarding the nature of my argument. I am not intending to use this single topic as a generalized assault on the application of either "scientific" or statistical methods to the study of politics. As I said in the preceding section, when these techniques are not misused by sectarian zeal, they help shed light into dark corners and add precision to our ways of thinking about politics. In any case, the debate on this issue is murky and conducive to considerable skepticism as to the rightful scope of any social explanation.

Rather, I am making three subsidiary contentions that relate to the general issue of method: they are analytically distinct as long as they remain purely theoretical, but they are inseparable in practice and application, particularly in regard to the exploration of political violence. The first is the appreciation of value-oriented research, focusing on such empirically intractable concepts as "justice," "purposefulness," and "legitimacy," as opposed to schemata where "is" and "ought" are regarded as reducible— via psychological filtration—to strictly material or quantitative dimensions. The second is the appreciation, at least for purposes of political understanding, of a concentration on the description and discrimination of politico-cultural situations (which may be retrospectively grasped as "structures") that receive or are progressively created by violence within the political order, as opposed to psychologistic attempts to grasp violence at its root and to extrapolate monads of individual frustration into a generalized theory of rebellion. (This may be attractive to psychology, but it short-circuits most of the major preoccupations of politics.) The third is the appreciation of the not merely formal need to cultivate a notion of what is and what is not politically germane, as opposed to the contention that politics is both diffuse and omnipresent in virtually all human subject areas, and that therefore they are properly assimilable to political science.

In the context of these arguments, it would be foolhardy to assert (without the attachment of a long epistemological memorandum) that the explanation of political phenomena, combined with prescriptions for political therapy, by way of psychologistic reductionism is complete flimflam. However, this approach often does lead us in false and uninteresting directions. If all human beings under stress have certain common modes of behavior, this hypothesis may be of constructive value in an age of existential anarchy, but it cannot possibly generate the kind of questions that help us understand collective diversity, which is the chief advantage of the comparative method. At best, empirical-psychological reductionism operates only as part of a sequence of various levels of interpretation and has no claim to being "queen of the social sciences" or the groundwork for a utopia of "general theory." Even John Stuart Mill's "ethology" did not attempt to press the point that far.

The. problem with the relative deprivation" thesis is not only that, for the sake of generality, it becomes exceedingly porous, but that its presumed constancy in violence would render it incapable of explaining the decisive specifics of individual cases or types. Since politics is a species of historical explanation that widely employs comparative models construed across space and time for the purpose not of combining disparate events but of particularizing with the aid of general constructs, such "root theories" are at best hypothetical points of departure and never ends in themselves. Even if "relative deprivation" is always with us (although I would opt, even here, for a typological discrimination of deprivations), the fact in itself is not very interesting if we want to understand how violence occurs in specific situations. Moreover, its limitations as an explanatory thesis need to be understood. As one writer, who supports the thesis in a set of cases where one might expect it to be most useful (millenarian movements), puts it: "It is always possible after the fact to find deprivations. What is important is to be able to predict either the types of deprivations that lead to certain ideological formations, or the degree of deprivation which characterizes a cult movement. To date neither of these goals is achieved, although we are closer to the first than the second.[34] I would of course go further than this to assert that the action ensuing from deprivations is understandable only in terms of the situations in which they occur and the aims and opportunities thereby presented and grasped by the organizers of the aggrieved.

I shall discuss the psychologistic theory of political violence with increasing specificity. But I should first like to dispose of my hanging assertion that contemporary political science fails to close the "loop of explanation" needed in a proper account of political violence. It has already been suggested that modern "power theorists" take a certain psychology of power for granted in order to construct their conception of the "political." Similarly, I have argued that genetic theories of violence centering around the psychology of the individual, while professing to explain violence and even to place it haphazardly in political settings, are incapable of probing its political structure. For purposes of the present discussion, we shall dwell on the second type of theory. If we imagine an illustrative circuit of political violence that proceeds in definite stages—expectations, frustrations, perceived grievances, perceived solidarity of grievances, organization for collective action, reaction by authority, violent confrontation, organization of repressive force, bilateral organized conflict, outcome, etc.—we can easily determine what a general theory of violence based on the hinge-concept of "relative deprivation" fails to supply.

It cannot, in the first instance, easily account for the distinction between material and "ideal" expectations and frustrations, except by polling people on the spot, performing content analysis on texts and tapes (if feasible), or some arbitrary form of reductionism based on theoretical preferences. If, on the other hand, material grievances tend to be translated into more "ideal" (i.e., ideological) ones as the collective political awareness of grievances becomes more advanced, then there is no cogent way of describing this transition except by naive agglutination. Properly political ideals and goals are, in fact, assigned a totally dependent or inert status, being disguised or conflated within the concept of "frustration" ensuing from the sense of relative deprivation. This has the logical consequence of reducing all utopianism or even reconstructive political theory to a banality that merely masks the wish to substitute a more efficient nurturant state for one sensed to be inadequate. Another possibility is that elites invent myths of reconstruction to organize the inchoately aggrieved by unifying their separate purposes. But this runs us into the complex problem of leaders and followers (their origins, their distinctive interests, their interplay, etc.), which "general" psychologistic theories of violence are hard-pressed to treat.

Even if we acquire a storehouse of reasons "why men (sometimes) rebel," we remain ill-equipped to understand the situations in which their rebellions take shape, which is a political question of the greatest importance. In fact, what is supplied here is a discontinuous theory: the preconditions and incidence of rebellion are explained through recourse to a general psychological axiom; the structuring of violence is canvassed and posited through quantitative computation of individual historical episodes, further refined into a few rough-and-ready categories by factor analysis.[35] There is an acknowledgement that political violence becomes structured, but there is no theoretical effort to explain these dynamic patterns (for this, both macroanalysis and a sense of diachronism and cultural differentiation would be required),[36] nor is it possible to obtain an effective linkage theory between predispositions and structures.[37]

I have suggested that there is something which I will call a *normative gap* in the type of theory I have been discussing. I do not mean by this the crude charge that empirical political science is literally empty of moral concern. What I mean is simply that political violence, wherever reasonably advanced, confronts prescriptive institutions with prescriptive alternatives. Violence may well be initially generated through psychological mechanisms of perceived deprivation, and a certain critical mass of these phenomena may allow for political structuration to intervene. Also, fear, jealousy, damaged pride, and other emotions may operate to transform latent hostility into violence. But none of this accounts for the input of the prescriptively political (often accompanied by a high sense of moral outrage) into the organization and intensification of violence. And yet it must come from somewhere. What I am speaking of here is somewhat akin to the dichotomy C. B. Macpherson constructs when he construes liberal-democratic theory as (up to now) a bicephalous mixture of the capacity to maximize one's materially acquisitive powers and the potential to develop one's ethical human attributes, or to Isaiah Berlin's famous discussion of "negative" and "positive" liberty.[38] In the latter case, for example, both "liberties" imply a perceived rather than a literal state of being. "Negative liberty," I think no less than "relative deprivation," is capable of being defined in descriptive terms, as "perceived satisfaction of wants and security." "Positive liberty," however, implies self-governance and self-fulfillment, things that are not easily reducible to psychologically reliable or generalizable axioms, as Rousseau knew when he wrote the fateful words about "forcing men to be free." Some men do not ardently desire political freedom as long as they are fed, while others, never in real danger of an empty stomach, not only find that freedom intoxicating (possibly because they can afford to cultivate "higher" needs) but are resolved to obtain it for others. Situations of political violence involve some of these same perplexities, which it would be absurd to ignore, and which unilateral psychological explanations cannot penetrate.

This is equally apparent when we examine the problem of political violence from the point of view, not of the rebel, but of the public authority. Obviously in the case of repression by the state (we shall say, for sake of example, beyond any conceivable lawful employment of force) of certain members and groups of society, it can make little sense to use the hypothesis of "relative deprivation" if we wish to preserve any semblance of a political context. To be sure, here we are not speaking of rebellion or why men do it; but we *are* legitimately speaking of political violence. At very least, we now see that a "general theory" of rebellion is not likely to be a general theory of political violence.

But there is more to the problem than just this. All known public authorities may be inherently unjust and may be violent conspiracies of exploitative power-seekers or their gerants; but,

if this should not always be the case, then we must at least con-
jure with the possibility that the overseers of the state have an
official or functional interest in its maintenance and eminence,
just as Scottish groundskeepers have in the condition of their
fairways. In such a case, not only would the state be a public
value transcending its mere nurturant efficiency, but the support
of that value would depend on some shared communication of the
goals of the commonwealth between rulers and ruled, including
a willingness for joint sacrifice—a condition that may, without
agonized analysis, be described as the existence of *authority*.
Authority depends on an acquiescence in certain forms and uses
of power; but it does not inhere totally in persons or even in
role-playing persons as a general rule. It is an intersubjective
sensing of patterns of conformity built on social or public confidence.[39]

However—and especially in the world we live in—authority so
defined is inherently unstable. Not only does the modern temper
of individual freedom and criticism, with its deep structures of
economic and technological change, corrode many of the ancient
givens of legitimate authority, but the pendular law of action and
reaction gives rise to a politics without stable boundaries. For,
on the one hand, prevailing authority is continually challenged
by new idols created by the response of the rebel consciousness
to the changing nature of things. And, on the other, existing
power is constantly overreacting to these challenges in illegal
and violent ways, in the hope of salvaging through coercion, even
overkill, attributes of stability that could no longer be maintained
by public confidence, tacit consent, constitutionalism, the rule
of law, and other mechanisms. Strategies on both sides become,
effectively, war strategies and are no longer seen as variant interpretations of the settlement of common disputes and the facili-
tation of common goals. The spirit of conquest replaces mediation.

It would of course be possible to say that this is merely another
instance of power confronting power, "incumbent" versus "in-
surgent." And it would be possible to analyze these situations
nonnormatively in terms of equilibrium theory: violent interruptions of social solidarity occur so that it may be restored at a
higher level, this being one of the regulatory functions of the
political system. But, even in these instances of insufficient explanation, psychologistic reasoning would appear powerless to

say why agents who act for the state act in the way they do. Psychology becomes an even more nebulous clue to the complexities of pro-state violence when we grant normative properties to the idea of the state, that is, when or if we concede that the state (including its symbols and associations) is capable of being an object of common veneration and cooperative undertaking, and that regimes sometimes, whether rightfully or mistakenly, seek to defend these values with violent and extralegal means when challenged by parts of society. De Gaulle has written of "a certain idea of France." His explanation of this was not good textbook social science; but the type of justification he evokes for his political acts has been a great deal more powerful in practice than many proposed by modern theory.

Modern political violence is, in its more advanced instances, a challenge to normatively perceived authority structures that are deteriorating[40] or a response by authorities whose position and conception of politics are imperilled. Only at this level can a satisfactory understanding be obtained, and only in terms of situations exceeding the aggregation of grievances; not by genetic explanations of how individuals cross the threshold from licit to violent behavior. Those mechanisms may, in any case, be conspicuously different for leaders and followers, for rebels and for state officials, and for persons of diverse cultural orientations.

The latter point may be worth making in somewhat more detail, since, for example, it is a cardinal factor in Gurr's quest for a theory "capable of accounting for the common elements of that much larger class of events called civil strife."[41] Gurr is indeed an outstanding example of what Kenneth Waltz, in another context, calls "first-image theorists," i.e., those who reason toward the condition of war from the indelible predispositions of a common human nature.[42] Gurr goes on to state:

> a general theory of civil strife [cannot] rest on culturally specific theories of modal personality traits, though it might well take account of the effects of these traits. . . . The only generally relevant psychological theories are those that deal with the the sources and characteristics of aggression in all men, regardless of culture.[43]

One's immediate response to this large claim by a noted political scientist is: what price are we expected to pay for the elegance of such a general theory? Evidently, the suppression of cultural traits and of historical analysis. Violence, as a pure concept, may lack those dimensions. However, it is equally clear that political violence cannot. As another political scientist, writing of Latin America, states: "The author believes that insights into the problems of instability and violence are to be gained by trains of analysis starting out from each of these points of departure: race, cultural heritage, geography, and economic structure."[44] The modest amount of empirical work I have done in connection with communal strife leads me to concur. While most theorists agree that "national character" (deriving from Montesquieu's *esprit général*) has its pitfalls as an explanatory concept, the difficulty lies more in capturing the concept than in using it. Corroboration comes from the historian Marc Bloch, who writes of the early feudal age that "violence became the distinguishing part of an epoch and a social system."[45] Whatever may be the primordial givens of human nature, it is surely possible, on analytic grounds, to distinguish a violent society from a *société policée.*" And it is certainly conceivable that political violence—if a violence within bounds—might be "functional" to the performance of certain societies. Let us follow Bloch's account:

> [Violence] played a part in the economy: at a time when trade was scarce and difficult, what surer means of becoming rich than plunder and oppression? . . . Violence entered into the sphere of law as well; partly on account of the principle of customary law which in the long run resulted in the legalization of almost every usurpation; and also in consequence of the firmly rooted tradition, which recognized the right, or even made it the duty, of the individual or the small group to execute justice on its own account. . . . Finally, violence was an element in manners. . . .[46]

The electoral process in some countries is traditionally accompanied by violence. For example, a UPI dispatch of November 11, 1969, tells us the following horror story from the Philippine Islands: "At least 13 persons were killed in political violence yesterday and early today, pushing the death toll to 63 since July 1, a record in presidential elections. Violence is part of every political campaign in the Philippines. More than 40 persons were killed in 1965 and about 100 in 1967." Since these episodes were recorded, we have become aware of political and ideological strife on a deeper level in the Philippines; but this does not negate the "traditional" dimension of political violence endemic in that country (again having little to do with the guerrilla warfare of the 1950s in Central Luzon or the more recent trouble in Mindanao). Should the political observer take this carnage as seriously as he would, say, the deaths in the Spartacus Rebellion of 1919 in Germany, or should he conclude that it was mainly lethal saturnalia or *duello* conducted around the polling places? Such problems becloud all quantitative surveys of the subject as well as the frequent attempts to locate a psychological genesis of violence that short-circuits any cultural diversity. However, sacrificing the elegance and parsimony of a general theory for complex middle-range interpretations is not likely to do much damage to reality. It means a return from psychology to sociology and, as I have previously argued, a reflection on certain normative aspects of the problem.

Cultural diversity is not the only problem. There is also that of the immediacy of what might be called a political situation or consciousness. If we deliberately examine cases that appear, at first glance, to be collective apotheoses of mass hysteria caused by going beyond the breaking point of "relative deprivation," we find even here prefigured patterns of political action based on wider and more articulate social premises. One such case is the Taiping Rebellion of 1851-1864 in China, a sequence of events that, clearly, fused imaginative eschatological motivations with more down-to-earth political ones. With respect to the former, it might be argued that deprivations fed both fantasy and violence. But in the latter category, there was, from the outset, a basic political focus: hatred of the "foreign" Manchu dynasty, resistance against corrupt administration, and refurbishment of native political traditions.[47] Another significant case is the famous "great fear" of the French peasants and petty artisans in 1789. No doubt famine and fear of aristocratic reprisal were powerful determinants of the situation and could be viewed as concrete evidence of a mass sense of "relative deprivation." But even here, as Georges Lefebvre writes, "the revolt produced by hunger could easily assume a political and social form."[48] Not only did deprivation swiftly coagulate and swell in rural France, but also, from the beginning (as Tilly has argued), protest and violence were directed against the public authority and violence immediately discovered political arguments to press and preformed political channels in which to operate. Lefebvre carefully checked 1789 against other major incidents of peasant unrest and concluded: "Thus, in 1848 as in 1703, aside from a feeling of insecurity naturally inspired by the economic setting and the political conditions, one finds at the base of the panic the idea that a faction or a social class threatens the life and possessions of a majority of the nation. It is this universal and ever identical fear that provides local uprisings, whose genesis and importance vary, with their emotional weight and their contagiousness."[49] The peasants of 1789, after all, knew what they were after: the seigneurial titles, which, during their invasion of the *châteaux,* they burned with heady abandon.

I believe the potency of the "psychological" thesis on violence has been seriously overrated, owing to, as I indicated, certain undiscriminating forms of data-collection and the euphoria of the "prediction and control" school. Even Samuel Huntington,[50] a scholar whose treatment of political violence is far removed from all this, concludes that "a satisfactory explanation of civil violence had to be grounded on [*sic*] psychological as well as material conditions"[51] and goes on to accept Gurr's theoretical approach and engraft it into his own species of developmental analysis. Illuminating as Huntington's writings have been, here he misses the essential issue. It is not between material conditions and psychological perceptions—the primacy of the latter can be easily allowed—but between analyses of the psychic genesis of violent action and of the politically relevant patterns in which such organized actions take place. Here the psychological premises and the paths of explanation that they provide, as they confront arbitrary and schematically pigeonholed quantitative data, tell us little of theoretical interest about political violence. No doubt a "total explanation" of the phenomenon would need to incorporate basic psychological propositions; but the notion of such an explanation is preposterous, at least for now. As Tilly (who, in a very sophisticated way, tends to accept the premises of the power theorists, but does so while carrying out very exhautive structural examinations, bolstered by statistics) puts it:

"[Gurr] eventually shapened a rather different axe from the one he was grinding."[52] In other words, Gurr's statistical work (though not his general theory) tended to substantiate a hypothesis concerning the negative correlation between political violence and modernization that Tilly accepted.

In this section I have tried to indicate some objections to the psychologistic explanation of political violence of the type offered by Gurr. I have canvassed some of the not too obvious issues and some that are more likely to be immediately visible. The most direct and articulate criticism has been voiced by an historian, who has no professional stake in either political philosophy or social science as practiced by Gurr:

> many factors must intervene [upon the effects of individual psychology] such as developments in the social and economic structure, conflicts and changes in the political system, the emergence of ideologies, and the like. Such factors are crucial to the dynamic causal properties of revolution [the word "revolution" in this author's usage alternates with "civil strife," "internal war," and the like, and is his preferred term]. Furthermore, they are not attributes of states of mind, but properties of political and social situations or systems. Gurr's theory, however, cannot take account of structural developments or political conflicts except as they are related to the psychological phenomenon of relative deprivation. This inability considerably diminishes both the significance and the possibility of analyzing adequately nonpsychological factors.[53]

Though these are the words of an intellectual historian, they express very well the reluctance of political theory to see psychologistic premises as a royal road to an understanding of the kinds of violence with which it is concerned. I am not specifically trying to unmask theories of violence that take their point of departure from generalizations about human behavior, nor am I attempting to assert some interlocking "levels of interpretation" scheme, as Kenneth Waltz did so brilliantly on the subject of war and international relations some years ago. I am simply asserting that fundamental political inquiry is best served by other techniques, though in the process it may be compelled to sacrifice both elegance and some pretense of science. More especially, it seems that a mixture of sociologically macroscopic, historically particularistic, and normative approaches will be more fruitful, if considerably messier, than what the regnant school has lately been offering.

## NOTES AND REFERENCES

1. Dating probably from Sorel's opposition of "violence" to "force." See *Reflections on Violence* (trans. T. E. Hulme, New York: Collier Books, 1961), p. 171 f. and also chapter 3.
2. Hugh Davis Graham and Ted Robert Gurr (eds.), *Violence in America: Historical and Comparative Perspectives* (New York: Bantam, 1969), "Introduction," p. xvii.
3. James C. Davies, "Violence and Aggression: Innate or Not?" *Western Political Quarterly,* September 1970, pp. 612-613.
4. Ted Honderich, "Democratic Violence," in *Philosophy and Public Affairs,* Winter 1973, pp. 190-214.
5. Hannah Arendt, *On Violence* (New York: Harcourt, Brace & World, 1969), p. 79.
6. E. V. Walter, *Terror and Resistance: A Study of Political Violence,* (Oxford: Oxford University Press, 1969), p. 13.
7. John Spiegel, "Toward a Theory of Collective Violence," paper for the American Psychiatric Association, November 15-16, 1968, pp. 3-4. In violence committed by the young, Herbert Moller goes so far as to write of "elemental, directionless acting-out behavior." "Youth as a Force in the Modern World," *Comparative Studies in Society and History,* April 1968, p. 260.
8. Cf. for example, Robert Paul Wolff's contention that a "distinctively political concept of violence" is incoherent and impossible to pin down; "On Violence," *The Journal of Philosophy,* 66 (1969), 601-615, 607.
9. Proudhon, as quoted in George Woodcock, *Anarchism* (Cleveland: Meridian Books, 1962), pp. 132/33. Cf. Sir Lewis Namier: "A gale blows down whatever it encounters, and does not distinguish. Revolutions are anonymous, undenominational, and inarticulate.... [They] are not made; they occur...." In "1848: Seed-Plot of History" (excerpt from *Vanished Supremacies,* London: Hamilton, 1958), in Melvin Kranzberg (ed.), *1848: A Turning Point* (Boston: Heath, 1959), p. 64.
10. Cf. especially, Max Gluckman, *Order and Rebellion in Tribal Africa* (New York: Free Press, 1963).
11. E. V. Walter, *Terror and Resistance,* p. 12.
12. Thus conforming to a supposition of the political motivation of collective violence that proceeds from the "realiist" definition of politics.
13. Charles Tilly, in Graham and Gurr (eds.), *Violence in America,* p. 10. The point is more extensively made in the context of a case study by David Snyder and Charles Tilly, "Hardship and Collective Violence in France, 1830 to 1960," *American Sociological Review,* XXXVIII, 5, pp. 520-532. As the authors put it: "... we suppose that the principal im-

mediate causes of collective violence result from changes in the relations between groups of men and the major concentrations of coercive power in their environments." (p. 520.)

14. Gurr, in *Violence in America,* p. 564.
15. Cf. Talcott Parsons. *The Social System* (Glencoe: Free Press, 1951), p. 126f: ". . . political reality cannot be studied according to a specific conceptual scheme . . . because . . . the political component of the social system is a center of integration for all the aspects of the system which analysis can separate, and not the sociological scene of a particular class of social phenomena. . . ."
16. Morris Janowitz, "Patterns of Collective Racial Violence," in *Violence in America,* p. 401.
17. Much of Tilly's published work has covered violence in nineteenth-century French society. It is interesting to note that although France has had a centralizing political ethos, the country was certainly not noted for strong government or an abundance of social services during much of this period.
18. See, for example, Ted Robert Gurr, *Why Men Rebel* (Princeton: Princeton University Press, 1970); Ivo K. and Rosalind L. Feierabend, "Aggressive Behaviors Within Politics, 1948-1962: A Cross-National Study," in *Journal of Conflict Resolution,* September 1966, pp. 249-271; and I. K. and R. L. Feierabend and Betty A. Nesvold, "Social Change and Political Violence: Cross-National Patterns," in *Violence in America,* pp. 632-687.
19. See Terry Nardin, *Violence and the State: A Critique of Empirical Political Theory* (Beverly Hills and London: Sage Publications, 1971), pp. 9-11.
20. Beyond this, there is the further possibility of political collapse, or what the present author has elsewhere called *dysarchy,* where the state is either too inchoate or too decomposed to be the primary focus of intergroup violence. See G. A. Kelly and L. B. Miller, "Internal War and International Systems: Perspectives on Method," Harvard University Center for International Affairs Occasional Paper No. 21, Cambridge (Mass.), August 1969.
21. Contrary to what is asserted by Robert A. Dahl, *A Preface to Democratic Theory* (Chicago: University of Chicago Press, 1970), p. 74.
22. G. Sartori, "What is Politics?" *Political Theory,* February 1973, p. 20.
23. *Ibid.*
24. *Ibid.,* p. 21.
25. See Roger Bigelow Merriman, *Six Contemporaneous Revolutions* (Oxford: Clarendon Press, 1938), esp. the précis of Gabriel Naudé's *Considerations politiques sur les coups d'estat* (p. 101). For Naudé, a seventeenth-century controversialist, the phrase refers exclusively to "acts of the existing authority in the state and not those of rebels against it. . . ."
26. H. L. Nieburg, *Political Violence* (New York: St. Martin's Press, 1969), p. 197.
27. T. Honderich, "Democratic Violence," p. 197.
28. Moreover, only one that can be predicted by an uncertain knowledge of existing circumstances easily subject to change.
29. Cf. Arendt, *On Violence,* pp. 44-48.
30. There is a cogent criticism of power theory along somewhat different lines in C. B. Macpherson, *Democratic Theory: Essays in Retrieval* (Oxford: Oxford University Press, 1973), Essay 3.

31. Or, as Eugene C. Meehan correctly observes: "An adequate explanation of a great many human actions can be made with no reference at all to motives, particularly when the individual is acting in a highly structured social situation—the usual case in much of politics." *Contemporary Political Theory: A Critical Study* (Homewood, Ill.: Dorsey Press, 1967), p. 81.

32. Ted Robert Gurr in "Psychological Factors in Civil Strife," in I. K. Feierabend, R. L. Feierabend and T. R. Gurr (eds.), *Anger, Violence, and Politics* (Englewood Cliffs: Prentice-Hall, 1972), p. 33.

33. Gurr, *ibid.,* p. 37: "My basic premise is that the necessary precondition for violent civil conflict is relative deprivation." Relative deprivation is generally defined as a negative discrepancy between legitimate expectation and actuality.

34. David F. Aberle, "A Note on Relative Deprivation Theory," in Sylvia L. Thrupp (ed.), *Millenial Dreams in Action* (New York: Schocken, 1970), p. 213.

35. As Tilly puts it, regarding Gurr ("Does Modernization Breed Revolulution?" unpublished seminar paper, April 1971, p. 12): "it takes quite an inferential chain to go from the structural conditions he actually indexes to the psychic orientations his theory deals with." I do not think that Gurr ever achieves any theoretical grasp of structure.

36. It is, after all, more meaningful to say that Yemen and Oman are both located on the Arabian peninsula or that Henri III and Charles X were both bad kings than it is to say that between 1961 and 1965 the total magnitudes of civil strife in Brazil and Chad were approximately the same.

37. Lest I be accused of placing too much weight on the concept of "structure" in my attempt to criticize the aggregative mode of psychological explanation, it seems useful to provide some clarification at this point. To the extent that aggregated frustrations provide the tinder for a violence that may quickly assume political forms and significance, situations are ready at hand in the social order or are created through the mediation of a politically conscious leadership that transforms the character of the violence (both the understanding of the participants and the historian's retrospective interpretation) to a collective, *zweckrational* level. It is generally proper here to speak of "patterns" or "situations," rather than "structures." However, the notion of structure is important in three senses: (1) we often cannot appropriately interpret instances of collective violence without an acknowledgment of preformed or traditional structures of political expression, or the structures within a given culture that tend to allow for such expression; (2) beyond a certain level of concentration, movements of violence, whose midwife has been "situations," tend to theorize and create patterns of strategy and action that can be legitimately regarded as structures, especially where they are opposed to existent structures and intended to replace them; and (3) retrospectively, as historians of politics, we tend to analyze collective violence in terms of structures, suggested by distance and our conception of intervening events and trends, even if the participants operated without any actual sense of structure, that is to say, more or less pragmatically within the parameters of a moving situation. Albeit, we should guard ourselves against overloading situations that were variable and subject to different outcomes with the deterministic connotations of "structure."

38. Cf. Macpherson, *Democratic Theory,* p. 11f; and Isaiah Berlin, *Two Concepts of Liberty* (Oxford: Oxford University Press, 1958).
39. My argument here is not dissimilar from Hannah Arendt's in "What is Authority?" in *Between Past and Future* (New York: Viking, 1954), pp. 91-141; but it differs in the respect that it defines authority as a shared confidence between the governed and governing (a structural relationship) and not a mere attribute of the latter.
40. Not necessarily in their nurturant functions, either; societies have often sustained inegalitarian austerities (even within the context of "relative deprivation") for the sake of other values.
41. T. R. Gurr, "Psychological Factors in Civil Violence," p. 33.
42. Kenneth N. Waltz, *Man, the State, and War* (New York: Columbia University Press, 1958), p. 16f.
43. Gurr, "Psychological Factors," p. 33.
44. Martin Needler, *Political Development in Latin America: Instability, Violence, and Evolutionary Change* (New York: 1968), p. 45.
45. Marc Bloch, *Feudal Society* (Chicago: University of Chicago Press, 1964), II, p. 411.
46. *Ibid.*
47. Eugene P. Boardman, "Millenary Aspects of the Taiping Rebellion," in Thrupp (ed.), *Millenial Dreams in Action,* p. 72.
48. Georges Lefebvre, *La Grande Peur de 1789* (Paris: Armand Colin, 1932), p. 33.
49. *Ibid.,* p. 64.
50. Cf. C. Tilly, "Does Modernization Breed Revolution?" p. 10: "the most attractive general feature of Huntington's scheme is its deliberate flight from psychologism. . . ."
51. Samuel P. Huntington, "Civil Violence and the Process of Development," Adephi Papers No. 83 (December 1971), International Institute for Strategic Studies, p. 1.
52. Tilly, "Does Modernization Breed Revolution?" p. 12.
53. Perez Zagorin, "Theories of Revolution in Contemporary Historiography," *Political Science Quarterly,* March 1973, p. 44.

> Hence it is evident that the state is a creation
> of nature, and that man is by nature a
> political animal.
> Aristotle POLITICS I,2 (1253a)

# 5

# THE POLITICAL ANIMAL

## LISA H. NEWTON

Any sentence that begins "Man is . . ." recalls an era not our own, an era of anthropological boldness, not to say arrogance, foreign to our tentative scientific temperament. No one can deny that we have gained more truth than we have lost in the retreat from generalization about our own species, nor that we have gained more humane social institutions than we have lost in the increased tolerance of human diversity that accompanied the retreat. But if "all generalizations about human beings are rash and probably false," then this one must be too; and it would be ultimately dangerous to ignore the threat to human dignity posed by slavish adherence to scientific skepticism on the subject. For we are beginning to worry that if man has *no* nature all his own, if no feature of humanity is rooted in objective fact, then permissible experimentation and manipulation can have no bounds. Our objections to the inhuman use of human beings are rooted only partially in abstract judgments of individual worth and the value of freedom, judgments that we are prepared to back up with argument; they rely just as heavily on an inherited sense of what is, literally, "human" and "inhuman," what is natural and unnatural for man. It is this sense primarily that is under attack in the advance of this particular skepticism, and before it is entirely eroded, we would do well to see what truth can be salvaged from it. I would like to consider the generalization about human nature formulated by Aristotle and heading this paper, that man is a "political animal." Clearly, some interpretations show the statement to be false;[1] but there seems to me to be one most valuable interpretation that shows it to be true, as well as useful as a guide and corrective to political institutions in our own day. It is the purpose of this paper to elicit that truth.

## CAN WE SPEAK OF "HUMAN NATURE"?

The first task must be to reduce this thorny part of the problem to manageable dimensions; metaphysical discussion of "nature" or "essence" in general is hardly possible or necessary in the limited space and scope of this paper. When we ask in the context of political philosophy, "Is there any such a thing as human nature?" what we want to know is, "Can the institutional (man-made) conditions under which people live ever be pronounced good, as tending to fulfill human nature, or bad, as tending to warp or injure it?" The purpose of this section is to show one way in which an affirmative answer can be given to this question.

Some perfectly straightforward senses of "nature" serve as the building blocks of which the more complex senses are constructed. For example, the Aristotelian "essence" or "nature" as including the notion of "purpose" is simply illustrated by any human artifact that is made with that purpose in the mind of the artificer. Thus, it is the nature of a knife to cut, since that is why the knife was made (and sharpness is its virtue). This sense of "nature" is purely prescriptive, it specifies that a knife *ought* to cut; even if we are familiar with only 43 knives and none of them cuts, our observations are logically incapable of modifying our certainty that it is natural for a knife to cut. For another example, the scientific use of "nature" as confined to the notion of "typical pattern of conformation and behavior" is simply illustrated by any ordinary general truth about a naturally occurring species. Thus, it is the nature of a "cat" (defined by certain physical characteristics, e.g., retractable claws) to chase mice when hungry, since that is the way a vast majority of cats, as defined, in fact react to mice that show up before meals. This sense of "nature" is purely descriptive and specifies only that we may expect that all cats in future observations *will in fact* chase mice when hungry. Speculation as to the manner in which it came about that this species has this "nature" is possible, but not necessary, within empirical discourse. We do not leap to a prescriptive mode when we ask how it happens that cats chase mice, but we definitely ask a different question, logically unrelated to the question of whether or not they do. This new question permits a correct answer in terms of evolutionary theory: in the wild, where small game is available and where other sources of food are rare and the food supply insufficient to support all of the cat population up to reproductive age (specification of environmental circumstances is required for any such explanation), a cat with a well-developed hunting instinct will be more likely to survive to reproductive age than a cat that lacks one (and its young will be more likely to be fed); a good hunting instinct is an inherited trait; hence in each generation, as long as the conditions hold, there will be more cats with a good hunting instinct and fewer without one.

This explanation is, again, perfectly straightforward, but some interesting hypothetical statements it entails deserve examination. First, *if* the cat lives in the wild,[2] *then* it is more likely to survive if its hunting instinct is strong. If the cat does not live in the wild, nothing follows. Second, from the above, *if* survival is a good, *then* a cat in the wild *ought* to have a strong hunting instinct, and prescriptive language enters the description. At this point we are dealing with a hypothetical imperative only, but it is the starting point for the type of confusion that convinced most of us that all talk of "human nature" was vain, probably dangerous, and probably self-contradictory. From "is" to "ought" is still the easiest slide in philosophy.

Consider the following example. My mother-in-law has a cat shaped like a basketball. It seems a healthy enough cat, and not unhappy (however bad-tempered), but through an abundance of rich food and no exercise, it has attained the size and shape of a basketball; and I object. I think it is wrong and unnatural not to allow the cat to exercise, to maintain the natural shape of a cat. But on what justification? We must distinguish between two types of condition, commonly held to be undesirable: first, a condition causing suffering, or *painful* condition, which is clearly felt and actively avoided by the creature; its avoidance behavior is the defining characteristic of such a condition. Second, a condition preventing the creature from doing something that it otherwise could do and, in normal, "natural," or "base" circumstances would do, an *unnatural* condition: the creature's potential to do such a thing is determined by observing similar creatures in those normal circumstances. Thus, from the fact that cats evolved in the wild, we take wildness as our base; from "if cats in the wild do not hunt, they will not live," we get "cats in the wild ought to hunt" by positing survival as a good, and as a necessary condition for the latter, "cats in the wild ought to be physically fit to hunt"; since wildness is posited as the "natural" condition for cats, we promptly conclude that "cats by nature ought to be physically fit to hunt" and object strenuously to basketball-shaped cats. All very understandable, but all very fallacious. This type of slide will not get us to true statements about the nature of any species, let alone human beings.

In becoming alert to the fallacy contained in that sort of reasoning, we have become alert to the slippery terminology that smooths the is-ought transit. "Nature," "natural," and "essential" are glaring examples already mentioned; "function" is another. If I say that it is the President's "function" to enforce the law, I mean that that's what he *ought* to do, and I intend to become annoyed with him if he does not. If I say that the "function" of a malarial swamp is to keep down the population in an area, I do not, unless my name is Malthus, intend to say that that is what it *ought* to do; I mean that that is what it in fact does, not just in one instance, but regularly. That "function" like "nature" can be either descriptive or prescriptive is clear enough. But there is also a clear area of overlap, as when we speak of the "function" of the kidneys. A logically unconfused description of the overlap is simple enough: ordinarily, kidneys in fact strain certain substances out of the blood, which substances, dissolved in water, are expelled from the body as urine, hence we say it is the "function" (descriptive) of the kidneys to clear the blood of these substances; if the kidneys do not in fact clear the blood in an individual case, the individual dies (fact); but human life is a good (posited value); therefore the blood ought to be cleared of those substances, and by the kidneys (nothing else in the body can do it); therefore it is the function (prescriptive) of the kidneys to clear the blood—it is what they *ought* to be doing. This description of the logic of "function" in such a case may be oversimplified; it does not take into account, for example, the fact that the "description" of what a kidney does "normally" (another slippery word) is really a description of the operation of an ideal kidney—one doing the best possible job of clearing out the blood, with nothing wrong with it at all—not a typical kidney. At least it separates the factual from most of the normative aspects of the word, and we will be able to use a similar analysis when we come to "functional" descriptions of the workings of a society.

The presence of slippery words, words that make illogical transitions imperceptible, is one indicator of buried presuppositions legitimizing the transitions. The presuppositions embedded in the is-ought slide are well known. One, historically important, reduces all of observed nature, man included, to the level of artifact, created specifically to fulfill a purpose in the mind of God the artificer. Then each thing has a "nature" in the sense of "purpose"; observation suffices to tell us what it is. (From the physical equipment of a cat, we conclude its purpose is to hunt; else why would it have been made with those claws and teeth?) Another, less theological, is that there is a "natural" condition for any thing; especially in the case of living things, the thing "strives" to reach that condition over a typical, if flexible, orderly course of development. The fact that this development occurs is, for Aristotle, sufficient to pronounce the necessary conditions for that development "good" for that creature. Neither of these presuppositions has many defenders today. As for the first, it is all very well to say that God has a specific purpose in mind for each creature—but how can be sure ever that we know what it is?[3] As for the second, even granted that *if* there is a natural condition for a thing, then it is good for that thing to attain it (and in the case of, say, malignant tumors, we might be inclined to doubt that), we have difficulty giving a meaning to that "natural" without importing the Divine Purposes we just got past. Or, settling on one of the circumstances in which the creature is found to use as a "base," (for the cat, the wild), we proceed to decide that what aids the creature's survival in those circumstances is universally good for it.

When we come to the special case of human beings, our difficulties increase. Not only do we inherit the problems set forth so far for any creature, but a convenient benchmark is denied us: there simply is no "wild" condition we can use as a base. Man is, to make the first generalization of the type criticized above, essentially a cultural, symbol-creating animal. He is *always* found in an artificial setting, one of his own making. Superficially, these settings vary drastically. Early twentieth-century anthropology was one long proof that "normal" behavior and accepted practice in any given society would be totally insane behavior and immoral practice in most of the rest of the societies of the world. What any one society regarded as "natural" was totally unthinkable in another. The anthropologists rapidly went beyond this superficial emphasis on the exotic to the actual workings of the society beneath, and found that we had more in common than we thought—but at the price of heavy reliance on that slippery notion of "function." Societies can be analyzed into functions that are the same the world over. When, and only when, we have decided (not unreasonably) that the survival of a society is a good, and the proper end of all activity within that society, then all activities of the society can be viewed as means to that end.[4]

Not all critical examination of the institutions of a society has to involve itself in the slippery notions discussed so far. It is entirely possible to advance criticisms of institutions and their operations simply by positing values for the society, explicitly or implicitly in the course of criticism, and deriving the value of the institutional operations under consideration from their tendency to enhance or diminish the realization of those values in the society. One obvious societal value, for example, is the happiness of the individuals involved; most of us will agree that human suffering ought to be minimized in the long run. To use the terms of the example above, we can agree that a painful condition is always undesirable, and if it can be shown that any social condition is the cause of individual pain, that social condition can be condemned.[5] Felt happiness is rarely the only value espoused by social critics: institutions are also on occasion expected to make people rational, free, moral, peaceful, loving, and/or industrious and are judged good or bad in proportion to their tendency to do so. Two different types of analysis must be carried out to make such judgments: an empirical inquiry into the social results of the institutions must determine what their effects on the people really are, and a normative inquiry into the meaning of the value posited and its relation to other social values must be carried out. If either inquiry fails to convince, the whole criticism fails.

A worse difficulty for this logically simple brand of criticism lies in the values posited to begin with. Where societies are concerned, these abstract terms have no accepted meaning outside of the institutions intended to implement them. The terms tend to become hopelessly enmeshed in the history of the institutions, their meaning warped out of shape in social practice, precipitating endless debates when they turn up in political discourse (as other than ritual approval-words). And this condition is unavoidable; it really is very difficult to decide whether freedom is more valuable than equality, or whether mercy should supersede justice, in general and in the abstract. Although we can often tell when a societal condition is thoroughly bad and needs correction, an abstract debate on values is not likely to reveal new and significant approaches to this correction.

The corrective to this overly abstract type of debate is found, in recent literature, in a revival of the anthropologists' functional analysis. Social criticism can fruitfully begin the last obervation above: that we can often agree that we recognize a thoroughly bad phenomenon, even if we cannot agree on the absolute or relative weights of the values we agree are violated by it. Over the last decades the example most frequently chosen as a starting point is, understandably, the rise of Nazism in Germany in the 1930s. Here we have a case where a nation of (we thought) thoroughly rational people espoused a thoroughly irrational doctrine and enthusiastically undertook a hopelessly evil course of action. Why? The problem demands a much deeper analysis of the working of any society than utilitarian economics and social-contract political theory were capable of providing. Somewhere, we knew, Nazism had played an essential part in the working of German society at the time; the challenge was to discover what it was, and what practice played that part in other societies, so that the Fascist phenomenon could be avoided elsewhere. The writers who took on the problem came up with a set of different but closely related solutions;[6] what interests us is that in their approach to a solution, they reintroduced the notion of "human nature" and presented a picture of man as a "social animal"— a term that perhaps needs more explanation.

Something must be wrong with a people that undertakes the extermination of a large part of its citizenry. The only sense the analysts could make of the Nazi movement was that it supplied something the people lacked, and wanted desperately. But this was to say, that people *by nature* needed that thing, whatever it was; that all people need it, that they will try to find it no matter what barriers are put in their way. But then there are *societal* needs, or drives, natural to men as a social species, needs which *ought* to be satisfied in ordinary society if its people are to be immune from aberrations like Nazism. Hungry people will fight for food; this need (drive, instinct, whatever) must be as universal to mankind as the need for food.

The societal need that was left unsatisfied in Germany following World War I was isolated differently by different writers, which is hardly surprising. Some called it a need for "love," others "security," others noted the failure of "authority" or "legitimacy" in that shattered society; increasingly, concepts of "solidarity" or "community" began to emerge from the literature. We may call the illness they found "anomie," after Durkheim; the symptoms are too similar not to come from the same social and psychological virus. This anomie—or frustration, social fragmentation, loneliness —resulted, they claimed, from a societal emphasis on individual rationality and individual advantage, the end-product of a process dating from the Enlightenment at least; to cure that illnes, we must reshape our institutions, keeping in mind that man is a *social* animal, a creature that needs love and companionship, acceptance and cooperation, before he needs individual freedom and competitive advantage. We could dispute the conclusion, but that is not the point. The point is that if that thesis is even intelligible, it entails the presupposition of a human nature whose invariable needs do not end with the physical, but continue into the structures of the institutions and the patterns of the culture, and dictate the broad limits of a good society.

Two criteria are now available to judge institutions by. Most obviously, if the direct result of a social practice is a *painful* condition, that institution is imperfect to the extent that it causes suffering; it ought to be changed unless it can be shown that the amount of suffering in society is on balance less (strictly speaking, the least possible) because of the operation of that practice. But it should be noted that the social condition brought into focus by Nazism in Germany is not necessarily a painful one for those who suffer from it. In the eventual dismantling of civilization that results from it, a great deal of pain is involved for almost everyone; but if avoidance behavior is, as it must be, the defining characteristic of pain, anomie is not painful. Indeed, since its most salient feature is the absence of felt restrictions and societal constraints, it is often regarded as pleasurable. But it is an evil condition, in that if people live this way, the will become destructive if the opportunity arises (and therefore the cause of suffering: eventually, human suffering is the easiest measure of disvalue); it is an *unnatural* condition. The housecat is not in the "normal" circumstances, i.e., the wild, that defined its nature; it does not have to hunt. But the human being, whether Trobriand Islander, Athenian of the fourth century B.C., German of 1930, or present-day American, *is* in his natural setting—he is living with other human beings in a society whose activities are structured by rules into accepted practices and established institutions, and these institutions can fulfill or fail to fulfill his natural, societal, needs. But that point, however limited it may be, is all we wanted to establish.

The notion of a "societal" need, while opening the door to the reintroduction of theories of human nature discredited in the past, is not itself fundamentally misconceived or self-contradictory. Its value element is easy enough to isolate: it lies in the condemnation of the item selected for analysis, e.g., National Socialism, ultimately on the grounds of the suffering it causes. Its observational element is clear enough, in the similar facts of human behavior in the Germans' reaction to the Nazi movement and an ordinary non-Nazi's reaction to some element in his own society. It does not entail a position on the question of physiological determination of mental processes: we can believe, with Robert Ardrey and other ethologists, that the source of these societal needs or tendencies is innate and inherited, a type of animal instinct; or we can believe, with Hans Kohn, that a "natural tendency" is simply "a tendency which, having been produced by social circumstances from time immemorial, appears to us as natural."[7] A societal need, innate or conditioned from time immemorial, is simply there, and must be dealt with. It does not deny the anthropologists' claim that all human behavior is culturally and ultimately historically conditioned; in fact it insists upon it. The only objects that could satisfy such needs as were found—needs for order, for community, for status and legitimacy—would have to be institutions, artificial, man-made, symbolic structures within the society. But then all things cultural are not arbitrary or accidental as far as human life is concerned; by nature, we need certain types of institutions in our societies, and if we do not have them, we will exhibit the erratic behavior and the tendency to accept harmful or inadequate substitutes which are characteristic of any deficiency disease known to medicine. The question for the next section concerns the consequences of this conclusion. On the assumption that we do not know precisely what types of institutions satisfy what types of societal needs—we are not anthropologists, and the matter is one for empirical research—we want to know what, if anything, concerning Aristotle's proposition is entailed by the fact that men seem to have needs that only man-made institutions can satisfy.

### THE POLITICAL NATURE OF MAN

The question can be approached most easily from Aristotle's side. We will attempt to show that in his demonstration that "man is a political animal," an essential thread of argument is identical with the conclusion from the last section: that man, by nature, requires what only human artifice can provide—and that this feature of his nature is the most important, defining, essential feature, the feature by virtue of which he is human.

Aristotle's proof that "man is a political animal" is elliptical in the extreme. Fleshed out, it works as follows.

1. Man is a social animal (one with curious deficiencies) (from *Politics* I, 2 1252a-b): Observation shows us that men, like the members of many other species, live together in association. They are drawn together into stable unions for many fundamental purposes, especially reproduction (union of man and woman) and cooperative work (master and slave). Without these associations the species would not survive. But these small associations are not

ultimately sufficient for survival, nor is the next larger association, the village. Among them, they can take care of daily recurring needs and some others, but long-range needs cannot be served.

The obvious solution is to expand, but here a curious deficiency appears in man's nature. People do not seem to have any elaborate instinctual pattern built in to tell them the *form* of their adequate association, as do the other animals. The capacity for justice, for wise administration of a good and practical ordering of a society is much better realized by a queen bee than by humans in these primitive groups: man rules woman, master rules slave, largely by brute strength or cleverness, and king rules tribal village by an Austinian "habit of submission" to the eldest of the family. Therefore, although "natural" (in the sense of physical or innate) drives and abilities are sufficient to explain the existence and, initially, the form of social units like the family, temporally the first and most basic unit, they are insufficient to explain the existence and form of the unit that is large enough to be self-sufficient, the *polis* or state. Yet the state must be reached if the long-range needs of the species are to be satisfied.

2. Man is a rational animal (*Politics* I, 2 1252b-1253a): We use the word "rational" in at least two senses, and both show up in Aristotle's demonstration. The more limited sense of "rationality" is as a (uniquely human) instrument of the appetites: the human ability to foresee consequences, conceive situations that at present are not, and adjust means to ends makes it possible for us to develop ways of getting what we want that are not available to other animals. The state is brought into existence by human rationality, in this sense, for "the bare needs of life"—to provide for the common defense by making available a common wall, a manpower pool, the facilities for training an army, and to promote the general welfare through a protected market for trade. In the pursuit of these goals, the power of speech is a necessary instrument, as it serves to set forth "the expedient and inexpedient," making possible concerted work.

By the other sense of the word, "rationality" is the human capacity to transcend and control the appetites, to live a life governed by principles of right and wrong, principles worked out by reason and tested in dialogue with reasonable men. The power of speech, defining characteristic of the species, is central to this sense of rationality; it is the means of setting forth "the just and the unjust." Man alone "has any sense of good and evil, of just and unjust, and the like," and he alone has the capacity to organize his life according to these perceptions. It is for the fulfillment of this capacity that the state is ultimately created. As the sole means of ensuring the leisure necessary for governing life by public reasoning (Aristotle is not here discussing the "life of contemplation," elsewhere proved to be the best life but reserved to philosophers) and as protector of the "public space" necessary for the dialogue, the state continues in existence "for the sake of the good life." Rationality in the limited sense brings the state into being; the state creates the possibility of a fully rational life.

3. Man is a political animal (*Politics* I, 2 1253a): Presumably, the life of reason is valuable enough to be pursued for its own sake, even by the angels, who have no societal needs to fulfill. But rationality plays an essential role in the most basic structure of human life and needs. Man is a gregarious animal, but, as noted above, he is instinct-poor; unlike other gregarious animals, he has no innate, specific, instinctual knowledge of the rules appropriate to life in society. Yet like the others, he *must* have forms of organization to structure the activities necessary for survival. In the absence of instinctive equipment, he must use his rational capacity. Alone of the animals, he can construct and understand rules or laws to which he can conform his behavior; he alone can construct his own institutions, organize his own cultural patterns, participate consciously in his own government. He can and he must—there is no other way they could come into being. The state is the necessary condition for, as well as the result of, the construction of the institutions required for human life; therefore man is by nature an animal that belongs in a state, a political animal. Q.E.D.

From the foregoing, the meaning of some of Aristotle's odd statements at the end of that chapter becomes clear. The "priority" of the state to the family and to the individual is a logical priority, stemming from the fact that the uniquely human capacities to be developed by the family can be realized only in the state; the humanity of the individual is defined by his participation in the process in which the state consists. Also, that "a social instinct is implanted in all men by nature" means no more than that man must live and work together with others of his species—he cannot be solitary; the means of doing this, for better or worse, are left to the rational efforts of men who do not always find it easy to be reasonable—hence "he who first founded the state was the greatest of benefactors." And since no instinct will keep the association together and working well, it is justice, the disposition to maintain the public space and keep to the laws, which is "the bond of men in states;" and the public reasoning or dialogue itself, "the administration of justice, which is the determination of what is just, is the principle of order in political society."

For Aristotle, the proof that there was such a thing as human nature was unnecessary; he simply assumed it. The proof that the nature was political was so obvious to him that he could summarize it in a page or so, indicating the major steps with unprovable propositions like "Nature, as we often say, makes nothing in vain" (1253a, referring to the power of speech). Yet the same observable, in fact undeniable, features of human existence and association lead us to the same conclusion that he reached: that the defining characteristic of *human* life is that its principle of order is the creation of, and adherence to, laws and institutions specific to the society. Man is, to make the second and last enormous generalization of this paper, by nature a lawmaker.

We began with the question, Can human institutions ever be pronounced good, as tending to fulfill human nature, or bad, as tending to warp or injure it? It seems clear from the foregoing that the answer is yes, and that Aristotle knew it all the time. As the cat in its natural setting must hunt to survive, so the human being in his natural setting must create, maintain, and live within certain practices in order to survive. These practices vary from society to society, but fulfill the common function of structuring, by rules, the activities necessary for survival; deprived of adequate structures, the human being goes haywire. As the cat in his natural setting (but not in domesticity) must be physically fit to hunt, so the human being must be psychologically and socially free to create institutions; we shall not find angels in the forms of men to be our leaders and lawgivers, so we must become ourselves capable of making the laws. The citizen must develop rationality, at least in the limited sense, and he must be free to operate upon his society through collective action undertaken after public reasoning. Rationality and freedom are not automatic products of a government that proclaims attachment to them, nor are they automatically destroyed when a government disclaims interest in them; the ideology of a gigantic nation-state has little to do with the actual structures in which the people live. It is at the most immediate levels of society, the township, municipality or region, that sufficient openness to allow the play of human reasoning must be preserved. Where such openness is found, the people can act collectively upon their common problems, i.e., can be political men; where it is not, the life available to human beings does not contain the elements essential to human nature; it is not a fully human life.

## NOTES AND REFERENCES

1. For example, see Richard Taylor's comments on one understanding of the assertion, in *Freedom, Anarchy and the Law* (Englewood Cliffs, N.J.: Prentice-Hall, 1973), pp. 1–2.
2. And all the other conditions just mentioned still hold. This qualification will continue to be part of what we mean in this paper by "the wild." I am assuming that the hunting instinct in a cat, like other instincts, is inherited.
3. See, among others, Kai Nielsen's essay on the difficulties of this sort of reasoning, "The Myth of Natural Law," in Sydney Hook, ed., *Law and Philosophy* (New York: NYU Press, 1964).
4. Be it noted, that ultimately, it is arbitrary to regard survival as a good. See Barry Miller, "Hart's 'Minimum Content of Natural Law,' " 43 *New Scholasticism* 425 (1969).
5. A difficult but enlightening task of institutional analysis is the isolation of the causal relationships between the social practices and individual sensibilities. In his notion of the "sociological imagination," C. Wright Mills catches the essence of this analysis.
6. The literature is huge, and in almost no case focused exclusively on Nazism; we shall be drawing freely in this discussion from at least Erich Fromm's *Escape from Freedom* (New York: Holt, Rinehart and Winston, 1941), Sebastian de Grazia's *The Political Community* (Chicago: University of Chicago Press, 1948), Hans Kohn's *The Idea of Nationalism* (New York: Macmillan, 1951), and the works of Erik Erickson, Bruno Bettelheim, Erving Goffman, *et al.* Examples of more recent social commentary using the same assumptions on related subjects, are Morton Grodzin's *The Loyal and the Disloyal* (New York: World Publishing Corporation, 1956), Philip Slater's *The Pursuit of Loneliness* (Boston: Beacon Press, 1970), Alvin Toffler's *Future Shock* (New York: Random House, 1970), Theodore Roszak's *The Making of a Counter Culture* (Garden City: Doubleday & Company, 1968), Robert Nisbet's *The Quest for Community* (New York: Oxford University Press, 1953). These carry on a tradition established by nineteenth-cen-

tury Continental sociologists, especially Emile Durkheim *(Suicide)* and Ferdinand Tönnies *(Gemeinschaft and Gesellschaft).* See Robert Nisbet's summary of this tradition and its influence, *The Sociological Tradition* (New York: Basic Books, 1966).

7. Robert Ardrey's works toward this point include at least *The Territorial Imperative* (New York: Atheneum, 1966) and *The Social Contract* (New York: Atheneum, 1970). Hans Kohn's definition is found in *The Idea of Nationalism,* p. 4.

# 6

## THE PRIORITY OF HUMAN NEEDS AND THE STAGES OF POLITICAL DEVELOPMENT*

### JAMES CHOWNING DAVIES

In this paper I will attempt to establish a relationship between the stages of development in human beings and the stages of development in polities. First I will consider the general question of priority, of hierarchy, in human needs. Then I will state specifically a theory of priority among basic needs and indicate how I believe the theory helps to explain the stages of political development. There neither is nor can be a holistic theory to explain political development, on psychological, sociological, or economic grounds. There is no one-to-one relationship between the development of individuals and polities. On the other hand, relationship is not random. What is presented here is a basic, necessary, though not a total explanation of the basic phe-

157

nomena that occur as polities develop out of elemental societies.

Everyone, everyday, everywhere can readily verify the priority of some of the basic needs over all others. These most basic needs are the physical ones, which are shared with all animals and which many natural and social scientists regard as the only basic needs. All an individual has to do to verify the priority of physical needs over all others is to stop breathing. If he can go for more than a very few minutes without becoming totally concerned with breathing, then he has empirically refuted the priority of the physical needs. If he goes without food for a few weeks, he has refuted the priority. And if he is injured or gets ill and pays no heed to his pain or ache, he has refuted the priority. Virtually no one who can intellectually contemplate the priority of human needs is preoccupied with meeting any of his physical needs. Unfortunately, the substantial majority of mankind, late in the twentieth century, still is preoccupied mostly with satisfying physical needs. For members of the middle class in advanced societies, satisfaction of the physical needs is only a mealtime and bedtime concern. For most of the rest of humanity, satisfaction of the basic but nonphysical needs is still, during most of their waking hours, a thing of the future.

The topmost priority of the physical needs has nevertheless been recognized by some writers and others who have experienced life in more fully human terms. In the Grand Inquisitor scene in *The Brothers Karamazov,* Dostoevsky has mankind say to the Church: "Make us your slaves, but feed us." In *Uncle Tom's Cabin,* Harriet Beecher Stowe has the slave Uncle Tom tell his master that he can control his body, but his soul belongs to God. There is a German saying: first comes food, then morality.

The retrogression in behavior that occurs when people are extremely deprived has been repeatedly observed. In the winter of 1846–47, among a group of California-bound pioneers, the Donner Party, while they were stuck by storm on the east of the High Sierra, some cannibalism occurred.[1] One woman ate parts of her dead husband; some children were fed parts of their dead father. In the Ukraine, as Khrushchev vividly reports, cannibalism broke out in the wake of the devastation of the Second World War.[2] In 1972, following an air crash high in the Andes on the 13th of October, sixteen survivors, who weeks before had been in the modern, civilized world, ate some flesh of the 29 men who had died before the final rescue on the 22nd of December.[3] In such circumstances, when hunger is strong, the social ties, let alone morality, are weak.

There has long been recognition that human beings have not only physical but also other innate needs, and there has long been more or less explicit recognition of the priority of physical needs over all others. Twenty-three hundred years ago, Aristotle regarded the family as the first social unit, noting that it is formed to satisfy minimally the "daily" physical needs of humans to eat ("as meal-tub fellows") and to procreate.[4] Man is thus by his nature a social animal[5]—and, Aristotle added, only in the political association can man pursue his highest good,[6] which is happiness. Two thousand years ago Jesus said that man does not live by bread alone, and he urged people to identify with each other in non-status, that is, in human or what Aristotle might call natural terms.

A hundred years ago Karl Marx hurled thunderbolts against the capitalist system as the cause of the inhuman reduction of poor people to mere appendages of machines. Because of this emphasis on the socioeconomic system in his *Capital* (1867, 1873), Marx's earlier and basic theoretical orientation has been neglected. In 1843 he wrote that "the root is man," adding that "theory is only realized in a people so far as it fulfills the needs of the people."[7] In 1846 he and Engels wrote that "life involves, before everything else, eating and drinking, a habitation, clothing, and many other things" and "that as soon as a need is satisfied . . . , new needs are made." The first new need is establishment of the family, the first social relationship, which itself later becomes subordinate to new social relations and new needs.[8]

It would be absurd to conclude that Aristotle, Jesus, and Marx agreed in their views of human beings, but it would also be absurd to fail to note the similarity in their starting points. Not being psychologists, none of these three ever elaborated on men's nature in ways that are now possible. Defining human nature as those tendencies to behave that are common to all human beings, we can note the growing acceptance of the existence of such common tendencies, one set of which consists of basic needs.

Building on a psychological tradition that includes William James,[9] William McDougall,[10] and Henry Alexander Murray,[11] Abraham Maslow hypothesized a hierarchy of needs. He made clearly explicit what was indefinitely explicit in such observations about human nature as those we have noted. He rank-ordered five needs, in descending priority, in his now well-known list: the physical, security, social-affectional, self-esteem, and self-actualization needs.[12] Since at least the 1950s, this hierarchy has begun to serve in political analysis. As far as I know, its first recognition was in my own doctoral dissertation in 1952 and its first basic theoretical integration in my *Human Nature in Politics* in 1963.[13] Others who have mentioned the hierarchy are Christian Bay and Robert Lane.[14] Some research based on it is mentioned below. Before the need hierarchy as Maslow stated it becomes fixated as unalterable natural law, it seems appropriate to revise the theory, including a revision (with some embarrassment) of my own prior formulation of it.[15] There is, I believe, a basic inconsistency in Maslow's formulation, and there are a couple of at least politically significant omissions. This revision of a thirty-year-old theory comprises the first part of this chapter.

## THE PRIORITY OF HUMAN NEEDS

A behavioral theory is supposed to conform to the way people actually behave, and not vice versa. The arrangement of the priority of basic human needs that appears to have the best fit with the way people actually behave is as follows:

first, the physical needs;

second, the social-affectional or love needs;

third, the self-esteem or dignity or equality needs;

fourth, the self-actualization needs.

While these categories are not definitive, they appear to include all the substantive needs common to all human beings, including of course those people whose major concern is with only their physical needs and the most elementary form of social needs. The substantive needs are those pursued primarily because they are inherently gratifying and only secondarily because they relate to some other, instrumental, desire. The instrumental needs are pursued in the process of satisfying a substantive need, to which their relationship is one of mode or means.

One minor note as to usage. The term "basic" is often used as though it meant "physical." On grounds that it is better to call all needs basic that are theoretically common to all human beings—

whether these needs exist in actual or potential form—all four of the substantive needs I have listed are here deemed basic, along with the instrumental needs to be considered later. The consistent assumption is that all these basic needs are organically, genetically programmed predispositions.

Let me briefly spell out the argument for establishing priority among the four categories of substantive need. In this chapter it is impossible to do much more than illustrate the relationships. A wide range of experimental and other evidence relating to the priority of needs is presented in my *Human Nature in Politics,* particularly the first two chapters.

The nearly self-evident fact is that most people who eat and sleep regularly and are in good health are not preoccupied with satisfying the physical needs. For this reason and perhaps because it is deemed too banal or embarrassing or frightening to discuss physical needs, these needs tend to be overlooked. Nevertheless, as I will suggest in the later section on political development, the physical needs remain of enormous importance in both political theory and political life, because mild physical deprivation weakens and severe physical deprivation often severs the most basic social ties, even within the family. This deprivation, whether as the consequence of never progressing beyond concern with their satisfaction or as the consequence of retrogressing to their concern, tends to produce anarchy in the struggle of each against all to survive. And this tends to maintain or produce tyranny.

In a provocative study of the effects of physical deprivation, Aronoff found striking differences on a Caribbean island between the life style and social interactions of physically more deprived cane cutters and physically more gratified fishermen. The physically insecure cane cutters led a fragmented, conflictful life of preoccupation with subsistence, more or less in isolation and social conflict—the Hobbesian war of each against all. The physically more secure fishermen were able to concern themselves fairly successfully with pursuit of the love and self-esteem needs.[16]

The social-affectional or love needs, which appear at or shortly after birth, are also rather often neglected or taken for granted by people who have experienced fairly stable emotional lives and thus are able productively to concern themselves most of the time with other things. Variously composed of quasiphysical (sexual) and nonphysical ingredients, the love needs form a continuously traveled bridge between a human being's most elemental physical needs and his/her more distinctly human needs as a unique individual. A person's demands for everything from food to recognition of his/her unique creativity are all transacted with other human beings. Aristotle was indeed understating it when he called man a social animal. Those who can calmly read or write about the need which, after survival, is the most basic do indeed take it for granted.

The deprivation of love needs helps demonstrate their high priority. Consider the mental condition of an individual who has become chronically preoccupied with love, as a consequence of either traumatizing childhood neglect or the capricious on-and-off concern of his/her parents or the breakup of a love attachment to girl or boy, betrothed, or spouse. At worst he/she will be continuously and neurotically preoccupied with his/her love life and social life, forever seeking affectionate interaction with others on an intense or casual basis. At best, when he/she does turn his/her mind to more distinctly human needs, he/she is likely to feel chronically insecure, because of the unstable emotional foundations on which he/she tries to build his/her life. (The awkward "he/she" pairing is used to emphasize that the innate desire for food, love, and any other thing is not a genetic endowment shared by only half the human race.)

Harry Harlow and his associates have extensively studied this need in its most elemental manifestation. They observed the effects of depriving infant monkeys of contact with their mothers and other monkeys. In some cases, the contact-deprived monkeys adopted a continuous catatonic crouch; in others they became incapable of defending themselves against the aggressive play of their nondeprived peers. In still other cases, when as adults they were involuntarily impregnated on what Harlow called a "rape rack," and had offspring, some tried to kill their infants and others merely ground their infants' heads against the floor.[17]

There are two more directly political studies relating to the deprivation of various needs, including the physical ones, affection, and status as it relates to the social-affectional needs. In a survey analysis using the need hierarchy as the theoretical basis, Knutson found, inter alia, that those higher on her indexes of political participation and of leadership were much less likely to mention deprivation of physical and affection needs.[18]

In a six-nation study in Europe, Inglehart found striking relationships between socioeconomic status and attitudes toward European integration. The lower-status people were more opposed to integration and the higher-status people (those who can concern themselves with lower-priority needs) were more in favor of integration. Similarly and perhaps more significantly, Inglehart noted an intergenerational difference, with the younger, postwar generation being less oriented toward acquisitive values and more toward what he calls "post-bourgeois" values. He also found a shift, in Germany, from 1949 to 1963, in which concern for "freedom from want" diminished in importance and concern for "freedom of speech" increased. This is precisely what a theory of the priority of needs would predict. Germans after the war were moving beyond their first concern, which was to get adequate food, clothing, and shelter. Inglehart offers a comparable explanation for the response of Frenchman of various classes to the May 1968 student-worker rebellion.[19]

The self-esteem needs are those most directly related to political analysis, for which they can more appropriately be labeled the recognition or equality or dignity needs. They include the expectation of being accorded equal worth and therefore equal right to participate in social and political life. They are the kind that begin to surface when individuals try to establish their equal independence from others while retaining their ties of affection to them. When dignity needs are prominent, individuals wish both to be apart and to be a part. They cannot establish their independence, and thereby their self-esteem, as equals to others, if they are too close. But they require interaction with others in order to establish and confirm their equal and independent worth. What Erik Erikson called the adolescent identity crisis has much to do with self-esteem needs.[20]

This set of needs manifests itself in interactions ranging from the child demanding recognition from its parents and the spouse demanding equal treatment by spouse to the citizen demanding equal political rights and equal justice under law. But the esteem needs are typically overridden by the physical and social-affectional needs. A poor man who is hungry enough will take humiliation by someone who tosses him a coin and laughs when he scrambles for it—because the poor and hungry man can get food with the money. An individual who is deprived or threatened with deprivation of his/her social-affectional needs will sometimes crawl abjectly to someone who, along with contempt, will give him/her a morsel of love. Many women stay married despite even physical abuse by their spouses and other actions by which their husbands depreciate and degrade them. Many men do likewise, to avoid the ache of solitude.

However, when people gain sufficient security, in the steady satisfaction of their physical and love needs, they begin to demand recognition as individuals meriting respect and dignification. Most recently, blacks in America and women in many countries have begun to demand equality, in a host of ways. They became able to do so when they reached a level of material self-sufficiency (nondependence) and of social integration that substantially freed them from subordination to whites and to men, respectively. The blacks and women who are not particularly concerned with asserting their dignity, for whom the esteem needs are not salient, fall on both sides of the esteem level in the hierarchy. Poor and isolated blacks and women, those who have not yet achieved relatively symmetrical interdependence in the process of satisfying their physical and affectional needs with whites and men, are not yet ready to assert their equal dignity. Prosperous, socially integrated, respected, and career-oriented blacks and women often prefer to forget that they have moved out and beyond those blacks and women whom they have left behind.

The self-actualization needs are those that are fulfilled when an individual becomes absorbed and proficient in—both lost and found in—work or a hobby that he/she enjoys, quite apart from its utility as a means of earning a living or as surcease from toil. A person loses his/her self when the boundaries dissolve between the self and some aspects of the environment, in activity that is inherently pleasurable as an end in itself. The aspects of the environment may include people. A person finds his/her self in the discovery that this interaction *is* pleasurable, is profoundly gratifying for its own sake and not just as a means of satisfying the need for food, sex, companionship, or dignity. Such activity is self-actualizing, *is* her or him. A person may actualize her/himself in the practice of medicine, machine-tool design, camping, collecting old bottles or new automobiles, writing, painting, composing, or just reminiscing about the good old days. Many people (but still only a small minority) find much inherent pleasure in their work—even as wives and mothers. For most, their work—including housework—remains toil.

The self-actualization needs first become manifest among children when, for example, they become totally absorbed in building a sandcastle, riding a bicycle, or writing down the words they have hitherto understood only orally. The self-actualization needs continue from their earliest childhood beginnings down to the end of old age. But only when the physical, social, and self-esteem needs are routinely met can the self-actualization needs become the central concern. Let an individual begin to doubt the significance, the importance, of what he/she does, and he/she will seek the recognition and approval of others, whether these others be other physicians (or patients), toolmakers, collectors, or even occasionally spouses. He/she needs others' approval of his/her self-actualizing activity in order to bolster self-esteem, a sense of worth. Let the person become lonesome after long hours in any actualizing activity, and he/she will seek the company of others. Self-actualization must not forever isolate him/her socially. Let him/her get sufficiently fatigued, and he/she will eat and sleep. His/her self-actualization must let him/her rest.

Three observations, peripheral to what has been said above, merit central emphasis at this point. The first is the often apparent reversal of priorities. Some people paint when they are hungry. Politicians have extraordinary stamina, particularly when campaigning. A composer may go without sleep for a night or so when in the midst of a symphony. A martyr, in the course of actualizing her/himself at the stake, may undergo everything from degradation (as people jeer and spit at her/him), to separation from all loved ones, to all-encompassing pain before the flames have seared her/him into unconsciousness.

People vary widely in their ability to stand hunger, pain, solitude, and degradation in the course of fulfilling themselves. Some individuals have enormous capacity to endure deprivation of higher-priority needs. But these reversals of the need hierarchy probably are very unusual in frequency and brief in duration. They are most readily explicable as the extraordinary behavior of extraordinarily strong individuals. Few—perhaps no—political purgees subjected to brainwashing have been able to withstand indefinitely the intense pain, isolation, and abuse of their inquisitors.[21] They are physically and mentally broken by their tormentors and then they either are killed or commit suicide. And even in his final agony on the cross, Jesus said: "My Lord, my Lord, why hast thou forsaken me?" Few people in the most nurturant environments are so single-mindedly absorbed, dissolved, in musical composition as Beethoven because of his deafness. For every Jesus Christ and Joan of Arc, there are hundreds of millions who prefer almost anything to deliberate martyrdom.

The second observation is that there is no clean-cut layering of overt acts such that any one of them can be categorized as satisfying only the physical, only the social-affectional, only the dignity, or only the self-actualization needs. The infant who is being breast-fed is also getting a healthy dose of affection. The adolescent who for the first time falls in love is experiencing not only love but also gratification of his/her need for recognition, esteem, and dignification, because another person makes him/her the object of attention, regard, and worth. Some people actualize themselves in the occupation or hobby of cooking—and tend to oversatisfy a physical need in the process. Some people actualize themselves in love, gaining their most profound pleasure not only in sex but in the intense love of one other person. And some people actualize themselves as leaders in minority groups that have been denied dignification by the large society. Such people are fulfilling also their esteem needs, in the course of intensively seeking the social and political recognition of those with whom they identify—those whom they love as a group of people—as fellow members of a rejected, degraded minority. In their work such leaders combine the satisfaction of their social-affectional, dignity, and self-actualization needs. Any theory or any research is fundamentally defective if it develops without a recognition that virtually all overt acts of all people are motivated by more than one basic need.

The third is that there is a retrogression from advanced to primitive modes of living whenever any individual or social group (including a nation) loses the satisfaction of a higher-priority need. The behavior of a seriously ill or injured musician is hard to distinguish from that of a seriously ill or injured workingman. An individual who has a self-actualizing life as a successful toolmaker or musician will act like a hungry child if he loses his job. Some prime political examples are the mental states in Germany of both the unemployed of the 1930s and those whom the Nazi government placed in concentration camps. Both unemployed and internees behaved primarily in response to their hunger. Civilization can neither emerge nor continue on a basis of physical deprivation. It disappears when people are compelled by dire circumstances to regress to a primary concern with physical survival.

The fundamental value of using the priority of needs in political analysis is that it explains what is superficially called "irrational" behavior: it explains why people seem to behave "like animals" when their normal daily life is interrupted by concerns whose force can be explained only by indicating that these concerns relate to the orderly priority of needs. What would be irrational for a self-actualizing person is to let himself die rather than eat or go to the doctor. What is irrational in political analysis is to pretend that hungry people do or can behave politically like those who are well fed, socially accepted, dignified, self-actualizing upper-middle-class members of the establishment. It is unnatural, irrational not to respond first of all to hunger.

And the priority of needs helps explain political behavior that is not hunger motivated. It helps explain why young men who are threatened with military service are responding to at least two basic needs when they demonstrate against a small war overseas. The highest priority need affected is the desire to live, to which the possibility of combat duty is a real threat. In addition, military service interrupts the expectations of such young men to be able to pursue a career that will actualize them. Opposition to the Vietnam conflict would have continued on the same high moral tone it had for many years among university students in America, if it were not for the fact that ending the draft ended the threat to them of various fundamental deprivations.

Similarly, an individual who feels isolated socially and ineffectual personally may join a totalitarian political party if it not only diminishes his isolation and gives him self-respect but also gives him something serious to do in a time of widespread social despair. The "appeals of communism" to American and other intellectuals during the 1930s depression ran this gamut of basic needs.[22] Physical hunger was not a major concern for most of these intellectuals.

### THE MEANS OF SATISFYING
### THE SUBSTANTIVE NEEDS

Earlier in this chapter I spoke of an inconsistency and some omissions in the Maslow need hierarchy. Both the inconsistency and the omissions can I think be corrected, first, by shifting one need out of Maslow's original set; second, by subdividing basic needs into two broad categories; and third, by an elaboration of the second of the two. The two categories are the substantive and the instrumental needs.

Maslow's formulation of the need hierarchy, as we have noted earlier, contains five needs, arranged in descending order of priority: the physical, security, affectional, self-esteem, and self-actualization needs. The problem is that security is inconsistent, in kind, with the other four needs. Maslow's inclusion of security among the other needs is akin to presenting a recipe in which the following are listed as ingredients: flour, milk, eggs, yeast, salt, and stir all these things together well. Stirring things together well is not an ingredient but a process. Feeling secure is like things being stirred together well.

A more totally coherent scheme of needs can be established if we conceptually separate out those desired, continuing mental states that are achievable in the *process* of seeking satisfaction of the physical, social-affectional, esteem, and self-actualization needs and categorize these latter as the substantive needs. The processual or instrumental needs are here defined to include security, knowledge, and power. *Each* of these relates to *each* of the substantive needs. Independently they do not appear to have any priority in relation to one another: knowledge does not as such appear to precede power, security does not precede knowledge, and so on. But each of these instrumental needs acquires priority as it becomes linked or attached to a substantive need. Figure 1 may help clarify the posited relationships.

Everyone needs and therefore seeks security. In the present conceptualization, individuals seek it as a state of mind that is achieved in the process of seeking satisfaction of their substantive needs and that is reinforced by adequate success at satisfying these needs. When they are generally succcessful at satisfying these needs, individuals feel secure, confident, that these needs can and will be fulfilled. In a relationship that is between means and ends, people want to be (optimally but not totally) secure in the ability to satisfy their physical needs, their affectional life, their esteem or dignity, and, while engaged in work that actualizes their unique potential capabilities, optimally secure in being free from unpre-

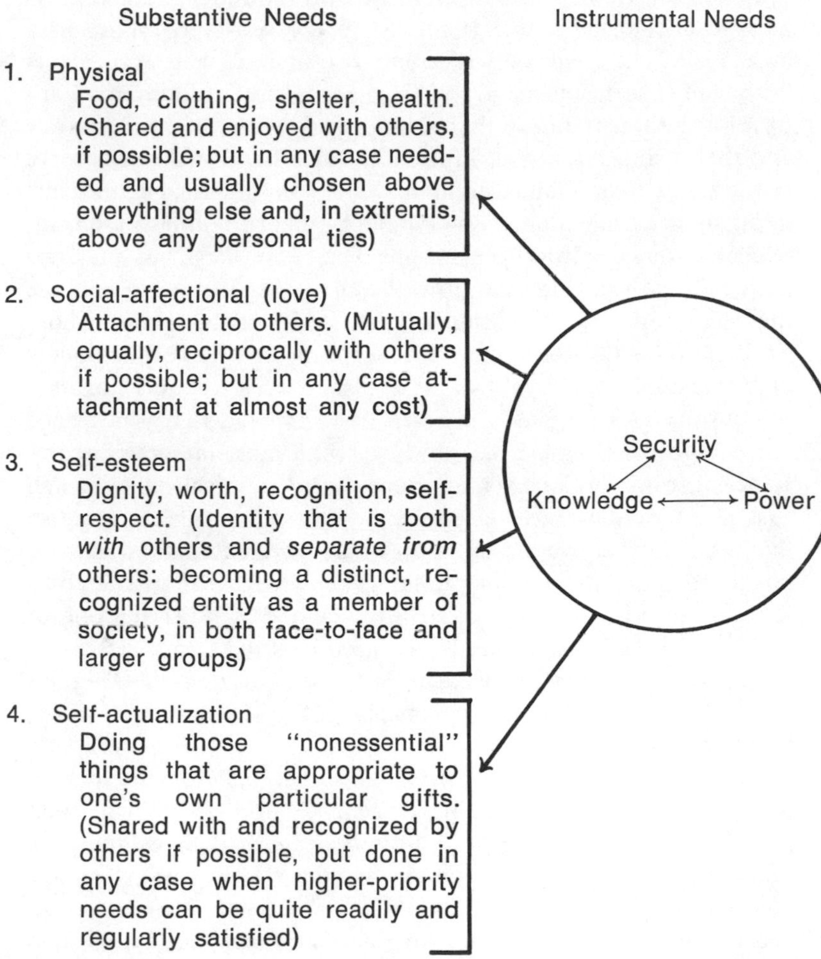

Substantive Needs                    Instrumental Needs

1. Physical
   Food, clothing, shelter, health.
   (Shared and enjoyed with others,
   if possible; but in any case needed and usually chosen above
   everything else and, in extremis,
   above any personal ties)

2. Social-affectional (love)
   Attachment to others. (Mutually,
   equally, reciprocally with others
   if possible; but in any case attachment at almost any cost)

3. Self-esteem
   Dignity, worth, recognition, self-
   respect. (Identity that is both
   *with* others and *separate from*
   others: becoming a distinct, recognized entity as a member of
   society, in both face-to-face and
   larger groups)

4. Self-actualization
   Doing those "nonessential"
   things that are appropriate to
   one's own particular gifts.
   (Shared with and recognized by
   others if possible, but done in
   any case when higher-priority
   needs can be quite readily and
   regularly satisfied)

Security

Knowledge ⟷ Power

Figure 1.   The Priority of Needs and the Means of Their Satisfaction

dictable interruptions by more urgent (higher need-priority) matters.[23, 24]

In some ways it is somewhat difficult to consider knowledge as an instrumental need that is related to the substantive ones as a means is to ends. Not only men but also animals and even plants "rationally" seek satisfaction of their needs, and at times it is hard for Homo sapiens to see the kinship between his natural activity and that of other forms of life. On the one hand, we can observe flowers and trees that respond to water, air, light, and nutrients in highly discriminating ways—without our attributing reason, intelligence, or knowledge to plant life. The "knowledge" of a plant is built into its genes. On the other hand, we tend often to suppose that philosophers, scientists, writers, and artists—those whose work may be the most integrated expression of men's uniquely high mental development—engage in their creative work for only the purest, least physical purposes. It is embarrassing—but need not be—to consider the fact that everyone must in some circumstances use his brainpower for purposes of physical survival and that in all circumstances he is using it to satisfy one or more of the basic substantive needs. For whatever combination of purposes, an individual is not pursuing knowledge for just *its* own sake but also for *his* own sake, in the course of satisfying one or more of his substantive needs. In need-priority terms, a scholar or scientist pursuing knowledge for its own sake is seeking his own self-actualization—and probably also satisfaction of other, higher priority, needs.

If a scientist like Gregor Mendel seeks, just for the fun of it, some abstract understanding of genetic variation among sweet peas in his monastery garden, he is here deemed to be pursuing knowledge as a means of actualizing himself. If a scientist like Norman Borlaug concentrates his experimental work in plant genetics on producing more abundant yields of rice, corn, and wheat that offer the prospect of ending chronic hunger in the world, the explanation is more complicated. This one-time Iowa farm boy presumably enjoyed the work in plant genetics for its own sake and was in this sense actualizing himself—doing it for his own sake. But he also helped nurture people and gained recognition (the Nobel Prize). He can be said to have gratified the entire range of his substantive needs, in extraordinary measure, in the pursuit of knowledge.

Unlike plants, people do therefore pursue knowledge, in order to understand the workings of the universe, of the earth, of society and individuals. The linkage between knowledge and the substantive needs may be nothing so intellectually challenging as Mendelian genetics or microbiology, pure *or* applied. It can be linkage whereby an infant who cries and then is fed soon learns —gains knowledge—that if it cries, mother will come and feed it. And a starving free citizen or a political prisoner learns that if he obeys the government he will survive.

Power similarly may be considered as a means used to achieve satisfaction of any and all of the substantive needs. Power is defined as the ability to produce intended effects. One can say that a child is exercising power when, by crying, it induces its mother to feed it, cuddle it, pay it some attention, and thereby give it some recognition. The power that one person uses to gain the affection of another (for example, sexual attractiveness and expressed or real concern for the other) is satisfied in the process of gaining and maintaining that affection. The power that a person exercises on others in pursuit of recognition of his dignity, his worth (e.g., getting them to say hello on the street, getting a promotion, getting a manuscript published, getting applause as a concert pianist) is similarly gratified *in the course* of his action (as a pedestrian, employee, writer, or pianist). Similarly a person who seeks power, in the course of actualizing himself as a highly influential public official or lobbyist, is gaining power while engaged in activity that is inherently satisfying.

A major reason for separating out security, knowledge, and power as basic needs that are instrumentally related to the substantive needs is this: there is a tendency to intermingle manner and substance in social analysis and thereby to overlook the relationship between social and political institutions as instruments and human wants as ends. In everyday life it often appears that instrumental goals are being pursued for their own sake and, correlatively, that institutions bear no significant relationship to what people substantively want. We forget that people cannot eat the constitution, just as we forget that style of dress in women relates or is supposed to relate to the very substantive need for sex. To ignore the distinction and the relationship is to mix means and ends, style and content, and therefore to avoid analyzing the means-end aspects of political behavior and—an even grosser oversight—to avoid examining the basic functions served by political structures.

Before relating the priority of needs to political development, one further matter must be mentioned: the distinction and the relationship between two phenomena. These are the initial emergence of the successive substantive needs in the course of an individual's development from infancy to maturity and their continual emergence in the course of everyday living.

The substantive needs generally emerge in the day-to-day lives of individuals consistently with the same priority that operates in the course of development from infancy to maturity. That is, priority is asserted in development and reasserted every day throughout life. Continuously, every individual moves back and forth from the most to the least basic of his needs, reiterating a process that began at birth. Figure 2, below, shows the relative saliency of the basic needs in the course of a normal lifetime and of a lifetime interrupted by illness, starvation, or other physical trauma. The last of these has enormous political portent. As the German case during the 1930s demonstrates—and regardless of other factors—hungry people are incapable of attaining political self-rule if they lack it or of keeping it if they have it. Figure 2 illustrates how various needs change in saliency in the course of a normal lifetime and in the course of one interrupted by such trauma as serious illness or imprisonment.

## THE STAGES OF POLITICAL DEVELOPMENT

The five stages of political development as I see them emerging in sequence are primitive anarchy, anomic anarchy, oligarchy, democracy, and civilized anarchy. The first and last of these involve so little politics—so little making of public policy—that they could be called pre- and postpolitical. But they do involve a little politics and they are integrally related to the three more intensely political stages of political development: anomic anarchy, oligarchy, and democracy.

*Primitive anarchy* prevails in a society that is confined to face-to-face contacts in virtually all its interactions. Almost everyone in such a society knows everyone else. Everyone trusts everyone, at least to the extent that each knows how each of the others interacts in various situations. Authority is exercised by persons

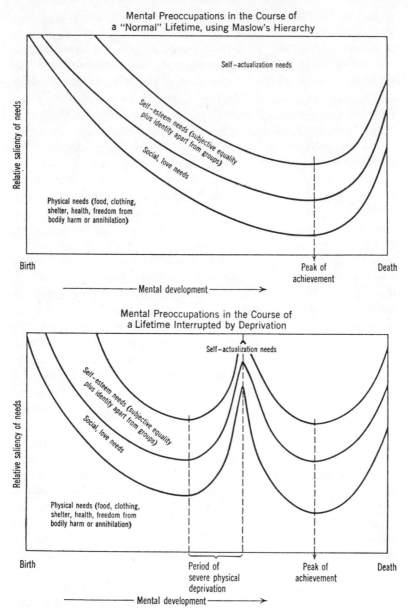

Figure 2.   From J. C. Davies, *Human Nature in Politics* (1963), p. 62. Used by permission of the publisher, John Wiley and Sons, Inc.

known to everyone as residents of the same small community. This society is overwhelmingly a subsistence society. Almost all its members are able to concern themselves only with staying alive, with satisfying the physical and the most elementary social-affectional needs. It is a fragile society, highly vulnerable to such catastrophes as drought, flood, epidemic disease, or to incursion by technical and morally more advanced societies and cultures. It is a routinized, compliant society that is profoundly disturbed at the thought of collective action against conventionally established and accepted—that is, authoritative—power.

In this stable, almost prepolitical society, a Hobbesian war of each against all is rare: an unchanging relationship among individuals has been established over centuries, in a constricted natural and social environment. The caprices of weather, disease, and of those who rule are not enjoyed. But they are accepted as part of life and as the price of survival. If there is a devastating flood, windstorm, or drought, it is acknowledged as the will of the gods or God—possibly as punishment for some unknown wrongdoing. If the landlord's son beats one's own son or if the landlord deflowers one's daughter before her marriage, these are accepted as inevitable—perhaps as punishment for one's own violence or promiscuity perpetrated against others who are weak.

These relationships to nature and one's fellow-men do manage the problems that arise in the course of survival, in a static social state. But they are not well equipped to handle even survival problems when natural catastrophe or foreigners from an advanced society suddenly intrude. Catastrophe and intrusion demand truly effective response if primitive people are not to be destroyed and if they are ever to begin developing toward larger social aggregations, toward individual dignification, and toward the individual's development of his/her own unique potential. Human intruders into such primitive societies typically possess superior economic technology, weapons technology, skill in social organization and administration (which may be called authority technology), and a value system that are radically different from most of the modes of interaction in a primitively anarchic society. The intruders use their skills to exploit the local population. Faced with such traumata, the society tends either to collapse or to die slowly, in encapsulated, often disease-ridden isolation.

At the same time, the exogenous influences trigger the emergence of those most distinctly human expectations that a primitive culture suppresses. Some or most individuals may survive—and commence at last to develop. Their ancestors and they have expended centuries in costly (psychic-energy consuming), unconscious, restless compromise with their human potential. They have had to sacrifice their potential in order to survive as somewhat more than typically social animals. At last, in the collapse of their primitive and static society, they see the opportunity of leading a nonsubsistence, nonprimitive life. They timidly embrace and gradually internalize a new and liberating way of life. In short, the collapse of primitive society and culture is rapid because, with all their pain and destructiveness, the outside forces represent the prospect of development. After roughly a thousand static years, European feudalism declined rapidly in the face of modern socioeconomic developments that included widening trade markets, the accumulation of capital, and the division of labor. People are now able to move from the fragile, unending, and stultifying search for subsistence to the tougher and more exciting dynamics of social life in which the development beyond subsistence is demonstrably possible.

The movement from stasis to development has occurred not once but repeatedly. In sketching the beginnings of Greek history, Thucydides describes the origins of the city states, and the occurrences he describes appear to be in some degree consistent with the transition from primitive anarchy to successive stages of political development. Once the Greeks became assured of steady provision of food and other physical necessities, relatively unified, interdependent societies came into existence, bearing such historic names as Athens, Corinth, Thebes and (far off to the west) Syracuse.[25]

The movement recurred in Western Europe when feudalism as a social system began to break down, trade and cities began to flourish, and nation-states began to form. It recurs in the twentieth century in isolated island communities of the South Seas and mountain communities in the United States, the Spanish Pyrenees, and Yugoslavia, and in backland communities in Turkey, Australia, Africa, and perhaps in every country. There is probably no static society anywhere, even in remotest New Guinea, that has not been infected with modernizing influences, but in even very advanced nations there remain small, encapsulated communities that have shown only the most tentative stirrings of development.

*Anomic anarchy,* the second stage, begins when people (both ordinary and extraordinary people) recognize the necessity for some degree of impersonalized control of the means of fulfilling those needs that begin to emerge when either or both of two events occur. They come to accept authority because of the intolerable chaos that follows radical disruption of established modes of life. The two alternative events are the autochthonous, indigenous development of discontent within a static community and the development of discontent as the result of intrusion from without. In Central and Western Europe, such discontent developed indigenously during the period before the sixteenth-century Protestant Reformation. Perhaps in most other places and at later times, such discontent developed exogenously.

During the transition from prepolitical stasis to political development, concern with satisfaction of the physical needs grows more intense, particularly among ordinary people. They have begun to move to the cities not just because cities are more exciting and liberating but, perhaps more elementally, because the countryside no longer provides its population a livelihood. This rural impoverishment came about in central and western Europe partly because of what in English history are called enclosure acts. These acts of Parliament gave "legal" sanction to landlords' assertion of their long-neglected and therefore uncontested "rights" to domain over the commons, the lands that had been usable since time out of mind by the local people for grazing and other purposes.

Landlords now began to use "their" commons to provide not just livelihood but wealth. They produced crops of grain, flax, and wool that enriched them in the national and international market and impoverished their tenants. As the sixteenth-century critic Thomas More put it, sheep began to devour people. Four centuries later, rural impoverishment in Vietnam came about because of defoliation and antipersonnel bombing and other wartime savageries that pushed people into the cities.

And so the struggle to survive, having become insufferable in the countryside, is continued in the cities. It produces an often frantic, individual, total, and lawless preoccupation on the part of poor people with seeking food, clothing, and shelter. The search goes on often at the cost of physical safety, when those who can and will and must settle for mere survival gamble with their very lives by stealing, robbing, and burglarizing. The victims are not only the intended ones—when the intended are those who are rich from their control of land, goods, commerce, and jobs—but also those who share poverty with their attackers but differ from them in having something, anything, that is worth taking by force or sleight of hand.

Numerically speaking, most of the victims of the poor are the poor. The warfare that results from this struggle is not one in which the poor fight the rich: it is not a class war as such. It is one in which the poor fight everyone, including those whose straits are as dire as their own. It is the struggle that goes on in slums and ghettoes in cities all over the world among people who have to gamble with their lives in order to survive and not with their wealth in order to get richer.

*Oligarchy, the third stage.* As a result of this often frantic preoccupation, the prospering extraordinary citizens—not to protect the poor but to protect themselves from predation—use the government, which becomes theirs, to establish strong, even harsh, means of eliminating anarchic violence and the arbitrary taking of lives and property by people whose only ruling law is the desire to survive. Then the war of each against all, which Hobbes described after observing in the seventeenth century the struggle to survive among London dockworkers, becomes intolerable even to its combatants. Ordinary citizens, including poor people, become willing not only to put up with but also at times to accept the power of a political elite, a government that will at least police the process whereby the overwhelming majority tries to stay alive. The near-anarchy of the struggle of individuals to survive produces its counterpart in the near-total exercise of power by government, and this power is popularly accepted. Autocratic, even totalitarian, government acquires authority. Oligarchy has succeeded anomic anarchy.

The archetypical example of this transition is the largely endogenous one whose English version Hobbes observed. The transition was from a relatively stable and static feudal economy to the dynamic of modernization. Some other examples, some of them occurring in the twentieth century, are largely exogenous, resulting from the imposition of forces that throw people into the battle for survival and induce their conformity to near-total power.

Slaves, seized and sold in Africa by Africans to Western traders

who transported and resold them in America, are one such exogenous example, one in which people were untimely ripped from
the womb of their ancestral ways and dragged in to a modernizing
and altogether frightening world across the seas. As described by
Stanley Elkins,[26] the process produced an incredible measure of
conformity to the power of both slave trader and slave owner, because the alternative was death or severe physical punishment. The
process resulted in a chronic concern for survival and a conformity
that continued down into and beyond the century following legal
emancipation in the United States. A finding that authoritarianism
has a higher incidence among American blacks than among whites
in the mid-twentieth century[27] is comprehensible only in light of
this centuries-long struggle among blacks to survive in a white society in which conforming was the prerequisite for their survival.
The relatively high incidence of authoritarianism that Lipset has
noted among working men[28] is similarly based, I would argue, in
their nearness to the struggle to survive and thus their limited readiness to move out of the third (oligarchic) to the fourth (democratic) stage.

In addition to slavery, there are other examples of exogenous
influences. One is the intrusion of Spanish civilization into Latin
America, starting in the sixteenth century. The initial reaction of
the indigenous Indian population was shock and an attempt at
withdrawal. A subsequent reaction has been a slow movement by
Indians out of semislavery into and, like onetime slaves in the
United States, toward integration in the modern polity. This interaction between an indigenous population and exogenous influences in the Americas began first perhaps in Mexico, but more recently appeared in such nations as Peru and Bolivia. In North
America, where Indians have not been virtually obliterated, they
seem at last to be following their remote Central and South American relatives into the early stages of political integration—in such
actions as the seizure of the town of Wounded Knee, South Da-
kota, in early 1973.

Another striking example of the initiation of political development as the consequence of exogenous factors is that incredible
phenomenon in the civilized modern world, the concentration camp.
Aside from their primitive savagery, such camps are awesome in
showing how even modernized people like Jews (and, less modernized, Slavs) retrogress when thrust backward into the ancient

but ever renascent struggle to survive. Internees in these camps, moved abruptly out of modern and presumably participatory life in Germany (and Poland, Russia, Belgium, the Netherlands, France, Denmark, Italy, and other nations), struggled like Hobbes's seventeenth-century London dockworkers to survive. They conformed to the manners and even the brutal way of life of their captors in order to do so. And in some of the camps, there were occasional, concerted, not altogether futile rebellions.[29] In complicated ways, the reversion of Germany itself, from the democratic beginnings in the 1920s to the anarchic and oligarchic stages under Nazism, was a consequence of both endogenous and exogenous forces.

Another example, similar in kind to the German concentration camp but attenuated in form, involves the internment of people of Japanese birth or ancestry in the United States during the Second World War. After being thrust back onto the task of survival, these people were at first in social chaos. But they then formed some kind of social community. Then, in several of the camps, the internees carried out riotous demonstrations that clearly demonstrated their demand for minimal rights to participate in the process of making decisions affecting the entire community—that is, political decisions.[30] Indeed, the disturbances in the German concentration camps and the American internment camps indicate not merely the first two stages of political development (primitive and anarchic anarchy) and the third (oligarchy), in which in the interests of survival power is surrendered to an elite. Concentration camp disturbances also indicate the beginnings of the fourth, to which we can now turn.

*The fourth stage of political development* tends to produce democratic government. This stage commences with the transition from concern for individual and nuclear family survival to concern with establishing and acting on a sense of wider community interest— of class solidarity, as Marx put it—against those who rule. This sense of communal interest begins in the first stage but does not then eventuate in collective action beyond the face-to-face community. Before the fourth stage can begin, there must generally be such an elevation above the level of mere subsistence as to make it possible for people to see that their individual interest is also their common interest. People then are no longer so totally preoccupied with staying alive and well. In a very elemental sense, they are now getting socially established and unified. They form groups on a semi-impersonal basis, like trade associations of merchants, bankers, and manufacturers; and trade unions of workingmen. The Gemeinschaft (the community of the primitive, prepolitical society and its urban counterparts, the neighborhood and the face-to-face factory work group) is supplemented in the modernizing polity by the Gesellschaften, the associations. Businessmen, farmers, workingmen (and blacks and concentration camp internees) no longer struggle impersonally with others in their own social group. Even without establishing face-to-face contact, they sense their common interest and begin to act as collaborating antagonists toward other groups and the government which they see to be dominated by other groups.

The fourth stage develops in successive waves, each of which (as in the growth of a river delta) witnesses the accretion of sequential, broad, and no longer closely personal ties within particular segments of society—but not within all segments at once or even in close sequence. Historically, in the industrializing world, this has meant that, first the middle class of entrepreneurs—merchants, miners, farmers, and manufacturers—diminishes its sense of individual competitiveness and increases its sense of common interest, against the government that entrepreneurs regard as responsive to feudal lords and perhaps to peasants, but not to themselves.[31] It is at the beginning of this stage that the Puritan and French Revolutions took place in the seventeenth and eighteenth centuries, respectively. Much later the working class—those whose struggle for survival after the English enclosures forced them into the cities produced the scene from which Hobbes drew his picture of the state of nature—develops a sense of common interest. More or less simultaneously with factory workers, small farmers (who are feeding the urban middle and working classes) develop a sense of common interest and no longer allow the value of the products of their labor to be determined solely by either supply and demand or by those who rule economically and politically in the cities.

As each of these successive groups becomes united, it begins to exert power against the government, which it sees as responsive only to other groups. Political power, once generally accepted in order to police the struggle of individuals to survive, is specifically rejected by protesting groups when it is seen as a threat to their group survival. In the case of the middle class in England, America, and France in the seventeenth and eighteenth centuries, group unification produced more-or-less violent revolution against the established government, and against the landed aristocracy, churches, and bureaucracies that the government was seen as supporting. In the case of farmers and workingmen in the nineteenth and twentieth centuries, there was no revolution. In all cases—bourgeoisie, farmers, and workers—the large and rather impersonal group became established and has remained so, as active political participants.

In America, in the case of later and less economically distinguishable groups, from blacks to women and to native Indians and Chicanos, the process of establishing a sense of common interest within each of these groups still continues in the 1970s. In many critical ways blacks, women, Indians, and such immigrant groups as Mexicans (Chicanos) have remained dependent for their material subsistence on the power of their opposites (whites, men, and Anglos) to allocate to them some ill-defined portion of the material and non-material goods of the society. These groups remain primarily preoccupied with developing their ability to control the means of satisfying the physical needs for food, clothing, shelter, health, physical safety, and (in the case of women, because of a persistent double standard) sex. The new demands of these groups for equality and power reflect their gradual moving beyond concern with the physical needs, as these become increasingly available to them without degradation, that is, without subordination. Women, for example, increasingly are demanding equal dignity because their physical needs (economic and otherwise) and their social-affectional needs are no longer so preponderantly under the control of men.

The precondition for developments in this fourth stage merits reemphasis. The precondition for increasing the awareness of members of a large social category that they have common, group interests, is that they get beyond the point where they are individually preoccupied with provision of the physical needs for themselves and their families. The middle class, that vanguard of limitation of governmental power in modern times, did not begin to develop a sense of common interest against the government until its members ceased to be totally preoccupied as individuals with their economic survival. The middle class then saw the government interfering with and not facilitating their preoccupation with the production and consumption of material goods.

The middle class was (and still is) so preoccupied with the creation of material wealth that, even in the process of moving well beyond the point of needing material goods in order to stay alive, most of its members have remained captives of a psychology of material deprivation. They have not emancipated themselves from the historic but to them no longer appropriate belief that material abundance is the only concern. The same has been true of the working class, which recalls widespread economic depression and occasional layoffs since the depression. Contradicting their ideologies of survival, first the middle class and then the working class got well enough established so that their survival was no longer in question. Then they fought government, won crucial battles against it, and at last joined it. At first they attempted, with more or less success, to dominate the government. Then they began to settle for codetermination of public policy.

The process is iterative. Those who have succeeded for a long time fail to understand the like motivations of those who are demanding recognition and participation. Middle-class people in colonial America did not become politically active at the time when they were trying to establish their businesses and plantations. They cooperated with the English colonial government, which in any case ruled rather lightly and absentmindedly. The colonials became politically active when new measures of the government in London threatened the continuing growth of their businesses and their wealth. After their successful revolution, they proceeded, before and after the Jefferson (1801-09) and Jackson (1829-37) administrations, to try to exclude all others from the government they regarded as their own.

And the same has been true of farmers and workingmen. They began to collaborate as farmers or as workingmen not when physical survival was really a serious threat to them as individuals but when they sensed their common interests and the threat to their survival as a collectivity. *After* their individual physical survival was assured, *then* they could join together against government whose actions (or inactions) threatened a *retrogression* to the time when they did have to worry individually about survival.[32] In turn, American farmers—notably in the South—and workingmen showed astonishment that black people, having gained some material advancement since the expansion of wartime factory work opportunities in the 1940s, should now collectively be demanding some nonmaterial goods: recognition, dignification, and participation in political life.

The expression, during the fourth stage, of group interest in universalist terms did not occur in human history for the first time in the American Revolution, with its declaration that "all men are created equal." In the German Protestant Reformation the expression was "the priesthood of all believers." Before that there were the mumbled incantations of churchmen, reciting in Latin (a language unknown to all but a tiny fraction of the population) the profound and easily glossed over exhortations of Christ, in whose name the churchmen professed to be acting but actually were only talking. And, a few years after the American Revolution, in France in 1789, it was "liberty, equality, fraternity." And in each case the new class, once it was established, served its own interests.

However, the result is never clear-cut nor are the lines among groups in society ever precisely defined and maintained. Some individuals in established groups begin really to broaden, in their actions, their identification with people whose conventional values and life-style are different from their own. Late in nineteenth-century America, some of the middle class began to identify and work with farmers and workingmen. In the mid-twentieth century, out of American Catholic and Protestant churches and private and public colleges, there emerged some of the earliest support, by upper-middle-class whites, of lower-working-class blacks. Some workingmen's organizations began to accept blacks who needed to work, to belong, and to gain self-respect. And even some men have begun to regard women as other than mothers, wives, mistresses, prostitutes, or physically mature and manipulable children. Eventually, dominant (that is, nonegalitarian) women's liberationists will come to regard men as other than physically mature and manipulable children. And priests in North America, South America, and Europe—bearing allegiance to the same first institution, founded in the name of the brotherhood of man, that fought the Protestant Reformation for a century until the 1648 armistice— have undertaken to act in support of degraded people rather than only talk about universal brotherhood.

The transition from the third, oligarchic stage (when people are primarily concerned with physical survival but are no longer fighting one another and are *beginning* to cooperate against tyrannical government) to the fourth, democratic stage (when people have begun to form solidary social groups and are *beginning* to act in ways that make their universal principles of human equality universally applicable) is rarely quick or nonviolent. Aside from the Hundred Years' Wars of the Reformation, the stalemate between oligarchic and democratic tendencies persisted in Germany at least to the end of the Second World War. In England, the major transition from oligarchic to democratic tendencies began in the seventeenth-century Puritan Revolution and may be said to have ended successfully in the Reform Acts of the nineteenth century—except with respect to half of the potential participants (women), who were not admitted until the twentieth. In France the transition did not commence until the late eighteenth-century Revolution and may be said to have been "completed" before the Second World War. In America, the *transition* toward democracy began with the Revolution and may be said to have ended in the savage struggle between oligarchy and democracy in the Civil War—except with respect to half the potential participants (women), who were not admitted until the twentieth century. Russia probably did not enter the first absolutist political stage until Ivan the Terrible's victory over the boyars in the sixteenth century, remained in it after the 1917 Revolution, and does not really appear to be out of that oligarchical stage in the 1970s. In Russia, as the purges of party members that have continued beyond the violent events of the 1930s indicate, not even the elite ruling class is secure in its own dignification. And the dignification of the peasantry and the working class is still far in the future.

The most advanced societies and polities in the twentieth century have moved into the fourth, democratic stage, but most of their political life remains at that stage. There is a growing consensus in principle and commitment in practice, among all segments of society, to securing to each individual adequate fulfillment of the physical needs—that is, to the achievement of material well-being. Increasingly individuals are assuming their right to participate as group members who can demand that the government do some things and not do others—except that, as each new group begins self-consciously to work together, it is still resisted. It has become acceptable at last that workers organize and bargain collectively with business and government. But is it all right for blacks to do so, or women, or schoolteachers, or professors? Some people doubt it, but more demonstrate a growing ability to move beyond the use of universalist principles for group interest—and with much less violence than attended the first struggles of the bourgeoisie to overthrow the dominance of the landed aristocracy, the Church, and absolutist government. As we slowly approach the fifth stage, the principles of equal human dignity and equal human worth, invoked to establish particular groups, are beginning to be applied universally.

*The fifth stage of political development is civilized anarchy,* when government begins to wither away and society starts to become metapolitical. It commences after physical survival and then group survival have been secured in preceding stages and when there is a real obliteration of the practice of measuring individuals' worth by their utility or their social origins. It commences, that is, when intergroup identifications have finally merged with interpersonal identifications. It begins when the universal principles in whose name progress toward group establishment has been achieved are actually practiced: when, universally and in no romantic or sentimental way, people regard one another as equals.

This fifth stage cannot be reached until each group has become secure in its own recognition and its participatory rights. Until then, each group tends to fear that the access of any other group to prestige and power is a threat to its own prestige and power as an already established group. No group or individual who is established wants to be disestablished, to retrogress to the point of being politically dominated by others. When a group becomes securely established and no longer fears losing power altogether by being compelled to share it, then it is able to diminish the intensity of its opposition to new groups demanding recognition and to increase its support for the universal application of the universal principles under which each successive groups gains power. Only then can the fifth stage commence, can government begin to wither away, and each individual citizen undertake his/her own individuation.

The later stages entail a kind of precession of ideas and values. The third stage, oligarchy, during which order is established, invokes such principles as the solidarity of the masses, the unity of the (Italian, German, Soviet, Egyptian, or Vietnamese) nation, the corporative state. In the fourth stage, during which groups become fully established, the principles are the equal rights of equally dignified men. In the fifth stage, during which government begins to wither away, individuals really are regarded as equal and the new, metapolitical principles pertain to such matters as the full realization of the human potential and the right of each individual to pursue his/her happiness as he/she sees fit.

The fifth stage calls for equal evaluation of individuals, as entities of inherent and not merely instrumental value, and for equal participation. All political power is then truly derived from the general public as a total community and all government is responsible to it. Unlike the individuals whom it serves, government has neither inherent nor instrumental value other than its utility as an instrument controlled by the public and not by any smaller group that invokes divine right, inherent power, or tradition—or that uses universalist principles for group purposes.

It is evident that societies thus far contain only a limited number of people who have internalized—or, more enduringly, sensed—their common identity with others or the very individual differences among them. Partly for this reason, no government anywhere has yet fully achieved the ability to serve with equal concern and effectiveness the interests of individuals as individuals, let alone of individuals as members of groups. In even the most advanced polities, such as Sweden, Denmark, England, and the United States, some citizens count for much more than others. But in some societies enormously portentous developments have taken place, in what Lasswell has called the sharing of deference and the sharing of power. The still only dimly visible plateau of the postindustrial society is here conceived as a necessary precondition not for completing but for starting the fifth stage of civilized anarchy.

Both the development and the direction of development of economic, social, and political institutions depend on the fundamentally innate demands, the expectations, of the human organism and the innate means of achieving these demands. Modern industrial economies with their division of labor, accumulation of capital, and the necessary collaboration and interdependence of people as "mass" producers and "mass" consumers could never have come into being without the fundamentally innate demand of people to live above the subsistence level, to collaborate in very complex ways, and—with their ability to remember, learn, and abstract—to organize institutions that serve the purposes of each individual human being.

Modern participatory governments began in the German, Swiss,

Scandinavian, Dutch, and English Reformations, when these ostensibly religious movements came to deny the principle of hierarchy and to assert the principle of equality—which of course they did not practice. These postfeudal beginnings—of the process of equalizing for all citizens the amounts of deference and power that each citizen exercises—would not have occurred if individuals (at first segmented and then individuated) did not, at the appropriate stage of their development, *naturally* expect and demand such deference and power.

In the "utopian" and hypothetical metapolitical society, government has at last withered away and people are in the condition of internalized universal identifications, values, and rules—in short, of civilized anarchy. By now it may be clear what has to be done successively before people can move from the war of each against all to the point when they can realize their full human potential. And by now it should be clear how far we are from the glorious dreams of such theorists as Peter Kropotkin and, in his ultimate goal, Karl Marx. No theorist or practitioner of political development has ever been able to really leap over successive stages. The Soviet Union, hastening to the classless society, probably remains politically one of the most class-dominated industrial societies in this modern world. Each person, each society, has to progress through each stage. Attempts to overleap them are as fatal as Macbeth's vaulting ambition.

There is no point in painting a chiliastic picture of what society is like when every individual is secure, knowing, and effectual in gaining satisfaction of his physical, love, self-esteem, and self-actualization needs. But we have some indication, partly from Maslow's growing preoccupation late in life with "the farther reaches of human nature," that such existence is far from being what Hobbes saw as man's abbreviated, empoverished, solitary natural condition.

One crucial matter requiring reemphasis relates to my postulating this "ultimate" human condition as a metapolitical one. Neither society nor government can achieve the paradox of effecting the self-actualization of the individual. He has to do it himself. But society and government have to provide the nurturant environment in which the individual can seek and find how to realize his/her utmost potential. There are no criteria on the basis of which the "success" of an individual in achieving his/her potential can be judged. The only criterion that can be established is that each individual, being of equal inherent (not of equal instrumental) worth, must have an equal opportunity with all others to develop his/herself as he/she sees fit and therefore may not interfere with the equal opportunity of all others to develop themselves as they see fit. At certain stages in the development of individuals from infancy to maturity, realizing this opportunity requires no diminution of interaction among people differing in skill and maturity. But it does not leave pedagogy to psychological operant conditioners or to other elites who can know no better what is the ultimate good of mankind than did Thomas More, Martin Luther, John Calvin, Jeremy Bentham, or Karl Marx. What such a metapolitical condition would make possible is the measure of fulfillment that has come, precociously in terms of political time, to such individuals as Beethoven, Lincoln, and Gandhi—it would make it possible for everyone to become himself, whether or not he has the potential of such giants.

The restraints necessary for each individual to reach the stage at which he/she can develop his/her full potential would of course have to be internalized, commencing at birth, as restraints do now. Each individual, in an ontogenetic process, has to pass through what society has been, and continues, passing through in the thousands of years of its still uncompleted phylogenetic process. But the restraints that are necessary are those consistent with the developing, emerging nature of individual human beings. The beginnings of control by operant conditioners appear to be false starts toward a good society. The beginnings of understanding by such developmental psychologists as Anna Freud, Jean Piaget, René Spitz, Harry Harlow, John Bowlby, and Erik Erikson are not false starts but are only beginnings. In short, we do not yet have the scientific means to propel us into civilized anarchy.

The seemingly accidental manner in which every society in recorded history has produced a few actualizing individuals is one of the major clues to what is possible when opportunities no longer result from genetic accidents or an elitist environment. The division of labor and capital accumulation have brought about an enormous productivity, which now for the first time provides the material part of the basis for moving society on to the post-industrial stage and, beyond that, to the metapolitical condition when all individuals can become self-actualizing—even if they are not Beethovens, Lincolns, or Gandhis. A major block to movement in that direction is the failure of empathy among actualizing individuals for those who are not. Unless the total developmental process is to come to a stop, the demand by increasing millions of individuals for the opportunity to fulfill themselves may diminish the opportunity for greatly gifted but egocentric individuals to do so. They may be killed or taxed to death. The material base is already being established. The empathy base remains as unformed as warm syrup and, among many actualizing people, as nurturant as helium.

The process by which first a tiny fraction, and then successively larger ones, have the opportunity of realizing their full potential is—to borrow a word from embryology that Erik Erikson used in his developmental psychology—a matter of epigenesis. Each successive stage of individual development depends on the prior and continuing satisfaction of those basic needs that have higher priority. No individual can proceed to actualize his/her own unique potential until he/she has come to expect regularly the satisfaction of his/her more basic, higher priority, needs—the dignity, love, and physical ones. Correlatively, only a tiny proportion of individuals will ever be able to actualize their potential until the society (including family, friends, and larger social entities) in which they develop has itself collectively developed the steady capacity to satisfy these higher priority needs. This takes us back to the basic equation: behavior is a product of the interaction of the organism and the environment.

Figure 3 may help to indicate how the process has evolved, and may continue to evolve, toward the maximum self-actualization of the maximum number of individual human beings.


### THE NEEDS OF INDIVIDUALS AND
### THE DEVELOPMENT OF POLITIES

Linking stages of individual development to stages of political development provides some benchmarks to help ascertain how far we have ascended as human beings and what foothills we must climb before we can all have what Abraham Maslow called "peak experiences." I have attempted here to continue the bold pioneering work of such people as Walt Whitman Rostow, Abraham Maslow, Karl Marx, and, before them all, Aristotle. I

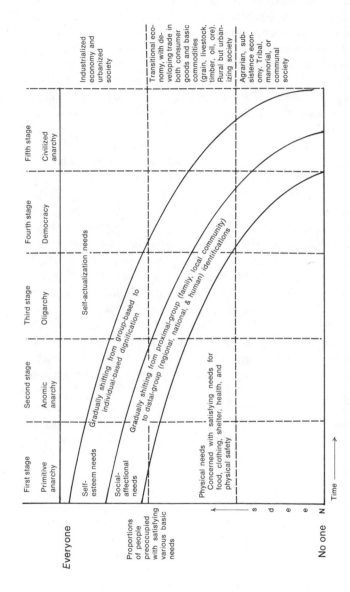

Figure 3. Stages of Political Development

The times that various peoples use to go through successive stages of (national) development are very variable, and so the time scale is not fixed or fixable. Only the *sequence* of stages is here regarded as invariable. I.e., it is not deemed possible for any people to avoid the disorder of transition from primitive anarchy to oligarchy; nor is it deemed possible for any people en route to civilized anarchy to avoid experiencing either capitalist elitism or its socialist alternative, the dictatorship of the proletariat's vanguard. It is also deemed impossible for capitalist or socialist oligarchy to outlive its utility for very long.

have tried to be more specific in mapping the stages—the plains and plateaus—that must be traversed on the way from here to utopia. All of these thinkers did indeed envision the good life, and they themselves lived it: they actualized themselves as human beings to a fantastic degree. But Rostow and Marx, I think, remained too preoccupied with the material bases—the plains— of the good life, while Maslow and Aristotle took these bases for granted as they climbed their own peaks.

We need not—and should not—bemoan or condemn the individual theoretical inadequacy of these bold men. Their elegant theoretical complementarity enables us to understand more clearly the *sequence* of steps toward the good society, with its provision of an opportunity for every person to scale the peaks of his/her individual actualization. But—the substance of their thought aside—neither the impatience nor the complacency of these or any other theorists—Thomas More and Peter Kropotkin, for instance—can help us. Indeed such hopes and moods—which is all that many critics see in such work—often impede progress toward closing the gap between the real and the ideal. Mental seven-league boots have never really turned out to be an efficient or even useful mode of transportation.

Unfortunately, perhaps all societies are as far from utopia as most critics say they are. And unfortunately no extant society has come very close to the utopia its advocates have predicted. Not even the most advanced society or polity has yet quite passed beyond the fourth stage, the democratic one, in which social integration and political participation gradually become universal. In no society that I know of are all citizens equal political participants. Even in such an advanced nation as Sweden, the Lapplanders remain largely outsiders, and people in lower skill and status positions still manifest much deference to those in higher skill and status positions. In any present society, any upper-middle-class individuals who presume that the opportunity for self-actualization is available to all, because it is available to them, live in a world apart. They are likely to be surprised and indignant when new groups, demanding not only food, social integration, social integration, and dignification but also the right to actualize themselves, show a readiness and determination to achieve their new demands. That is what underlay much of the unrest and violence in universities in Japan, the Soviet Union, the United States, and France in the 1950s and 1960s. In Japan, part of the cause was suffocating custom; in the Soviet Union, a suffocating political leadership that kept running by rote through the prayer-beads of Marxist-Leninist dogma; in France and the United States, a futile imperialism in the Indo-Chinese sub-Continent and a cloying materialism at home. In none of these nations were either the students or their opponents aware of the differences in their stages of development. In all these nations university students generally were more advanced than either their elders or the degraded groups with which they identified at home and abroad. Students were relatively comfortable economically and socially, enjoyed recognition, and were able to prepare themselves for fulfilling careers. And students understood elders and degraded no better than elders and degraded understood them. They were like the nineteenth-century nihilists in Russia, in their dedication and their innocence.

Some violence has occurred at the transition points from each stage of development to the next—less, it seems, after the initial gigantic first-stage wars between feudal and bourgeois segments that began in the sixteenth and continued into the twentieth century than in later-stage transitions. Some violence is likely to occur when not material needs but social identification, dignification, and self-actualization needs are involved, and when those who have reached one stage lack empathy with those who are at any earlier or later stage.

All people have the right and may gain the opportunity to become themselves fully, but they will never be able to do so without the prior and continuing means of satisfying the higher-priority—the more basic—innate needs. The demand for self-actualization is deep and universal: no less universal than the demands for dignity and for social integration that precede the emergence of the demand for self-actualization. If the natural origin of the demand is recognized, then perhaps mature, fulfilling people will not forget the sequential way in which they developed from infancy to maturity and will not deny the same step-by-step epigenesis to other individuals and other nations.

## NOTES AND REFERENCES

\* It has been no easy task to try to integrate the ideas joined together here. Preparing this latest but not final statement on the theoretical problems was much facilitated by the very substantial help of James W. Clarke, Robert S. Frank, Seymour Martin Lipset, Darien A. McWhirter III, J. Roland Pennock, and the participants in a panel of the Western Political Science Association in San Diego, California, on 5 April 1973.

1. George R. Stewart, *Ordeal by Hunger* (1936) (New York: Ace Books, 1960, ch. 16, "The Will to Live," esp. p. 123; Bernard de Voto, *The Year of Decision: 1846* (1942) (Boston: Little, Brown, 1943), p. 421.
2. Edward Crankshaw and Strobe Talbott, eds., *Khrushchev Remembers* (Boston: Little, Brown, 1970), pp. 234-235.
3. *Facts on File,* Sunday, 24 December to Sunday, 31 December 1972, p. 1073.
4. Aristotle, *Politics* I. i. 4–7, H. Rackham, transl. (Cambridge: Harvard University Press, 1932), pp. 5-7.
5. *Op. cit.,* p. 9. Rackham's translation of *politikon zoön* is the literal one, "political animal," but by this term Aristotle is deemed to mean that man is a member of the city community, including the political community. The Greek word *polis* did not distinguish the polity from the general society.
6. *Op. cit.,* p. 9, and Aristotle, Nicomachean Ethics I. ii. 7, H. Rackham, trans. 1926) (Cambridge: Harvard University Press, 1934), pp. 5-7.
7. Marx wrote this in his 1843 critique of Hegel's *Philosophy of Right.* Citation is to Robert C. Tucker, ed., *The Marx-Engels Reader* (New York: W. W. Norton, 1972), pp. 18-19.
8. Quoted from *The German Ideology* (1846). Citation is to Lewis W. Feuer, ed., *Marx and Engels: Basic Writings on Politics and Philosophy* (Garden City: Doubleday Anchor Books, 1959), pp. 249-250.
9. See William James, *The Principles of Psychology* (1890) (New York: Dover Publications, 1950), vol. 2, ch. 24, "Instinct." And for an extended discussion of the evolution of some politically relevant psychology, see J. C. Davies, "Where from and Where to?" ch. 1 of Jeanne N. Knutson, ed., *Handbook of Political Psychology* (San Francisco: Jossey-Bass, 1973), pp. 1-27.
10. See William McDougall, *An Introduction to Social Psychology* (1908) (Boston: John W. Luce, 1918), pp. 51-92.
11. See Henry Alexander Murray, *Explorations in Personality* (New York: Oxford University Press, 1938), pp. 77-83.
12. Abraham H. Maslow, "A Theory of Human Motivation," *Psychological Review,* 50 (1943), 370-396.
13. The full citations are: J. C. Davies, *The Political Implications of Psychoanalytic and Academic Psychology,* Ph.D. dissertation (Berkeley): University of California, 1952), pp. 123-124; and *Human Nature in Politics* (New York: John Wiley & Sons, 1963).
14. Christian Bay, *The Structure of Freedom* (1958) (New York: Athenem, 1965), pp. 11–12, 327–328; Robert E. Lane, *Political Life: Why People Get Involved in Politics* (Glencoe, Ill.: The Free Press, 1959), ch. 8, esp. pp. 102, 105-108; and Lane, *Political Thinking and Consciousness* (Chicago: Markham Publishing Co., 1969), pp. 26-27, 31-47.
15. In *Human Nature in Politics,* chs. 1 and 2.

16. Joel Aronoff, *Psychological Needs and Cultural Systems* (New York: Van Nostrand Reinhold Co., 1967), esp. ch. 4.

17. Harry F. Harlow and R. R. Zimmerman, "The Development of Affectional Responses in Infant Monkeys," *Proceedings of the American Philosophical Society,* 102 (1958), 501-509; H. F. and M. K. Harlow, "Social Deprivation in Monkeys," *Scientific American,* 207 (1962), 136-146; H. F. Harlow and S. J. Suomi, "Induced Psychopathology in Monekys," *Engineering and Science* (California Institute of Technology), 33 (April 1970), 8-14.

18. Jeanne N. Knutson, *The Human Basis of the Polity* (Chicago: Aldine-Atherton, 1972), esp. chs. 2 and 4, and pp. 204-206, 341, 342.

19. Ronald Inglehart, "The Silent Revolution in Europe: Intergenerational Change in Post-Industrial Societies," *American Political Science Review,* 65 (1971), 991-1017; and Inglehart, "Revolutionarisme Post-Bourgeois en France, en Allemagne et aux Etats-Unis," *Il Politico* (Università di Pavia, 36 (1971), 209-235.

20. Erik Erikson, *Childhood and Society* (1950) (New York: W. W. Norton & Co., 2d ed., 1963), Part 4, "Youth and the Evolution of Identity."

21. Robert Jay Lifton's *Thought Reform and the Psychology of Totalism* (New York: W. W. Norton & Co., 1961) is a sensitive and somber appraisal of the brainwashing process in China in the 1950s.

22. Gabriel Almond, *The Appeals of Communism* (Princeton: Princeton University Press, 1954).

23. In an article published a year before his 1943 need hierarchy theory, Maslow offered some comments on security that appear to me more consistent with my way of relating it to the substantive needs and less consistent with his placement of it after the physical needs in his hierarchy. In this earlier article he sees the security feelings as "a general flavor that can be detected or savored in practically everything that a person does, feels, or thinks." In summary, Maslow says that secure people are generally optimistic, calm, outgoing, cooperative, sympathetic, and generally feel their own capacity to solve problems. He does not touch upon the theoretical problem of showing how, if security is the second need in the hierarchy, a person could be secure or insecure about such things as love, self-esteem, and self-actualization. See Maslow, "The Dynamics of Psychological Security-Insecurity," *Character and Personality,* 10 (1942), 331-344. As S. M. Lipset noted in a personal communication, people in Sweden who are in the professions show evidences of tension with respect to their careers. Neither Lipset nor I would claim that the phenomenon is limited to Sweden. Professional people everywhere are actualizing themselves probably more fully than those whose occupation is routine tending of machines. This frees them from some insecurities but not from insecurity.

24. Kinship is evident between the following briefly outlined stages of political development and Walt Whitman Rostow's stages of economic growth. Two basic differences between the two schemata, as I see them, are these: first, Rostow's have a heavy economic emphasis and a coherent but not very systematic psychological foundation; mine offer a superficial economic analysis and a systematic psychological foundation. Second, I make a more specific statement of political structures (primitive anarchic, anomic anarchic, oligarchic, democratic, and civilized anarchic).

It is difficult to criticize Rostow's approach to the growth problem radically without denying the phenomenon of growth, economic and otherwise, or without picking nits. His analysis of the preconditions and the economic takeoff points makes enduring theoretical sense. See his *Stages of Economic Growth* (Cambridge, England: The University Press, 1960), ch. 3.

However (and I hope this is not picking an interpretive nit), I would place the takeoff point for France at about the beginning of the eighteenth century rather than in the middle of the nineteenth (cf. Rostow, *op. cit.,* ch. 4, esp. p. 38). My argument depends partly on the criterion of increased agricultural productivity and population and partly on the "glorious" consequence of French political unification under autocratic rule, during and after the reign (1643-1715) of Louis XIV. During most of the eighteenth century France was able to sustain a succession of largely colonial wars overseas, against England. By the theory I have advanced here, France was well into its third stage of political development in that century. The relation of the basic phenomena of population growth and health to the infrastructure for aggressive war needs to be emphasized. The French economic historian Labrousse notes a decline in the death rate and a rise in the total population, starting in the eigtheenth century. See C. E. Labrousse, "The Crisis in the French Economy at the End of the Old Régime" (1943), R. W. Greenlaw, transl., in R. W. Greenlaw, ed., *The Economic Origins of the French Revolution* (New York: D. C. Heath & Co., 1958), pp. 59-72, at pp. 62-63. Here are some very approximate figures on French population growth:

| Time | Population (in millions) | Percentage growth over prior century |
|------|------|------|
| 15th century | 16 | — |
| 1700 | 19 | (19% over a 200- to 300-year period) |
| 1750 | 24 | — |
| 1800 | 27 | 42 |
| 1900 | 39 | 44 |

From: R. R. Palmer, ed., *Atlas of World History* (New York: Rand McNally & Co., 1957, p. 193).

25. See Thucydides, *The Peloponnesian War,* R. Crawley, trans., 1874 (New York: Modern Library, 1934, esp. pp. 3–15.
26. Stanley M. Elkins, *Slavery* (1959) (Chicago: University of Chicago Press, 2d. ed., 1968).
27. C. U. Smith and J. W. Prothro, "Ethnic Differences in Authoritarian Personality," *Social Forces,* 35 (1957), 334-338.
28. Seymour Martin Lipset, *Political Man* (Garden City, N.Y.: Doubleday & Co., 1960), ch. 4, "Working-class Authoritarianism," presents an argument and data that are highly consistent with my general argument about the third (oligarchic) and fourth (democratic) states of political development.
29. See Elie A. Cohen, *Human Behavior in the Concentration Camp* (New York: W. W. Norton & Co., 1953), which formed much of the basis for Stanley Elkins's analysis of the traumatic impact of enslavement. On concentration camp revolts and disturbances, see Jean-François Steiner, *Treblinka* (London: Weidenfeld & Nicolson, 1967), esp. chs. 13-17; and Eugen Kogon, *The Theory and Practice of Hell* (1950) (New York: Berkeley Publishing Corp., paperback, n.d.), ch. 20, "The Underground Struggle."

30. Alexander Leighton, *The Governing of Men* (Princeton: Priceton University Press, 1945) is based on the author's experiences during the formation of a community among the Japanese interned in the Poston, Arizona, camp. A little rebellion that broke out in another camp, at Manzanar, California, is analyzed in George Wada and J. C. Davies, "Riots and Rioters," *Western Political Quarterly* 10 (1967), 864-874. The conclusion was that the rioters were marginally caught between the land of their parents and the land of their own birth. For a general analysis of these camps, see Dorothy S. Thomas and Richard S. Nishimoto, *The Spoilage* (Berkeley and Los Angeles: University of California Press, 1946).

31. Barrington Moore, Jr., in his *Social Origins of Dictatorship and Democracy* (Boston: Beacon Press, 1966), pp. 17-20, emphasizes that it was large capitalist farmers and urban bourgeoisie who united against the government, as the Puritan Revolution approached.

32. The general theory of the gap between expectations and gratifications as it tends to produce revolution and rebellion is contained in J. C. Davies, "Toward a Theory of Revolution," *American Sociological Review*, 6 (1962), 5-19. See also Davies, "The J-Curve of Rising and Declining Satisfactions as a Cause of Some Great Revolutions and a Contained Rebellion," in H. D. Graham and T. R. Gurr, eds., *The History of Violence in America* (New York: Bantam Books, 1969), pp. 690-730, where the theory is somewhat more precisely stated.

# HUMAN NATURE
# AND RADICAL
# POLITICAL THOUGHT

Davies's chapter at the close of the preceding Part constitutes a fitting transition to Part II, in which three authors all deal, in various ways, with the place of human nature in radical thought. Donald Keim leads off with a discussion of the theory of human nature evidenced by the counterculture. He discusses the "new man" of the counterculture in terms of each of its elements (as he analyzed it): personalism, potentialities, fluidity, creativity, and phenomenal experience. After a discussion far richer than any summary can suggest, he concludes that the counterculture's conception of human nature is riven with contradictions. In this respect, one might add, it may be true to the reality of human nature; but at the same time, as Keim argues, it may fail of its visionary objective.

197

Marvin Zetterbaum, like Keim, examines the problem of protean man. Not claiming to have succeeded in the search for human nature, he nonetheless holds that "our overwhelming sense of the transhistorical identity of man" attests that history is more than "some ultimate 'we know not what' of human nature." The search must go on.

Sargent finds seven different theories of human nature that have been held by various radical political theorists. After considering them, in turn, he concludes that each is too simple for the facts and that the good society will probably be "much more diverse and complex than we have tended to think of it because the interactions of heredity, socialization, and environment will continue to produce people with widely diverse needs and desires."

# 7

## "TO MAKE ALL THINGS NEW"—
## THE COUNTERCULTURE
## VISION OF MAN AND POLITICS

DONALD W. KEIM

As a decade of social unrest reached a crescendo with Cambodia and Kent State bookracks trumpeted a dust-jacket prophecy of revolution.

> There is a revolution coming. It will not be like revolutions of the past. It will originate with the individual and with culture, and it will change the political structure only as its final act.[1]

This transformation will go beyond anything in modern history; "beside it, a mere revolution such as the French or the Russian, [will seem] inconsequential."[2] For "what is coming is nothing less than a new way of life and a new man."[3]

The years since have clouded the prophetic vision but the dream of making all things new remains alive behind disillusioned eyes. The present moment thus seems propitious for a closer look at the "new man" so recently proclaimed.

Actually several species of "new man" appeared during the 1960s. This essay is concerned with the version produced by the counterculture. Because distinctions among the counterculture, New Left, youth, students, hippies, and so forth often become matters of controversy, a brief definition may be helpful. By counterculture I refer to the radical critique of technological society that rejects structural explanations and solutions and instead identifies society's problems and their resolution in terms of self, consciousness, and culture or worldview. In other words, the counterculture is distinguished precisely by its vision of "a new way of life and a new man."

Rather than casting about in the more ephemeral materials of the counterculture, I concentrate upon the works of a few well-known spokesmen.

I do so because my purpose is not to represent the full dimensions of the counterculture but to examine critically the underlying conception of human nature that informs the counterculture vision. I am interested in the kind of "new man" envisaged and in the kind of politics such a being would be likely to undertake. Along the way I shall try to assess the basic presuppositions the counterculture brings to its project of "making all things new."

## THE NEW MAN

The "new man" of the counterculture may be described in many ways. I wish to emphasize five elements—personalism, potentiality, fluidity, creativity, and phenomenal experience—each of which adds something distinctive to his character.

1. *Personalism*.[4] The counterculture gives pride of place to the individual. Despite the attention lavished on community, few contemporary movements have been so militantly individualist. Charles Reich gives clear expression to this point when he declares that "the individual self is the only true reality" and that the first commandment of the "new man" is "be true to oneself."[5] Each individual is unique and possessed of singular merit and therefore ought not to be judged, evaluated, or compared according to uni-

versal criteria.[6] Moreover, since the self alone is real and able to create authentic values, the individual must be treated as an end, never as a means. "It is a crime to allow oneself to become an instrumental being, a projectile designed to accomplish some extrinsic end, a part of an organization or machine." [7]

2. *Potentialities.* "Men have unrealized potential for self-cultivation, self-direction, self-understanding, and creativity"—so professed the authors of the 1962 *Port Huron Statement.*[8] Their optimism resounds through the writings of the counterculture. The possibilities before man, his potential for a full, rich, and meaningful life, mark the present age as one of extraordinary promise.

The converse is, of course, a sense of betrayal engendered by society's failure to realize man's potential. Man's life has been flattened into a one-dimensional existence. The materialism of the consumer is mirrored by the instrumentalism of the producer. Reason is reduced to a linear calculation of efficient means. Sensitivities are deadened and the creative impulse is either prostituted on Madison Avenue or relegated to the oblivion of the "coffee table" and bookstore sales of "publishers' remainders."

The potentialities of man, notable for their lack of fulfillment, take on a variety of meanings. To some members of the counterculture they are the spiritual forces that lie buried beneath the reductive rationality of technological man. Resurrected, these energies could carry man beyond the plane of objective consciousness into alternative realities long deserted save for the occasional mystic or poet.[9] To others the potentialities are seen as human faculties that are underdeveloped or even atrophied from disuse. In the new society men will have the opportunity to develop their faculties and become full human beings.[10]

Regardless of form, the potentialities of men provide a focal point for the counterculture's indictment of technological society and for its vision of the new Adam.

3. *Fluidity.* No longer obliged by scarcity to occupy a slot in the program of production, man is able to contemplate a style of life that expresses a broader range of possibilities for self-realization. This opportunity has been grasped by many individuals who have thereby adopted a life-style which is distinguished by fluidity and experimentation. Youth, the segment of society most actively engaged in this project, has come to be regarded by many as harbingers of the "new man."

In addition to the promise of material abundance, a number of other developments have helped to generate the fluid self identified with today's youth. According to Robert Lifton, the rapidity of change, together with the spread of mass communications and the threat of nuclear annihilation have disrupted man's sense of the continuity of life.[11] This disruption, which he terms "psychohistorical dislocation," is seen in the fading efficacy of traditional symbolic media of immortalization such as nature, religion, and art.[12] Though this condition is not unique to the present age, the problem has been exacerbated by historical events. The consequence is the emergence of a new style of "self-process."

> What this means is that more and more people are experiencing certain psychological processes in common, and that these, generally speaking, involve changing self-definition, or at least blurring of perceptions of where self begins and ends.[13]

The result is Protean Man, whose "self-process"[14] is "characterized by an interminable series of experiments and explorations—some shallow, some profound—each of which may be readily abandoned in favor of still new psychological quests."[15] This new self displays an openendedness and a fluidity that are cultivated through introspection and conscious experimentation.

4. *Creativity.* The fluid self is achieved through the deliberate manipulation of experience. Gone are the last vestiges of the spirit of resignation in the face of unfathomable purpose. Man is the creator of his own "self-process." In the words of Roszak, "The task of life is to take this raw material of [one's] total experience—[the] need for knowledge, for passion, for imaginative exuberance, for moral purity, for fellowship—and to shape it *all,* as laboriously and as cunningly as a sculptor shapes his stone, into a comprehensive style of life."[16]

Man's identity as creative being has been submerged in recent decades by complex organizations and behavioral psychology. But the future holds the promise of regaining man's creative nature. "Man once more can become a creative force, renewing and creating his own life and thus giving life back to his society."[17]

5. *Phenomenal Experience.* Man is a sensate animal before he is an intellectual being. Given the programmed, plastic quality of technological society, experience keeps the self alive and open. It becomes "the most precious of all commodities."[18] "All experi-

ence has value, all of it has something to teach, none of it is rejected because it fails to accord with some pre-existing scheme of things."[19] From the fragments of phenomenal experience man self-consciously builds his new self. Experience also serves to revitalize deadened senses, thus expanding consciousness.

These tasks require the direct absorption of experience. Immediate phenomenal experience is regarded as somehow "truer," more authentic, and therefore more expressive of self, than mediated experience. Hence young people eschew traditional education and puritan renunciation and are instead writing poetry and hitchhiking through Europe at an age when their elders were reading novels and viewing travelogues.

## DUAL SELVES

Thus far we have drawn the "new man" as a single, composite figure. Yet when one begins to scrutinize the writings of the counterculture, this figure begins to divide in two. It is as if the counterculture had produced its vision with two different optical instruments: a microscope to discover the natural man trapped beneath the layers of technological society and a telescope to define the contours of the "new heaven and new earth." The strain created in using these two instruments has generated a radical discontinuity in the counterculture vision. Indeed, as we shall see, it has virtually sundered the "new man," producing two distinct notions of man.

The dual selves of the counter culture are reflections of a schism in radical political thought between the critical and visionary evaluations of human nature. As social critics, radicals often assail society for its stultifying effects upon men. Society prevents them from fulfilling their full human potential. Instead, a "second nature" is imposed to ensure the efficient and productive functioning of society. As visionaries, however, radicals conceive men in a different light. They have the capacity to make qualitative changes, not only in their condition but in their very nature. Massive social change may be required, but this task also lies within men's power, given an adequate understanding of society's mainsprings.

In this essay I will consider the counterculture's vision in terms of these two models of man—the critical model: "man fulfilled" and the visionary model: "man transformed." In general these two models coincide with the critical and visionary components of counterculture thought. But the schism which has led to the dual focus also generates tensions within both components, thereby dissolving simplistic classifications. Ultimately we will also ask whether either model is adequate to the task of describing man's nature.


## THE CRITICAL MODEL: "MAN FULFILLED"

Throughout the writings under consideration man is portrayed as alienated, manipulated, and reprogrammed by society. Man's hope is to break out of this straitjacket and rid himself of the pernicious ideas and oppressive institutions that prevent him from becoming the autonomous, integrated, fulfilled human being he could be. The message is clear: man's psychological and moral growth has been stunted by technological society. But the hope remains that through revolutionary change the obstacles to self-fulfillment can be removed and man will be able to realize the promise of his human nature.

The counterculture hs shown no hesitancy in criticizing the unsavory features of society. Alienation, conformity, exploitation, inequality, invasions of privacy, bureaucracy, domination—all receive extensive comment. Characteristically these concerns are viewed not as isolated problems amenable to reform but as expressions of a deeper malaise. This affliction Reich has diagnosed as the "loss of self."

> Of all the forms of impoverishment that can be seen or felt in America, loss of self, or death in life, is surely the most devastating. Beginning with school, if not before, an individual is systematically stripped of his imagination, his creativity, his heritage, his dreams, and his personal uniqueness, in order to style him into a productive unit for a mass, technological society. Instinct, feeling, and spontaneity are repressed by overwhelming forces. As the individual is drawn into the meritocracy, his working life is split from his home life, and both suffer from a lack of wholeness. Eventually, people virtually become their professions, roles, or occupations and are thenceforth strangers to themselves.[20]

The phrase "loss of self" misleads somewhat because the problem is not precisely the elimination of the self but its evacuation.

A shell remains which is filled by a "substitute self."[21] This is clearly signified by the terminology employed which indicates a process that surpasses garden-variety socialization. The "natural" self is suppressed and a surrogate is manufactured to the specifications of technological society. The individual is absorbed by society.

The process operates in two ways. First, men become dependent upon social roles and artifacts for their sense of self (identity). As Reich develops the argument in several discussions of social "role-playing," individuals have become their occupations and they have molded their identities in relation to society's products.[22] The television image of the young couple sipping Mateus in a ski lodge becomes, not a measure of success or the good life, but a fragment of one's self. One goes skiing and drinks Mateus not for the pleasures they afford but to live that image.

The second, and more subtle, occurrence derives from the ascendancy of what Roszak calls "single vision."[23] Science and its great monument, urban-industrial society, have narrowed men's sensibilities to the point where men have lost the capacity to envisage alternatives to the prevailing technocratic order. Pragmatic rationality has turned men into instrumental beings. Nature is regarded as raw material. Life oscillates between production and consumption while happiness is measured in mounds of material possessions. "Single vision has become the boundary condition of human consciousness within urban-industrial culture, the reigning Reality Principle, the whole meaning of sanity."[24] Once again the result is man's identification with the prevailing social order.

The critical attempt to explain the "loss of self" and the formation of the "substitute self" takes the form of an explanatory theory that boils down to the claim that man's nature is molded by the prevailing sociohistorical forces. Theories of this type have, of course, been widespread since the early nineteenth century. Maurice Mandelbaum, in a recent study of these and related theories of human nature, has referred to this view as "organiscism,"[25] which he defines as "the doctrine that human thought and action are invariably dependent upon the forms of organization of social institutions."[26] The contemporary exposition of the "loss of self" reflects the main tenets of organicism as they emerged in the early nineteenth century.

Experience was claimed to play a dominant role in *all* aspects

of thought and of action, and it was widely claimed that, in the
course of his experience, an individual acquires wholly new capacities which become, quite literally, a second nature to him.
They are to be viewed as a second nature because they become
so deeply ingrained in him that they are experienced as wholly
natural, as being an essential part of his nature.[27]

The same perspective is maintained in the account given of the creation of the "substitute self."

The counterculture explains this social dependency in terms of
the relationship between world view, consciousness, and the self.
Sociohistorical forces are manifested in the prevailing world view,
which in turn shapes man's conception of self. As Roszak explains
it, the world view is nothing we learn in a conscious way. "It is,
rather, something we absorb from the spirit of the times or are
converted into, or seduced into by unaccountable experiences."[28]
By shaping consciousness, the prevailing world view defines the
boundaries of reality in a particular period and thus circumscribes
what one conceives to be "normal" life.

> But what is more important about consciousness is that which
> remains unconscious at the core of the mind, subliminally shap-
> ing our powers of perception and intellection, screening, filter-
> ing, censoring without making its presence known. This is the
> level at which society most decisively governs the psyche. . . .
> Unless we realize, at least dimly, what portions of our personal-
> ity lie buried, forgotten, perhaps ruined in this submerged quar-
> ter of the mind, there is no chance of challenging official re-
> ality.[29]

A full discussion of this matter would have to recount the complex processes involved, since they constitute a distinctive contribution to radical theory. However, we are concerned here with the
broader implications of this thesis of social dependency.

Organicism contains an obvious discontinuity between its explanatory and normative premises. The explanatory theory propounds the historicity[30] of human nature. The self is a product of
sociohistorical forces; therefore it is both temporally variable and
substantively malleable, perhaps even fluid. Yet this explanatory
theory is fused with a normative theory that indicts society for its

failure to provide the conditions necessary for the fulfillment of man's nature. To sustain the latter, *critical,* viewpoint, the counterculture must postulate a "potential" or "natural" self that has not been realized. But to postulate a "potential self" appears to contradict the historicity of human nature, which, if it means anything, must signify the absence of constant traits that distinguish human beings as possessors of a unique nature.

The source of difficulty, both logically and historically, is the *axiom of authenticity.* By this I mean the assumption that the individual possesses a "natural" or "true" self that has been obscured by artificial societal accretions. Invariably such imagery conveys a connotation of "depth": the deeper one goes, the closer one approaches the "true self" which has been enveloped by layers of artificiality which must be peeled away like an onion.

The axiom of authenticity provides the basis for the indictment of technological society. In the words of the *Port Huron Statement,*

The goal of man and society should be human independence: a concern not with the image of popularity but with finding a meaning in life that is personally authentic . . .[31]

The critical images invoked invariably contrast the authentic with the artificial, the unique self with a standardized social role. Solutions to society's problems also follow this path: remove the (external or internal) impediments to the actualization, realization, or fulfillment of the authentic self.

This is not the place to discuss the origins and sustaining power of the axiom of authenticity. Such a discussion would require a review of centuries of Western thought and symbolizations.[32] However, it is necessary to assess briefly the compatibility of this axiom with the concomitant explanatory theory.

To find solid ground for a reconciliation of the authentic self and the historicity of human nature is difficult. The problem derives from the strong implication contained in the explanatory theory that human nature is infinitely malleable. Of course, if the malleability thesis is taken in a weak sense to mean that changes in culture and society that generate new experiences will bring about changes in attitudes, ideas, and behavior, then there is no formal contradiction. But this weak sense hardly characterizes the thrust of the counterculture's critique. If on the other hand malleability is taken in the strong sense to mean that there are no constant attributes or features of human nature (excepting those biological or other elements associated with men as a "class"), then a deep fissure appears. And unless the authentic self is interpreted in a completely formal sense, without substance, (i.e., as pertaining to the "class" of men), or, alternatively, in the Romantic sense as idiosyncratic to each individual, then there must be specific attributes or constants that are potentially present but are systematically thwarted by social forces. Otherwise authenticity would be a vacuous notion and the grounds for criticism would have disappeared.

This problem has long plagued radical theorists. The most familiar solution is, of course, Marx's. Though the nature of man will always reflect the prevailing productive forces and attendant social relations, man's opportunity to make the most of his potential can be evaluated for any given period. The core of the argument was recently summarized by Lobkowicz when he wrote:

> [Marx believed] that it is possible to measure man's present existence by a potentiality revealed by this existence itself. For alienation is something like a negated *ought* embodied in facts, a kind of existence which reveals an ideal to be pursued and which, precisely in light of this ideal, appears as denying man his ultimate completion.[33]

Thus without postulating a transhistorical essence, indeed while recognizing man's so-called nature as simply the sum of the productive forces and social relations at a specific stage of history, the gap between promise and performance can be measured within a historical period.[34]

Whether this overcomes all difficulties is a question long debated.[35] The purpose of mentioning Marx's answer is not to recommend it but to note the longevity of the problem for radical thought. Although our authors have been preoccupied with issues of consciousness, little effort has been made to address the problem in their writings—a commentary no doubt on the degree of theoretical sophistication displayed.

They share with Marx another problem central to the malleability thesis. The qualitative transformation of man is accomplished by molding experiential fragments into a new self. The "new man" thus generated transcends the capacities of technological man. He has overcome the barriers to self-realization that have restraind him previously. He has acquired a new nature.

Now, if men are the products of their age, how can one account for their sudden acquisition of the ability to bring about such a transformation? One familiar answer is "objective conditions." The counterculturists do assert that the present social "crisis" has abruptly wakened men in some fashion to their true condition.[36] But they do not rely upon the inevitability of revolution to carry the burden of human transformation. Indeed, they are precluded from doing so by their perception of the problem characteristic of technological society: the absence of revolutionary changes in the face of propitious social conditions.[37] Rather, they proclaim that man possesses the power to reorient himself—to alter his life and thereby to change society.[38] The presence of this power is precisely what the counterculture movement is understood to represent. Man has the capacity to transform himself!

Yet, the capacity for self-transformation must be possessed without regard to historical period, i.e., it must be part of an essential nature—a constant element—if the counterculturists expect men to realize qualitative transformation. Without this presupposition they would have to rely upon the *automata* of history to fulfill their vision.[39]

In its brief life the counterculture has recapitulated most of the theoretical problems of radical thought. Explanation of the persistence of the prevailing order is purchased with high-risk capital. To prevent a collapse into historicism the counterculture must buttress its social theory with the axiom of authenticity. In the critical model of man authenticity is expressed in terms of potentialities. Social impediments have blocked the fulfillment of man's potentialities and, therefore, the achievement of an authentic life.

In the end the axiom of authenticity is a dubious aid. It runs counter to the historicity of human nature contained in the explanatory theory of social dependency. At the same time it drains the self of all substance, leaving only a receptacle for the deposit of one's favorite prejudices as authenticity becomes the warrant for "doing one's own thing."

The other aspect of the explanatory theory imposes an equal burden. To retain the malleability thesis the authors must either vitiate the critical argument or rely upon the familiar *deus ex machina* of radical thought—"true" consciousness—to animate the transformation process.

The discontinuities we have thus far traced are, of course, familiar aspects of radical thought. That contemporary thinkers have not overcome these problems is not surprising. It is useful nonetheless to recall the relationship between the counterculture and the radical tradition in light of breathless assurances that the counterculture signals a breakthrough in the transformation of the human condition.

With these remarks we have passed from critical theory to a vision of "man transformed." We must now take a more careful look at this vision.

## THE VISIONARY MODEL: "MAN TRANSFORMED"

The visionary model of man does not suffer the tensions that mark the critical model. Instead one is confronted with a straightforward expression of messianic humanism, i.e., "that strand of political thought which seeks to transform the quality of man's existence, to transcend the limitations and inequities of the human historical situation as it has hitherto been experienced and make a fundamentally new beginning." [40] This qualitative change in existence (*metastasis*) entails "the establishment of a new world populated by new men—with 'new' in both instances being taken to mean a condition qualitatively different from that which preceded it." [41] Beyond asserting that the counterculture, like virtually all radical thought of the past two centuries, is an expression of messianic humanism, I shall not refine the notion further at this point. [42]

Rather I wish to emphasize the paramount significance of qualitative transformation for the visionary model. This notion contrasts sharply with the conception of self-fulfillment that provides the core of the critical model. Notwithstanding the importance of self-fulfillment in providing a critical account of society's betrayal, it is the transformatory vision that provides the counterculture with its distinctive character. The metastatic vision of "man transformed," a judicious blending of extrapolations from emerging life styles with long-familiar millennarian speculations on the "new man," distinguishes the counterculture from the other sections of contemporary radicalism. The former propounds a change of consciousness while the latter seek to change the structure of society through seizure of, or accession to, political and/or economic power. This distinction is evidenced in Reich's remark that "the great error of our times has been the belief in structural or institutional solutions."[43] In fact, "the enemy is within each of us," in our warped and stunted consciousness.[44] Transformation thus demands a change of conciousness.[45]

The emphasis on transformation is a clear effort to draw free of the determinism bequeathed by "organicism" and, more generally, by the tradition of social dependency. Men *can* transcend their condition by a change in consciousness. This change is within the power of men to perform.

The resulting tension between transformation and social dependency is obvious; it will be examined in greater detail below. For the moment, however, it is important that the nature of the transformation process be clearly understood.

### THE TRANSFORMATION PROCESS

Transcendence is a key term for unpacking the meaning assigned to the transformation process. In *The Greening of America,* for instance, Reich tells us that "the foundation of Consciousness III is liberation. It comes into being the moment the individual frees himself from automatic acceptance of the imperatives of society and the false consciousness which society imposes."[46] Further on he amplifies this by pointing out that "the central fact about Consciousness III" is summed up in "the power to choose a way of life."[47]

> The power of choice, the power to transcend, is exactly what has been missing in America for so long. That is why a new life-style is capable of dismantling the Corporate State. . . . The elements of that life may vary and change; the supreme act is the act of choice. For the choice of a life-style is an act of transcendence of the machine, an act of independence, a declaration of independence. We are entering a new age of man.[48]

The power to choose is the power to transcend; transcendence is achieved by choosing a life style rather than accepting the patterns imposed by society.[49]

Choosing a life style is also an assertion of independence—mastery of one's life—autonomy. Man has been deprived of that mastery; he has become the servant of the machine, and of the social structure erected to serve it. Transformation requires the reacquisition of control over these artifacts. Transcendence means liberation which in turn means autonomy. In the words of Reich, "The meaning of liberation is that the individual is free to build his own philosophy and values, his life style, and his own culture from a new beginning." [50]

Transcendence on this reading involves dismantling the cages of self. The autonomy sought is universal: autonomy vis-à-vis other individuals in the long tradition of self-determination, but also autonomy vis-à-vis the "reality" that surrounds the self. This becomes evident when one considers what "choosing a life style" entails.

As Lifton argues, the adoption of a life style involves the stitching together of experiential fragments with the thread of self-conscious experimentation. Each new experience becomes a dynamic bond between outer and inner worlds. Traditional boundaries between private and public life are pulled down; the self becomes creative process; and dislocation is transcended through deliberately expanded and heightened experience. [51]

The stance of the counterculture with respect to experience is brought sharply into focus at this point. Despite the professions of openness, the counterculture seeks to dominate experience, to manipulate it, rather than to draw sustenance from it. As Roszak insists, "the task of life is to take this raw material of his total experience—[the] need for knowledge, for passion, for imaginative exuberance, for moral purity, for fellowship—and shape it *all,* as laboriously and as cunningly as a sculptor shapes his stone, into a comprehensive style of life." [52] The effect is to mold the fragments of experience into a new, protean self. In so doing, the individual achieves a measure of autonomy otherwise lacking. Furthermore, to insure this autonomy, the individual must impress his own pattern on experience, lest it encapsulate him once again. He must, that is, construct a new reality that mirrors his new, autonomous self. Protean man becomes Prometheus. [53]

## THE RECONSTRUCTION OF REALITY

The vision of qualitative transformation becomes the promethean reconstruction of reality. This is the conclusion one must necessarily draw from the account of the transformation process. That this conclusion would be steadfastly denied by defenders of the counterculture hardly needs to be added. Yet it is implicit in the assumptions they bring to the discussion.

The construction of a "second reality," a reality created by man in accordance with his infinite will, is the inevitable consequence of the underlying conceptions of human nature embraced by the counterculture. Its distinctive form is received from the interplay of the normative (critical) and explanatory (social dependency) theories, as can be seen if we examine three elements of the new life style: autonomy, creativity, and phenomenal experience.

The preoccupation with autonomy is dictated by the critical model of human nature. The specific form by which autonomy is expressed—control over the ideas and artifacts that constitute social reality—is inspired by the axiom of authenticity, which posits a "natural" self anterior to society's accretions.

The motive force for qualitative transformation is provided by the creative impulse. Creativity is the essence of "natural" man. This assumption the counterculture obviously shares with a long list of radicals, including Marx. The results are also the same: the self is conceived as a process of autogenesis; reality likewise is created by man.[54]

Phenomenal experience is the medium for transformation. The equation of experience with social phenomena is derived from the presuppositions of the social dependency thesis. The "second nature" of man is produced by the impress of technological rationality and social artifacts upon the plastic substance of human nature. Thus, man, whose nature is a product of sociohistorical forces, must enlist social dependency in the service of self-fulfillment. He must shape his world out of phenomenal experience in order to create the conditions for the realization of his authentic self.

When autonomy, creativity, and experience are collapsed into a transforming life style, then to adopt a new life style expresses more than rebellion against social conventions or the search for autonomy. It is nothing less than an effort to transcend man's "second nature" through the creation of a "second reality."

Many persons otherwise sympathetic to the counterculture have expressed concern over the implications of this conception of transcendence. For example, Lifton detected in some contemporary youth an attempt to overcome the dislocations of everyday life by replacing the "discontinuity of history" with the flow of experience. "Romantic totalism," as Lifton terms this effort to achieve "experiential transcendence," may lead to the confusion between mind and its material products typical of China's "Great Proletarian Cultural Revolution." There attempts were made to control the external world and achieve technological goals through mental exercises and assertions of revolutionary will.[55] More commonly, "romantic totalism" involves the effort to evade what Camus described as modern man's surrender to history by "replacing history with experience."[56] It takes the form of "a stress upon . . . experiential transcendence, upon the cultivation of states of feeling so intense and absorbing that time and death cease to exist."[57] The pitfall has become familiar: to reinforce these feelings one is tempted to victimize intransigent obstacles, whether people or things.[58]

Roszak is another writer who, though generally sympathetic to the counterculture, has been disturbed by certain tendencies within the movement. In particular he has criticized the identification of authenticity with spontaneity. Flinging themselves into an assortment of "mad passions," many young people "allow their understanding to stop at the level of surface conduct . . ."[59] In this preoccupation with the surface of experiences they reflect the shallowness of the world that surrounds them.

Experience, Roszak would say, has a "deeper" mode. It is something "felt": a resonance within man, in a nonintellective sensorium, which penetrates to "root meanings."[60] Alternatively, this may be expressed as the openness of the self to "root meanings." Seen as such, experience in its depth dimension becomes the path to transcendence. The opening of the soul to the transcendental dimension of existence is Roszak's prescription for the narrow, one-dimensionality of life in urban-industrial society. "The orthodox consciousness in which most of us reside most of the time . . . is very cramped quarters, by no means various and spacious enough to let us grow to full human size."[61]

Roszak's work is something of an anomaly. Much of it points beyond the metastatic vision we have been discussing. In his endeavor to resurrect those portions of the psyche that have been buried by the scientific world view he has sought to recover the sense of life as multidimensional existence—a life that participates in multiple realities.

To discuss the full scope of Roszak's argument would, however, carry us beyond the scope of this essay. For despite his status as a spokesman for the counterculture, the thrust of his argument points in a direction few are prepared to follow. For most, the transformatory vision is tightly bound up with what we have called personalism. They see it as an effort to go beyond social convention; to realize one's potential as an autonomous and self-sufficient being; to move from alienation to authenticity; in other words, to realize the vision of qualitative change in man and his world.

Nevertheless, we cannot leave Roszak without commenting briefly on his position. His professed aim is to revitalize man's multileveled consciousness—to regain insight into hidden truths of nature and religion which have been lost to the "single vision" of science. He denies that his examples of Romanticism, mysticism, and the Old Gnosis are meant to be anything more than evidence of multiple realities. They are not intended, he says, as specific prescriptions.[62] Notwithstanding this fact, it is difficult to square his professions with the overall impression conveyed by his writings. He makes a plausible case for the multidimensionality of existence. Yet one is ultimately driven to the conclusion that he is advancing a species of millennarian gnosticism when he insists that the road to the New Jerusalem demands total conversion to the "magical vision of life" in which is revealed a deeper, truer reality.[63] In place of the multiple realities he professes to seek, one uncovers a version of classic gnosticism complete with hermetic knowledge and Third Realm symbolisms.

Although Roszak's thought is atypical, it does suggest the problems posed by the counterculture's notion of transcendence. It also illustrates the ease with which the tensions generated by the dual selves can push a theorist into positions he might otherwise wish to avoid!

With these examples in mind, the dual conception of human nature can be placed in a broader context.

## THE RADICAL HERITAGE

Throughout this essay we have remarked upon the discontinuities that are present in the thinking of the counterculture, in particular the dual selves and their divergent presuppositions. It is now clear that the dualisms are reflections of the long-lived tensions within radical thought between promethean and social determinist elements. The prospect of self-fulfillment clashes with a reductionist psychology that views man as a function of society, history, or economic forces. Thus, the critical vision is buffeted between a sociohistorical account of man's alienated condition and a critique couched in intensely personalistic terms. Similarly, the transformatory vision seeks to turn social determinacy to use as a mechanism for the realization of an authentic self. To accomplish this task the passive, plastic victim of social dependency must discover the remarkable capacity to generate a new self through the manipulation of the social environment.

It is hardly surprising that the resulting conception of human nature is riven with contradictions. Man is both passive and creative. He strives for self-fulfillment yet he remains malleable and without a fixed nature. The tensions generated by these conflicting presuppositions doubtless contribute to the internecine conflicts that beset radical movements periodically. Nonetheless, new versions continue to appear, as the counterculture attests.

This vitality of radical thought stems in no small measure from the presumption of human "perfectibility."[64] Within the transformatory vision, the conflicting aspects of the dual selves have been fused together into a composite model that utilizes the notions of "natural" self, malleability, and promethean autogenesis to create the image of an authentic man who will come into existence "after the revolution."

Because the radical vision of human "perfectibility" shares many elements with the liberal notion of "improvement" the contradictory implications of radical "perfectibility" have often gone unnoticed.[65] However, one element has provided a consistent differentia between radical and liberal thought: the promethean urge.


## THE LABOR OF PROMETHEUS

Two aspects comprise this urge—man conceived as *homo faber,* and a mechanical conception of transformation.

Earlier I alluded to the programmatic consequences of prometheanism when defining messianic humanism. Here I am concerned with showing how this radical element has led the counterculture to repudiate its own vision of human "perfectibility."

The difficulties commence with the conception of man as a creative being. Creativity may take many forms of expression. For the counterculture, as with most radical thought, it is expressed through a material medium. Man is *homo faber*. The scope of creative activity is circumscribed by the horizon of intramundane experience.

This view is allied with a narrow, mechanistic conception of transformation. In principle the mechanistic conception presents two alternatives. Either the self will be transformed into a new being, or society must attain a new, nonalienating condition. In both cases qualitative transformation is understood as involving the substitution of an harmonious condition for one beset by contradictions and conflict. Human existence is radically altered, indeed, transformed.

Significantly, the framework of alternatives ignores a third possibility: a change in man's orientation *toward* existence. This possibility would also involve a qualitative change in man, but it would be a change *within* man—the sort of change that a Plato or an Augustine might contemplate.

A change in man's orientation toward existence (*metanoia*) may be differentiated conceptually from a change of existence (*metastasis*). The latter transformation could in principle involve either a change of self or a change of society. However, a spontaneous change of self is precluded by the radical's insistence upon man's social dependency. To reclaim man's autonomy, his authentic self, therefore requires a social transformation. A qualitative change in man will be achieved *en passant* as the social impediments to self-fulfillment are removed. Thus, transformation means *metastasis,* a qualitative change of existence—the creation of a new society.[66]

Therefore despite its language of transcendence, the counterculture prohibits man from seeking the "vertical transcendence" provided by a reorientation of the soul toward existence. The scope of human experience is narrowed rather than expanded. As *homo faber,* man is imprisoned within the world of phenomenal experience which alone is subject to his will. Ultimately, the labor of Prometheus issues in contradiction. Animated by a desire to recover the autonomous self by means of experiential transcendence, the counterculture ends its journey of renewal in a closed, solipsistic universe.

## THE POLITICS OF PERSONALISM

The contradictory consequences of the radical conception of man have been often remarked. There would be little need to reiterate these consequences beyond the examples already adduced were it not for the frequent assertion by the counterculture's supporters that it has escaped the difficulties of earlier radical theories. In this concluding section, therefore, I will briefly outline three features of the politics of personalism, each of which demonstrates that the counterculture has not escaped the fate of its paternity.

The first feature is the negation of politics. In the eyes of the counterculturists politics is a badge of social dependency, of inauthentic life. Man is good; society corrupts him. The authentic man would have no use for politics because domination would no longer exist. Metastatic transformation would be the last act of politics. The qualitative transformation of society would render politics superfluous.

In identifying politics with domination the counterculture perpetuates the modern disregard for the "horizontal" notion of politics as an expression of men's efforts to order their common participation in existence, to organize for action in history.[67] The counterculture's ignorance of politics as an expression of man's essential nature reduces collective existence to a Hobbesian condition, which must then be transcended through *metastasis*.

Implicitly, order is here regarded as a psychological phenomenon that exists "naturally" within an authentic self. Once the sociohistorical impediments are removed, this order will spontaneously emerge.

An extended discussion of the consequences of this view is tempting but it must be resisted. Instead, I will simply note that the substance of the counterculture argument presents a *prima facie* case for the inadequacy of its anthropology. To create the conditions for the spontaneous order of the authentic self man must overcome a recalcitrant reality. This will be accomplished by adopting a new life style through which he imposes his own order on reality. The individual thus shapes experience to conform to his will—a task that obliges him to ignore all experience that poses a potential threat to his autonomy. The inevitable result is a "second reality" which provides the spontaneous order of a solipsistic universe.

Though self-delusion is the likely outcome of the politics of personalism, twentieth–century experience attests to man's ability to mold the world in accordance with his will. Thus we must take account of a second result of the counterculture: the effort to transform existence may lead to political messianism.

We have heard Lifton's expression of concern in the regard. So too have many others voiced their unease despite assurances that the goal of autonomy precludes the imposition of one man's will upon another's.[68] One needs only to read Philip Slater's prescription to understand the insufficiency of benign intent:

> Past efforts to build utopian communities failed because they were founded on scarcity assumptions. But scarcity is now shown to be an unnecessary condition. . . . Hence the only obstacle to utopia is the persistence of the competitive motivational patterns that past scarcity assumptions have spawned. Nothing stands in our way except our invidious dreams of personal glory. Our horror of group coercion reflects our reluctance to relinquish these dreams. . . . If we can overcome this horror, however, and mute this vanity we may again be able to take up our original utopian task.[69]

Much could be said about the actual practice of members of the counterculture when confronted with man's "horror of group coercion,"[70] but I wish to emphasize the broader consideration that emerges from their conception of human nature. The fusion of the axiom of authenticity with the promethean urge produces the critical mass of messianic humanism. Camus has given us an unforgettable description of the result.

> Here ends Prometheus' surprising itinerary. Proclaiming his hatred of the gods and his love of mankind, he . . . approaches mortal men in order to lead them in an assault against the heavens. But men are weak and cowardly; they must be organized . . . ; they must be taught to refuse . . . immediate rewards. Thus Prometheus, in his turn, becomes a master who first teaches and then commands . . . [Men] must be saved from themselves. The hero then tells them that he, and he alone, knows the city. Those who doubt his word will be thrown into the desert, chained to a rock, offered to be vultures . . . Prometheus

alone has become god . . . [;] he is no longer Prometheus, he is Caesar.[71]

Since radical thought makes liberal use of paradox, it is appropriate to end with a paradox of personalism. The counterculturists have condemned others for seeking structural solutions to the problems of technological society. Yet their dual conception of man has obliged them to seek qualitative change through *metastasis*. Despite the personalist mechanism of life style, with its dialectic of malleability and autogenesis, transcendence requires the transformation of reality. In the end the self remains a derivative category.

And so, the counterculture, which begins with the Beatles' advice

> You tell me it's the institution,
> You'd better free your mind instead.[72]

ends by seeking freedom through the metastatic transformation of society's institutions.

## NOTES AND REFERENCES

1. Charles Reich, *The Greening of America* (New York: Random House, 1970), p. 4. (Cited hereafter as *Greening*.)
2. *Ibid.*, p. 350.
3. *Ibid.*
4. The term is taken from Theodore Roszak, *The Making of a Counter Culture* (Garden City, N.Y.: Anchor Books, 1969), p. 56. (Cited hereafter as *Making*.)
5. *Greening*, p. 225.
6. *Ibid.*, pp. 225-227.
7. *Ibid.*, p. 225.
8. Quotations from the *Port Huron Statement* are taken from the excerpts included in Robert A. Goldwin (ed.), *How Democratic Is America?* (Chicago: Rand McNally, 1911), pp. 1-15. The quoted passage is found on pp. 5-6.
9. See for example Roszak, *Making*; and *idem., Where the Wasteland Ends* (Garden City, N.Y.: Doubleday, 1972). (Cited hereafter as *Wasteland*.)
10. See in particular Reich's discussion of the middle class and the blue-collar workers in *Greening*, pp. 281 ff.
11. Robert J. Lifton, *History and Human Survival* (New York: Vintage Books, 1971). This theme of disrupted continuity runs throughout the essays that comprise this volume. Lifton's views are summarized in his essay on "Protean Man" which is reprinted in this collection, pp. 316-331.
12. *Ibid.*, p. 318.

13. Lifton, *Boundaries: Psychological Man in Revolution* (New York: Vintage Books, 1970), p. 39.
14. Lifton follows Erik Erikson and Kenneth Keniston in abandoning terms like "character" or "personality" on the ground that they convey a fixed, static sense inconsistent with the actual psychological state they wish to describe.
15. "Protean Man," *History and Human Survival*, p. 319.
16. *Making*, p. 235.
17. Reich, *Greening*, pp. 5-6.
18. *Ibid.*, p. 257.
19. *Ibid.*
20. *Ibid.*, p. 9.
21. *Ibid.*, pp. 29-30, and p. 131.
22. *Ibid.*, pp. 80-85, and chapter vi, significantly entitled, "The Lost Self."
23. *Wasteland*, chapter 3, esp. p. 76.
24. *Ibid.*, p. 413.
25. By "organicism" Mandelbaum and I do not refer to the variety of social theory which, based upon organic analogies, emphasizes the primacy of the whole and the developmental process. Nonetheless, organicism as a theory of human nature has historical and logical affinities with organicist social theory.
26. Maurice Mandelbaum, *History, Man, and Reason* (Baltimore: The John Hopkins Press, 1971), p. 170. The ensuing discussion is inspired by Mandelbaum's work.
27. *Ibid*, p. 143. Actually, the passage quoted occurs in Mandelbaum's discussion of geneticism, "another nineteenth-century version of social determinancy. However, he argues explicitly that "geneticism" and "organicism" are alike save for the mediative element, which in the former case is the individual and in the latter is culture or the "spirit of the age." See chapters 8-9.
28. *Making*, p. 81.
29. Roszak, *Wasteland*, pp. 76-77.
30. I use the term "historicity" here because: (1) "Historicism," while more felicitious, has acquired so many meanings that its use is apt to convey more than is intended; (2) I agree with Mandelbaum that indiscriminate use of "historicism" undermines its basic meanings as a philosophy of history and a normative outlook. See Mandelbaum, *History, Man, and Reason*, Part I.
31. *Loc cit.*, p. 6.
32. Several recent works have addressed the notion of authenticity: Marshall Berman, *The Politics of Authenticity* (New York: Atheneum, 1970), and Lionel Trilling, *Sincerity and Authenticity* (Cambridge: Harvard University Press, 1972). The *locus classicus* remains the work of Rousseau.
33. Nicholas Lobkowicz, *Theory and Practice* (Notre Dame: University of Notre Dame Press, 1967), p. 421.
34. See *ibid.*, p. 314, and Shlomo Avineri, *The Social and Political Thought of Karl Marx* (New York: Cambridge University Press, 1968), chapter iii, esp. p. 85.
35. A good recent discussion of the relevant issues is found in Allen W. Wood, "Marx's Critical Anthropology: Three Recent Interpretations," *Review of Metaphysics*, XXVI (Fall 1972), pp. 118-139.
36. One "objective condition" generally accepted is the conquest of scarcity.

Roszak alone among the counterculture writers with which I am familiar rejects this assumption. He is persuaded that urban-industrial society will have to be judged an experiment that failed. (*Wasteland*, "Introduction," esp. p. xxix.) Roszak notwithstanding, abundance is assumed to create an unprecedented opportunity for a new way of life. [See Edward Shils, "Of Plenitude and Scarcity," *Encounter*, XXXII (May 1969), pp. 37-57.]

The other "objective condition" is more difficult to state with precision. There is a vague notion that things have come to a head, that life is in danger of extinction, viz., nuclear weapons, environment, resource depletion; consequently, men have a visceral awareness of the need for transformation. Reich exemplifies the "awakening" caused by the confluence of historical forces when, after reciting America's problems, he observes that men have begun to develop a new consciousness "as a matter of urgent biological necessity." (*Greening*, p. 18.) There is an unmistakeable echo here of Marcuse's instinctual argument as expressed in *An Essay on Liberation* (Boston: Beacon Press, 1969).

37. This, too, is most extensively expounded by Marcuse. In a broader sense, however, this perception is the *raison d'être* of the counterculture insofar as the movement itself constitutes a conscious alternative to the structural approach of "obsolete" Marxism.

38. The next section attempts to explicate this point. Of course it should be noted that the counterculture is no more precise about the mechanism of transformation than have been other radical schools.

39. See Mandelbaum, *History, Man, and Reason*, chapter xii, for a persuasive argument on the necessity of the "constant" of self-transformation within "organicism." I have also been influenced in my interpretation by Avineri's discussion of Marx wherein "anthropogenesis" is shown to be a "constant" in Marx's writings. (*The Social and Political Thought of Karl Marx*, p. 85.)

40. Dante Germino, *Modern Western Political Thought: Machiavelli to Marx* (Chicago: Rand McNally, 1972), p. 16.

41. Dante Germino, *Beyond Ideology: The Revival of Political Theory* (New York: Harper & Row, 1967), p. 31.

42. In his recent text (note 40, *supra*) Germino confesses to a change of opinion regarding radicalism and messianic humanism. He now thinks the emphasis should be on "inner" rather than "outer" transformation (p. 16). He would also disagree with (at least) some of the conclusions I shall draw below regarding the counterculture. (See chapter xiv, esp. pp. 385-386.)

43. *Greening*, p. 356.

44. *Ibid.*, pp. 356-357.

45. Roszak makes almost the identical point in *Making*, pp. 49, 55; see also the *Port Huron Statement*.

46. P. 225.

47. *Ibid.*, p. 354.

48. *Ibid.*

49. *Ibid.*, p. 363.

50. *Ibid.*, p. 225.

51. See "Protean Man," *passim*.

52. *Making*, p. 235.

53. In its posture toward experience the counterculture confirms its identity as a species of messianic humanism. "The master assumption of mes-

sianic humanism is that reality can be molded to conform to the infinite will of man." (Germino, *Beyond Ideology,* p. 31.)

54. The classic expressions of these results are provided by Marx in Part One of *The German Ideology* and the section on "Alienated Labor" in the *1844 Manuscripts.* See also the discussion in Avineri, *The Social and Political Thought of Karl Marx,* pp. 71 ff. On the relationship between creativity and autonomy consult the interesting discussion in Eric Voegelin, *Science, Politics and Gnosticism* (Chicago: Henry Regnery Co. [Gateway Edition], 1968), especially pp. 34-35.

55. Lifton refers to this extreme form of "romantic totalism" as "psychism." Lifton, "The Young and the Old: Notes on a New History," *History and Human Survival,* p. 368. See also his *Revolutionary Immortality* (Harmondsworth: Penguin Books, 1969).

56. Lifton, "The Young and the Old," p. 361. For Camus's view, see Albert Camus, *The Rebel,* translated by Anthony Bower (New York: Vintage Books, 1956), esp. p. 30.

57. Lifton, "The Young and the Old," p. 362.

58. *Ibid.,* pp. 362 ff. Lifton does not believe that "romantic totalism" is typical of radical youth.

59. *Making,* p. 81.

60. *Wasteland,* chapter x, esp. p. 356.

61. *Ibid.,* p. 77.

62. *Ibid.,* p. 393. An example of a review that interprets Roszak in this fashion is George Stade's review of *Where the Wasteland Ends* in *The New York Times Book Review* (September 24, 1972), pp. 1 *et seq.*

63. *Making,* pp. 50-51.

64. I have borrowed the term from John Chapman's discussion of the modern conceptions of human nature in "The Moral Foundations of Political Obligation," *Political and Legal Obligation,* ed. by J. Roland Pennock and John W. Chapman, Nomos XII (New York: Atherton Press, 1970), pp. 142-176. However, the meaning I give the term here diverges somewhat from Chapman's.

65. For reasons I cannot go into here, I believe that "improvement" is a more faithful characterization of the liberal impulse than "perfectability." Nevertheless, I agree with Chapman (*vide* note 64) that the liberal and radical anthropologies share many elements.

66. Here my disagreement with Germino's revised interpretation of the radical tradition (note 42, *supra*) comes to a head. While I concede that the counterculturists envisage an "inner" transformation, the burden of this essay has been to show that they cannot accomplish this goal without smuggling in notions of social dependency that are inconsistent with their "transformatory vision." Moreover, there remains the question of the kind of "inner" transformation. The counterculture is far removed from the "change of heart" envisaged by either Plato or Augustine. Germino fails to acknowledge this difference in his revised interpretation, though he was obviously attentive to it in his earliest work.

67. For a recent discussion of the nature of politics that utilizes the horizontal/vertical distinction, see Giovanni Sartori, "What Is 'Politics,' " *Political Theory,* I (February 1973), pp. 5-26. A similar distinction is to be found in Donald W. Keim, "Participation in Contemporary Democratic Theories," *Participation in Politics,* ed. by J. Roland Pennock and John W. Chapman, Nomos XVI (New York: Lieber-Atherton, 1975).

68. Examples are Shils, "Of Plenitude and Scarcity," and John Passmore,

"Paradise Now: The Logic of the New Mysticism," *Encounter*, XXXV (November, 1970), pp. 3-21.

69. *The Pursuit of Loneliness* (Boston: Beacon Press, 1970), p. 150.
70. For example, Lyman Tower Sargent, *New Left Thought* (Homewood, Ill.: The Dorsey Press, 1972).
71. *The Rebel*, pp. 244-225.
71. *The Rebel*, pp. 244-245.
72. Quoted in Slater, *The Pursuit of Loneliness,* p. 116.

# 8

## HUMAN NATURE
## AND HISTORY*

MARVIN ZETTERBAUM

I

In the penultimate chapter of *The Prince,* Machiavelli
speculates on how much control man may be said to have over
his own life and how much his life is dependent on things outside
his own control—on nature, chance, Providence, other men's actions—all of which we may, for present purposes, gather under
the general title of "fortune." While an audacious individual is
generally apt to be more successful in confronting the vicissitudes
of fortune than a cautious one, it is undeniable that any kind of
fixity in one's nature is a bar to complete success. Such success
requires a human nature that is fundamentally malleable, and so
Machiavelli voices his fateful aspiration:"If [man] were to change
his nature with the times and the circumstances, his fortune would

225

never change."[1] Man can thus come near neutralizing fortune altogether only if he is successful in storming the last bastions of his own nature. The conquest of nature necessitates the conquest of human nature. Man must overcome—himself.

Whatever the success of the first enterprise, the conquest of nature, there are those who have been alerting us to the realization of the second, the emergence, in Robert Jay Lifton's terms, of "a new kind of man—a 'protean man,' " one who defines himself by the absence of any fixed human nature and who is engaged in a "continuous psychic re-creation"[2] of his self-image. It is as if man, shorn of any conception of himself as a being endowed with certain permanent, inalienable, characteristics, were free to give himself his nature simply by changing the definitions of his own being. For some, the understanding of man as self-conscious creator, as the being whose nature, paradoxically, is not to have a nature, represents the final philosophical insight about man. Moreover, it is one for which the evidence, it is alleged, can be found in the record of man's history, or, alternatively, the conception of man as self-maker justifies looking at human history as the record of man's hitherto largely unself-conscious alterations or perceptions of his own being, and hence also as a record of man's changing nature. Thus the contemporary phenomenologist and psychotherapist van den Berg inaugurates a new science, *metabletics,* specifically to study the changes in man's nature through his history: "Whereas," he tells us, "in traditional psychology, the life of a previous generation is seen as a variation on a known theme, the supposition that man does change leads to the thought that earlier generations lived a different sort of life, and that they were *essentially* different."[3] Collingwood and Ortega offer virtually identical formulations. Collingwood tells us that "the value of history . . . is that it teaches us what man has done and thus what man is,"[4] while Ortega declares that "Man is what has happened to him, what he has done . . . *Man, in a word, has no nature; what he has is . . . history.*"[5] Nor have political scientists failed to add their voices to the growing chorus. Hwa Yol Jung, for example, affirms that "historicity presupposes the ultimate existential thesis that man *is* what he does, that is, the idea of active self-making or of man as history maker."[6]

Whether we consider the doctrine in its essentially psychological-idealistic version wherein man alters himself as he alters his definition of self, or in its economic–materialist version (Marx) wherein man by altering his environment alters also himself, it is generally acknowledged that Vico is the spiritual father of the doctrine that man, having no determinate nature, makes himself. Vico is also identified as the author of the even more far-reaching doctrine that truth itself is a kind of making, that we know only that which we have made ourselves. Not having been made by man, nature remains, contrary to what Descartes had supposed, ultimately mysterious, while the things that have come from man's own hands, his culture, institutions, his history, are in principle intelligible—as a carving formed by our own hands is intelligible to us since both conception and execution are of our own doing. Whether or not Vico is truly the originator of these views or whether the honor ought more properly to be given to Machiavelli, to Hobbes, or even, as some have contended, to such fifteenth-century figures as Nicolas of Cusa or Pico della Mirandola, is not within the scope of this particular article. The history of the doctrine of man as self-maker, tracing the contributions of the men already mentioned along with such others as Rousseau, Kant, Hegel, Marx, Nietzsche, Heidegger, and Sartre, has been the object of much critical scholarship by such contemporary writers as Hannah Arendt, Löwith, Mandelbaum, Strauss, Lobkowicz, Rosen, and Fackenheim, to name only a few.[7] Moreover, the elaboration of a complete and wholly accurate account of the coming into being of the doctrine that man is his coming into being, his making and doing, would not establish the truth of the doctrine in question, or even, perhaps, make it altogether intelligible. We are all empiricists to the extent that no one would speculate on the nature of man without taking into account what it is that man has done; but what man has done is precisely that —what he has done. To assert, further, that what he has done is his *nature* is, as Fackenheim reminds us,[8] to add an essential postulate: that man's being and his acting or doing are identical, and this postulate is not confirmed or confirmable by the recital of man's historical activities.

Man has no nature. Man is what he does. Man makes himself. Man is . . . his history. Such notions remained wholly outside the tradition of Western philosophy until the last two or three centuries. That they are widely disseminated and even accepted today makes one look attentively for some decisive human experience, at the least some fundamentally original interpretation of human experience that has come to serve for modernity as the defining human experience, one by which we claim to know what was so completely hidden from our predecessors. For it could not (and, of course, did not) escape the observation of men until modern times that human beings are essentially different from all other animate beings in that only humans are apparently free to articulate their lives in a seemingly endless variety of ways: as herdsmen, farmers, shopkeepers, soldiers, statesmen, artists, scholars, and the like. Differentiation of activities exists in other species as well, but no bee chooses or can choose to be a worker, a drone, or queen bee, or, still more remarkably, to be a worker in the morning, a drone in the afternoon, and a queen bee in the evening. In this respect, then, human being has a degree of indeterminacy about it that is not so of other natural beings, but such indeterminacy need not be inconsistent with a permanent human nature: the nature of man may be that he is endowed with the capacity to vary his manner of living. So, when Pico, in his celebrated oration on the dignity of man [1487], remarks that only Adam of all the creatures has no "fixed seat," while all others are bound by the laws imposed upon them, and that man has been given "free judgment" by which to determine his nature for himself—when he thus concludes that man is the "moulder and maker" of himself, he can be understood in a wholly traditional sense.[9] That is, such self-making, along with the judgment to determine and evaluate the ways of life so chosen are entirely consistent with and may even presuppose a permanent capacity to make such choices, as well as access to fixed criteria by which the choices may be evaluated. What man is essentially is the invariable principle of variance—reason.

In exercising his choices, man actualizes one or more of his latent possibilities and in so doing he becomes what it was always in his capacity to become. What he can do or make is limited by his human capacities, by his nature, by that which is the very basis of his doing or making. What he cannot do is remake that nature, of which, of course, he is not the cause or originator. Thus making and doing and the articulation of men's lives have not only seemed to be compatible with an unchanging human nature but have also been thought to be intelligible only on such a foundation. Change without an anchor in permanence, in the unchanging, is unintelligible.[10] Classical philosophy, then, indeed most philoshophy until the discovery of history in late modern times, took as its task the search for the unchanging—the immutable characteristics of human nature as well as the permanent horizon or permanent "whole" that that nature opens into—amid or behind the changing human things: behavior, laws, institutions, regimes, artifacts, and the like. It was only by identifying such constants that man could hope to erect a just social and political order, one that paralleled and reflected the natural order of man and of the whole. If we are to discover that human experience or interpretation which makes the modern doctrine of man as self-maker intelligible, it must be one that comprehends change on the basis of change; one, moreover, in which the vehicle of change is itself altered in its being as a result of the making or doing it initiates or participates in. Such an interpretation would be as sweeping in its scope as the Galilean assertion that a body in motion will continue indefinitely in motion without the intercession of any applied force.

The quarrel between the one interpretation and the other, between the ancients and the moderns, is perhaps most visible today in the work of Professor Leo Strauss.[11] His critique of positivism and historicism, for example, may be viewed as an attempt not only to lay bare the fundamental inadequacies of these respective doctrines, but also to restore to the contemporary world the classical view of human acting. To comprehend human making or doing within a permanent horizon, a permanent whole, is at least part of Strauss's intention in his now famous exchange with Alexandre Kojève over Strauss's interpretation of Xenophon's *The Hiero*.[12] But while the issue between the permanent and the changeable is joined, it is, alas, not resolved. Like a Socratic dialogue, this particular exchange ends with an admission by Strauss that the exchange must be considered inconclusive inasmuch as it scarcely touched upon, let alone resolved, the differences in their presuppositions regarding the nature of being. According to Strauss, classical philosophy was understood as the "quest for the eternal order or for the eternal cause or causes of all things." This quest presupposes "an eternal and unchangeable order within which History takes place and which is not in any way affected by History." In such an order, any "realm of freedom," that is, the sphere within which human actions take place, is only "a dependent province within the 'realm of necessity.' " Finally, classical philosophy presupposes that "Being is essentially immutable in itself and eternally identical with itself." Strauss concedes that that presupposition is not self-evident and notes that Kojève (following Hegel) replaces it with the view that "Being creates itself in the course of History."[13]

Strauss is not unaware that in the classical view events within the dependent province may provide the occasion or the preconditions for access to knowledge of the eternal order. As he remarks in an essay on Collingwood, "To say nothing of other considerations, one may be chiefly concerned with the permanent or recurrent, and yet hold that a given unique event (the Peloponnesian war, for example) supplies the only available basis for reliable observations which would enable one to form a correct judgment about certain recurrences of utmost importance,"[14] in this case about the nature of war and peace in the affairs of men. Or it may be suggested that such an event provides access to what Strauss has called the "fundamental problems" or the "fundamental questions," questions which, belonging as they do to the nature of man as man, disclose themselves to men at least as early as men begin to undertake philosophic inquiry.[15] While it may appear paradoxical it does not seem incompatible to assert, on the one hand, that man is in principle capable of grasping the fundamental problems at any time and in any place and, on the other, to maintain that, it is only consequent upon a particular event that man may indeed have access to the eternal questions. All other things being equal, the nature of war is more likely to be disclosed in a major battle than in a frontier skirmish; more apparent to a general than to a private; to an accomplished general than an untried one; and *a fortiori,* to the greatest general in the greatest war. Or, at least, to the greatest intelligence reflecting on the greatest war. So, of course, was the claim of Thucydides. The decisive importance of some events within the dependent realm is, then, consistent with the assertion of a permanent human nature and of an eternal order.[16] The difficulty lies elsewhere.

It was maintained, above, that no one would argue that it is wholly unnecessary to see what man has done in order at least to begin the investigation by which we may arrive at what man is. The question, though, is how much looking you have to do or when you can safely stop looking. We would all agree, I believe, that if man has existed on the earth for some four to fourteen million years, it would have been unwise and misleading to have formulated and offered as final a definition of man with the experience of man up to the point, say, of three hundred thousand years ago. Some contend that the evidence available to those who began the tradition of philosophy in fifth–century Greece was sufficient. But to so argue is to assert that nothing additional might be learned (if we were to continue looking at what man does) that could in any way be decisive in coming to understand what man is. It is to assert, in other words, that all future history—specifically, of war, of practical affairs, of technology, of the arts, of philosophy itself—could not provide any evidence that might be decisive in altering the definition of man. There might be a certain plausibility for this view—as is implied in the Hegelian understanding—if the cutoff point coincided with a late or mature age in human history (though what age has not viewed itself as a mature one?)—but it is certainly surprising to have the cutoff at the Greek period, which everyone acknoyledges to be the beginning of philosophic inquiry. In actual fact, it matters not at all what specific cutoff point is chosen, or what specific event in the dependent realm is singled out as somehow decisive. That is, it matters not whether the cutoff be one century or another, or whether the decisive event be the Peloponesian war or the second World War. For in each case what is being asserted is that a point in time has been reached in which the final truth about man has become available, if not in practice, at least in theory. This being so, no future evidence need be of any interest. In both the traditional and Hegelian views this amounts to maintaining that the future will be characterized only by relatively insignificant variations on a known theme, the essential constants of human nature. While the past is of some significance in coming to know what man is, the future that beckons him can hold no genuine surprises. If, then, we are seeking that human experience or interpretation that makes the doctrine of man as self-maker intelligible, it is evident that that experience will involve an intensely deepened awareness of the significance for man of the future, and of a future which is essentially mysterious, concealing unknown and even unknowable possibilities. Yet, since we do not *experience* the future (although we may have expectations from it) our view of the future derives not from any particular experience but from reflections on the fundamental problems, reflections that led finally to the conclusion that there was neither any permanent human nature nor, in fact, any immutable fundamental problems.

As to the persistence of the fundamental problems, it is instructive to note that Karl Löwith (who has himself been in the forefront of those critical of the doctrine of man as self-maker) contends that the existential question, "Why is there anything at all rather than nothing?" *"could not emerge"* in the thought of Aristotle "because he was a Greek thinker for whom existence as such—that there is something—was an unquestionable element within the essential structure, order, and beauty of an always existing cosmos without beginning and end, including the existence of rational animals called men." [17] If this is the case, a very dark cloud is cast over the view of man possessing a permanent nature able to grasp the permanent problems, for Löwith's assertion encapsulates even the greatest thinkers within horizons set for them by their own time and place. It is not possible to enter into the historicist strains that enter somewhat inexplicably into Löwith's thought. Instead, we may ask whether the fact that the problem of radical contingency does not arise in the thought of Aristotle may not be explicable on grounds other than the one Löwith offers. In so doing, we cannot avoid asking the rather fundamental question of whether or not the question of radical contingency is itself a fundamental question. Is it, perhaps, only a pseudo-question, a blind alley to which modernity has been led by pursuing some labyrinthian error of thought? Obviously, this question in turn revolves around the identification of the fundamental questions or even around the demonstration of the existence of such questions. Other candidates for the category of "fundamental question" may readily suggest themselves, but only a comprehensive vision of the nature of the whole and of human nature within it could possibly enable us to distinguish the genuine questions from the pretenders. The identification of the "existential" question as a fundamental one presupposes just such a demonstration or comprehensive vision, one moreover itself free from the perspectival limitations of time and space. We are not lacking such comprehensive visions, but those we have have lost their evidency for us. Even what we will accept as evidence has become problematic. The question of what we will accept as evidence, of what it is upon which we will ground our grasp of ourselves and of the whole, provides, I believe, the most direct entry into man as self-maker.

II

Before the problem of man as self-maker arises and is seen in all its fullness we observe the successive steps, begun already in Descartes and Vico, which culminate in the total "denaturing" of man, the removal of man altogether from that eternal and unchangeable province of which Strauss speaks. While the classical view insisted upon the distinction between the human and the natural or the nonhuman, it nevertheless encompassed both within a natural whole.[18] Modern natural science, and the movement of positivism arising from it, preserved the idea of a natural whole but one which denied altogether any genuine distinction between the human and the natural. Kant rescued the human world, preserved it as a human world, but did so in such a manner that its articulation with the natural world was ultimately mysterious; and Hegel's heroic effort at a new synthesis was scarcely successful. The edifice he constructed seemed to some of his successors either to have effected a fundamental transmutation of human reality or to have lost sight of human reality altogether, subsuming it under absolute spirit or cosmic time. What appeared to be lacking was the full realization and appreciation of that human reality, unalloyed and uncontaminated. As Löwith observes, "Hegel brings to an end the truly metaphysical definitions of man, which define him from the standpoint of something absolute. Starting with Feuerbach, man was considered anthropologically, from the conditional standpoint of the finite individual. Only this individual man, based upon himself, gives rise to an actual problem of man."[19] It is not, then, accidental that Ortega, one of the contemporary figures who is unequivocally identified with the position of man as self-maker can say, "Human reality is a strange reality concerning which the first thing to be said is that it is the basic reality, in the sense that to it we must refer all others, since all others . . . must in one way or another appear within it."[20]

The radical separation of man from nature, the attempt to confront unalloyed human reality, entails the rejection altogether of the perennial definition of man as some sort of animal—the rational, the risible, the tool-making or image-making animal —for while such adjectives differentiate man from all other animate beings that which they modify ties him to the rest of the animal kingdom. No full understanding of what is essentially and distinctly human is thought to be possible so long as this alleged link is not severed. Marx, for example, alludes to this necessity in one of his early writings when he notes, "For a starving man, the *human* form of food does not exist, but only the abstract character of food,"[21] Of course, for Marx, the starving man has not yet come upon his humanity since he is still enmeshed altogether in the realm of necessity, or of nature. Martin Buber comments on a passage in Husserl: ". . . The depth of the anthropological question is first touched when we also recognize as specifically human that which is not reason. Man is not a centaur, he is man through and through . . . Even man's hunger is not an animal's hunger. Human reason is to be understood only in connection with human non-reason. The problem of philosophical anthropology is the problem of a specific totality and of its specific structure."[22] In attempting to delineate this specific totality, in narrowing and concentrating attention upon this primal reality alone, the traditional question, what *is* man? is replaced by the question, what is the *manner of being* of the creature, man?—a question whose form purportedly focuses attention upon human reality as it is directly perceived or lived from within, as it is experienced by the agents themselves. In its own way, this shift in the question being asked about man already reflects a deeper shift in man's perception of the so-called fundamental questions. It reflects, that is, the view that there are no essences properly speaking, and that we must then turn instead to man's existence, to his way of being in the world.

What, then, is the manner of being of man? More specifically, what are those aspects having a direct bearing upon man as self-maker? According to Ortega, the primary facet of man's reality is that he is never wholly integrated with his environment or his circumstances. In contrast to all other beings in nature, man is the only entity whose life is not exhausted by a description of its organic or biological necessities, whose life "does not coincide, at least not wholly, with the system of his organic necessities."[23] Again unlike any other creature, man's behavior and activities are not given to him ready made; they are not, as it were, drawn out of a repertoire with which he is equipped at birth. All the other things in the world are precisely that, "things," that is, entities whose manner of being consists in being what they already are, whose potentialities coincide at every moment with their actuality.

At every moment, a dog, a stone, an atom, is what it must be at that moment. "Things," Ortega tells us, "are given their being ready made." Since man, on the other hand, is not identical with his nature or his circumstances, he is rather to be understood as "an entity whose being consists not in what it is already, but in what it is not yet, a being that consists in not-yet-being." [24] A vacuum arises upon the fulfillment of man's strictly biological or natural life, and in this vacuum man erects (indeed cannot help but erect) his truly human life. Human life "is not given to man as its fall is given to a stone or the stock of its organic acts—eating, flying, nesting—to an animal. [Man] makes it himself, beginning by inventing it." [25]

The critical issue here is the one of invention. It is acknowledged by just about everyone (save, perhaps, certain positivists who, in making the counter-claim call into question the very claim they are making), that man is not in nature as are other animate and inanimate beings. The Greeks were aware that man alone causes to come into being a "second" or "historical" world, one that would not have come into being without man's explicit decision and act. Aristotle, for example, acknowledges every man's indebtedness to the first man who constructs a political regime.[26] Still, the city is "natural." It is natural because the city is the specific locus in which man can actualize his social and intellectual potentialities, in which he can become a complete human being; it is natural because man has the innate capability of discovering the specific form appropriate to his fulfillment; and it is natural because this specific form is not arbitrary. The city is not one of several alternatives in which man might fulfill himself; it is the only alternative. Few words in the literature of political philosophy have proved to be as ambiguous and as indispensable as the term "natural." These meanings already suggest themselves: that whose origin lies outside itself (man as well as all other animate and inanimate beings); that whose activities cannot be other than they are (all animate and inanimate beings except, perhaps, man); that which is itself not given "spontaneously" by the free hand of nature, but arises out of the activity of one of its natural creatures, man (the city); a construct, again not arising spontaneously out of nature, but one which as it were completes the intention of nature (the city); and so on. It is obvious that the first two senses, conveying as they do some notion of necessity, may seem to bruise against the latter two, those requiring an apparently free act, albeit in the service of necessity. So it is that man may appear as naturally "unnatural." [27] In any case, the issue is not whether man can or does "cultivate, pervert, and negate his own nature," but rather whether in so doing, in inventing or calling into being that second world, man has any awareness of or access to extrahuman or natural standards in the consciousness of which he may generate his second nature. This possibility is of course emphatically denied in the doctrine of man as self-maker. There is, it is alleged, no finite fixed form that may be taken as the definition of a complete human being; indeed, what man is, that is, what he is capable of becoming, will not be fully known until the last man is expiring.[28] Man does not have a self already determined and given which he has only to actualize: "Man must not only make himself: the weightiest thing he has to do is to determine *what* he is going to be." [29]

In determining what he is going to be, each individual imagines or invents various conceptions of life, and in the circumstances in which he is placed he constructs for himself a project of being or doing; he may find such a project at hand in the lives of those around him, or he may quite literally invent a new one. "This vital program is the *ego* of each individual, his choice out of diverse possibilities of being which at every instant open before him." [30] To choose a project of being is not to create something out of nothing; man is always limited by the past, by circumstances, by the situation. Thus, Ortega affirms, ". . . man makes himself in the light of circumstances . . . he is a God as occasion offers, a 'second-hand God.'" [31] Nor is it possible for man *not* to choose to construct a project for himself. Man is constitutively free; he is "free by compulsion," whether he wishes to be or not.

> Freedom is not an activity pursued by an entity that, apart from and previous to such pursuit, is already possessed of a fixed being. To be free means to be lacking in constitutive identity, not to have subscribed to a determined being, to be able to be other than what one was, to be unable to install oneself once and for all in any given being. The only attribute of the fixed, stable being in the free being is this constitutive instability.[32]

Thus, freedom, or constitutive instability, the nonbeing of the being of man, replaces rationality as the principle of variance. Man's freedom is not genuinely constitutive of his being if that freedom is understood solely as the capacity to be a yea-sayer or a nay-sayer to nature, to affirm or to turn his back upon those standards or modes that nature has previously established and has given him the capacity to discover and the will to act upon. The concept of man as self-maker thus seems to eventuate in the realization that all human projects are equal, that no standards exist by which to evaluate or objectively guide the construction of truly human projects. Whether this is so or not, our initial obligation is to be faithful to the reality we are trying to grasp, the nature of being human.

Our grasp of that reality will not be complete unless we acknowledge also the way in which human making differs from such making as may take place in nature itself. Collingwood maintains that, even if we accept the evolutionary concept that the forms in nature are undergoing change, a fundamental difference remains in that evolution "abolishes one specific form in creating another. The trilobites of the Silurian age may be the ancestors of the mammals of today, including ourselves; but a human being is not a kind of wood-louse. The past, in a natural process, is a past superseded and dead." [33] On the other hand, in the process that is human making the human past is actively preserved in the human present, and "the historical change from one way of thinking to another is not the death of the first, but its survival integrated in a new context . . . ." [34] The same thought is expressed by Ortega quite graphically:

With the evolutionary thesis still unproved, whatever its probability, it can be said that the tiger of today is neither more nor less a tiger than was that of a thousand years ago: it is being a tiger for the first time, it is always a first tiger. But the human individual is not putting on humanity for the first time . . . . He finds at birth a form of humanity, a mode of being a man, already forged, that he need not invent but may simply take over and set out from for his individual development. . . . Man is not a first man, eternal Adam: he is formally a second man, a third man, etc. [35]

The separation of the human historical process from the natural process completes the "denaturing" of man. At the same time it discloses the intimate tie of the doctrine of man as self-maker to the legitimate concerns of poltical philosophy, for the world into which man enters, his "social uterus" (in the language of Adolf Portmann) is inevitably not only a natural world but, for him, a social and political world as well, a repository of the projects of countless generations of men before him.

### III

It must be evident that a doctrine of historical self-making is internally paradoxical. Throughout the present essay the term "man" has been used (e.g., "man as self-maker") as if, despite the claim that it is precisely man who is changing in the very process of self-making, the term maintained a fixed denotation. In more concrete terms, it may not be thought possible, on the assumption of the impermanence of human nature, to recognize *as human* our ancestors or as human products the products of our ancestors, especially those of our ancestors who are separated from us by many generations and many changes of human institutions. If the human past were totally superseded and dead (as in the natural process), it would not be possible at all. Collingwood readily acknowledges this when he affirms that, if the historical process of human thought were analogous to the natural process, "It would follow that the ways of thinking characteristic of any given historical period are ways in which people must think then, but in which others, cast at different times in a different mould, cannot think at all. If that were the case, there would be no such thing as truth . . ." [36] If I cannot think *at all* like my ancestors, if I can enter into the life of that other through no process of memory, thought, or imagination, if between us there is thus a total barrier, then I cannot even recognize him as one of my own kind.

For Collingwood, however, the difficulty is overcome once we recognize that the human present includes, ineluctably, the human past. Greek mathematics, for example, is not inaccessible to us because it is Greek; rather, our own mathematics is erected, and erected necessarily, upon the foundation of Greek mathematics. By unraveling the process by which the one became the other, we come to see Greek mathematics.[37] So, too, with other more specifically human things. Still, human being is not like an onion, or like the rings of a tree, in that by peeling off one layer after another we successively uncover the human being of former ages. For, if human being is a historical self-making, the past that is incorporated is not simply accumulated in an additive fashion; the past must be so taken up that it alters the very being of that into which it is incorporated. As Ortega remarks, "The European of today is not only different from what he was fifty years ago, his being now includes that of fifty years ago."[38] If, then, standing in my present, I peel off an outer layer, I find that I am not then happily regarding a human being of a former age—I *am* that human being. In fact, of course, the attempt cannot even be made, for I am the whole onion; I exist in my present entirety; I am my present entirety; the thought of a self-removal of a part of myself is self-defeating. Only a being standing outside the historical process could so remove the layers and see the generations of human beings. But such a being is not, as Collingwood and Ortega understand it, a *human* being. As Collingwood insists, the historian's business "is not to leap clean out of his own period of history but to be *in every respect* a man of his age and to see the past as it appears from the standpoint of that age."[39] Furthermore, "This point of view is valid only for him and people situated like him, but for him it *is* valid. He must stand firm in it, because it is the only one accessible to him, and unless he *has* a point of view he can see nothing at all."[40] Upon such a view, man is always encapsulated by the perspective of his situation, and he brings this situation to his confrontation of the past. When I understand Plato, I am always conscious in some way that it is *I* who understand Plato, and this I is not and cannot be some transcendental ego—it is I in all my wholeness, historicity, and subjectivity. The past, then, cannot be seen as the past, as it understood and experienced itself. The past as past is, after all, despite Collingwood's distinction between natural and historical process, a "past superseded and dead," and my forebear must remain as mysterious to me as a trilobite to an ape.

Yet Collingwood needs no help from us in rescuing himself from absurdity. Whatever the metaphysical perplexities to which his position is exposed, he would have no more difficulty in recognizing as human one of his forebears than we would have in refuting Zeno's proof that motion is impossible. Just as in the latter case we would casually take a step forward, so Collingwood would grasp the hand of his fellow and say "Well met." In each case, we would act upon the belief in a permanently subsisting "world" and of ways of being in the world that could not have arisen from religious, scientific, or philosophic reflection about that world. In actual fact, our awareness of other individuals as human beings, for example, necessarily precedes and undergirds any inquiry into the "nature" of human being.[41] *How* we know that a given creature is human or not is deeply mysterious, but we cannot deny that such knowledge exists or that it constitutes part of our common sense prescientfic, prephilosophic, natural mode of being in the world. Strauss remarks that "political science stands or falls by the truth of pre-scientific awareness of political things. . . . Our perceiving things and people is more manifest and more reliable than any 'theory of knowledge'—any explanation of how our perceiving things and people is possible—can be; the truth of any 'theory of knowledge' depends on its ability to give an adequate account of this fundamental reliance."[42] Phenomenologists, in particular, have been zealously pursuing this original life-world ever since the impetus for it was given by Husserl's discovery of the *Lebenswelt*. But zeal has not necessarily been rewarded with concrete achievements. Among contemporary scholars, there is very little agreement on the constituent makeup of the natural world, how one arrives at it, or even knows when one is there. Not one but several different life-worlds have been identified or postulated.[43] To indicate the difficulty of arriving at what might be thought to be most accessible to us, there are those, like Strauss, who maintain that the concrete reality at which some recent philosophers finally arrive is but an abstraction from an abstraction, namely from a world already saturated by philosophy and natural science, and hence not the original concrete reality at all.[44]

There is agreement, though, that however necessary it is to grasp our prescientfic awareness of things, it is equally important not to remain at that level; in some fundamental way, our natural awareness is either deficient or defective, though only from it (and by remaining faithful to it) can we remedy those deficiencies. In the traditional, classical view, the world of opinions (the ordinary human world), must be transcended in the direction of truth. The moderns, on the other hand, refusing to accept everyday opinions as constitutive of the authentic life-world, argue that we must go beneath these to the permanent basic *structures* of existence, of human being in the world, structures that make having and holding opinions possible at all. What are sought are Kantian *a priori* categories of existence, now broadened to encompass not only man's cognitive grasp of the world but the entire range of his experience in and with the world. As we have already seen, the view that man is a historically situated self–maker is not incompatible with, and in fact is thought to disclose, at least one permanent structure of being human: man's radical freedom, his no-thingness. Hans Jonas identifies three modes of the freedom man expresses in transcending nature: tool-making, image-making, and tomb-making, and argues that these can serve as "universal 'coordinates' of understanding valid for the whole course of human history."[45] The number of basic structures proffered by one or more investigators has grown very large: lived body, lived space, lived time, intentionality, being-toward-death, basic guilt, basic anxiety, and so forth. This has prompted one critic to suggest that what has been brought to light is less a description of the basic ontological structures of existence than a variety of ontological autobiographies.[46] Indeed, it is true that the identification of the basic structures has met with no more certain success than the similar attempt to identify man's basic *needs* as a way to cut through the fact/value dilemma and to provide objective values for man and political order.[47]

We noted earlier that our primary obligation was to gain an adequate account of human reality even if such an account were to lead to the conclusion that no objective means exists by which to choose or evaluate human projects. Yet almost every version of the doctrine of man as self-maker includes the assertion that the ontological description of man has prescriptive significance. Ortega looks to the application of "concrete historical reason" not only for the clarification of human reality but also, "along with this, for light on the nature of the good, the bad, the better, and the worse."[48] John Wild notes that ". . . every clarification of a necessary ontological pattern is normative in character."[49] However, whereas traditional philosophy found in the nature of man specific recommendations for a truly human life (a life of reason, a life of virtue, a life as citizen, etc.), the contemporary views we have been considering stress the purely formal but nevertheless universal prescriptions embodied in the ontological categories of existence. Thus, for example, Maurice Natanson finds that "the 'what' of the norm undoubtedly varies historically and anthropologically, but the 'that' of the norm is unchanging. It is universal for the human condition that men everywhere and at all times recognize *that* there is a course of action which is considered fitting and proper for certain situations. . . . Claims about what the proper act should be in given situations vary, within a culture as well as between different cultures, but *that* something is expected as normal behavior is a constant of human experience." [50] This may strike some as less than helpful, and it may be thought to be caviling to remark that if the basic structures of existence are genuinely universal and *a priori*, if they are the condition of our experiencing the world as a world and of our being in the world, there is scarcely much that may be done about them. Possibly for this reason is it rather maintained that the good life is the life in accordance with the proper *mode* of experiencing the basic structures, authentically or inauthentically, in full recognition of the demands imposed upon us by our essential freedom, or in flight from such awareness. To attempt to live by denying the no-thingness of man, to seek to fall back upon a pregiven being and thus to reintegrate man into nature (or to give him a "thinglike" nature) is thus to live inauthentically, not as a man lives or ought to live.[51] Still, if it should finally appear that man is indeed constitutively free, if he cannot look to any pregiven pattern for guidance in his project-making, it is difficult to see how this may be reconciled with the view that if man is to live in a truly human fashion he must make himself in a particular way or live in the light of a particular awareness. If man is free in this special sense, what could be the source of this obligation? Moreover, even if there is only a "form" of the truly human life, can it nevertheless be said that man is constitutively free?

We must confront again (but for the last time) the apparently limitless varieties of projects that men have articulated for themselves throughout human history. Surveying this medley, Ortega affirms that "Man is an infinitely plastic entity of which one may make what one will, precisely because of itself it is nothing save only the mere potentiality to be 'as you like.' . . . [and] it is impossible to see what frontiers can be set to human plasticity." [52] Yet we may be reminded of our previous contention that history only discloses that men have, in fact, articulated their lives or their projects in various ways, and be invited to state what, finally, this has to do with human nature. In the face of such evidence Hannah Arendt avers, "Not the capabilities of man, but the constellation which orders their mutual relationships can and does change historically. Such changes can best be observed in the changing self-interpretations of man throughout history, which, *though they may be quite irrelevant for the ultimate "what" of human nature,* are still the briefest and most succinct witnesses to the spirit of whole epochs." [53] Arendt thus distinguishes between the changing self-interpretations and the ultimate "what" of human nature, while Ortega identifies the two. Man's self-interpretations made concrete in his projects constitute his human reality.[54]

The doctrine of man as self-maker is not incompatible with the view that man's capabilities, his bodily and rational faculties, for example, remain constant throughout, but to look to these constants for the being of man is to miss, it is claimed, what genuinely constitutes human reality.[55] It is thus not a matter of indifference whether human nature is sought in whatever it is that all men have in common—existential structures or basic needs or innate passions—or in what separates them. In fact, there is something almost classical in the rejection within this vew of any appeal to uniformity (or of law expressing that uniformity), of any search for the lowest common denominator that embraces each and every instance of the human species, of any identification of the constant features expressed beneath the cultural and institutional practices of all nations. We may be reminded that when Aristotle comes to speak of regimes, he stresses that what distinguishes them from one another is far more important than what they may have in common.[56] Of course, this is not to deny the natural base upon which whatever is taken to be genuine human reality is erected, man's need for food and shelter, his susceptibility to disease, and so forth. Nor is this to deny that the classics, unlike the moderns, identify genuine human reality with a form of excellence, the virtuous or philosophic life, attainable not by all but even in some cases by just a few. The contemporary view of man as self-maker seeks, paradoxically, the uncommon in what is characteristic of all, lived human life as it is experienced by each participant himself. It is thus less interested in man's capacity for speech than in what men say, less in their ability to reason than in the products of their thought, less in their common appetites for food or sex than in their ways of breaking bread and regarding the object of their sexual desire. When Shylock urges upon us the awareness that he, too, bleeds upon being pricked, we are not indifferent to the fact that it is Shylock who urges this upon us, and it is his being Shylock, defender as he sees it of his own people, that constitutes his reality, not, or not essentially, the common physiological properties he shares with the rest of us.

We may now finally affirm, with Ortega, that human reality is indeed "a strange reality, the basic reality, in the sense that to it we must refer all others, since all others . . . must in one way or another appear within it." This thought, too, is not very different from the original impulse animating classical political philosophy. As expressed by Strauss, this is the belief that "Adequate 'speaking about' in analytical or objective speech must be grounded in and continue the manner of 'speaking about' which is inherent in human life." [57] It is precisely such a speaking about, one that remains faithful to the reality of human life as it is experienced by each of us, that is purportedly attained in the awareness of human nature as an historical self-making. Yet every description of human reality must already be at some remove from that reality; our experience is other than our reflection upon that experience. If it be asserted, as we saw above, that genuine human reality is constituted by the groundlessness of our being, that we neither have nor can have any awareness of extrahuman or natural standards in the light of which we may formulate our projects of being, it must be evident that both the assertion and the awareness are derivative, that they are not immediately given in experience. Of course, I may be taught and even come to believe and act upon such a view, as I may come to believe in the reality of Platonic Forms. Still, while the experience and the analysis or description may differ, we have no warrant for asserting that the one is less "real" than the other, for our reflections are surely part of our human reality. In fact, they structure and often determine the manner in which we experience the way we are in the world. The search for basic human reality is analogous to the search for the state of nature from the perspective of civil society, an effort finally abandoned through the efforts of Rousseau. We possess no Archimedian consciousness from which, immune from the reality in which we are immersed, we may nevertheless see ourselves as we really are.[58] While the doctrine of man as self-maker understands and even underscores this inevitable limitation (if indeed it can be called that), it is not itself free from the illusion of having transcended that limitation. A case in point is its view of man and nature. That view achieves a radical separation of the two spheres on the basis of which the peculiarly human things may come to be understood. Yet must we not acknowledge, as Erwin Straus reminds us, that "The boundaries of possible realization that precede all self-realization are not established by the self,"[59] that, in other words, we are not only from nature but also in it and that the lines between the two cannot so finely be drawn? A radical separation of man and nature in which man forgets the origin of man out of nonman, be it God or nature, is forgetful also of an aspect of human reality, and it verges on the arbitrary to identify the "genuinely human" with that which is said to be of man's own making as if that making is wholly free of any natural component.

The concern for the basic structures of human existence arose out of an attempt to meet the objection that the doctrine of man as self-maker cannot account for our overwhelming sense of the transhistorical *identity* of man. Only by an appeal to such universal structures, common to all men as men, or to universal basic needs, or to what others have termed the universal constants of history, only on some such basis can we account for what we know to be the case—that our ancestors were, as we are, members of the same human species. These structures, it is readily acknowledged, are purely formal, contentless, objective; meaning, content, and subjective experience are the empirical components that are added by the successive generations of men. Still, it was in the uniquely constituted projects of man that we sought, above, the reality of being human, and it is to the real or alleged incompatibility between these two perceptions of man—the purely formal and the empirically rich—that some have attributed the irreconcilable conflict between phenomenology and existentialism, the one taking as its goal objective *knowledge* of human reality and the other emphasizing the *task* of being human.[60] Does the former solve the problem of the identity of man while losing sight of the reality of being human?

In the final analysis, we cannot abandon the search for human nature as we abandoned the concept of the "state of nature." We may discard this or that understanding of human nature; we may at one time or another acknowledge the genuinely human in reason, or virtue, or fear, or passion, or faith, or in the making of projects; in sociability or in asociability; in what is universally true for all men or in what is uniquely lived and experienced by each particular individual. Whatever else may be true of our nature, this search, this seeking for understanding of ourselves is constitutive of our being. This search cannot eventuate in showing that the identification of what constitutes genuine human reality or the interpretation of the same phenomena, the changing self-interpretations of man, is itself a matter of arbitrary choice. We are not simply free to decide either that the medley of human projects is man's nature, that man is his history, or that this history is but an epiphenomenon thrown up by some ultimate we know not "what" of human nature. We are thus not free to decide if man is a self-maker or not; the concept of man as self-maker cannot be, if it purports to be the truth about human being, merely another self-interpretation. We shrink from asserting, with Nietzsche, "Supposing that this also is only interpretation . . . well, so much the better."[61]

## NOTES AND REFERENCES

* I am very grateful to Professors Martin Diamond (Northern Illinois University), Victor Gourevitch (Wesleyan University), Hwa Yol Jung (Moravian College), Eugene Miller (University of Georgia), and to my colleague Larry Peterman for criticisms and comments on an earlier draft of the present paper. They are, of course, not responsible for the views expressed here.

1. Niccolò Machiavelli, *The Prince,* tr. and ed. Mark Musa (New York: St. Martin's Press. 1964) p. 213.
2. Robert Jay Lifton, *History and Human Survival* (New York: Vintage, 1971), p. 316.
3. Jan Hendrick van den Berg, *The Changing Nature of Man* (New York: Norton, 1961), pp. 7-8.
4. R. G. Collingwood, *The Idea of History* (New York: Oxford University Press, 1956), p. 10.
5. José Ortega y Gasset, *History as a System* (New York: Norton, 1962), pp. 216-217.
6. Hwa Yol Jung, "Leo Strauss' Conception of Political Philosophy: A Critique," *Review of Politics,* Vol. 29, No. 4 (Oct. 1967), p. 512.
7. See e.g., Hannah Arendt, *Between Past and Future* (Cleveland: Meridian, 1963); Karl Löwith, *Meaning in History* (Chicago: University of Chicago Press, 1949); Maurice Mandelbaum, *History, Man, and Reason: A Study in 19th Century Thought* (Baltimore: John Hopkins Press,

1971); Leo Strauss, *Natural Right and History* (Chicago: University of Chicago Press, 1953); Nicholas Lobkowicz, *Theory and Practice* (Notre Dame: University of Notre Dame Press, 1967); Stanley Rosen, *Nihilism* (New Haven: Yale University Press, 1969); and Emil L. Fackenheim, *Metaphysics and Historicity* (Milwaukee: Marquette University Press, 1961).

8. Fackenheim, pp. 13, 26.

9. Cited in Lobkowicz, p. 135.

10. cf. Karl Löwith, *Permanence and Change* (Cape Town: Haum, 1969), p. 12, ". . . even if we were to assume that there were an historical transformation in the *essence* of man, this transformation too could only occur when man remained essentially the same, through all changes and transformations. For only that which remains permanent can also change. Otherwise one could in no way recognize that which has altered and transformed as such."

11. See, in addition to *Natural Right and History, What is Political Philosophy?* (Glencoe: Free Press, 1959), and *The City and Man,* (Chicago: Rand McNally), 1964). For an extremely perceptive analysis and critique, see Victor Gourevitch, "Philosophy and Politics, I-II," *Review of Metaphysics,* Vol. XXII, No. 1, pp. 58-84, and Vol. XXII, No. 2, pp. 281-328.

12. Leo Strauss, *On Tyranny* (Ithaca: Cornell, 1968). The French edition, *De la Tyrannie,* deuxième edition (Paris: Gallimard, 1954), contains some passages not translated into the English edition. See also G. P. Grant, "Tyranny and Wisdom: "A Comment on the Controversy between Leo Strauss and Alexandre Kojève," *Social Research,* Vol. 31 (Spring, 1964), pp. 45-72.

13. Strauss, *De la Tyrannie,* pp. 342-344.

14. Leo Strauss, "On Collingwood's Philosophy of History," *Review of Metaphysics,* Vol. 4, No. 4, June 1952, p. 569.

15. On the "fundamental problems," see Gourevitch, II, 284 ff., 315-316.

16. Berthold Riesterer, in his *Karl Löwith's View of History* (The Hague: Martinus Nijhoff, 1969), reaches (mistakenly, I believe) an opposite conclusion in commenting upon Löwith's assertion that historicism "fails to recognize the possibility that a certain historical situation could have been far more favorable for the discovery of truth than any other." Riesterer contends, p. 87, that "A genuine extratemporal search for truth . . . is not dependent upon any particular historical situation or age, it can occur at any time and under any and all circumstances." Cf. also Strauss, *City and Man,* pp. 155, 236.

17. Karl Löwith, "Heidegger: Problem and Background of Existentialism," *Social Research,* Vol. XV (1948), pp. 359-360.

18. Cf. Eugene F. Miller, "Political Philosophy and Human Nature," *The Personalist,* Vol. 53, No. 3, Summer 1972, p. 212.

19. Karl Löwith, From *Hegel to Nietzsche* (Garden City: Anchor, 1967), p. 305. Cf. Martin Buber, *Between Man and Man* (New York: Macmillan, 1965), p. 147, "One could say that Hegel in the position he assigns to man, follows the first creation story, that of the first chapter of *Genesis,* of the creation of *nature,* where man is created last and given his place in the cosmos, yet in such a way that creation is not only ended but also completed in its significance now that the 'image of God" has appeared; while Feuerbach follows the second creation story, that of the second chapter of *Genesis,* of the creation of *history,*

where there is no world but that of man, man in its centre, giving all living things their true name."

20. Ortega, *History*, p. 165.

21. Karl Marx, *Economic and Philosophical Manuscripts*, tr. T. B. Bottomore, in Erich Fromm, *Marx's Concept of Man* (New York: Frederick Ungar, 1966), p. 134.

22. Buber, p. 160. Cf. Martin Heidegger, "Letter on Humanism," in *The Existentialist Tradition*, ed. N. Langiulli (Garden City: Anchor, 1971), p. 212. Löwith, [in Reisterer, p. 95] argues that man's uniqueness "extends to his embryonal development; it manifest itself in the way he satisfies his most primitive natural needs; and it is attested in the specifically human possibility of suicide. Man alone, of all living creatures, can cultivate, pervert, and negate his own nature." Contrast these views with the earlier, very different, tradition. See Aristotle, *Ethics* 1098ᵃ 1, Metaphysics 1016ᵇ 30, Thomas's *Commentary on the Ethics*, V. 8, 877, Dante, *Monarchy*, tr. D. Nicholl (Nicolson: London, 1954), Bk. I, Ch. III, p. 7. See also Collingwood, p. 227.

23. Ortega, p. 93, Cf. Löwith, *Permanence*, p. 58; Reisterer, pp. 94-96.

24. Ortega, pp. 112-113.

25. *Ibid.*, p. 108. Cf. Joseph Cropsey, "Political Life and a Natural Order," *J. of Politics*, Vol. 23, 1961, pp. 55-56, and also Hans Jonas, "Change and Permanence: On the Possibility of Understanding History," *Social Research*, Vol. 38 (Autumn, 1971), pp. 517-518.

26. Aristotle, *Politics*, 1253ᵃ 32.

27. Cf. Reisterer, pp. 94-95.

28. Cf. Ortega, pp. 203-204.

29. *Ibid.*, p. 202.

30. *Idem.*

31. *Ibid.*, p. 206.

32. *Ibid.*, p. 203.

33. Collingwood, p. 225.

34. *Ibid.*, p. 226.

35. Ortega, p. 220.

36. Collingwood, p. 225.

37. *Idem.*

38. Ortega, p. 218. Cf. Collingwood, p. 229, ". . . since the historical present includes in itself its own past, the real ground on which the whole rests, namely the past out of which it has grown, is not outside it but is included within it."

39. Collingwood, p. 60, my italics.

40. *Ibid.*, p. 108.

41. See Miller, pp. 209-210; Jonas, pp. 502, 524; Ortega, p. 168, Löwith, *Permanence*, p. 12.

42. Leo Strauss, "An Epilogue," in *Essays on the Scientific Study of Politics*, ed. Herbert Storing, (New York: Holt, Rinehart and Winston, 1962), p. 315.

43. See, e.g., John Wild, *Existence and the World of Freedom*, (Englewood Cliffs, N.J.: Prentice-Hall, 1963), Ch. 4; and James M. Edie, ed., Introduction to Pierre Thevenez, *What is Phenomenology?* (Chicago: Quadrangle, 1962), p. 28. Cf. Victor Gourevitch, in *Phenomenology: Pure and Applied*, ed. Erwin Straus (Pittsburgh: Duquesne University Press, 1964), p. 200, ". . . the Lebenswelt is [n]ever, in any sense, directly available to be lived, or experienced, or described."

44. Strauss, *What is Political Philosophy?*, p. 28.
45. Jonas, pp. 517-18. On existential "structures," see also Fackenheim, pp. 77 fn. 44, 80 fn. 45, 84-88 fn. 47; Edie, pp. 25-28, 168 fn. 17; Maurice Natanson, "Philosophy and Psychiatry," in Straus, Natanson, and Ely, *Psychiatry and Philosophy* (New York: Springer-Verlag, 1969), pp. 108-110; Reisterer, p. 4.
46. William Earle, "Phenomenology and Existentialism," *J. of Philosophy*, Vol. LVII, No. 2, p. 81. See also Richard F. Grabau, "Existential Universals," in James Edie, ed., *An Invitation to Phenomenology* (Chicago: Quadrangle, 1965), pp. 147-160. For the contrary view, see Michael Gelven, *A Commentary on Heidegger's "Being and Time"* (New York: Harper Torchbooks, 1970), pp. 39-42.
47. Cf. Marvin Zetterbaum, "Self and Political Order," *Interpretation*, Vol. I, No. 2, Spring 1971, pp. 243-245. See also Marvin Zetterbaum, "Equality and Human Need," *American Political Science Review*, Sep. 1977 (forthcoming.)
48. Ortega, p. 218; cf. *ibid.*, p. 222 fn. 17.
49. Wild, p. 165.
50. Natanson, p. 95.
51. Cf. Fackenheim, fn. 47, pp. 84-88. See also Leo Strauss, "Relativism," in *Relativism and the Study of Man*, ed. Helmut Schoeck and James Wiggins (Princeton: D. Van Nostrand, 1961), p. 155.
52. Ortega, pp. 203-204.
53. Arendt, p. 62, my italics.
54. Cf. Ortega, pp. 165-169. In an unpublished manuscript on Rousseau's *Discourse on Inequality*, Victor Gourevitch notes, "What differs from time to time and place to place is not just how men live or what they do and believe, but, *since these are the properly constitutive elements of their being, what they are*" (italics mine). Fackenheim observes, p. 15n, "If there is a [permanent] human nature, then the historical changes of human self-understanding are as irrelevant to that nature as are the changes in the physical sciences to physical nature. But if human being is an historically situated self-making, then the historical changes in human self-understanding (itself a form of human self-making) must necessarily affect human being."
55. Cf. David Hume's remark, "Mankind are so much the same, in all times and places, that history informs us of nothing new or strange in this particular. Its chief use is only to discover the constant and universal principles of human nature . . ." [cited in Miller, p. 217], with Ortega's view, pp. 204-205, that what *does* change is the reality "human life."
56. Aristotle, *Politics*, Bk. III, Ch. 1.
57. Strauss, *What is Political Philosophy?* p. 29.
58. Cf. Arendt, p. 86.
59. Erwin Straus, "Psychiatry and Philosophy," in Straus, Natanson, and Ely, *Psychiatry and Philosophy*, p. 11.
60. See Grabau, "Existential Universals," *passim.*
61. Friedrich Nietzsche, *Beyond Good and Evil*, I, 22.

# 9

## HUMAN NATURE AND THE RADICAL VISION

### LYMAN TOWER SARGENT

If it is possible to make a nontrivial statement that applies to all human beings, i.e., if there is a human nature, there must be some significance for political philosophy. This must be particularly true for a political position that holds that (1) the world is in a serious, even an intolerable, situation; (2) it is possible to improve this situation and produce a society in which everyone, or almost everyone, will be at least content, perhaps even happy; (3) this happy state can be brought about only through fundamental changes in the economic, social, and/or political systems. One holding such a position must take account of human nature, and it is at least possible that the position dictates certain conclusions about human nature.

In this essay, I wish to explore the implications for radical thought of this admittedly simple statement of the relationship between radical thought and conceptions of human nature. If my brief characterization of what almost all radicals believe and my definition of what must be entailed in any conception of human nature worth talking about can be accepted as valid, it seems worth exploring the relationship. Radicals are perhaps the only truly optimistic political thinkers, and they are often accused of naïveté regarding human nature. And it seems fair to say that radical thought has been rightly accused of such naïveté and may also be guilty of some rather basic confusions where human nature is concerned.

Obviously not all radicals take the same position regarding human nature, but, it must be asked, can any single position explain (1) the present mess, (2) the conditions that will satisfy man in the future, and (3) the means of getting from here to there? The problem is a central one for the radical. He needs to have some explanation for human behavior that allows him to comment on all these points in some detail, and such a conception must, it seems, entail some definition of human nature.

But the assumptions of radical thought in this area have been fundamentally confused in three ways. First, the question of human nature has rarely been faced; it has simply been assumed or ignored. Second, when it is discussed it is often discussed in a contradictory or unclear manner. Third, the linkages between human nature and the various other aspects of their political theory or programan are often unclear or unformulated.

Such failings constitute a basic flaw in the thinking of most radicals, although one that, I think, can be remedied. This is particularly true now since we are learning so much more about the biological basis of human behavior and the range of genetic determination. The new evidence must be carefully weighed and older conceptions rethought. Regarding this new knowledge, radicals have tended toward an anti-intellectual approach. Ideas that conflict with radical formulations have been rejected as untenable rather than subjected to the rigorous analysis that might make it possible to reject them on factual grounds.

But detailed consideration of the new data is not my purpose here. In this paper I am exploring solely the implications of theories of human nature that radicals have held or could hold. I shall attempt to show where each conception leads, and I shall comment on the problems that each conception entails, particulary in light of evidence for a significant degree of genetic determination. My approach will be critical and analytical rather than historical. In doing this I shall focus on the relationship between particular conceptions of human nature and the three contentions about contemporary society and the possibility of change that radical thought postulates. Obviously a single conception should apply in all three cases.

There are, rather unbelievably, seven different conceptions of human nature that self-proclaimed radicals have held: men are good; men are bad (actually held, but added here more for symmetry than significance); each man has an authentic self that can be found or created; there is no such thing as human nature; human nature is evolving; human nature is malleable; human nature is genetically or biologically determined. It might be accurate to say that they could all be reduced to an environment-genetic continuum, but this would miss the complexities and confusions of the actual positions. Of course, the overwhelming tendency is to the environmental rather than the genetic or biological. I shall look at each in turn.


## MEN ARE GOOD

Tradition has it that radicals believe that man is by nature good, or even perfectible,[1] and that changed social conditions will allow that nature to be expressed. And, of course, the anti-radical argument has also contained a major element to the effect that people are not like that—that they are either bad or a mixture of the two. Certainly some radicals, such as Godwin or Morris, have believed man to be basically good.

The traditional attitude has two parts. First, there is such a thing as human nature which can be judged to be essentially good, bad, etc. Second, social conditions, environment, control the expression of that human nature. Setting aside the question of the quality of human nature, we are left with two propositions, the existence of human nature and its ability to find expression.

Most radicals assume the existence of human nature. Such an assumption must mean that there is something nontrivial that can be said of *all* human beings that cannot be said of any other species. Additionally, in this context, this one element must be socially and politically relevant. No importance could be attached to a statement lacking any relevance to social and political thought.

Such a view of man is perhaps the easiest one for radicals to hold because it allows them to say that man acts evilly in contemporary circumstances only because of those circumstances. It says that the environment, which we all admit is unsatisfactory, makes man apparently incapable of expressing his true, good nature. And, obviously, since this true nature is good, a vision of the good society is possible. One of the difficulties that has often been pointed out to radicals is the absence of evidence in contemporary circumstances that man can create a good society or even live in one.

For the environmental determinist who believes that man is by nature good, this poses no problem: if we can construct a better society, men will behave better, and no problem in fitting man's nature to the good society arises. The problem in such a conception relates to change. How can man be moved from stage one, our present distress, to stage three, the good society? There are two possible routes, both of which leave some questions. First, even in contemporary circumstances, some good men are produced. The fact that they are produced can pose serious problems for the radical. How are good men produced by a bad environment? Since good men are produced, against the expectations of the environmental approach, is it not possible that that approach is wrong? Secondly, if social change is taking place and if progressivist assumptions are made, the environment that controls man's nature will improve and man will change and gradually get better. But without the progressivist assumptions, there is no reason to assume that the world is getting better and that man's nature will change for the good as opposed to the world getting worse and man's nature thus changing for the worse. It is also a much better argument for reform than for radical change, since most radicals tend to believe that rapid rather than gradual change is essential to bring about a good society.

Thus, while the conception of human nature is directly linked with both the analysis of present circumstances and the good society, the conception of human nature is not directly linked with the possibility of change from one to the other. It requires a set of subsidiary assumptions about the process of social change to fill in this gap. And these assumptions are of the sort for which there is no evidence, or even for which no evidence is possible. One might even conclude that there is considerable negative evidence regarding the assumption of progress.

The assumption that man is good and that only certain changes are needed in the environment to bring out his basic goodness is fundamentally flawed and includes a set of secondary assumptions that we can no longer accept.


## MEN ARE BAD

I include this merely to balance the picture. The only people known to me who are self-styled radicals holding this position might best be labeled Fascists. However, there are people who hold that men are bad but that a good society can be produced through a strong central government which controls all aspects of men's lives. The present circumstances are easily attributed to the inherent evil in man; the creation and continuation of a good society is based on control.[2]


## AUTHENTIC SELF

There is an authentic self within each of us to. be discovered, and social conditions largely determine our ability to discover it. Not only is this authentic self usually different for each of us, but it is very likely to be so. Hence an assertion of diversity usually accompanies this conception.[3] It may be approached in either of two ways. First, it may be assumed that it is possible to discover and accept this self. Second, it may be assumed that it is possible to create this self. The difficulty of this conception of human nature is that it is virtually meaningless because the concept of the authentic self has no content. It tells us nothing about man's ability to live in changed circumstances. It assumes that if we all discover or create our authentic selves, we will become psychically well adjusted, will overcome alienation, and will thus be able to get along with all of our fellows. But no evidence is offered for such a position.[4] However, it does hang together to some extent.

The position is that (1) there is an authentic self to be discovered or created; (2) on the whole we are not now in touch with our authentic selves; (3) we are thus alienated from our selves;

(4) we are thus alienated from our fellows; (5) once we achieve contact with our authentic selves we will no longer be alienated from our selves and therefore will no longer be alienated from our fellows; (6) thus a significantly better society will be possible.

Of course one is bothered by what all this means. Even though this model can fit all three components of radical thought, it tells us little or nothing about the content of any stage—which is exactly the point many contemporary radicals make. Contemporary society is dislocated because we are all alienated. The good society will be fine because we will no longer be alienated. But what is the content of the good society? It is impossible to tell, of course, because we are now alienated, and we cannot in any way tell what we would be like in a nonalienated society. We cannot tell how we would interact with others in a nonalienated society. Thus, a good society is possible, but we cannot define it.

Hence the radical loses a major element of his appeal. He can only say that you will be better off, and that you will feel better because you will no longer be alienated. But he cannot say what this means. He can appeal to the person who feels psychically unwell today, but he has no way of appealing on the basis of a vision of a good life. All he can say is that it will be a better life because you will no longer be sick because you will no longer be separated from yourself. But the traditional radical has been able to appeal on a somewhat more concrete basis. Although Marx did not specify the particulars of his good society after the withering away of the state, he was talking in a tradition in which most people would understand that certain things would take place in such a society, and Marx did specify some of those characteristics. There was a shared tradition and Marx did nothing to deny much of that tradition.[5] Thus, because no shared tradition exists today, the modern radical who argues for the acceptance or creation of self and the diversity that implies has lost one of his major attractions.

## NO HUMAN NATURE

Sartre says that there is no human nature, there is only the human condition.[6] This has become a popular position among radicals because it allows for the three stages as well as or better than most other conceptions. And it does not involve the number of implausible or unprovable assumptions that so many of the other positions require. Since we have no evidence about human nature, why bother to assume it?

It is an appealing position because it puts the onus for our lives solidly on ourselves. We create the social conditions in which we live. They come entirely from our own actions and inactions. Therefore we can change them at will. Obviously it is not quite so simple as that, but it gets back much of the élan of the traditional radical. You can do something about your lives now if you will only try.

But this position is running up against the difficulties of our growing knowledge of the genetic and physiological basis of human behavior. It is becoming a little hard to say that there is no human nature. It is not yet impossible but it is becoming difficult and thus the possibility of such a position is being eroded. The radical has tended to dismiss this growing body of evidence as unworthy of consideration since it is not conclusive. It would appear to be much more sensible to try to deal with the direction our knowledge now seems to be taking rather than to dismiss it because it has not yet been perfected.

This poses a considerable problem for the modern radical. If human behavior has some genetic or physiological basis, it may well be that some things simply cannot be changed, at least with our current knowledge. It will be impossible for the radical to change the XYY chromosome. Thus he can no longer argue that in the good society there will be no criminally insane.[7] Some problems will always require concerted social action to limit and control violence against other persons. And such action will of course produce fundamental inequalities in society. To be fair, even William Morris believed that the rare murder might occur, but he also believed that such actions were entirely within our ability as individuals to control.

Also, rejection of human nature raises questions about the possibilities of the good society. If nothing can be said about all men, why can the assumption that a better society is possible still be made? If it is possible to say nothing about all men, how can we say that life can be improved for all men? Is this not contradictory? What then is the radical's position? Does he say "no I cannot provide any way in which life will be better for everyone, but most people's lives will become better?" Again he loses part of his case. He must then argue solely in measurable terms. He must be able to say that by doing X we will improve the lives of this set of people in these ways. And he must demonstrate that this is in fact true. He becomes a social scientist or a reformer, or both. In this situation the force of his contentions depends entirely on how horrible we believe the current situation to be.

## HUMAN NATURE IS EVOLVING

"Natural biological evolution in man is slow, but cultural evolution has become a part of natural evolution and has accelerated it at a dizzy rate. In a way it has changed human nature radically. One might even say whether post-modern man is still *Homo Sapiens* remains to be seen."[8] Borghese's position is another way of denying the importance of human nature. If human nature is constantly changing and evolving, even if the implication is that it is getting better, then we are again saying nothing useful about all men. And all the criticisms made about the rejection of human nature apply equally here.

## HUMAN NATURE IS MALLEABLE

"Human nature is a convertible commodity, and can be made good or bad by circumstances."[9] The same point holds true here—if human nature is completely malleable, there is no such thing or it is completely determined by environment. If it is completely determined by environment, the environment has to change independently of man before man can begin to act better. In this case, the argument is being made for an Owenite community which would provide a new and better environment within the old, bad environment and make it possible for more and more good men to be produced. The assumption is that society can include many different environments all producing diferent types of human nature. But there is also the assumption that men, even those from bad environments, will choose the good with no explanation for why that choice would be made.[10]

## GENETIC OR BIOLOGICAL BASIS
## FOR HUMAN NATURE

Traditionally this position was held by Kropotkin and purported to provide a scientific basis for anarchism. Kropotkin argued, on the basis of his observations of animals in Siberia, that species were inherently cooperative. Thus it could be argued that social conditions made men competitive and that if cooperative social institutions were established, man would improve.[11]

Today Marcuse holds a remarkably similar position. "Prior to all ethical behavior in accordance with specific social standards, prior to all ideological expression, morality is a 'disposition' of the organism, perhaps rooted in the erotic drive to counter aggressiveness, to create and preserve 'ever greater unities' of life."[12] But for Marcuse this foundation is itself malleable by social conditions. Thus while there is a biological basis for human solidarity, it need not always be expressed. This of course neatly explains all three stages. Once certain social changes, brought about by technological changes, make the expression of solidarity possible, more rapid change becomes possible, and the good society can come.

There is of course one basic problem—evidence. And of course for Marcuse evidence is almost impossible owing to the nature of the argument; proof will be possible only when this "disposition" can be expressed. But even so Marcuse's explanation on this point fits better than most others. Still we must hesitate to believe before the evidence is available; if one chooses to argue that there is a biological basis for socialism one must expect to be held to fairly rigid standards of evidence. So far the evidence is not adequate, but Marcuse's position, or even Kropotkin's cannot be simply thrown out. There is not yet adequate evidence against them.

In conclusion it may be useful to look briefly at one part of a recent controversy that has raged between the hereditarians and the environmentalists—the question of the mixture of inheritance and environment in the development of intelligence. I shall focus on the issues raised by R. J. Herrnstein[13] because he carefully avoids the racial question that some others raise explicitly.[14] I do this not to avoid the racial question, but because so far I am convinced that Herrnstein raises the most serious questions for radical thought.

Herrnstein's position, put succinctly by him, is as follows: "(1) If differences in mental abilities are inherited, and (2) if success requires those abilities, and (3) if earnings and prestige depend on success, (4) then social standing (which reflects earnings and prestige) will be based to some extent on inherited differences among people."[15] The radical can easily respond that the good society will be based on equality in earnings and prestige or that in such a society all service to society will be rewarded equally, and that the problem will thus be obviated. But this response, while tempting, ignores the deeper issue. If significant differences in mental abilities cannot be eradicated by environmental change, (1) does the vision of an egalitarian society make sense any longer, and (2) even if it makes sense, is that society possible? What sort of egalitarian society can be achieved when its members know that certain significant differences in mental ability cannot be changed by an improved environment? What radical response can be made to the conclusion that their best will not be enough?

Three responses seem possible. The first, genetic engineering, has not yet been treated in radical thought, partly because of the difficulties in conceptualizing the needed social decision-making apparatus, and partly because the issue has not yet been seriously faced. A second response, eugenic manipulation of the population, has not been dealt with recently for the same reasons. In addition, of course, both responses have been rejected a priori because of the perceived conflict between social need and individual freedom that both seem to involve. Since these responses are possible solutions to a very serious problem, radical thinkers must soon attempt to deal with the relationship between freedom and the goal of an egalitarian society when human equality is assumed to be unachievable by nonmanipulative means. The third response is the only one given, and it avoids all the hard questions. Although Herrnstein's case is an impressive one, admittedly it has not been conclusively proved. And it may not be provable without experiments that will force us to answer the questions posed by the first two responses. In addition, it is still possible that changes in the environment could reduce the range of differences in mental abilities sufficiently for the differences not to be considered socially significant. Clearly, much more thought about and research into these questions is needed. While the important questions may not be answerable outside a radically transformed society, it should be possible to clarify many of the issues.[16] The specifics of this particular issue, while potentially significant, are much less important than the more general question of unchangeable characteristics of human nature postulated by the genetic or biological approach. If the existence of such characteristics is demonstrated conclusively, radical thought must change.

The question, finally, is what can then be said about the future position of radical thought regarding human nature. In all probability nothing will change until biological evidence of the most concrete kind forces a change, but it now seems likely that that day is not far off. Obviously, the nature of the biological evidence will determine the nature of the response, but a few comments are still possible. First, it will no longer be possible to say that there is no such thing as human nature. Second, it will no longer be possible to argue that environmental change can completely solve our problems. Third, radicals will be forced to look more carefully than they have so far at the complex interactions among heredity, socialization, and environment.[17]

All this can be very enriching for radical thought. It is probable that the good society will be much more diverse and complex than we have tended to think of it because the interactions of heredity, socialization, and environment will continue to produce people with widely diverse needs and desires.

## NOTES AND REFERENCES

1. See John Passmore, *The Perfectibility of Man,* 2nd. ed. (London: Duckworth, 1972) for an excellent consideration of the question of perfectibility.
2. See, for one example, [Jacob W. Horner] *Military Socialism,* by Dr. Walter Sensney (pseud.) (Indianapolis: Author, 1911).
3. See my *New Left Thought: An Introduction* (Homewood, Illl.: Dorsey, 1972), pp. 11-23.
4. It is being argued by some that group therapy and the like are providing such evidence. See, for example, Carl R. Rogers, "Interpersonal Relationships: U.S.A. 2000," *The Journal of Applied Behavioral Science,* #3(1968), 265-280. But, alternatively, see Sigmund Koch, "The Image of Man in Encounter Groups," *American Scholar,* 42(Autumn, 1973), 636-652.
5. See Daniel Tarschys, *Beyond the State; The Future Polity in Classical and Soviet Marxism,* No. 3 of Swedish Studies in International Relations (Stockholm: Läromedelsförlagen for Scandinavian University Books, 1971), pp. 48-86.
6. Jean Paul Sartre, *L'Existentialisme est un humanisme* (Paris: Nagel, 1966), p. 52 and *passim.*
7. In all fairness it must be noted that even this is debatable. First, the radical can subscribe to genetic engineering as a possible solution, albeit one that does not recommend itself to most radicals. Second, the connection between the XYY chromosome and behavior patterns has not

yet been fully established. See Joshua Lederberg, "The Genetics of Human Nature," *Social Research,* 40(Autumn, 1973), p. 388.

8. Elisabeth Mann Borghese, "Human Nature Is Still Evolving," *The Center Magazine,* 6(March/April 1973), 4.

9. James Casey, *A New Moral World, and a New State of Society* (Providence, R.I.: Author, 1885), p. 3. Cf. "The unlimited malleability premise is almost surely false. The raw material of human nature—the product of evolution—cannot be molded into all shapes and forms by environmental engineering. Certainly there is a wide range of human flexibility. But unless the environment is organized in highly specific ways, inherent human needs will be thwarted and individuals will fail to pass through the development experiences they require." Daniel Yankelovich, "The Idea of Human Nature," *Social Research,* 40(Autumn 1973), 423.

10. Cf. B. F. Skinner's *Walden Two* (1948).

11. See particularly his *Mutual Aid; A Factor of Evolution* (Boston: Extending Horizons, 1955).

12. Herbert Marcuse, *An Essay on Liberation* (Boston: Beacon, 1969), p. 10.

13. See R. J. Herrnstein, *I.Q. In the Meritocracy* (Boston: Little, Brown, 1973).

14. See Arthur R. Jensen, *Genetics and Education* (London: Methuen, 1972); and Jensen, *Educability and Group Differences* (London: Methuen, 1973).

15. Herrnstein, pp. 197-198.

16. Cross-cultural studies now could illuminate certain of these questions. For example, what is the situation in the Communist world? Does it vary significantly from what is shown in studies such as those by Herrnstein?

17. See Robert Theobold and J. M. Scott, *Teg's 1994; An Anticipation of the Near Future* (Chicago: Swallow, 1972), for an attempt to explore such a complex future.

# RATIONALITY AND
# HUMAN NATURE

Richard Brandt's discussion of "The Concept of Rationality in Ethical and Political Theory" leads off his final Part. While the term "human nature" seldom appears in his essay, the concept of rational desires is central to his argument; and what desires are rational for given individuals, he contends, depends upon their basic natures. The best key to man's nature is provided by cognitive psychotherapy. He does not quite contend that a single, constant pattern of human nature characterizes all men: but he does argue that rational individuals with all the relevant considerations vividly before their mind's eye will arrive at similar principles and that they will attach importance to the outcome of collective, impartial choice, partly in order to secure the cooperation of others, and partly for reasons of benevolence.

The two succeeding papers in this Part, while agreeing with much of Brandt's argument, take issue with certain aspects of it. Felix Oppenheim is particularly concerned to assert that rational men, lacking information that would enable them to advantage themselves, would not necessarily agree upon the benevolence principle. As a matter of fact, he argues, most men are not benevolent. Bernard Gert, in his discussion of "Irrational Desires," agrees with Brandt that the concept of rationality should be extended to desires and that some desires are properly designated "irrational." But he believes that Brandt is "completely wrong" in turning to empirical psychology, specifically psychoanalysis, to determine the content of rational desires. "There is no account of any therapy," he concludes, "that could serve as a defining characteristic of rational desires."

John Chapman concludes the Part and the volume with his essay, "Toward a General Theory of Human Nature and Dynamics." Although approaching the matter very differently, he concludes, with Brandt, that it is by focusing on rationality rather than on the irrational that the most distinctive and significant features of human nature can be discovered.

# 10

## THE CONCEPT OF
## RATIONALITY IN ETHICAL
## AND POLITICAL THEORY

### RICHARD BRANDT

The most important contribution philosophers can make to the appraisal and justification of moral systems and political institutions is to identify and formulate the fundamental questions, and to explain why the questions claimed to be fundamental really are so.

Without any further preliminaries, I propose to plunge in and state what seems to me the fundamental question for both political theory and moral philosophy.

The basic question appears to be this: Which moral code, or political system, would all rational persons choose collectively for a society in which they believed they and/or their children would spend their lives? And for what reason would they choose it? I suppose this question, stated as I have without any interpretation of its central terms, would be accepted as the fundamental question by various classical and contemporary writers, going back at least to Hobbes, and including such present figures as John Rawls, R. M. Hare, William S. Vickrey, John Harsanyi, Russell Grice, David Richards, and perhaps A. K. Sen. However, once we start to define the terms of the formulation more precisely, the agreement diminishes. For instance, Rawls would want to construe the term "choose collectively" to mean "choose in the absence of information which would enable anyone to advantage himself," and in this he would be followed by some but not all of the writers mentioned.

From here on I shall not attempt to identify any consensus among writers, but simply discuss the problem on my own account.

First let me call attention to one consequence of framing the question as I have. I am *not* assuming that the prior problem is to identify sound or acceptable *moral* principles and then later consider how political institutions must be framed in order to conform to these principles. I am assuming that if certain political institutions would be chosen collectively by rational persons, that is enough justification; indeed, I would call this "moral justification." Moral principles are the principles proper for individuals to employ in choosing what to do as individuals, and it will sometimes happen that an individual, if he acts according to acceptable moral principles, will find himself breaking the *law,* even when the law is part of a system that would be chosen by rational persons. Institutions are public entities and necessarily rather clumsy instruments; moral principles can be more delicate. For instance, there are relations in the family or between friends which moral principles properly govern, but from which the law had better stay away. Institutions and the moral code presumably are closely related, and presumably people would not be rational if they collectively chose moral principles quite incoherent with their public institutions. But there is a difference. In fact, it is not clear that a legislator would be bound by moral principle to vote for the institutional system that would be chosen collectively by rational persons, if his constituency were strongly opposed to it. At any rate, such considerations are my reason for regarding the question which institutions are morally justified (would be chosen collectively by rational persons) as a question coordinate with the one which moral principles rational persons would collectively choose, and not as a posterior question to be answered only after we have identified a sound system of moral principles.

Let us turn to the interpretation of our proposed fundamental question. What are we to mean by a "rational person?" Or, if you prefer, a "rational choice?" In ordinary use, the term "rational" is vague. The *Shorter Oxford Dictionary* gives, as the meaning of what seems the relevant sense, "agreeable to reason; reasonable, sensible, not foolish, absurd, or extravagant." We might add to this, perhaps, that in ordinary use "rational" is a term of commendation, like "good" and "right," although among some of the younger generation it may have to be argued that it is a good thing to act rationally. Among writers on rational decisions a more precise definition has become popular, which comes somewhere close to stating the properties many people would want to find in a person before they would call him "rational." First, a rational person would have a *transitive* and *complete* preference ordering of possible states of the world, including lotteries. Second, if the agent has certain knowledge of the outcomes of alternative actions open to him, he is rational only if he chooses the action that will produce an outcome to which none other is preferred. If, however, he does not have certain knowledge of the outcomes of alternative actions, he is rational only if he chooses in conformity with a strategy, the employment of which may be expected in the long run to give him the most preferred set of outcomes.

With some trepidation I am going to adopt a different definition of "rational person" or "rational action," although it is one that in the end has many of the same implications for what we are to identify as rational actions. If you do not like my definition as a definition of "rational," I shall be content to use a different word instead. Only, then I happen to think that the fundamental question for political and moral philosophy should be stated in terms of this other word that you assign me. But I think it useful, for various purposes, some of which will become clear as we proceed, to explicate the term "rational" in my perhaps perverse way. At any rate, I would call attention to the fact that the decision theorists' definition is hardly a mere account of the accepted English usage, which is far too vague to fit their definition. Professor Patrick Suppes, in a paper in *The Journal of Philosophy* in 1961 (p. 607), remarked that the disagreements in decision theory show that we "do not yet understand what we mean by rationality," or, as he put it in the very next sentence, "it turns out to be extremely difficult to characterize what we intuitively would want to mean by a rational choice among alternative courses of action." I find these statements puzzling; but rather than go into an account of what would justify defining "rational" in one way rather than another, I shall give my own account, in the hope that it will be useful and clarifying. I shall briefly state, later, where I think it differs from the decision theorists' concept.

The definition of "rational" I prefer permits both (1) basic or intrinsic *desires* (desires for something for itself, not because it is expected to lead to something else that is wanted), and (2) *choices (actions)* to be appraised as rational or irrational. Roughly, the *generic* sense of "rational" is "informed," where "informed" does not imply omniscience, but the *vivid* presence of *available* knowledge. The generic sense has to be specified in slightly different ways for the two contexts of application. (1) Roughly, I call a basic or intrinsic *desire, aversion,* or *preference* rational if and only if it is not different from what it would have been if the agent had brought vividly to mind (on optimal occasions in the past, sufficiently frequently so that the full impact could occur) all the relevant knowable facts—relevant in the sense that they would make a difference if brought vividly to mind. I shall explain this more fully below. (2) I call a *choice* or *action* rational if and only if it is not different from what it would have been if, first, the agent's basic desires had been rational, and second, he had in mind at the moment of choice, with perfect (or at least equal) vividness, all the available information relevant to the choice. Thus the *generic* meaning is such that either a basic desire or an action is said to be rational only if it is not one that results from some kind of *cognitive* mistake, some inaccuracy or inadequacy of representation of knowable facts. Notice that this concept of rationality does not enable us to identify a rational desire or choice in a simple way; for that we need more facts, about human nature in general or particular individuals, and especially the data of empirical psychology (presumably facts about human nature).

Let me explain the above concepts of the rationality of a basic desire (etc.) more fully, since it is widely held that basic desires, aversions, and preferences are not subject to rational appraisal. Let me point out first that the view that basic desires are not subject to objective criticism is not one we take seriously when we visit a psychotherapist. On the one hand we may go to him because we know that some deeply ingrained emotional response to something, say a fear response, is inappropriate in view of the inherent character of the object, and we want help in removing the response. Similarly, we may notice that we have angry or distrustful responses to almost everyone, responses that get in the way of pursuing important goals, and we may wish help with respect to these responses. What I wish to say is that in general it is also proper to classify basic desires and aversions as rational or irrational, for there are basic desires and aversions that we have acquired from praise or blame or modeling by parents or teachers, or by accidental associations of the objects of desire/aversion with aversive or delightful states of affairs, or from false beliefs about them— desires or aversions that would never have developed as a consequence of experiences with typical examples of the states of affairs desired (or aversive). In saying this I am of course assuming that desires and aversions can develop (and are "rational" if they do) from direct interaction with the states of affairs desired (or aversive) or with states of affairs relevantly like these, and from the person's merely just liking or disliking this interaction natively (or in a learned way not distorted by prior "irrational" processes). Moreover, just as phobias tend to diminish with attention to the nondangerous character of the objects when this is made vivid (say, by modelling behavior by others, or experimental efforts by the person himself), so desires and aversions, acquired otherwise than by direct association with typical examples of the things wanted or aversive, will tend to diminish, as a result of repeated attention to what their objects are like. It follows from my definition of "rational" that any desire or aversion which will extinguish as a result of such discriminative reflection is irrational. Or, to put it in different words, any desire or aversion which will extinguish through "cognitive psychotherapy" is irrational. For example, I suspect that most cases of strong motivation for personal recognition or achievement (in the sense of one-upmanship), and aversion to many nonprestige occupations, are irrational in this sense. Some values, which writers like Marcuse regard as false, a result of manipulations by the social system, may be irrational in my sense. Incidentally, we should note that the concept of a rational desire is *person-relative,* in the sense that a desire that is rational for one person may not be so for another. Some desires (aversions) may be rational or irrational for everybody (e.g., possibly an aversion to pain), a consequence of human nature as such, but, possibly as a result of native physiological differences (e.g., in level of energy), a desire rational for one may not be for another. Hence, decision whether a given desire (e.g., for power) is rational for a given person may be a task as difficult as it may be important. Again, where some degree of desire (e.g., for achievement) may be rational (because everyone enjoys acquiring complex skills or "competences"), a higher degree of it, resulting from childhood deprivation of love, may be irrational; and it may be no easy matter to separate the two.

Let me now contrast this usage with the concept of a rational *choice* or *action,* as I conceive it. I said a rational action is one that would occur if the agent's desires are rational (but for many purposes we may want to ignore this, and take the agent's actual desires as the given fact), and if he had in mind, *at the moment of choice,* with perfect or at least equal vividness, all the relevant available information. Now can this concept enable us to make any general statements about which choices are rational? It can, if we make use of the psychological "theory of action"—if, for instance, we make use of the theories of a line of writers including Lewin and Tolman, and more recently, Atkinson, Ryan, Irwin, Vroom, and experimentalists on human decisions. This theory contains a network of laws of wide application that enables us to predict with high probability what a rat will do, when he knows which alley leads to food and when he is hungry, and equally well what a human being will do, when we know which outcomes are valenced for him (wanted or aversive) at the time, and when he knows his position in the world at the time and has beliefs about which actions of his will likely lead to these outcomes. In order to use this theory to determine which kinds of action are *rational* for a person, we have to draw inferences about what a person *would* do, in certain types of situation, given his valences (actual or rational), *if he represents to himself vividly the relevant knowable facts about his situation.* If we do this, we can infer, say, that a rational agent, choosing between one act that will produce one desired outcome, and a second act that will achieve the same outcome and also another desired outcome, and at the same cost, will choose the second. (This follows from the empirical laws of choice, given that the agent represents to himself that the likely outcomes will be as stated.) Again, we can infer that a rational person, who is considering two actions that produce the same desired outcomes, but one with more effort or expenditure than the other, will choose the plan with the lower effort or cost. Again, we can infer that a rational person, considering two options, both expected to lead with equal cost to the same desired outcome, but one with greater probability to the desired outcome, will take the one with the greater probability. So, if we identify the "rational" man as the agent who vividly represents to himself available knowledge, we can go a long way toward inferring what a rational man will do in certain circumstances. Rationality, incidentally, excludes action on impulse —which essentially is action taken because the prospect of certain outcomes was not present to the mind at the time of choice. And it excludes "action from fear," when this means that aversive outcomes were represented vividly at the time of choice, with other outcomes (either desired or aversive) excluded from the focus of attention.

Clearly the identification of actions as rational requires both reference to human nature (the principles of psychology) and the definition of "rational."

Where does this concept of a "rational" person lead to conclusions different from those to which the concept of rationality employed by decision theorists would lead? Let me mention a few of the more important points. Most obviously, my concept makes it possible to talk of basic desires and aversions as being themselves rational or irrational; the other theory does not. Second, my concept has the implication—although the chain of inference requires some explaining—that future wanted states of affairs may not be discounted just because they are future, although they may be discounted because the associated probability is lower; further, it has the consequence that future desires, aversions, and preference-rankings are to be weighed as heavily as present ones. Third, my concept does not render it an analytic truth that a decision is rational only if it occurs in the context of a *transitive* preference ordering of states of the world, although it probably leads to refusals to recognize as rational some of the money-pump behavior that has been thought characteristics of a person with intransitive preferences; but the transivity of preferences is a difficult topic, and I do not wish to lay any weight on this difference. There are other differences, some deriving from the fact that my concept involves a limitation to *available* information, some deriving from the fact that there is no supposition that a rational person would have preferences among many lotteries. But at many or most points the two concepts lead to the same identifications of behavior as rational, since a fully informed person, "rational" in my sense, would choose an action to achieve his ends that he knew conformed to a policy that in the long run would probably succeed more frequently than any other policy for action. I cannot claim, however, that the psychological theory of action enables us to say that a rational person in my sense would prefer one sophisticated strategy for action under uncertainty to another; but then, as far as I am able to make out, neither have decision theorists offered very good reason for choosing among various strategies for action under uncertainty.

Perhaps the most interesting difference between defining "rational action" in my way and defining it as the decision theorists tend to do, lies in the reasons that may be offered *why* a person should be interested in acting rationally, in other words, in why the showing that an action is rational constitutes a recommendation of it. If one defines "rational" as I do, the correct answer to this question seems to be that a person who wishes to appraise his behavior by intellectual means at all can hardly fail to take an interest in desire or action which he knows he would have to take except for failure to represent vividly to himself available relevant information. A person who seriously doubted whether he should act rationally in my sense must apparently in consistency do whatever came into his head at any moment and stop reflecting about the best course of action. In contrast, I think some value judgments would have to be offered in defense of doing the rational thing in the way this is often defined by decision theorists; but there does not seem to be much discussion of this point, and it sometimes seems decision theorists think it is enough to weigh their intuitions about what is rational, mysterious as this process seems to be.

Let us return now to our initial question about moral codes and political institutions: "Which moral codes, or political system, would all *rational persons* (rational in desire and in action) *choose collectively* for a society in which they expected they and/or their children would spend their lives?" I have indicated that some writers would construe "choose collectively" as "choose impartially' or "choose under conditions of ignorance of facts which would enable them to advantage themselves"; and, of course, some writers are using a different concept of rationality.

I wish to discuss briefly two problems about this question. First: Can it be shown that rational persons would collectively choose *any* particular moral code or set of institutions? If not, our question may be a good one but there is no way to answer it. Second: Suppose you do identify some moral code or set of political institutions as the one which would be *chosen collectively* by rational persons, what does this prove anyway? Why should a rational person take an interest in which institutions or moral code would be the *collective* choice of rational persons? I begin with the second of these questions. Incidentally, it is worth bearing in mind how well our question compares in these respects with what seems at first a simpler choice of a basic question: Which moral code, or political institutions, would *maximize utility* over the long run? But I will deal with my question only.

If any given individual could believe that a certain moral code or political system would be given top preference by *him,* if he were rational, it is obvious that nothing needs to be said about the importance of this showing for *him;* there could hardly be a higher recommendation of something than to be shown it would be your top choice if you were rational. But what is the importance to anyone, or everyone, of knowing that a certain moral or political system would be chosen by all rational persons including *him, if* they were choosing impartially, or collectively? Why is it important to identify such a system? Some philosophers, like R. M. Hare, would argue, on the basis of their analysis of the use of "ought" or "moral" in English, that, if the system that were impartially chosen were identified, people must agree that they "morally ought" to live by it; but I do not think it a strong recommendation of acting in a certain way, to show that, as the phrase "morally ought" is used in English, a person cannot consistently deny that he "morally ought" to act in that way. He could always avoid the conclusion by deciding that he preferred to use "morally ought" in some other way. (This is to ignore the serious doubts about the cogency of Hare's analysis of "morally ought".) I think we must do something else: try to show at least why a rational person would be motivated to behave in a certain way, if he knew that a certain moral code or political institution would be chosen collectively, or impartially, by all rational persons.

I do not think we can show that all *conceivable* rational persons, for instance, all dictators with absolute power, would want to support, teach, or recommend a system, moral or political, that all rational persons would choose collectively, although, of course, every rational person must want to live in some sort of moral and political system. But I think we can show that most rational persons, in ordinary circumstances, would want to do so. Why? In the first place, in order to obtain a moral code or political system that comes as near as possible to insuring his own welfare, he must convince other people. Other people, in the long run, cannot be enlisted to cooperate in supporting a moral or political system that disadvantages them for no good reason. A person's best realistic possibility for getting cooperative activity toward a moral and political system that will benefit him maximally, then, is to engage others in the support of a system that can be identified as one they can all choose, impartially or collectively. A system of morality, it should be remembered, requires collective action if it is to be taught to the coming generation. In the second place, other people will willingly submit, for the adjudication of conflicts of interest, to a moral and legal system, at least in the long run, only if it is one which can be collectively or impartially chosen. On the one hand, each will see that no reason can be given why he in particular should be disadvantaged; and on the other, each will see that all others will take the same view; so, if there is to be a compromise that all can accept without strong temptation to resort to violence, it will be a system of rules that can be chosen collectively. If there is to be an accepted system for peaceful resolution of conflicts of interest, the system must be one which can be chosen collectively. Third, in a society whose public morality and political institutions could be collectively or impartially adopted by all rational persons, there can be a quality of life that cannot exist in a society without such morality or institutions. There can be relaxed mutual trust, openness, absence of need for being on one's guard, friendly warmth among persons, a cooperative spirit, the freedom with others that derives from knowledge that one is not prospering at their expense. I would claim, then, that in the human situation a rational person would choose to escape from the state of nature to a moral and social system that could be collectively or impartially chosen by all rational persons.

To say this is not at all to say that it is always to the advantage of a given person to obey the law in a well-ordered society, or to follow the rules of a moral system that all rational persons would choose collectively. Far from it. I am only saying that it is to the advantage of each person, in the long run, to support, proclaim allegiance to, preach, and demand an educational system that teaches and explains a moral and political system that all rational persons can accept. In so far as our actual moral and political system is of this kind, it is to the advantage of every individual to support it, over the long run, although not necessarily to live by it on particular occasions.

I must acknowledge that I have not fully demonstrated that a rational person would choose to support a moral and political order that could be chosen collectively, or impartially, by all rational persons. All I have shown is that a rational person would choose to support such an order in so far as it regulated the interaction among persons with whom he has to deal and *who can be a threat to him*. If a morality that could be "impartially" chosen requires equal rights for members of future generations, imbeciles, unborn fetuses, or even animals (to the extent that they are equally capable of suffering or enjoyment), then it is not obvious that a rational person would choose to escape from a state of nature to such a moral system; at least, it is not so obvious how self-interest could be served thereby. And the same, if we are talking of a moral or institutional system that could be "chosen collectively," if we require that the collective choice be a matter of agreement by members of future generations, imbeciles, animals, etc. (assuming this even makes sense). I suggest that we can show that a rational but selfish person would choose to escape from a state of nature to a moral and political system only of a somewhat "minimal" sort, one that provided rules that could be chosen impartially or collectively by all the adults from whom this person could hope to gain or might have something to fear and only for regulation of their mutual interactions. A moral and political system that goes beyond this in its system of rights and protections can, I believe, be justified, not to wholly selfish persons, but only to those with a strain of benevolence. This restriction is perhaps not very important, if, as I think is the case, it is at least rare that a rational person will be without a strain of benevolence not because, as Hume thought, benevolence is a part of human nature, but because human beings who have experienced a normal process of child-rearing will, if they are rational, develop a degree of benevolence. To the extent that a person is benevolent, he will be disposed to support a moral and political system that extends rights and protections to being from whom he has nothing to fear—future generations, animals, fetuses (perhaps), imbeciles, and so on.

With the foregoing reservations, then, let me repeat that a rational person, in view of the fact that he is living in society, would choose to support the moral and political system that all rational persons can collectively or impartially prefer. This fact is the one that gives importance to identifying which system of morals and politics rational persons would collectively or impartially prefer.

Let us return now to our first question—whether it can seriously be shown that rational persons would, collectively or impartially, prefer one set of moral rules and political institutions. I naturally do not expect to get far with an answer to this question in the space remaining, but perhaps I can make some points that will be helpful in reflection on the issue.

So far I have left vague the conception of choice "collectively" or "impartially" by all rational persons. What is a collective or impartial choice? Let us begin with the notion of "impartially." One line of philosophers, currently most vocally represented by R. M. Hare, would explain an impartial choice roughly as one that would be made by a person with an equal positive concern for the welfare of all persons including himself. A second group of philosophers, among whom Professor Rawls has given the view the fullest statement, would explain an impartial choice as one that would be made by a person who had no information that would enable him to advantage himself. The notion of the collective choice of an institution has received less attention recently, although Russell Grice has advocated a form of it in connection with moral philosophy, and the concept is related to discussion of principles of collective bargaining by economists. The notion of "collective choice" that seems to me worth further exploration is one of rational people (and, as rational, provided with available relevant information), voting preferentially among many possible moral and political systems incorporating "planks" put forward in nomination by rational persons (and hence *not* including planks a fully rational person would not want), with permission to make trade-offs (so that one could abandon support of a scheme including his pet plank or restrictive rule, in return for others' abandoning support of restrictive rules unpalatable to him), under the constraints that the system chosen must command the loyalty of all to an acceptable degree, and that none may be preferred to another when it is known that the former would provide for the satisfaction of interests less than the latter.

These are all possible notions, and there may be others that are better. How are we to choose what kind of "collective" or "impartial" choice we want to include in our formulation of the basic question? Some of these notions may lead to inconsistencies or causal impossibilities; these must of course be rejected. Among those that are left, I think we must make a choice on the basis just discussed; that is, we must show that a rational person would, in the long run, prefer to support a moral or political system selected by the use of one of these concepts rather than the other. I shall not, however, comment further on the relative merits of these various conceptions here. I shall only remark that there is nothing sacrosanct about an impartial choice, particularly choice behind a veil of ignorance about how to advantage one self, or about a collective choice in the sense suggested. If one of these conceptions leads to identically the same consequence as another, the differences among them are unimportant. Moreover, none of them can well make claim to be a self-evidently proper guide to either ideal moral rules or ideal political institutions; each of them must, as I see it, commend itself by showing how a selection of it rather than another would permit a choice among moral codes and political institutions of a kind that would elicit the most support from rational persons.

A majority of the writers who set out to identify the moral system, or political institution, that rational persons would choose collectively or impartially, in one or the other of the senses explained above, arrive at the conclusion that the moral and political system chosen would be utilitarian in some form or other. That is, the moral and political systems would be identified as those that would maximize expectable utility for everyone, perhaps with some restrictions. Roughly speaking, the argument is that whether you are impartial (or want the welfare of all equally) or are choosing in ignorance so that you do not know how to advantage yourself, you will want a system that maximizes expectable utility, either because in such a system you will stand the best chance to do well or because you want everyone maximally benefited. Similarly, if you think of the choice as a collective voting system. of the kind sketched a moment ago, the equilibrium system that will be chosen is one that on the evidence appears to maximize expectable utility. Of course, in so far as utility cannot be precisely measured and compared, there will be some margin of imprecision in the identification of the ideal moral or political system.

Most of the writers, I suggest, come to this conclusion. Some others do not, notably Professor Rawls. Rawls argues that a person who is unable to advantage himself over others because of the absence of relevant information must move to protect himself against calamity in social institutions, by adopting a maximim strategy—that is, one of maximizing the worst off one can be. This leads him to adopt some nonutilitarian principles. I do not find Rawls's argument wholly convincing, but this is not the place to debate the details of the various proposals. I would urge only that the main issues in political and moral theory are (1) exactly how to construe the idea of rationality, (2) how to construe the idea of a collective or impartial choice, (3) why a rational person would attach importance to the outcome of a collective or impartial choice, and (4) what kind of moral and political system such a choice would select—whether some kind of utilitarian system, or a system that satisfies Rawls's maximin rule, or something a bit different.

It would be a mistake to think that these various conceptions of collective or impartial choice, or the conceptions of maximin strategies versus maximize-expectable-utility strategies, will lead to vastly different conclusions about justifiable moral or political institutions. When we take human nature and the facts of society into account, the maximize-expectable-utility program is going to lead to very similar, if not the very same, moral principles and political institutions to which the maximin principles will lead. Professor Rawls seems to acknowledge that the difference may be very largely in the matter of what appears as a basic principle of a moral system or system of justice, and what appears as a derived principle, reached from the basic principle with the help of factual assumptions. The practical difference is rather small. But the theoreticians will naturally continue the debate as long as necessary in order to get things straight.

It is clear that, whichever of the somewhat different theoretical views we take, some features of both moral and political systems will be invariant. Any rational person will want a moral system that prescribes assistance to others at times of dire distress when the assistance is not very costly, which forbids unprovoked assault, and which requires keeping promises under certain general conditions. Again, a rational person is certain to choose a political organization that includes a system of criminal justice; and he will choose a political system that guarantees certain rights, including the right to freedom of speech of some sort, and of political association.

The question might be raised how the various systems sketched might deal with the possibility of choosers among moral or political systems, who want to require only certain things such as privileges for the highborn or for philosophers, or the prohibition of stripteases. Since these desires seem prima facie not to be self-interested desires, how, if at all, are they to be dealt with? I would propose to show that the desires are not rational, so that rational persons would not want such arrangements in the first place. Professor Hare would seem to reply that such desires are usually quite weak, and hence cannot properly weigh much in moral and political decisions. Professor Rawls rules them out because, on his view, the veil of ignorance is so far-reaching that choosers cannot even know what their particular desires are, but can know only desires that are common to the human species. This problem, however, and doubtless various others require discussion by proponents of the various theories.

In closing, let me say a word about where all this leaves issues about the justification for some sort of democratic system of government, about majority voting, about the obligations of an elected legislator to vote the views of his constituency; and so on. The answer is, of course, that any opinion about these matters must be a theorem, derived from the basic principles about moral or political institutions on the abstract level we have been discussing, conjoined with a mass of factual material about man and society.

# 11

# RATIONALITY AND EGALITARIANISM

FELIX E. OPPENHEIM

## I

Any rational person, Professor Brandt claims, would opt for a moral and political system based on egalitarian utilitarianism (which is the one all rational persons would choose collectively). I must disagree with this claim, for I must deny that rationality can be predicated of basic desires at all.

I do agree with Brandt's conception of rational choice, which is the generally accepted one. To make a rational choice in a given situation, the actor must (1) determine all alternative courses of action open to him; (2) predict the probable outcome of each alternative action as best he can on the basis of the information available to him; (3) establish a probabilistically weighted preference rank order among the alternative possible outcomes in terms of some given standard of evaluation; (4) select the course of action leading to the predicted outcome that corresponds to his highest preference.

The rationality of the actor's *predictions* of the alternative outcomes can in principle be ascertained objectively by the standards of inductive and deductive reasoning. So can the rationality of his *preferences* among these possible states of affairs—but only relative to some general standard of evaluation to which he has committed himself, i.e., *his own* basic desires or intrinsic goals[1] or general moral principles. Now, according to Brandt, it follows from the meaning of rationality that the adoption of a basic desire itself can be judged to be rational or not (p. 269). I draw the opposite conclusion. On the basis of the criteria of rational choice, it is quite meaningless to ask which of two incompatible *basic* desires or *intrinsic* moral principles, e.g., benevolence or egoism, it would be rational to adopt—unless one subscribed to some cognitivist metaethical theory claiming certain intrinsic normative views to be demonstrably true.

This does not imply that the criteria of rationality can be applied only to means to some given end, but not to the end itself. The actor's choice of an ultimate goal may be irrational because he holds mistaken factual beliefs (not due to the unavailability of pertinent information in the given situation). It seems to me that Brandt's examples of irrational "basic desires" are instances of such factual errors: "irrational phobias"—fears that go beyond the inherent dangerousness of the object (p. 269); values that are "false" as a result of social manipulation (*ibid.*); "unauthentic desires or aversions [which] will extinguish when faced with vivid awareness of relevant *facts.* "[2] The choice of a goal may also be irrational because it is utopian (unrealizable in the given situation by any given means); or because it is incompatible with some other of the actor's goals; or because the total outcome of realizing the goal includes features that are more disvaluable to the actor than the goal itself is valuable to him. However, if the actor does not commit such errors in predicting alternative outcomes or in evaluating them in terms of his own standard of evaluation, his choice cannot be qualified as more rational, or less rational, than if he had adopted some different normative principle. At one point Brandt himself states that in order "to determine which kinds of action are rational *for a person,* we have to draw inferences about what a person would do, in certain types of situation, *given his valences,"* (p. 270; italics added) i.e., his desires and aversions. But this statement is incompatible with Brandt's claim that "a basic desire may or may not be rational." I agree with the first statement but disagree with the second.

## II

If it cannot be said that having any basic desire or adhering to any intrinsic moral principle is rational or irrational, then it is surely not *logically* necessary that all rational persons adopt the same moral code, let alone the specific moral code of benevolence and a political system that "would maximize expectable utility for everyone" (p. 278). Such a political system would be collectively chosen by a group of rational actors only if one particular condition were fulfilled; namely, if all of them happened to be committed to benevolence as a basic moral principle, according to which everyone is to count for one. If a person is benevolent in this sense, it follows of course by definition that he supports egalitarian political institutions. If he lives in an inegalitarian society and is among the deprived, it will be rational for him to want to transform the system into an egalitarian one which would give everyone the same rights and opportunities. If he is one of the privileged, he will—if he is a rational egalitarian—gladly give up his privileges and join the disadvantaged in the creation of an egalitarian political and social system.

Now let us assume again an inegalitarian society, made up of rational actors committed to one and the same basic ethical principle, but this time to the ethics of elitism rather than of benevolence. According to this moral code, members of the power elite have the moral right to pursue their own (common) interest, while all other members of the society have the moral duty to serve the interests of the former, but no right to pursue their own. (Let us remember that, if I am correct, it makes no sense to say that it is not rational to adopt an elitist moral point of view or that it is more rational to adopt an egalitarian one.) In this case different types of institutions will be the rational choice for those at the top and for those at the bottom of the social hierarchy. The former will rationally defend the status quo. For the latter it will be rational to try to bring about at least a more egalitarian system, or, better still from their point of view, a regime based on inegalitarianism in reverse, in which the present "exploiters" will become the "exploited."

This is not to deny that there are hypothetical or even actual situations in which it will be rational for anyone to opt for egalitarian moral and legal rules, regardless of his basic ethical views. Thus, I agree with Brandt (and Rawls) that this might be the rational choice of "a person who had no information that would enable him to advantage himself" (p. 276). Indeed, since there is an equal chance that he might find himself among the disadvantaged half of an inegalitarian regime, he had better opt for an egalitarian one. However, Rawls himself considers a state of nature under a "veil of ignorance" a mere fiction. In fact, everyone knows his station in society. Surely it would not be rational for those who monopolize political or economic power to want to become "their own gravediggers," *unless* they happened to be committed to an ethic of benevolence.

I also agree that all rational persons, regardless of their basic moral point of view, would subscribe to rules prescribing assistance to others or keeping promises under certain conditions or prohibiting unprovoked assault (p. 279). These are again situations in which anyone may be at both the receiving and the giving end. But the question is: will all rational persons opt for egalitarian institutions beyond such limited instances? Only those who are among the disadvantaged, if egalitarian institutions are the "best" they can hope for, and those who have adopted egalitarianism as a basic ethical principle.

There is yet another, empirical, reason why, according to Brandt, egalitarianism is the rational choice for anyone. To insure his own welfare, everyone needs the cooperation of others. To that effect, "he must convince other people" to do so (p. 274). But he cannot convince others to cooperate if they live under a "political system which disadvantages them for no good reason" (*ibid.*). Yet, throughout the ages, wielders of absolute power have had little difficulty in translating their elitist ethics into "slave morality," and thus in convincing their subjects that it is their moral as well as legal duty to serve "the interest of the stronger," or to work for the realization of some higher goal that the leaders themselves allegedly pursue in an unselfish way. The subjects will then cooperate with their tyrants because they have been persuaded that it is for *good* reasons that they have been disadvantaged. Furthermore, while the power of absolute rulers is the more effective the better they can make it appear legitimate to their subjects, the former are often able to elicit the latter's cooperation through the use of coercive sanctions.

### III

That rational human beings are benevolent may mean either that it is rational for everyone to be benevolent or that rational persons do in fact adopt the ethics of benevolence. I disagree with the latter claim no less than with the former. Is it true that anyone who has been raised in a "normal" way and who is rational "will develop a degree of benevolence" (p. 276)? A small degree, perhaps. He may be charitable and helpful; and, as mentioned before, he is likely to favor certain specific egalitarian rules and their impartial application even for his own sake. But Brandt goes much further and affirms that most rational persons would opt for an all–out egalitarian moral and political system, except perhaps only "dictators with absolute power" (p. 274). (Incidentally, Brandt would have to consider such dictators irrational persons.)

It seems to me that those who enjoy political, social, and especially economic advantages are seldom benevolent to such a degree as to make it rational for them willingly to forgo these benefits for the sake of bringing the underprivileged up to an equal common level. They may make relatively small concessions, especially when doing so is the only, or the least costly, way of preserving the status quo in the long run. But how many within the upper–income brackets would opt for a complete equalization of incomes (which would also require the abolition of inheritance)? Or would any industrialized nation go beyond limited foreign aid and reduce the average wealth of its own citizens to the point of bringing about a world–wide common living standard (even in the equally unlikely case that the other developed countries were disposed to do the same)?

It might be objected that these considerations apply only to inegalitarian societies, but that an egalitarian system would be supported by most of its members, at least if they are rational. My reply is that up to now all large-scale societies have been essentially inegalitarian. Egalitarianism as a characteristic of institutions—i.e., the equal distribution of all burdens and benefits (including opportunities)—is an extreme type that no actual society has even approximated. How great the probability that societies will become egalitarian in the future, and to what degree, is a matter of speculation.

Within any inegalitarian system—and that means practically everywhere and all the time—most people are not benevolent, at least not whenever the stakes are high. But even if most people were benevolent, that would of course not prove that the ethics of benevolence and the politics of equality must be the rational choice of everyone. To raise the question in those terms is not even meaningful.

## NOTES AND REFERENCES

1. In this case, the positive value (to the actor) of the goal outweights the negative value of any other features of the outcome—e.g., means, side effects, further consequences.
2. This last example is taken from R. B. Brandt, "Rational Desires," *Proceedings and Addresses of the American Philosophical Association,* Vol. XLII (1969-70), pp. 43-64; at p. 55. Italics added.

# 12

## IRRATIONAL DESIRES

### BERNARD GERT

Philosophers seem to have a very odd way of proceeding. They usually have no doubt about the conclusion they hope to reach but are primarily concerned with whether they can reach the conclusion in some special way. As Mill pointed out some time ago, and as Brandt repeats in "The Concept of Rationality in Political and Ethical Theory" above, philosophers who regard themselves as holding very different ethical theories differ very little in their moral judgment of particular actions. What the philosopher seems most interested in is to show that his system is the best at allowing one to arrive at these judgments. With respect to ethical theories, this approach is quite acceptable; in fact, I have adopted it in *The Moral Rules* (1970). But when it is used for the concept of rationality, then I think it does not work.

We are all aware that there are irrational actions. No one doubts that a person who, prompted by a momentary desire to see how it feels to have no legs, has both of his legs cut off, acts irrationally. It is equally evident that it is irrational for someone who simply wants to know how it feels to be blind to blind himself. Would anyone deny that a person who, wanting to do something really different, kills himself in the most painful fashion possible is acting irrationally? Note that I am not saying that everyone would agree that cutting off your legs, or blinding yourself, or killing yourself in the most painful fashion possible are always irrational actions. There are reasons and circumstances that might make any of these actions rational. It would be rational to cut off your legs to prevent the spread of gangrene, thereby saving your life. It would be rational to blind yourself, if you believed that only thereby could you gain an understanding of the problems of the blind that would enable you to improve their situation significantly. (Of course, it would also be rational not to blind yourself, even though you had this belief. Reason allows a wide variety of actions). It would even be rational to kill yourself in the most painful way possible if you believed that only thereby would you earn eternal bliss after death. (I am not now concerned with the rationality of these beliefs.)

What I am maintaining is that cutting off your legs, blinding yourself, or killing yourself in the most painful way possible simply because you desire to do so, is to act irrationally. If taken as basic, that is, not as the result of considerations of other consequences, such desires are irrational. What Brandt has realized is the standard philosophical account of rationality provides no sure way of labeling such desires as irrational. By the standard account of rationality, the only way one can label such a desire irrational is to show that it conflicts with other more important desires. That is, the standard account does not deal with the rationality of a desire on its own: only its relationship to other desires can make it irrational.

What Brandt has done is to propose a new account of rationality, one that will enable us to evaluate individual desires as rational or irrational. This certainly is an improvement over the standard account. I shall simply quote his account of a rational desire. "I call a *desire, aversion,* or *preference* rational if and only if it is not different from what it would have been if the agent had brought vividly to mind (on optimal occasions in the past, sufficiently frequently so that the full impact could occur) all the relevant knowable facts—relevant in the sense that they would make a difference if brought vividly to mind" (p. 268). After offering this account of a rational desire, Brandt notes that it "does not enable us to identify a rational desire or choice in a simple way; for that we need many more facts, and the results of empirical psychology."

Here, it seems to me, is where Brandt goes completely wrong. It cannot depend on the facts of empirical psychology that desires to cut off one's legs, to blind oneself, or to kill oneself in the most painful way possible, (for no reason, one simply wants to do it) are irrational desires. If anything, the dependence is the other way around: we evaluate empirical psychology by seeing if it classifies such desires as irrational. Brandt has, I believe, gone back to the very error that he seemed to be out to correct. By the standard account, one could not call any desire irrational unless it conflicted with that person's other actual desires. Those holding the standard theory simply took it for granted that a person had other desires that would outweigh the desire to mutilate, blind, or kill himself, so that they would be assured that such desires would be labeled irrational. The plausibility of their accounts of rationality depends on this unstated assumption. However, suppose that (whatever the way desires are weighted) it were to be evident that the desires to blind and otherwise mutilate oneself and then kill oneself in the most painful way possible form the most important set of one's desires, and that one has a very minor desire to see a psychiatrist about ridding oneself of these desires. On the standard account, it is the desire to see the psychiatrist that is the irrational desire.

In Brandt's view, this is not the case, for he can say that if these desires to mutilate, blind, and kill oneself were subjected to "cognitive psychotherapy" they would be extinguished and that they are therefore the irrational desires. Thus, Brandt's view undoubtedly offers a considerable improvement over the standard view of rationality held by almost all moral, political, and economic thinkers. I do not claim that their views are similar in all respects, but simply that they all demonstrate at least the fundamental inadequacy I pointed out above. None of them has any way of assessing the rationality of individual desires, what Brandt calls "basic desires," and hence all leave open the possibility that genuinely irrational desires form the most important set of one's desires. However, though Brandt has a way of assessing individual desires, his method does not assure that genuinely irrational desires are ruled out. Suppose we subject a person to cognitive psychotherapy in approved fashion, such that before we know the results of the therapy we are convinced that whatever desire he has now is not going to be extinguished by further cognitive psychotherapy. Suppose further that after undergoing this therapy he still desires to blind and mutilate himself and then kill himself in the most painful fashion possible. Brandt, if he abides by his definition of rational desire, must now say that these desires are rational for this person. I consider this an unacceptable conclusion. I think that we would conclude that somehow cognitive psychotherapy had not worked and that a diffrent therapy should be tried.

This is not merely an outlandish example. Many people suffering from mental illness, e.g., depression, anxiety, or hostility, have desires such as I have described, and cognitive therapy of the kind described by Brandt is very likely to have no impact whatever on these desires. Indeed, sometimes the more vividly the person becomes aware of the harmful consequences that he is going to inflict on himself, the stronger his desire becomes. Mental illness frequently causes one to have irrational desires. Such desires are now often treated by relieving the underlying mental illness, usually by drugs. Merely making the consequences of the desires fully vivid is not always sufficient to eradicate the desires.

The important philosophical point is that no one will be satisfied to accept as a criterion, let alone a definition, of rational desires the survival of a certain technique unless it is guaranteed that this technique rules out certain desires as irrational. Since no one can guarantee that any technique will do this, it follows that defining rational desires in terms of any technique will be unsatisfactory. Thus Brandt's definition of rational desires does not fail because of any lack of sophistication in his account of cognitive psychotherapy. There is no account of any therapy that could serve as a defining characteristic of rational desires. It is almost too obvious to state that this point against Brandt holds with equal force against those Brandt is attacking (Hare and Rawls, etc.), for their account of rationality does not, in fact, even come as close as Brandt's does to guaranteeing the right content for rational desires.

It is clear that a person who desires to kill himself, cause pain to himself, disable himself, or deprive himself of freedom, opportunity, or pleasure, when he has no reason to desire these things, i.e., has no beliefs that he or anyone else will benefit now or anytime thereafter from his carrying out these desires, has irrational desires. Why then not say so and have done with it? It is very difficult to answer this question. There is a tradition in philosophy that you do not merely state your conclusions, but that you must derive them from more basic premises. As I said at the beginning of this paper, this is a valuable tradition. If one stated his conclusions, and nothing more, there could be no argument, no way of resolving disputes between philosophers who put forward diffrent conclusions. Obviously, however, the attempt to derive all conclusions from more basic premises must stop somewhere: some basic premises must simply be accepted.

Rationality is the most basic concept in philosophy, not only in moral and political philosophy but in theory of knowledge and metaphysics as well. Most philosophers presuppose that all men ought to act rationally at al times. For anyone who did not accept this assumption, the whole notion of giving reasons would lose its point. Thus Brandt is seriously misleading when he makes the casual remark "among some of the younger generation it may have to be argued that it is a good thing to act rationally" (p. 267). There is no way to argue this point. A satisfactory account of acting rationally must be such that no one who understands it would ever not want to act rationally. Indeed Brandt attempts to show that by his definition of rationality no one will seriously doubt whether he should act rationally. But I believe I have shown that Brandt's definition of rational desire is inadequate, for, by it, one could and sometimes should seriously doubt whether to act rationally.

The inadequacy of Brandt's account of rational desires has important consequences for any ethical or political theory that is based on it. Brandt correctly points out that "any rational person will want a moral system that prescribes assistance to others at times of dire distress when the assistance is not very costly, which forbids unprovoked assault, and which requires keeping promises under certain general conditions. Again, a rational person is certain to choose a political organization that includes a system of criminal justice; and he will choose a political system that guarantees certain rights, including the right to freedom of speech of some sort, and of political association" (p. 279). But on Brandt's account of rationality, none of this is certain at all. Only if we include as part of our definition of a rational person that he wants to avoid certain evils can we be certain that all rational men will choose a moral and political system with the features Brandt mentions. Since the standard account of rationality held by Hare, Rawls, etc., is, as was pointed out earlier, even less adequate than Brandt's this criticism of Brandt also has important consequences for the moral and political theories these philosophers put forward.

# 13

## TOWARD A GENERAL THEORY OF HUMAN NATURE AND DYNAMICS

### JOHN W. CHAPMAN

In his essay on Georges Sorel, Sir Isaiah Berlin remarks that "the ideas of every philosopher concerned with human affairs in the end rest on his conception of what man is and can be." [1] He goes on to show that Sorel thought of us as, above all, creative creatures, whom only conflict brings fully alive and whose ultimate worth consists in moral heroism. Exemplars of mankind are those early Christians who pitted their faith against pagan hostility.

A host of alternative interpretations of man immediately comes to mind. Perhaps for the student of political theory these will be associated mainly with the names of Plato and Aristotle, Saints Augustine and Thomas, Machiavelli, Hobbes and Locke, Montesquieu, Hume and Rousseau, Bentham and the Mills, Nietzsche, and Sigmund Freud. And most notably, Hegel and Marx. Others will wish to add the names of Tocqueville, Weber and Durkheim, Parsons, Sartre, Wittgenstein, and Claude Lévi-Strauss.

Each of these thinkers offers, explicitly or implicitly, a distinctive interpretation of human nature and dynamics. Man is the rational and political animal. Our will bends our minds, and that will is bad; we are diseased with "original sin," in the grip of motivational forces that pervade and corrupt all thought and action. We are dualistic creatures, compounds of spirit and flesh, but each of us has his natural destination in the great plan of life. Men are mechanisms, open to entirely causal explanation. They are envious, anxious, and prideful, afraid of one another, and rightly so. We are essentially rational, aware of the moral law, but must be on guard against associational processes at work in the mind; custom and habit can obscure the natural law. Climate and institutions shape our nature in special ways. Our nature is passive, and our similarity is the result of uniformity of experience. We are alienated, distorted, and thwarted by our institutions, but man is "naturally good" and capable of "perfectibility." Man is conditionable, and hence is the progressive animal. Human history is the history of man's will to power. We are crooked, disunified, basically irrational, endowed with incompatible urges and drives. Human nature is the product of interaction and is to be interpreted in historical and sociological terms.

Human character varies systematically with the stresses to which it is exposed. Man is a religious animal, whose cultural dynamics may be understood as the outcome of his instrumental and individualizing rationality. Human personality is internalized and institutionalized culture; our rationality translates instrumental activism into institutionalized individualism. We are our own inventions; we create and inhabit forms of life. Culture is prior to society and is the expression of reason mediating the polarities of existence.

The key to human nature lies in our variousness. Our nature is plastic and malleable; we are symbolizing, self-designing cultural artifacts. Or rather, our nature is essentially fixed, an amalgam of permanent attributes and tendencies, confronted by variety of circumstance and meaning. Otherwise humanity would display invariance.

For many generalizations about man's nature, there appears to be an equally plausible and compelling opposite. Some theorists emphasize innate tendencies and autonomous organizing processes, while others look outward to cultural structures for the explanation of human behavior. And the theories of man clearly incorporate diverse interpretations and appraisals of his rationality. Can a coherent and general theory of man be attained?

Along with theoretical diversity, one thinks also of the diverse forms of human character revealed by historians and the diversity of cultures portrayed by anthropologists.[2] And of the instabilities and retrogressions that men display, notably in this century, Apparently there are differing modes of human individuation. What is the explanation of cultural diversity and historical inconstancy? What elements of regularity can be detected in our nature? Are there any fundamental characteristics of men that are independent of their institutional and cultural environments? If there be psychological universals, how should these be conceived, as permanent attributes and properties, or as innate tendencies and processes, or both? What is the significance for understanding human nature of those psychosocial needs that arise out of social interaction? To understand ourselves, should we catalog autonomous needs and propensities, or investigate inner dynamic tendencies, or look for cultural commonalities? Should we look to history or to culture? The fact is that we remain unsure even as to how to think about ourselves.

I very much doubt that these perplexities will be resolved by any great, new, and fundamental discoveries about our nature. The shape of human nature must be already present in the record of our experience. It does not imply Hegelian arrogance to think that we now know everything there is to know about ourselves. Our trouble is that we are wandering in a jungle of fact and interpretation. I think a general theory of human nature and dynamics will look more like a map of the paths in that jungle than it will resemble the general theory of relativity.

## CAPACITIES, POTENTIALITIES, AND DYNAMICS

I propose to begin the construction of such a theory by taking the advice of Clifford Geertz, the anthropologist, and applying it to the history of western political philosophy. He advises attention not only to human capacities, potentialities, and behavior, but also and especially to human dynamics. "Man is to be defined neither by his innate capacities alone, as the Enlighten-ment sought to do, nor by his actual behaviors alone, as much of contemporary social science seeks to do, but rather by the link between them, by the way in which the first is transformed into the second, his generic potentialities focused into his specific per-formances." [3] Geertz agrees with Max Weber that man is an essen-tially religious, meaning-seeking animal, and so he finds the "link" in culture and in ideology, conceived as symbolic ways of trans-forming human sentiment and feeling into spiritual significance. Man is, "The agent of his own realization, he creates out of his general capacity for the construction of symbolic models the spe-cific capabilities that define him." [4]

Although Geertz would have us look to cultural variance for an understanding of human nature, as a poltical theorist I find it more congenial to begin by reflecting on the record of Western political thinking. And I assume it does not greatly matter where one begins. If there are patterns to be found in human thought and experience, then the findings of philosophers, psychologists, an-thropologists, and historians should all point to mutually support-ing cartographical conclusions. Along with his variousness, the natural, universal, and the invariant in man should show itself in all the spheres of his thought and action.

## HUMAN NATURE IN POLITICAL THEORY

In Western political thinking there appear to be three persisting psychological theories. One of these is what we call today "behaviorism" or "geneticism," the view that man is thoroughly plastic and malleable.

Although he was essentially a "developmentalist," Aristotle recognized the importance of the habitual in human conduct, and Hobbes was the first modern thinker to recommend systematic indoctrination, while both Locke and Rousseau cautioned against the irrational influence of mental associations. Hume was prepared to explain nearly all of thought and behavior in terms of the prin-ciples of association, and James Mill based his educational theory on straightforward stamping in of the principle of utility. A Humean, individualistic, and psychological account of human plasticity finds today an unbending advocate in B. F. Skinner.

The organicist version of the doctrine of malleability is based on our presumed dependence on our institutional, historical, or cultural environments. Historicism, in both its Hegelian and Marxist forms, assumes that we are extremely malleable, although both Hegel and Marx discern in human interaction a drive toward individuality and freedom. John Stuart Mill rejected both historicism and organicism and based his view of man as a progressive being on self-transformation through associational processes in which new capacities and motives are acquired. Divorce organicism from historicism, and you open the way to contemporary cultural interpretations of human nature.

A second perennial psychology is that of instinctivism or nativism. Plato's conception of the soul included subterranean drives, and the doctrine of original sin implies that self-centered instincts are decisive for thought and motive. Many have pointed to the force of self-interest in behavior, even as did Hobbes; they see plenty of scope for conditioning. Nietzsche's conception of the "will to power," and his vision of man as inveterate rationalizer and ideologist are expressions of instinctivism. Freud's view of man is based on the incongruity of his instincts. William McDougall's hormic theory of motivation is clearly an elaborate version of instinctivism. And more recently some anthropologists, geneticists, and students of animal behavior have chosen to emphasize, and are prone to exaggerate, the importance of inherited and seemingly unalterable patterns of behavior.

Carried to an extreme, instinctivism may take the form of an Augustinian or Nietzschean belief that all our characteristics are to be seen as expressions of some basic and ineradicable force labeled will. More usually it sees us as composed of a multiplicity of propensities or dispositions, more or less independent and autonomous, and yet sufficiently compatible to render us ambivalent rather than incongruent creatures.

Thirdly, there is "developmentalism," a term which I use to cover all those theories in which man is conceived as a bundle of potentialities which may be thwarted or fostered by his institutions and beliefs. Rousseau is the outstanding representative of this tradition which has its beginning in the moral psychology of Plato and Aristotle. Our nature is neither fixed nor indefinitely malleable. Rather we are endowed with dynamic tendencies such as our sense of justice. The institutions and beliefs appropriate to man are those that operate to neutralize discordant inclinations so as to release and to consolidate moral feeling. In this view, man's reason is not regarded in purely instrumental or cognitive terms. Rather it is seen as a pervasive force that shows through all psychological processes, a force that operates to form the psychological and moral unity that we call human personality. Contemporary exponents of developmentalism include psychologists as different as Solomon E. Asch, Abraham Maslow, and Zevedei Barbu. James Davies has elaborated his own version of it and applied it to politics in the present volume. John Rawls's theory of justice is based on a developmentalist interpretation of our moral psychology, central to which is the unifying and harmonizing pressure of reason.

Now it is likely, indeed certain, that each of these great psychological thoeries has formulated some aspect of the truth about our nature and its dynamics. On the basis of his monumental study of nineteenth-century thought, Maurice Mandelbaum declares that there is "... no necessary antagonism between some features of geneticism, some features of organicism, and some of the types of propositions concerning human nature and moral psychology which nativists have always sought to uphold."[5] There is a level of automaticity in human life, and there is an inertia in psychological and social processes, for both of which behavioristic psychologies are needed to account. But we are also hormic and purposive beings, deeply affected by our social and cultural surroundings. Human growth and behavior have both inner and outer dimensions, and these testify to the presence of unifying and organizing processes, some of which must be psychological, while others are social and cultural.

At the very minimum, therefore, I think we may reasonably conclude from the record of Western thought about man that we are plural beings. That is to say, we are endowed with, or come to acquire, a purality of needs, both physical and psychological, motives, desires, dispositions, and dynamic tendencies. Since some of our needs are fixed, some plastic, and others developmental, psychic consolidation is a stark and central necessity of the human condition.

## AN IMPULSE TO COHERENCE

Yet another important conclusion about human nature

may legitimately be derived from Western political theory. The great theories have an inner consistency, a compelling feeling of unity and coherence, which is something more than a matter of logic. By this I mean that the basic philosophical, psychological, and ethical components of a political theory are more than merely mutually consistent and compatible. If one accepts the theory's vision of reality, its metaphysical foundation, then it feels only natural and reasonable that men should live as the theory prescribes. Here I believe we have a dynamic manifestation of human rationality.

This drive or pressure toward meaning and coherence apears to be a phenonenon of universal significance. Geertz points out that, "In sacred rituals and myths values are portrayed not as subjective human preferences but as the imposed conditions for life implicit in a world with a particular structure." World views and religions, according to Geertz, set as the goal for man to live realistically; they offer ". . . the genuinely reasonable way to live . . . , given the facts of life . . . ." For example, "In the doctrine of original sin is embedded . . . a recommended attitude toward life, a recurring mood, and a persistent set of motivations."[6]

Further evidence of this human impulse to coherence comes from various quarters. Maurice Mandelbaum holds that ". . . we inveterately believe (as the normative senses of the term 'nature' constantly recall) that what is good and what is morally obligatory have their foundations in the underlying properties of being."[7] Richard B. Brandt has shown how differences in ethical beliefs and attitudes depend in a meaningful way upon differences in metaphysical views.[8] And there is the even more fundamental phenomenon of the functional dependence of emotional upon intellectual processes, given special attention in the work of Solomon Asch.[9]

I find striking the contention of John Casey that from our conceptions of rational choice and rational action may be extracted an unchanging picture of the good man. "It may . . . be that there are certain unchanging values that have their base in an unchanging human nature, and that these values are expressed in the traditional concepts of the virtues. It may also be that there are unchanging relations between these values. A good man is, perhaps, one who is courageous, temperate, wise, prudent, liberal and just; and whatever the moral or ideological fashion of the times, such a picture of the good man cannot change." [10] I suggest that Casey's analysis of what constitutes a good man presents a psychologically coherent set of qualitities. These qualities hang together in a way that can arise only from rational appreciation of human life and action.

These conclusions about our capacities, potentialities, and dynamics may be formally combined to construct a simple, and yet realistic, model of man.

## AN INTERPRETATIVE MODEL OF MAN

I propose now to proceed by working out some of the more important implications of three postulates about our nature, namely: that we are constituted of a plurality of needs, motives, and forces; that we are deeply rational beings; and that we are unequal and differentiated in endowment and development. As far as possible we shall wish to test the implications of the model against historical experience.

The first two of these postulates I infer from Western political thought which, as we have seen, contains contrasting images of man and which exhibits the power of that human dynamic I have called the impulse to coherence. These postulates, either one or both, find a place in the psychological propositions contained in the work of William McDougall, Solomon E. Asch, Maurice Mandelbaum, Clifford Geertz, John Rawls, and Zevedei Barbu.[11] Given our assumption of the basic unity of human thought and experience, this is what one would expect.

That inequality is a salient characteristic of man is plain both upon the historical record and from current preoccupations. Let us further subscribe to Geertz's claim that we are the unfinished, the uncompleted animal.

## THE AMBIGUOUS NATURE OF RATIONALITY

That our nature is pluralistic, unfinished, and rational imposes a task, that of psychic consolidation and motivational integration. So conceived, our nature imposes also a problem, that of interpretation, and poses a risk, that of instability, frustration, and imbalance. For pluralistic and unequal creatures such as we, even our vaunted rationality may prove to have ambiguous implications.

To begin with the problem of interpretation, among political philosophers this has taken and continues to take the form of unresolved questions about our moral psychology. Are we, despite our psychological ambivalence and cultural variance, ultimately unifiable and "perfectible" beings, for whom there is one right and good way of life, which once achieved would be steadily adhered to? Or is our nature so deeply and thoroughly pluralistic as to deserve to be described as contradictory, a condition that forces us to choose among drastically different values and ways of life, and that would account for the variety of human cultures?

Surely the foremost contemporary spokesman for the latter interpretation of the human condition is Sir Isaiah Berlin.[12] To believe that we can have all that we hold valuable, and to which human beings can rightfully aspire, is to take an unempirical view of life and morality. For Berlin it was Machiavelli who was the first to appreciate, at least implicitly, this central truth about our situation. For Machiavelli saw that paganism, life in accordance with a natural instinctual order, offered a genuine alternative to Christian ideals. This insight Berlin generalizes to account for what he regards as the irreducibility of a plurality of authentic and ultimate values. Presumably these are grounded in specific, independent, and autonomous propensities basic to human nature.

In Berlin's view, the unwillingness or failure to recognize that man lacks ethical unity accounts for much of the disorder and destruction of human society and history. As Kant discerned, our rationality, our impulse to coherence, tends to run wild. Then it becomes a metaphysical craving for a unity and a symmetry that nature and our nature lack. We misinterpret and mutilate ourselves by trying to impose on life gestalts that it rejects. Rationalist thirst produces the mirages of scientific politics and scientific history, both of which owe more to presumptuous metaphysical intuition than to genuine, empirical science. In the twentieth century it is metaphysical addiction, in the guise of ideology, that is at the root of the politics of extermination. To Berlin the human condition and history are finally paradoxical in that much that is apparently irrational is to be explained by our compulsive rationalism. Like cargo-culters we create murderous nonsense by attempting to impose meaning and coherence upon our situation beyond that which the evidence can bear.

Another illustration of the ambiguous implications of human rationality may be seen in our attitudes toward equality and efficiency. Reason inclines us toward both, but given human inequalities efficiency requires hierarchy. In consequence, according to Raymond Aron, a central tension of modern society is generated.[13] Or, as is the case with socialism, in both theory and practice, concern for greater equality and freedom may misfire when centralized control and planning are used to promote the former at the expense of the latter.[14] In both cases, the ethical and the economic implications of rationality diverge, to our consternation and institutional discomfort.

Somewhat less pathological, but nonetheless very disturbing, aspects of the influence of reason in human affairs may be connected with the thinking of Max Weber and Talcott Parsons. The long-term trend toward rationalization of life in the West results in emotional constriction and deprivation; the "formal" and the "substantive" aspects of rationality come into opposition; our instrumental activism locks us into bureaucratic cages. Hence, according to Parsons, there are to be anticipated periodic expressive outbursts, the most recent of which has come in the university.[15]

Here again apparent irrationality may well have a rational foundation, this time in the tension between individual and collective rationality. It is surely collectively rational and to the public benefit that as many persons as possible get as much education as they can absorb. But Raymond Boudon points to an "aggregation paradox," the consequence of which is that increasing expenditure of effort and resources is required merely to maintain achieved status. He says that ". . . one of the main effects of the aggregation paradox is that people who are exposed over time to an ever-increasing number of years of education receive no personal dividends from this increase." [16] Moreover, Boudon doubts that increasing equality of educational opportunity, contrary to its initial effect, will in the longer run promote social and economic equality. *"Other things being equal, and under broad conditions, educational growth as such has the effect of increasing rather than decreasing social and economic inequality, even in the case of an educational system that becomes more equalitarian."* [17] If Boudon is right, then the force of both collective and individual rationality will work against the goal of greater equality and so blight the liberal hope that freedom, in the form of equality of opportunity, will harmonize with social justice. Again, perhaps Berlin would say, authentic and ultimate values, clearly expressions of permanent human attributes and dynamics, collide and do not consort.

More benign interpretations of the implications and the influence of human rationality form the mainstream of Western thought. From Plato onwards reason has been generally regarded as the prime unifying and harmonizing force in personality and politics. Even Hobbes considered us sufficiently rational to bring our mutual anxiety and antipathy under institutional control. Among recent thinkers representative of the rationalist tradition we need single out by way of illustration only Nicolai Hartmann and John Rawls.[18] In the work of both, reason is conceived as a synthesizing force, basic to our moral psychology, at work in the formation of a singular ideal of the person, the source of moral unity in the midst of motivational and value plurality. Indeed, as we look down the historical road from Plato and Aristotle to Rousseau and Kant, what we witness is not a depreciation of rationality, rather its relocation, from nature to human nature. And even Hegel's metaphysical and historical conception of rationality may be interpreted in terms of the dynamics of human development.

Clearly we would not be the creatures that we are were it not for the presence within us of that dynamic force we call reason. Without its presence we would not merely be troubled by inconsistency of belief and behavior. We would not have the feelings, the sentiments, the motives, and the purposes that we have. Nor would we conceive of ourselves as the bearers of rights and duties; we would not have a sense of justice. Our reason is that which transforms inherent tendencies into moral sentiments and standards. It is the source of our impulse to coherence, even as it may operate also to unbalance, frustrate, or distort human aspirations.

We need not attempt to settle here the ultimate significance of human rationality as this issue emerges in the discordant visions of Berlin and Rawls, whether we are capable of achieving and institutionalizing a reflexive moral equilibrium or are doomed to moral instability. Our analysis does suggest, however, that their different appraisals of the human condition may arise in part from differences in perspective. In Berlin's historical and diagnostic perspective, human "perfectibility" is a metaphysical illusion masquerading as an impossible moral ideal; we continue to try to make our own truths, where only toleration and respect for human freedom and variousness will do. On the other hand, Rawls's conception of "perfectibility" seems devoid of metaphysical taint and based rather on the laws of moral psychology, which are open to further empirical investigation. From this perspective, compulsive rationalism may be seen less as an irrational response to ethical plurality than as a mode of individuation encouraged by certain species of metaphysical belief or insecurity of social circumstance. In any event, that the human impulse to coherence should be able to run to extremes is striking evidence of its centrality and strength in our nature.

I think, therefore, that it is enough for present purposes, and not open to serious challenge, to notice that the model of man embedded in Western political thought, and articulated in various ways in the writings of our contemporaries, does go very far to account for and to accommodate enduring and recurring features of human experience and reflection on that experience. Creatures who are by nature plural, rational, and unequal cannot do other than formulate interpretations of themselves and their condition. The record shows that man is not a candidate for monistic definition. His very nature renders him prone to moral speculation, to cultural differentiation, and to social and political experimentation. In this light, our reason is best conceived not as a defining and distinctive faculty, nor as a purely instrumental capacity, but rather as a dynamic and ambiguous force within, the source of the coherence of our beliefs and attitudes as well as a contributor to social disorder, political and cultural oppression, and personal disappointment.

There is, moreover, a pattern in Western experience of which we have yet to take account. This is the correlation between emphasis on rational thought and action and that feeling of inner authority and integrity that is characteristic of human individuality. The appearance of individualism in ancient Greece and modern Europe comes with surges in rational thinking. This phenomenon forces us once again to consider the inner and outer dimensions of our motivational integration and to confront head-on the cultural interpretation of man.

## THE DRIVE TO INDIVIDUALITY

That man's nature is pluralistic, unfinished, and rational poses for him a task beyond self-interpretation, that of motivational integration. How are our tendencies and capacities expressed in psychological processes and through institutional structures?

In Clifford Geertz's view, organization and integration of psychological and social processes are accomplished by cultural patterns, which he conceives of as analogous to templates or blueprints. It is culture that provides modes of individuation, that shapes, integrates, and focuses thought and activity. Culture is the expression of the human capacity for symbolization. And, "The reason such symbolic templates are necessary is that . . . human behavior is inherently extremely plastic." [19]

Geertz's conception of the mobilizing and totalizing functions of culture seems to be based on a thoroughly generalized conception of human capacities. There is no such thing as "natural" man, no common and universal human nature, no Man with a capital "M," who would stand revealed if only we could peel away his cultural skins. In a kind of resonance with Berlin, Geertz speaks of the quest for such a creature as a quest for a metaphysical, supraempirical entity. Hence he rejects what he perceives as the uniformitarian or "Enlightenment" doctrine of human nature. And he chides Lévi-Strauss for attempting to resurrect Rousseau's rational man in the myth-spinning of the "cerebral savage." Geertz is skeptical of human reason, an opinion for which he finds support in history, especially recent history. He does, however, affirm that, "The drive to make sense out of experience, to give it form and order, is evidently as real and pressing as the more familiar biological needs." [20]

It seems that this combination of highly generalized capacities, that is, plasticity, and deficiency of rationality, opens the way to Geertz's version of the cultural interpretation of man. We are essentially symbolizing, conceptualizing meaning-seekers. And evidently the scope of the humanly significant is so wide and great that there can be no Man, only men. Our innate capacities and tendencies are so inchoate as to preclude crystallization in the form of universal moral standards or ideals of personality.

As did the Enlightenment, so too does Geertz see in cultural variance the clue to the malleable nature of men.

Of special interests for us is Geertz's brilliant analysis of Balinese personality. These are a people seemingly the very antithesis of Western individualists. They really do seem appropriately described as cultural artifacts. Their personalities are integrated through processes that Geertz describes as anonymization, detemporalization, and ceremonialization. Their main fear in life is that social formalities may suddenly collapse and reveal the persons behind the masks. In Geertz's words, they suffer continually from "stage fright." The Balinese conduct their life oriented by reference to their cultural blueprints.

Now if we are so plastic and so completely cultural creatures as Geertz alleges, why should the Balinese experience any tension in their lives? Is their perpetual "stage fright" properly to be read as the outcome of misplaced significance or cultural incoherence, or is it that the Balinese may be, or were, the victims of inappropriate, constricting, and stultifying beliefs about themselves and the world? Is is not possible that their lack of individuality is connected with their dearth of rational thinking about life and society?

In any event, from the standpoint of an occupant of Western personality the Balinese mode of individuation looks both repressive and retarded, and it feels unstable. The Balinese personality may well be culturally integrated, but the cognitive and emotional configuration that Geertz analyzes appears to be inherently strainful and constantly on the verge of breaking down. And so it is. According to Geertz, "The sort of individualism which Burckhardt saw the Renaissance princes bringing, through sheer force of character, to Italy, and bringing with it the modern Western consciousness, may be in the process of being brought, in rather different form, to Bali by the new populist princes of Indonesia."[21] It is quite consistent with his cultural conception of man for Geertz to think of individualism as something that is being "brought" to Bali; it could not come otherwise, as the endogenous expression of human tendencies. Western individuality is just another cultural template that a people may or may not happen upon.

I am concerned, of course, with Geertz's cultural theory of man, because it seems to imply, despite what appears to be evidence of his own to the contrary, that the Western personality is accidental, only one of many possible forms of stable individuation, and hence does not express a universal human dynamic in the shape of a drive to individuality. Can it be merely a cultural accident that Augustine renounced Platonism and went over to Christianity? Or was it not because the latter enabled him to make more sense out of his life, gave meaning to those abysmal depths of his own personality?

In the West what I am calling the drive to individuality has surely shown itself more than once. Indeed, it has shown itself in too many times and too many ways to afford a cultural, symbolic explanation. We have Adkins's portrait of the unification of Greek personality, incomplete though this process may have been. There is Augustinian voluntarism, with its emphasis on choice and will, that liberates men from replication through Platonic forms. We have Zevedei Barbu's explanation of the appearance of the liberal, or bourgeois, personality in terms of the dynamic and interrelated processes of individuation and rationalization. Everett C. Hagen claims to detect the emergence of individualistic self-trust and self-reliance in England centuries before these qualities became characteristic of men on the continent—evidently the British have always been individualists! And there is the great fact of the concomitant rise of science and individualism in political and economic activity. What we know as Western individuality may well be connected with both religious and rational attitudes toward life, but both attitudes appear to be expressions of inner forces, whatever the relative weight one may wish to assign to them. However one reads the story, I do suggest that it is evident that much more than the force of character of Renaissance princes, of which Geertz speaks, has gone into the making of modern man.[22]

In this connection, consider also Erik Erikson's psychoanalysis of Gandhi and the Indian experience of political liberation, and notice the similarities to the way in which Martin Luther's assertion of freedom of conscience resonated through European civilization. Additional evidence of what I call the drive to individuality may be found in the life of Mao Tse-tung and Lucian Pye's analysis of the strains that exist in Chinese personality.[23]

I am very much inclined to conclude from these studies that a drive to individuality is present in human nature, indeed, that it constitutes an inner requirement of our nature. As such it is a human potentiality that takes the form, not of a permanent and universally manifested attribute, rather of a universal psychological and moral dynamic. This inner force may be thwarted by institutional or cultural structures, or it may lie dormant until released by cognitive or religious concerns. In either case, the result is some form of felt constriction and distortion, as illustrated by those brittle Balinese, whom Geertz so sensitively and persuasively probes.

This conclusion is quite in line with the way Geertz himself urges us to think about our nature. As we have seen, he says not to look for what is natural or universal, in the sense of fixed, in man. This is, in his view, an eighteenth-century mistake. Rather look for systematic relations among diverse phenomena, which I have taken to be his way of referring to human dynamics. But we seem to be something more than systematic and imaginative symbolizers.

Because he assumes that our native capacities are highly generalized, it appears to me that Geertz jumps too quickly, and contrary to his own findings and Western experience, to the conclusion that we are best understood as plastic and cultural, even ideological, creatures in whom symbol formation and direction operate autonomously. These are the psychodynamics that transform our generalized capacities into a myriad of disparate cultural performances.

That Eastern societies have exhibited astounding cultural inertia cannot be gainsaid. But cultural inertia, however much it may help to account for human diversity, does not justify a purely cultural theory of man. Its explanatory power is limited. For the fact of cultural inertia neither logically nor psychologically precludes the presence in men of an individualizing psychodynamic. Even the great organicists, Hegel and Marx, recognize the force of this psychodynamic and so fail to carry through their cultural and sociological interpretations of man.

Cultural programs and templates, or philosophies of life, may arise (and obviously have arisen especially in the East) that serve to deflect, obscure, or submerge the drive to individuality. There is no guarantee that human beings will automatically acquire beliefs, interests, and institutions that are appropriate to their potentialities. Systematic and long-term self-stultification is a risk inherent in the human enterprise, but it will not go unfelt and unresisted.

There is some further evidence that Geertz has pushed his thesis too far. This comes out in his explication of the function and significance of ideology. "The function of ideology is to make an autonomous politics possible by providing the authoritative concepts that render it meaningful, the suasive images by means of which it can be sensibly grasped." [24]

## INDIVIDUALISM AND IDEOLOGY

Whatever the case may be in Indonesia, this is hardly the way one would describe the role of ideology in Western history and politics. But Geertz goes on to argue, and with deliberately universal reference, that, "It is a confluence of sociopsychological strain and an absence of cultural resorces by means of which to make sense of the strain, each exacerbating the other, that sets the stage for the rise of systematic (political, moral, or economic) ideologies." [25] And with specific reference to Indonesia, he says, "The cultural failure is appearent from the growing, seemingly unquenchable ideological din that has engulfed Indonesian politics since the revolution." [26]

I do not mean to question Geertz's understanding of Indonesian politics in terms of cultural deficiency and institutional incongruity. This interpretation he fully substantiates, and it is an interpretation fully consistent with his theory of man. For this theory implies that the source of strain in a society lies in a disjointedness of its culture and institutions, and not in an incongruence between beliefs and institutions, on the one hand, and human nature on the other. Ideological "din" is the troubled roaring of meaning-seekers exposed to sociocultural incoherence. Cultural man becomes ideological man when his life loses outer consistency.

But can Geertz's interpretation of ideology be generalized to account for the appearance and the significance of ideologies in Western politics? Here the appearance of ideology, first noticed by Hume in the mid-eighteenth century, does not follow upon cultural disintegration. Rather, it seems to me, ideological politics in the West is one of the unanticipated outcomes of individualism.

For men who have become individuals—aspiring, purposive, and possessed of a sense of what Barbu calls "inner authority"— take to ideology when their hopes and expectations have been disappointed. They are internally integrated personalities who are regressing emotionally and intellectually, not culturally and externally integrated beings who have lost their moorings. In the West, as Frederick Watkins has shown,[27] ideologies have been self-generating, taking the form of reactions to successive and specific discontents. Since the eighteenth century there has been a meaningful procession of ideologies, a procession and not a steady "din." Just as the development of Western political theory displays a moral direction from achievement of security through acquisition of liberty to the demand for social justice, so does the parade of ideologies reflect a dynamic of wants and needs as economic liberalism gives rise to nationalism and socialism in various forms. It is a record of the expression of demands that arise from within the human personality as that is subjected to the processes of competitive industrialization, and the Western experience would be ill-conceived as a searching for cultural blueprints. Hence I think that Geertz's conception of the function and significance of ideology tends to slight that inner form of integration characteristic of Western man. His view of the meaning of ideological politics is a projection of his cultural theory of man and seems more applicable to the East than the West.

The coming of ideological politics to the West may very well illustrate, if not demonstrate, something of great importance about psychological processes. If we think of the character of Western man as the outcome of beliefs and institutions that are fitting, in the sense that these encouraged the natural inclination to acquire rational and individualized attitudes toward society and politics, once this type of character has been consolidated, then processes that have previously been veiled, latent, or only sporadic, may become salient. Throughout Western history there have been isolated millenarian groups and movements, but only in recent times has human rationality shown itself as a mass capacity for rationalization. Then metaphysical beliefs no longer shape and stabilize moral and political attitudes, but operate rather to serve and to rationalize emergent needs and motives. Thus aggressiveness, born of insecurity and frustration, may be mobilized and justified in the name of such metaphysical entities as history, class, or race. Modes of individuation, previously sporadic and isolated, tend to become universal in Western populations.

Evidently the psychic craving for coherence shows itself no longer in the dependence of moral and poltical attitudes on philosophical outlook, as it does in the great political theories. Now the situations in which men find themselves generate interests, needs, and motives that function to shape their projective beliefs. This emergent psychodynamic is the fount of the irrationality characteristic of ideologies. Moreover, this reversal of the dynamics of rationality will come as a surprise, as it has in this century.

In this perspective it is only paradoxical that the culmination of Western political thinking in the eighteenth and nineteenth centuries should be accompanied by the arrival of ideological politics. Thinkers such as Rousseau and even Hegel may be regarded as seeking institutional ways to stabilize rational individualism. Their aim was to neutralize, contain, or use Western man's self-centeredness and self-assertiveness in order to release and foster his moral and social potentialities. And the broad movement toward democray and constitutionalism testifies to their success. But inevitably perhaps industrialization and national competition created passions and fears to which the ideologists would minister. Those active characters, of whom John Stuart Mill spoke, would simply not resign themselves to fate in a manner characteristic of the passive peoples of the East.

These remarks on the Western experience are not inconsistent with what Geertz has to say about the East. His cultural conception of personal integration may be viewed as a variation on the theme of dependence of moral and political thinking on philosophical belief, in which symbolic modes displace or dominate rational modes of thought. The human proclivity for coherence and realism in the conduct of life may very well take on alternative, that is, inner or outer, emphases. In consequence, there are genuinely alternative modes of human individuation and integration.

In this theoretical perspective, what does appear to be special in the Western experience is the extent to which men grew internally integrated and moved historically from the claim to religious freedom to the assertion of moral, economic, and political freedoms. Probably the earlier Augustinian, institutional demarcation of the realms of church and state facilitated this development, for this imposed upon the Western European an inner necessity that no Greek or Roman ever faced, to consider and to reconcile within his own mentality the claims and purposes of both. In this manner also the bifurcated origins of Western civilization in Greek rationalism and Christian voluntarism may have exerted steady pressure toward individualization. That cultural duality should promote individuality is quite consistent with Geertz's observations on the coming of individualism to Indonesia.

And quite possibly, as I have suggested, the more inwardly organized men are, as distinguished from being culturally programmed, the more intense will be their propensity to rationalize once their emerging needs and expectations have been thwarted. Moreover, ideological thought and politics follow a historical pattern that can only be the expression of the nature of beings who have grown rational and autonomous.

From these reflections I conclude that a general theory of human nature and dynamics will have to take into account the experience of both Western and Eastern civilization as they have faced the need for self-interpretation and self-organization.

## THE SCOPE AND SIGNIFICANCE OF DIVERSITY

Even if we could establish conclusively that there is a universal tendency toward the active mode of personal integrity dominant in the West, much room remains for diversity of culture and character—given man's need to complete and furnish himself—as well as manifold opportunity for mistake, catastrophe, and ruin.

Clearly the drive toward individuality can be defeated or suppressed by inauspicious combinations of belief, institutions, and circumstance. This appears to be the case with Indian and Chinese civilization. Certainly the record of Chinese moral and political thought, from Confucius to the Legalists, is thoroughly averse to cultivation and appreciation of human individuality. One notices with special dismay the injunction of the Tao-Te-Ching that people be treated like "straw dogs." [28] And it is difficult to conceive of a doctrine less conducive to individualism than that of filial piety. The peoples of the East may simply have got off on the wrong cultural foot: the spiritual founders of their civilizations did not have the grasp of human potentialities we find in the work of Aristotle or the life of Christ. These peoples appear to have been in the sleep of cultural inertia and, until recently, were not exposed to a flow of competing philosophies of life. They are now moving from primordial cultures to ideologies (mostly manufactured in the West) without having gone through the Western trial of rationalization and individualization.

Less dramatic manifestations of human diversity are also inherent in the model of man with which we are working. The variousness of men presents itself in a number of regular and intelligible ways. Perhaps most striking of all is the proliferation of psychological analyses and moral ideals. Again and again we are invited to single out and to fasten upon some human capacity, potentiality, or presumed defect and to regard this as man's defining characteristic, and hence of paramount ethical and political importance. All of our ways of looking at men carry with them, explicitly or implicitly, requests to take up an attitude toward life, to complete oneself by acquiring a distinctive set of sentiments and motivations.

Hegel perceived an intelligible and progressive history of human interpretation and ideal. There certainly is oscillation, as the repeated clash between rationalists and romanticists bears out. Perennial attitudes toward life may well appeal to some persons in every generation: James Mill was a stoic, his son informs us. All of this questioning, agonizing, and dogmatizing about ourselves is fully consistent with our puzzling endowment of hormic plurality and unifying, systematizing rationality. It could not be otherwise unless we were purely instinctive animals or Hobbesian machines.

Diversity manifests itself in different psychological structures, from the Greek and the Roman, through the medieval and the Baroque, to the modern liberal personality, and the aberrations of twentieth-century fascist and communist man. Our model can also accommodate the nuances of national character that we see, for example, in the differing emotional configurations of present-day Englishmen and Frenchmen.[29] And in every age and country there are those men whom political theorists from Plato to Lasswell fear, the power-seekers, those who wish and need to run things despite their disqualifying debilities.

Given our native endowment, it is apparent that not only can we conceive of ourselves variously but also can become structured differently, perhaps especially so within a mode of individuation that is inward in its emphasis. If an entirely cultural interpretation of man were valid, would we not be stiffer than we are, less resilient and subtle in our responses to the exigencies of life? In the West it is those who lack internal consolidation who embark on cultural experimentation, who seek identity from imported blueprints.

It is possible too that genetic inheritance exerts significant influence on character and conduct. Perhaps, as C. D. Darlington and others allege, those peoples who did not experience the discipline of the agricultural revolution are not really like the rest; perhaps there are natural criminals, men who have been bred to their trade.

Lastly, the argument continues over how to cope and deal with human differences that are considered inequalities, now brought once again to sharp focus in the debate over John Rawls's compensatory theory of justice. From Aristotle through Machiavelli to Nietzsche, there are those who urge us to accept and to make use of human differences for the sake of ideals of excellence. They confront thinkers who would correct and compensate for unequal capacity and potentiality, who hold that morality cannot be based on the contingent and accidental. In the West the historical trend has been toward an enlargement of the sense of justice, and it must be significant for understanding our moral psychology that this trend has accompanied individualization as well as firmer reliance on rational thinking. This trend, however, has been reversed in conditions of insecurity and may be reversed again in the face of massive scarcity.

These diverse interpretations of man, the historical differences of psychological structure, and the persisting issues of moral and political philosophy are all sensible, that which is to be expected, in the light of our model of man as the unfinished, unequal, pluralistic creature, endowed with reason. The implication of the model is that we are political animals in a more than Aristotelian sense, not merely deeply interdependent. We are the innately philosophical animal, moral and political theoreticians by trade, forced to an unending concern with what we are and who we can and should be.

## SOME PATHS IN THE JUNGLE

Our political and cultural history must contain the truth about human nature and its dynamic properties. The problem is how to interpret the human experience, taking due account of both its Western and Eastern dimensions. Can we identify paths or patterns that point to the presence of man, or are there only the ramblings of men?

In accordance with our pluralistic model of man, I take it that in addition to our general cognitive and emotional capacities our psychological constitution includes autonomous tendencies, tendencies that are neither instinctive nor learned, the appearance and strength of which depend on human relations, both personal and institutional. Among these are the morally and politically significant feelings of sympathy, gratitude, envy, and pride. Even Machiavelli, who made so much of the envious nature of men, recognized their inclination to reciprocity and saw in it the origin of their sense of justice.

Given that we compose a constellation of psychological capacities and processes, some of which run contrary to others, it is clear that the distinctively human necessity is that of both psychological and social organization. The pattern of Western history and the facts of cultural variation together indicate that these processes operate in both inner and outer modes. We are institutional creatures whose sense of integrity derives from both cultural structure and inner sentiment.

Those who offer a cultural interpretation of man treat culture as the fundamental characteristic of life, and from cultural variance flow the distinctive forms of human society and personality. They may, as does Clifford Geertz, emphasize the way in which our capacity for symbolizing, understood as an autonomous tendency, brings our other and highly generalized capacities into social and personal focus. Others take a less symbolic and more instrumental view of the operations of human reason. For Lévi-Strauss, reason mediates the polarities of life. For Parsons, cognitive rationality supplies the instrumental link between culture and society. Weber conceives of religious and economic structures as instrumentally related, the one serving to legitimize the other. He is a cultural structuralist.

These cultural theories of man share an overly narrow and specific conception of the functions of human reason. It works to translate belief into personality and practice. This is the great path the culturalists detect in human experience. But, as Zevedei Barbu remarks about Weber's theory of man, ". . . such an interpretative model is bound to eliminate from the structure of social action almost anything pertaining to the mental structure of the actor as an individual." [30] According to Barbu, Weber reduces man to ". . . a puppet played on the strings of culture." [31]

On the other hand, those who take a developmental view of man—Rousseau, Rawls, Asch, Piaget, Maslow—stress organizing processes that arise in the course of institutionalized interaction from within the individual personality. This is a pattern central to human experience, and historically it may take either a progressive or regressive direction. In either case, the causal path leads from society to personality and culture. In the developmental view of man, what becomes of us depends more on institutional than on cultural structures.

Hence from the cultural standpoint we look like plastic, self-designing instrumentalists. In contrast, the developmentalists portray us as institutional and self-organizing creatures and look to history for vindication. That we can be and have been both constitutes the pattern in our experience for which a general theory of human nature must account.

## LEGALITY, RATIONALITY, AND INDIVIDUALITY

In contrast with the civilizations of the East, Western civilization is characterized by legality, rationality, and individuality. Our presumption is that these characteristics are causally connected through dynamic processes in human nature.

Western political theory displays something more than an impulse to coherence and a drive to individuality. Its rationalist and voluntarist traditions are united by an overarching legalism. So it was from the beginnings of the civilization in the legalistic ethics of the Hebrews and the legal unity of the Greek polis. According to William H. McNeill: "In sixth-century Ionia, human affairs were regulated quite successfully by impersonal, uniform, necessary, and—hopefully—just laws. Obviously, the laws of nature, which the Ionian philosopers thought they could detect in the universe at large, bore a striking resemblance to the laws of the polis, which surely, though invisibly, governed their own individual lives. The beginnings of Greek philosophy, therefore, may be viewed as a naïve but enormously fruitful projection upon the cosmos of the busy, ordered world of the polis." [32] Not only has Western cosmology tended to be legalistic, as in the work of Aquinas, but so has its ethics. Rousseau and Kant conceive of moral freedom in terms of self-imposed rules, and today western legalism shows its ethical face in the Rawlsian insistence on the priority of the right over the good. Or, as Hayek puts it, "Man is as much a rule-following animal as a purpose-seeking one." [33]

Western legalism has had intellectual as well as cultural and ethical consequences. Frederick Watkins points out that "When various civilizations are compared ... it becomes apparent that styles of thought are hardly less variable than styles of architecture or dress." [34] According to Watkins, the legal basis for social unity in the West had the decisive consequence of fostering analytic thinking. To the East, bureaucratic imperialism led to arbitral, ethical, and totalizing modes of thought, the function of which is to blur and transcend issues, issues that the legal mind and profession seek to sharpen. Gandhi, one recalls, was to the end opposed to making society a legal order.

Whereas the rational impulse to coherence appears to be universal, the inclination to analytic reasoning is peculiar to Western civilization. In this perspective, it is legalism that encourages the attitudes and ways of thinking that culminate in scientific achievement, and, as we have noticed, Western science and individualism have gone hand in hand.

These genetic considerations suggest that what becomes of men depends on the kind of social and political unity they achieve. The internal and the external modes of integration are but the outcomes of different kinds of society, which favor different forms of rationality, analytic and synthetic thinking as contrasted with symbolizing and totalizing modes. In this vital respect, human dynamics depend on political organization. Hence a comparison of Western and Eastern experience points to a political theory of man as the general theory. For it is political man who stands historically behind both the cultural men of the East and the legal men of the West.


## RATIONALITY AND THE THEORY OF MAN

Human rationality shows itself in numerous ways. Some are theoretical, others practical; some are analytic, others instrumental. Reason may operate to unify or to unbalance the human personality, and it may create tension as well as equilibrium. Rationality appears in both the reality-directed character of psychological functions and in the inner, often silent and unnoticed, processes that result in individuality. These outwardly directed and inwardly operative manifestations of reason may or may not work together. The externalized, cultural mode of human integration may support or conflict with the internal laws of human development. For creatures whose innermost properties depend heavily on institutionalized relations, freedom under law is likely to be the galvanizing ideal. Such creatures will be deeply concerned with justice, and their ethics will become more and more imbued with analytical precision.

In the West institutional arrangements, philosophical beliefs, and human dynamics came increasingly into congruence. In particular, moral and political thinking reflect and support a long-term trend against arbitrariness and injustice that culminates in liberal constitutionalism. There is a line of moral development in which man's capacity for reciprocity overcomes his mutual fear and hostility through an expansion of his sense of justice. Freedom and justice under law together represent the trajectory of a civilization that is legal in its origins.

I do not mean to assert, of course, that Western history is a tale of smooth and linear progression. Given the dual foci, both outward and inward, of our reason, that is most unlikely. Rather oscillation, confict, and shift of emphasis; and all this too is present in the historical record. The various forms of moral and political rationalism, from the Platonic universals to Thomistic natural law, testify to the reality-directed, projective mode of psychological organization. But according to Plato, reason gives us access to the universals, and according to St. Thomas, our reason enables us to participate in the universal law. What happens is that the outer gives way to the inner mode of individuation as men come to conceive the natural law as endowing them with natural rights. But before this transition takes place there is a moment at which both sets of processes are present with comparable strength. This is the Reformation, and in Martin Luther's life we can witness the struggle between the outer and the inner as he tries to reconcile his incompatible beliefs in religious truth and freedom of conscience. We have also seen how human rationality can become perverted into projective rationalizations in the form of metaphysically tainted ideologies.

These great figures in Western experience, these paths down which Western man has come, are obscured if we look only to or overemphasize the facts of cultural variation. No adequate theory of man can neglect those of his dynamic processes that show themselves only over time. Concentration on cultural differences leads to a view of man as the plastic animal, whose shape depends on symbolizing or instrumental processes. In either case, reason is given an interpretation that conceals our political nature. A general theory of human nature and dynamics begins in ancient wisdom. Man is indeed the rational and political animal.

## NOTES AND REFERENCES

1. Isaiah Berlin, "Georges Sorel," *The Times Literary Supplement,* No. 3, 644 (Friday 31 December 1971), 1617-1622, p. 1617.
2. On Western types of character, see especially: Zevedei Barbu, *Problems of Historical Psychology* (London: Routledge & Kegan Paul, 1960), and Bernard G. Rosenthal, *The Images of Man* (New York: Basic Books, 1971).
3. Clifford Geertz, *The Interpretation of Cultures: Selected Essays* (New York: Basic Books, 1973), p. 52.
4. *Ibid.,* p. 218.
5. Maurice Mandelbaum, *History, Man & Reason: A Study in Nineteenth-Century Thought* (Baltimore: The Johns Hopkins Press, 1971), p. 268.
6. Geertz, *op. cit.,* pp. 131, 130, and 124.
7. Maurice Mandelbaum, *The Phenomenology of Moral Experience* (Glencoe, Ill.: The Free Press, 1955), p. 17.
8. Richard B. Brandt, *Hopi Ethics: A Theoretical Analysis* (Chicago: The University of Chicago Press, 1954), and *Ethical Theory: The Problems of Normative and Critical Ethics* (Englewood Cliffs, N.J.: Prentice-Hall, 1959).
9. Solomon E. Asch, *Social Psychology* (New York: Prentice-Hall, 1952).
10. John Casey, "Human Virtue and Human Nature," in Jonathan Benthall, ed., *The Limits of Human Nature* (London: Allen Lane, 1973), 74-91, pp. 89-90.
11. In addition to the works cited above, see William McDougall, *An Introduction to Social Psychology* (23rd ed.; London: Methuen, 1936), John Rawls, *A Theory of Justice* (Cambridge: Harvard University Press, 1971), and Zevedei Barbu, *Society, Culture and Personality: An Introduction to Social Science* (Oxford: Basil Blackwell, 1971).
12. See his *Four Essays on Liberty* (London: Oxford University Press, 1969), and "The Originality of Machiavelli," in *Studies on Machiavelli* (G. C. Sansoni Editore, n.d), 149-206.
13. See Raymond Aron, *Progress and Disillusion: The Dialectics of Modern Society* (London: Pall Mall Press, 1968).
14. See Anthony Giddens, *The Class Structure of the Advanced Societies* (London: Hutchinson University Library, 1973), Chapter 15.

15. Talcott Parsons and Gerald M. Platt, *The American University* (Cambridge: Harvard University Press, 1973).

16. Raymond Boudon, *Education, Opportunity, & Social Inequality: Changing Prospects in Western Society* (New York: John Wiley, 1974), p. 198.

17 *Ibid.*, p. 187. Author's italics.

18. Nicolai Hartmann, *Ethics,* trans. Stanton Coit (3 vols.; London: Allen & Unwin, 1932), and Rawls, *A Theory of Justice.*

19. Geertz, *op. cit.*, p. 217.

20. *Ibid.*, p. 140.

21. *Ibid.*, pp. 409-410.

22. See A. W. H. Adkins, *From the Many to the One: A Study of Personality and Views of Human Nature in the Context of Ancient Greek Society, Values and Beliefs* (London: Constable, 1970); Charles Norris Cochrane, *Christianity and Classical Culture: A Study of Thought and Action from Augustus to Augustine* (London: Oxford University Press, 1944); Barbu, *Problems of Historical Psychology,* and *Democracy and Dictatorship: Their Psychology and Patterns of Life* (New York: Grove Press, 1956); and Everett E. Hagen, "British Personality and the Industrial Revolution: The Historical Evidence," in Tom Burns and S. B. Saul, eds., *Social Theory and Economic Change* (London: Tavistock, 1967), 35–66.

23. See Erik H. Erikson, *Gandhi's Truth: On the Origins of Militant Nonviolence* (New York: W. W. Norton, 1969), and *Young Man Luther* (New York: W. W. Norton, 1958); Stuart R. Schram, *Mao Tse-tung* (Baltimore: Penguin Books, 1969); and Lucian W. Pye, *The Spirit of Chinese Politics: A Psychocultural Study of the Authority Crisis in Political Development* (Cambridge: M.I.T. Press, 1968).

24 Geertz, *op. cit.*, p. 218.

25. *Ibid.*, p. 220.

26. *Ibid.*, p. 224.

27. Frederick M. Watkins, *The Age of Ideology—Political Thought, 1750 to the Present* (Englewood Cliffs, N.J.: Prentice-Hall, 1964); and consult also John Plamenatz, *Ideology* (London: Macmillan, 1971).

28. Sebastian de Grazia, ed., *Masters of Chinese Political Thought: From the Beginnings to the Han Dynasty* (New York: Viking Press, 1973), p. 253. See also Richard H. Solomon, *Mao's Revolution and the Chinese Political Culture* (Berkeley: University of California Press, 1971), and Karl A. Wittfogel, *Oriental Despotism: A Comparative Study of Total Power* (New Haven: Yale University Press, 1964).

29. See Nathan Leites, *The Rules of the Game in Paris,* trans. Derek Coltman (Chicago: The University of Chicago Press, 1969).

30. Barbu, *Society, Culture and Personality,* p. 139.

31. *Ibid.*, p. 146.

32. William H. McNeill, *The Rise of the West: A History of the Human Community* (Chicago: The University of Chicago Press, 1963), p. 214. See also Carl Joachim Friedrich, *The Philosophy of Law in Historical Perspective* (Chicago: The University of Chicago Press, 1956).

33. F. A. Hayek, *Law, Legislation and Liberty: Rules and Order* (Vol. I; Chicago: The University of Chicago Press, 1973), p. 11.

34. Frederick Watkins, *The Political Tradition of the West: A Study in the Development of Modern Liberalism* (Cambridge: Harvard University Press, 1948), p. 10.

# BIBLIOGRAPHY

## JOHN W. CHAPMAN

The following list of books and articles does not attempt to be comprehensive and exhaustive. It does not duplicate the bibliographies to be found in the first set of books listed. And it has been designed with the student of political theory and philosophy primarily in mind. It gives special attention to historical studies. *The Harvard List of Books in Psychology* (4th ed., Cambridge: Harvard University Press, 1971) should also be consulted. The catalogue on *Psychology* issued by Basil Blackwell's of Oxford is very useful.

*Books which contain bibliographies*

Greenstein, Fred I. Personality and Politics: Problems of Evidence, Inference, and Conceptualization. Chicago: Markham, 1969.

Gurr, Ted Robert. Why Men Rebel. Princeton: Princeton University Press, 1970.

Heine, Patricke Johns. Personality and Social Theory. London: Allen Lane, 1972.

Kelly, George Amstrong. Idealism, Politics and History: Sources of Hegelian Thought. Cambridge: Cambridge University Press, 1969.

Knutson, Jeanne N. The Human Basis of the Polity: A Psychological Study of Political Men. Chicago: Aldine-Atherton, 1972.

Shklar, Judith N., Ed. Political Theory and Ideology. New York: Macmillan, 1966.

Yankelovich, Daniel, and William Barrett. Ego and Instinct: The Psychoanalytic View of Human Nature—Revised. New York: Random House, 1970.

*Works of special interest for political theory and philosophy*

Arendt, Hannah. The Human Condition. Chicago: University of Chicago Press, 1958.

Asch, Solomon E. Social Psychology. New York: Prentice-Hall, 1952.

Barbu, Zevedei. Democracy and Dictatorship: Their Psychology and Patterns of Life. New York: Grove Press, 1956.

Berlin, Isaiah. Four Essays on Liberty. London: Oxford University Press, 1969.

Boudon, Raymond. Education, Opportunity, & Social Inequality: Changing Prospects in Western Society. New York: John Wiley, 1974.

Brandt, Richard B. Ethical Theory: The Problems of Normative and Critical Ethics. Englewood Cliffs, N.J.: Prentice-Hall, 1959.

Cumming, Robert Denoon. Human Nature and History: A Study of the Development of Liberal Political Thought. 2 vols. Chicago: University of Chicago Press, 1969.

Darlington, C. D. The Evolution of Man and Society. New York: Simon & Schuster, 1969.

Erikson, Erik H. Young Man Luther. New York: W. W. Norton, 1958.

Friedrich, Carl Joachim. Man and His Government: An Empirical Theory of Politics. New York: McGraw-Hill, 1963.

Geertz, Clifford. The Interpretation of Cultures: Selected Essays. New York: Basic Books, 1973.

Hartmann, Nicolai. Ethics. Trans. Stanton Coit. 3 vols. London: Allen & Unwin, 1932.

de Jouvenel, Bertrand. The Pure Theory of Politics. Cambridge: Cambridge University Press, 1963.

Kojève, Alexandre. Introduction to the Reading of Hegel. Ed. Allan Bloom. Trans. James H. Nichols, Jr. New York: Basic Books, 1969.

Macpherson, C. B. The Political Theory of Possessive Individualism: Hobbes to Locke. Oxford: Clarendon Press, 1962.

Mandelbaum, Maurice. History, Man, & Reason: A Study in Nineteenth-Century Thought. Baltimore: The Johns Hopkins Press, 1971.

Passmore, John. The Perfectibility of Man. London: Duckworth, 1970.

Plamenatz, John. Man and Society. 2 vols. New York: McGraw-Hill, 1963.

Rawls, John. A Theory of Justice. Cambridge: Harvard University Press, 1971.

Skinner, B. F. Beyond Freedom and Dignity. New York: Alfred A. Knopf, 1971.

Strauss, Leo. The City and Man. Chicago: Rand McNally, 1964.

*Studies of a general nature that bear directly or indirectly on human nature in politics*

Barbu, Zedevei. Society, Culture and Personality: An Introduction to Social Science. Oxford: Basil Blackwell, 1971.

Benthall, Jonathan, Ed. The Limits of Human Nature. London: Allen Lane, 1973.

Berelson, B. R., and G. A. Steiner. Human Behavior: An Inventory of Scientific Findings. New York: Harcourt, Brace & World, 1964.

Bienen, Henry. Violence and Social Change. Chicago: University of Chicago Press, 1968.

Boden, Margaret A. Purposive Explanation in Psychology. Cambridge: Harvard University Press, 1972.

Cantril, Hadley. Human Nature and Political Systems. New Brunswick, N.J.: Rutgers University Press, 1961.

Chapman, John W., "Personality and Privacy" in Pennock, J. Roland, and John W. Chapman. Eds. Privacy: Nomos XIII. New York: Atherton Press, 1971.

Chein, Isador. The Science of Behavior and the Image of Man. London: Tavistock, 1972.

Chomsky, Noam, "Psychology and Ideology" in Reasons of State. New York: Random House, 1973.

————. Problems of Knowledge and Freedom. London: Barrie & Jenkins, 1972.

Coles, Robert. Erik H. Erikson: The Growth of His Work. Boston: Little, Brown, 1970.

Davies, James C. Human Nature in Politics. New York: John Wiley, 1963.

Dollard, John, et al. Frustration and Aggression. New Haven: Yale University Press, 1939.

Eysenck, H. J. The Inequality of Man. London: Temple Smith, 1973.

————. The Psychology of Politics. New York: Frederick A. Praeger, 1955.

Festinger, Leon A. Theory of Cognitive Dissonance. Stanford: Stanford University Press, 1957.

Freud, Sigmund. Civilization and its Discontents. Trans. Joan Riviere. London: The Hogarth Press, 1930.

Gedo, John E., and Arnold Goldberg. Models of the Mind: A Psycho-analytic Theory. Chicago: University of Chicago Press, 1973.

Hall, Calvin S., and Gardner Lindzey. Theories of Personality. New York: John Wiley, 1957.

Herrnstein, R. J. I.Q. in the Meritocracy. Boston: Little, Brown, 1973.

Human Nature: A Reevaluation, Social Research, 40 (Autumn 1973).

Jencks, Christopher, et al. Inequality: A Reassessment of the Effect of Family and Schooling in America. New York: Basic Books, 1972.

Knutson, Jeanne N., Ed. Handbook of Political Psychology. San Francisco: Jossey-Bass, 1973.

Koestler, Arthur, and J. R. Smythies, Eds. Beyond Reductionism: New Perspectives in the Life Sciences. Boston: Beacon Press, 1971.

Le Bon, Gustave. The Crowd: A Study of the Popular Mind. New York: Macmillan, 1896.

Leighton, Alexander. The Governing of Men. Princeton: Princeton University Press, 1945.

Lindzey, Gardner, Ed. Handbook of Social Psychology. Vol 2. Reading, Mass.: Addison-Wesley, 1954.

Macpherson, C. B. Democratic Theory: Essays in Retrieval. Oxford: Clarendon Press, 1973.

Maslow, Abraham H. The Farther Reaches of Human Nature. New York: Viking, 1971.

McDougall, William. The Group Mind. Cambridge: Cambridge University Press, 1920.

McIntosh, Donald. The Foundations of Human Society. Chicago: University of Chicago Press, 1969.

Mead, George H. Mind, Self, and Society. Chicago: University of Chicago Press, 1934.

Money-Kyrle, R. E. Psychoanalysis and Politics: A Contribution to the Psychology of Politics and Morals. London: Duckworth, 1951.

Niebuhr, Reinhold. The Nature and Destiny of Man. 2 vols. New York: Charles Scribner's Sons, 1941.

Nott, Kathleen. Philosophy and Human Nature. London: Hodder and Stoughton, 1970.

Pennock, J. Roland. Liberal Democracy: Its Merits and Prospects. New York: Rinehart, 1950.

————, and David G. Smith. Political Science: An Introduction. New York: Macmillan, 1964.

Piaget, Jean. Structuralism. Trans. and Ed. Chaninah Maschler. New York: Basic Books, 1970.

Platt, John R., Ed. New Views of the Nature of Man. Chicago: University of Chicago Press, 1965.

Polanyi, Michael. The Study of Man. Chicago: University of Chicago Press, 1959.

The Proper Study. Royal Institute of Philosophy Lectures. Vol. Four. 1969-1970. London: Macmillan, 1971.

Quinton, A. M., "Contemporary British Philosophy" in O'Connor, D. J. Ed. A Critical History of Western Philosophy. New York: The Free Press, 1964.

Raphael, D. D., Ed. Political Theory and the Rights of Man. London: Macmillan, 1967.

Ricoeur, Paul. Fallible Man. Trans. Charles Kelbley. Chicago: Henry Regnery, 1965.

Riezler, Kurt. Man: Mutable and Immutable: The Fundamental Structure of Social Life. Chicago: Henry Regnery, 1950.

———. "On the Psychology of the Modern Revolution," Social Research, X (September 1943), 320-336.

Rogow, Arnold A., Ed. Politics, Personality, and Social Science in the Twentieth Century. Chicago: University of Chicago Press, 1969.

Shils, Edward. "Plenitude and Scarcity: The Anatomy of an International Cultural Crisis," in The Intellectuals and the Powers. Chicago: University of Chicago Press, 1972.

Singer, J. David, Ed. Human Behavior and International Politics. Chicago: Rand McNally, 1965.

Storing, Herbert J., Ed. Essays on the Scientific Study of Politics. New York: Holt, Rinehart and Winston, 1962.

Suttie, Ian D. The Origins of Love and Hate. London: Routledge & Kegan Paul, 1935.

Thorson, Thomas Landon. Biopolitics. New York: Holt, Rinehart and Winston, 1970.

Wallas, Graham. Human Nature in Politics. 4th Ed. London: Constable, 1948.

West, Ranyard. Conscience and Society: A Study of the Psychological Prerequisites of Law and Order. New York: Emerson Books, 1945.

Wolfenstein, E. Victor. Personality and Politics. Belmont, Mass.: Dickenson, 1969.

Young, J. Z. An Introduction to the Study of Man. Oxford: Clarendon Press, 1972.

*Studies in historical psychology*

Adkins, A. W. H. Moral Values and Political Behavior in Ancient Greece: From Homer to the End of the Fifth Century. London: Chatto & Windus, 1972.

———. From the Many to the One: A Study of Personality and Views of Human Nature in the Context of Ancient Greek Society, Values and Beliefs. London: Constable, 1970.

———. Merit and Responsibility: A Study in Greek Values. Oxford: Clarendon Press, 1960.

Arendt, Hannah. The Origins of Totalitarianism. New York: Harcourt, Brace, 1951.

Banfield, Edward C. The Moral Basis of a Backward Society. Glencoe, Ill.: The Free Press, 1958.

Barbu, Zevedei. "Soviet Historiography and the Concept of Man," Acta Philosophica et Theologica, II (1964), 69-79.

———. " 'Choisme': A Socio-psychological Interpretation," European Journal of Sociology, IV (1963), 127-147.

―――. Problems of Historical Psychology. London: Routledge & Kegan Paul, 1960.

Barker, Ernest. National Character and the Factors in Its Formation. 4th and Rev. Ed. London: Methuen, 1948.

Bauer, Raymond A. The New Man in Soviet Psychology. Cambridge: Harvard University Press, 1952.

Berlin, Isaiah. "The Concept of Scientific History," in Dray, William H. Ed. Philosophical Analysis and History. New York: Harper & Row, 1966.

Berman, Marshall. The Politics of Authenticity: Radical Individualism and the Emergence of Modern Society. New York: Atheneum, 1970.

Brogan, D. W. The American Character. New York: Alfred A. Knopf, 1944.

Cassirer, Ernst. An Essay on Man. New Haven: Yale University Press, 1944.

Cochrane, Charles Norris. Christianity and Classical Culture: A Study of Thought and Action from Augustus to Augustine. Oxford: Clarendon Press, 1940.

Cohn, Norman R. C. The Pursuit of the Millenium. 2d Ed. Rev. New York: Harper, 1961.

de Condorcet, Antoine-Nicolas. Sketch for a Historical Picture of the Progress of the Human Mind. Trans. June Barraclough. New York: The Noonday Press, 1955.

Dodds, Eric R. The Greeks and the Irrational. Berkeley: University of California Press, 1951.

Feuer, Lewis S. The Conflict of Generations: The Character and Significance of Student Movements. New York: Basic Books, 1969.

Foucault, Michel. The Order of Things: An Archaeology of the Human Sciences. New York: Pantheon, 1970.

Groethuysen, Bernard. Anthropologie philosophique. Paris: Librairie Gallimard, 1952.

Hartz, Louis, et al. The Founding of New Societies. New York: Harcourt, Brace & World, 1964.

―――. The Liberal Tradition in America. New York: Harcourt, Brace & World, 1955.

Kristeller, Paul Oscar. Renaissance Concepts of Man and Other Essays. New York: Harper & Row, 1972.

Lifton, Robert Jay. History and Human Survival. New York: Randon House, 1970.

Lovejoy, Arthur O. Reflections on Human Nature. Baltimore: The Johns Hopkins Press, 1961.

Mumford, Lewis. The Transformations of Man. New York: Harper, 1956.

Murphy, Gardner. Psychological Thought from Pythagoras to Freud: An Informal Introduction. New York: Harcourt, Brace & World, 1968.

Perry, Ralph Barton. Puritanism and Democracy. New York: Van-guard, 1944.

Polin, Raymond. Le Bonheur considéré comme l'un des Beaux-Arts. Paris: Presses Universitaires de France, 1965.

Potter, David M. People of Plenty: Economic Abundance and the American Character. Chicago: University of Chicago Press, 1954.

Quinton, Anthony, "Horizons of the Mind: Ideas and Beliefs of the Twentieth Century," in Bullock, Alan, Ed. The Twentieth Century: A Promethean Age. London: Thames and Hudson, 1971.

Ranulf, Svend. Moral Indignation and Middle Class Psychology: A Sociological Study. New York: Schocken Books, 1964.

Rosenthal, Bernard G. The Images of Man. New York: Basic Books, 1971.

Schler, Max. Ressentiment. Trans. William W. Holdheim. New York: The Free Press, 1961.

Schoeck, Helmut. Envy: A Theory of Social Behavior. Trans. Michael Glenny and Betty Ross. New York: Harcourt, Brace & World, 1970.

Starobinski, Jean. The Invention of Liberty: 1700-1789. Trans. Bernard C. Swift. Cleveland: World Publishing, 1964.

Ullman, Walter. The Individual and Society in the Middle Ages. Baltimore: The Johns Hopkins Press, 1966.

Walzer, Michael. The Revolution of the Saints: A Study in the Origins of Radical Politics. Cambridge: Harvard University Press, 1965.

Weinstein, Fred, and Gerald M. Platt. Psychoanalytic Sociology: An Essay on the Interpretation of Historical Data and the Phenomena of Collective Behavior. Baltimore: The Johns Hopkins Press, 1973.

*Some appraisals of historical and contemporary conceptions of man*

Aarsleff, Hans, "The State of Nature and the Nature of Man," in Yolton, John W., Ed. John Locke: Problems and Perspectives. Cambridge: Cambridge University Press, 1969.

Barnard, F. M. Herder's Social and Political Thought: From Enlightenment to Nationalism. Oxford: Clarendon Press, 1965.

Berlin, Isaiah, "The Originality of Machiavelli," in Studies on Machiavelli. G. C. Sansoni Editore, 1972.

———. "Georges Sorel," The Times Literary Supplement, 3,644 (Friday 31 December 1971), 1617-1622.

Burrow, John W. Evolution and Society: A Study in Victorian Social Theory. Cambridge: Cambridge University Press, 1968.

Cohler, Anne M. Rousseau and Nationalism. New York: Basic Books, 1970.

Chomsky, Noam, "The Case Against B. F. Skinner," The New York Review (30 December 1971), 18-24.

Cranston, Maurice, "Herbert Marcuse," in Cranston, Ed. The New Left. London: The Bodley Head, 1970.

Derathé, Robert, "L'Homme selon Rousseau," in Études sur Le Con-

trat Social de Jean-Jacques Rousseau. Paris: Societé les Belles
Lettres, 1964.

Fromm, Erich. Marx's Concept of Man. New York: Frederick Ungar,
1961.

Geertz, Clifford, "The Cerebral Savage: On the Work of Claude Lévi-
Strauss," in The Interpretation of Cultures. New York: Basic
Books, 1973.

Lively, Jack, "Introduction," to The Works of Joseph de Maistre. London: Allen & Unwin, 1965.

MacIntyre, Alasdair. Marcuse. London: Fontana/Collins, 1970.

Manuel, Frank E. Shapes of Philosophical History. London: Allen &
Unwin, 1965.

Oakeshott, Michael, "The Moral Life in the Writings of Thomas
Hobbes," in Rationalism in Politics. London: Methuen, 1962.

Odajnyk, Walter, "The Political Ideas of C. G. Jung," The American
Political Science Review, LXVII (March 1973), 142-152.

Ollman, Bertell. Alienation: Marx's Conception of Man in Capitalist
Society. Cambridge: Cambridge University Press, 1971.

Roazen, Paul. Freud: Political and Social Thought. New York: Alfred
A. Knopf, 1968.

Ryan, Alan, "The Nature of Human Nature in Hobbes and Rousseau,"
in Benthall, Jonathan, Ed. The Limits of Human Nature. London: Allen Lane, 1973.

Schaar, John H. Escape from Authority. New York: Basic Books,
1961.

Searle, John, "Chomsky's Revolution in Linguistics," The New York
Review (29 June 1972), 16-24.

Shklar, Judith N., "Hegel's Phenomenology: The Moral Failures of
Asocial Man," Political Theory, I (August 1973), 259-286.

Taylor, Charles, "Marxism and Empiricism," in Williams, Bernard,
and Alan Montefiore, Eds. British Analytical Philosophy. London:
Routledge & Kegan Paul, 1966.

Veatch, H. B. Rational Man: A Moden Interpretation of Aristotle's
Ethics. Bloomington: University of Indiana Press, 1962.

Waltz, Kenneth N. Man, the State and War: A Theoretical Analysis.
New York: Columbia University Press, 1959.

Wiener, Martin J. Between Two Worlds: The Political Thought of
Graham Wallas. Oxford: Clarendon Press, 1971.

Wild, John. Plato's Theory of Man. Cambridge: Harvard University
Press, 1948.

Wood, Ellen Meiksins. Mind and Politics: An Approach to the Meaning of Liberal and Socialist Individualism. Berkeley: University
of California Press, 1972.

*Political culture*

Almond, Gabriel A., and Sidney Verba. The Civic Culture: Political
Attitudes and Democracy in Five Nations. Boston: Little, Brown,
1965.

Apter, David E., and James Joll, Eds. Anarchism Today. London: Macmillan, 1971.

Aron, Raymond. Progress and Disillusion: The Dialectics of Modern Society. London: Pall Mall, 1968.

Bennis, Warren G., and Philip E. Slater. The Temporary Society. New York: Harper & Row, 1968.

Dahrendorf, Ralf. Society and Democracy in Germany. Garden City, N. Y.: Doubleday, 1969.

Deutsch, Karl W. Nationalism and Its Alternatives. New York: Alfred A. Knopf, 1969.

Doob, Leonard W. Patriotism and Nationalism: Their Psychological Foundations. New Haven: Yale University Press, 1964.

Eckstein, Harry. Division and Cohesion in Democracy: A Study of Norway. Princeton: Princeton University Press, 1966.

Erikson, Erik H., "Reflections on the Dissent of Contemporary Youth," Daedalus: The Embattled University, 99 (Winter 1970), 154-176.

Gerth, Hans, and C. Wright Mills. Character and Social Structure. London: Routledge & Kegan Paul, 1954.

Hacker, Andrew. The End of the American Era. New York: Atheneum, 1970.

Heilbroner, Robert L. An Inquiry into the Human Prospect. New York: W. W. Norton, 1974.

Inkeles, Alex, and Daniel J. Levinson, "National Character: The Study of Modal Personality and Sociocultural Systems," in Lindzey, Gardner, and Elliott Aronson, Eds. The Handbook of Social Psychology. IV. 2d Ed. Reading, Mass.: Addison-Wesley, 1969.

———, and Raymond A. Bauer. The Soviet Citizen. Cambridge: Harvard University Press, 1961.

Kahn, Herman, and Anthony J. Wiener. The Year 2000: A Framework for Speculation on the Next Thirty-three Years. New York: Macmillan, 1967.

Kamenka, Eugene, Ed. Nationalism: The Nature and Evolution of an Idea. Canberra: Australian National University Press, 1973.

Kornhauser, William. The Politics of Mass Society. New York: The Free Press, 1959.

Leites, Nathan. The Rules of the Game in Paris. Trans. Derek Coltman. Chicago: University of Chicago Press, 1969.

Lipset, S. M. Political Man: The Social Bases of Politics. New York: Doubleday, 1960.

McClelland, David C. The Achieving Society. Princeton: Van Nostrand, 1961.

Money-Kyrle, R. E. Man's Picture of His World: A Psycho-analytic Study. London: Duckworth, 1961.

Ortega y Gasset, José. The Revolt of the Masses. New York: W. W. Norton, 1932.

Parsons, Talcott, and Gerald M. Platt. The American University. Cambridge: Harvard University Press, 1973.

Pye, Lucian, "Culture and Political Science: Problems in the Evolution of the Concept of Political Culture," in Schneider, Louis, and Charles Bonjean, Eds. The Idea of Culture in the Social Sciences. Cambridge: Cambridge University Press, 1973.

———. Politics, Personality, and Nation Building. New Haven: Yale University Press, 1962.

———. The Spirit of Chinese Politics: A Psychocultural Study of the Authority Crisis in Political Development. Cambridge: The M.I.T. Press, 1968.

Riesman, David et al. The Lonely Crowd: A Study of the Changing American Character. New Haven: Yale University Press, 1950.

Rudolph, Lloyd I., and Susanne Hoeber Rudolph. The Modernity of Tradition: Political Development in India. Chicago: University of Chicago Press, 1967.

Sargent, Lyman T. New Left Thought: An Introduction. Homewood, Ill.: Dorsey, 1972.

Schram, Stuart R., Ed. Authority, Participation and Cultural Change in China. Cambridge: Cambridge University Press, 1973.

Solomon, Richard H. Mao's Revolution and the Chinese Political Culture. Berkeley: University of California Press, 1971.

Turnbull, Colin M., The Mountain People. New York: Simon & Schuster, 1972.

Walter, E. V. Terror and Resistance: A Study of Political Violence. New York: Oxford University Press, 1969.

*Political culture and climates of opinion: historical studies*

Becker, Carl L. The Heavenly City of the Eighteenth-century Philosophers. New Haven: Yale University Press, 1932.

Bell, Daniel, Ed. The New American Right. New York: Criterion Books, 1955.

Braudel, Fernand. Capitalism and Material Life: 1400-1800. Trans. Miriam Kochan. New York: Harper & Row, 1973.

Burckhardt, Jacob. The Civilization of the Renaissance in Italy. New York: New American Library, 1960.

Cassirer, Ernst. The Philosophy of the Enlightenment. Trans. Fritz C. A. Koelln and James P Pettegrove. Princeton: Princeton University Press, 1951.

Cobban, Alfred. In Search of Humanity: The Role of the Enlightenment in Modern History. London: Jonathan Cape, 1960.

Dunn, John. Modern Revolutions: An Introduction to the Analysis of a Political Phenomenon. Cambridge: Cambridge University Press, 1972.

Erikson, Erik H., "Hitler's Imagery and German Youth," Psychiatry, I (1942), 475-493.

Fromm, Erich. Escape From Freedom. New York: Avon Books, 1941.

Gay, Peter. The Party of Humanity: Essays in the French Enlightenment. New York: Alfred A. Knopf, 1964.

Giddens, Anthony. The Class Structure of the Advanced Societies. London: Hutchinson, 1973.

Goldmann, Lucien. Le dieu caché. Paris: Librairie Gallimard, 1955.

de Grazia, Sebastian. The Political Community: A Study of Anomie. Chicago: University of Chicago Press, 1948.

Groethuysen, Bernard. Origines de l'esprit bourgeois en France. 4e éd. Paris: Librairie Gallimard, 1956.

Gunnell, John G. Political Philosophy and Time. Middletown, Conn.: Wesleyan University Press, 1968.

Hagen, Everett E., "British Personality and the Industrial Revolution: The Historical Evidence," in Burns, Tom, and S. B. Saul, Eds. Social Theory and Economic Change. London: Tavistock, 1967.

Halévy, Élie. The Era of Tyrannies: Essays on Socialism and War. Trans. R. K Webb. London: Allen Lane, 1967.

Heimann, Eduard. Reason and Faith in Modern Society: Liberalism, Marxism, and Democracy. Middletown, Conn.: Wesleyan University Press, 1961.

Hofstadter, Richard. The Paranoid Style in American Politics. New York: Alfred A. Knopf, 1965.

Howard, Michael. The Franco-Prussian War: The German Invasion of France. London: Macmillan, 1961.

Institut International de Philosophie Politique. L'Idée de Philosophie Politique: Annales de Philosophie politique 8. Paris: Presses Universitaires de France, 1969.

Janik, Allan, and Stephen Toulmin. Wittgenstein's Vienna. New York: Simon & Schuster, 1973.

Lerner, Daniel. The Passing of Traditional Society. New York: The Free Press of Glencoe, 1958.

Lifton, Robert Jay. Thought Reform and the Psychology of Totalism: A Study of "Brainwashing" in China. New York: W. W. Norton, 1961.

Lukes, Steven. Émile Durkheim: His Life and Work. London: Allen Lane, 1972.

MacIntyre, Alasdair. Secularization and Moral Change. London: Oxford University Press, 1967.

Moore, Jr., Barrington. Social Origins of Dictatorship and Democracy: Lord and Peasant in the Making of the Modern World. Boston: Beacon Press, 1967.

Pocock, J. G. A. Politics, Language and Time: Essays on Political Thought and History. New York: Atheneum, 1973.

Shils, Edward A. The Torment of Secrecy: The Background and Consequences of American Security Policies. Glencoe, Ill.: The Free Press, 1956.

Shklar, Judith N. After Utopia: The Decline of Political Faith. Princeton: Princeton University Press, 1969.

Speier, Hans, "Folly," in Force and Folly: Essays on Foreign Affairs and the History of Ideas. Cambridge: The M.I.T. Press, 1969.

Stillman, Edmund, and William Pfaff. The Politics of Hysteria: The

Sources of 20th Century Conflict. New York: Harper & Row, 1964.

Talmon, J. L. Political Messianism: The Romantic Phase. London: Secker & Warburg, 1960.

Trevor-Roper, H. R., "The Phenomenon of Fascism," in Woolf, S. J., Ed. European Fascism. London: Weidenfeld and Nicolson, 1968.

————. The Crisis of the Seventeenth Century: Religion, the Reformation and Social Change. New York: Harper & Row, 1968.

Trilling, Lionel. Sincerity and Authenticity. London: Oxford University Press, 1972.

Venturi, Franco. Roots of Revolution: A History of the Populist and Socialist Movements in Nineteenth Century Russia. New York: Alfred A. Knopf, 1960.

Woolf, Leonard. After the Deluge. 2 vols. New York: Harcourt, Brace, 1931, 1939.


*Ideology*

Bluhm, William T. Ideologies and Attitudes: Modern Political Culture. Englewood Cliffs, N.J.: Prentice-Hall, 1974.

Corbett, Patrick. Ideologies. London: Hutchinson, 1965.

Cox, Richard H. Ed. Ideology, Politics, and Political Theory. Belmont, Cal.: Wadsworth, 1969.

Geertz, Clifford, "Ideology As a Cultural System," in The Interpretation of Cultures. New York: Basic Books, 1973.

Gregor, A. James. The Ideology of Fascism: The Rationale of Totalitarianism. New York: The Free Press, 1969.

Ionescu, Ghita, and Ernest Gellner, Eds. Populism: Its Meaning and National Characteristics. London: Weidenfeld and Nicolson, 1969.

Lane, Robert E. Political Ideology: Why the American Common Man Believes What He Does. New York: The Free Press, 1962.

Montefiore, Alan, "Fact, Value and Ideology," in Williams, Bernard, and Alan Montefiore, Eds. British Analytical Philosophy. London: Routledge & Kegan Paul, 1966.

Partridge, P. H., "Politics, Philosophy, Ideology," in Quinton, Anthony, Ed. Political Philosophy. London: Oxford University Press, 1967.

Plamenatz, John, Ideology. London: Macmillan, 1970.

Rejai, M., Ed. Decline of Ideology? Chicago: Aldine-Atherton, 1971.

Sargent, Lyman Tower. Contemporary Political Ideologies: A Comparative Analysis. Rev. Ed. Homewood, Ill.: Dorsey, 1972.

Sartori, Giovanni, "Politics, Ideology and Belief Systems," The American Political Science Review, 63 (June 1969), 398-411.

Shils, Edward, "Ideology," in The Intellectuals and the Powers. Chicago: University of Chicago Press, 1972.

Watkins, Frederick M. The Age of Ideology—Political Thought, 1750 to the Present. Englewood Cliffs, N.J.: Prentice-Hall, 1964.

Wolfe, Bertram D. An Ideology in Power: Reflections on the Russian Revolution. New York: Stein and Day, 1969.

Woolf, S. J., Ed. European Fascism. London: Weidenfeld and Nicolson, 1968.

## Political biography and psychohistory

Barber, James David. The Presidential Character: Predicting Performance in the White House. Englewood Cliffs, N.J.: Prentice-Hall, 1972.
Brodie, F. M. Thaddeus Stevens. New York: W. W. Norton, 1966.
Clark, L. P. Lincoln: A Psycho-Biography. New York: Charles Scribner's Sons, 1933.
Cohen, Stephen. Bukharin: A Political Biography. New York: Alfred A. Knopf, 1973.
Erikson, Erik H. Gandhi's Truth: On the Origins of Militant Nonviolence. New York: W. W. Norton, 1969.
Freud, Sigmund, and William C. Bullitt. Thomas Woodrow Wilson: A Psychological Study. Boston: Houghton Mifflin, 1967.
George, Alexander L., and Juliette L. George. Woodrow Wilson and Colonel House: A Personality Study. New York: Dover, 1956.
Glad, Betty. Charles Evans Hughes and the Illusions of Innocence. Urbana: University of Illinois Press, 1966.
Langer, Walter C. The Mind of Adolf Hitler: The Secret Wartime Report. New York: Basic Books, 1972.
Lifton, Robert Jay. Revolutionary Immortality: Mao Tse-tung and the Chinese Cultural Revolution. New York: Random House, 1968.
Mazlish, Bruce. In Search of Nixon: New York: Basic Books, 1972.
Rogow, Arnold A. James Forrestal: A Study of Personality, Politics and Policy. New York: Macmillan, 1963.
Tucker, Robert C. Stalin as Revolutionary, 1879-1929. New York: W. W. Norton, 1973.
Ulam, Adam B. Stalin: The Man and His Era. New York: Viking, 1973.
Wolfe, Bertram D. Three Who Made a Revolution: A Biographical History. New York: Dial Press, 1948.
Wolfenstein, E. V. The Revolutionary Personality: Lenin, Trotsky, Gandhi. Princeton: Princeton University Press, 1967.
Womack, Jr., John. Zapata and the Mexican Revolution. Cambridge: Harvard University Press, 1968.

## Psychological, social psychological, and sociological studies

Adorno, T. W. et al. The Authoritarian Personality. New York: Wiley, 1950.
Allport, Gordon W. The Nature of Prejudice. Garden City, N.Y.: Doubleday, 1954.
Berkowitz, Leonard. Aggression: A Social Psychological Analysis. New York: McGraw-Hill, 1962.

Bettelheim, Bruno, "Individual and Mass Behavor in Extreme Situations," Journal of Abnormal and Social Psychology, 38 (October 1934), 417-452.

Bowlby, John. Attachment and Loss. London: Hogarth, 1973.

Buss, Arnold H. The Psychology of Aggression. New York: Wiley, 1962.

Christie, R., and M. Jahoda, Eds. Studies in the Scope and Method of "The Authoritarian Personality." Glencoe, Ill.: The Free Press, 1954.

Coser, Lewis. The Functions of Social Conflict. New York: The Free Press, 1956.

Dror, Yehezkel. Crazy States: A Counterconventional Strategic Problem. Lexington: Heath, 1971.

Durbin, E. F. M., and John Bowlby. Personal Aggressiveness and War. London: Kegan Paul, Trench, Trubner, 1939.

Follett, Mary P. Creative Experience. New York: Longmans, Green, 1924.

George, Alexander L. The "Operational Code," a Neglected Approach to the Study of Political Leaders and Decision Making. Memorandum RM-5427-PR. Santa Monica: The Rand Corporation, September 1967.

Giddens, Anthony. Capitalism and Modern Social Theory: An Analysis of the Writings of Marx, Durkheim and Max Weber. Cambridge: Cambridge University Press, 1971.

Greenstein, Fred I., and Michael Lerner, Eds. A Source Book for the Study of Personality and Politics. Chicago: Markham, 1971.

Hagen, Everett E. On the Theory of Social Change. Homewood, Ill.: Dorsey, 1962.

Hocking, William Ernest. Human Nature and Its Remaking. New and Rev. Ed. New Haven: Yale University Press, 1923.

Homans, George. The Human Group. New York: Harcourt, Brace & World, 1950.

Hoffer, Eric. The True Believer. New York: Harper & Brothers, 1951.

Horney, Karen. The Neurotic Personality of Our Time. New York: W. W. Norton, 1937.

Janis, Irving. Victims of Groupthink. Boston: Houghton, Mifflin, 1972.

Kardiner, Abram. The Psychological Frontiers of Society. New York: Columbia University Press, 1945.

Kariel, Henry A., "The Political Relevance of Behavioral and Existential Psychology," The American Political Science Review, 61 (June 1967), 334-342.

Knight, Frank H., "Human Nature and World Democracy," in Freedom and Reform: Essays in Economics and Social Philosophy. New York: Harper & Row, 1947.

Lane, Robert E. Political Thinking and Consciousness. Chicago: Markham, 1969.

Lasswell, Harold D. Power and Personality. New York: Viking Press, 1948.

Leites, Nathan. The Operational Code of the Politburo. New York: McGraw-Hill, 1951.

Matthews, Donald R. U.S. Senators & Their World. New York: Random House, 1960.

May, Rollo. The Meaning of Anxiety. New York: Ronald Press, 1950.

Merton, Robert K., "Social Structure and Anomie," in Social Theory and Social Structure. Glencoe, Ill.: The Free Press, 1949.

Pear, T. H., Ed. Psychological Factors of Peace and War. London: Hutchinson, 1950.

Rochlin, Gregory. Man's Aggression: The Defence of the Self. London: Constable, 1974.

Rogow, Arnold A., and Harold D. Lasswell. Power, Corruption, and Rectitude. Englewood Cliffs., N.J.: Prentice-Hall, 1963.

Sampson, R. V. The Psychology of Power. New York: Random House, 1966.

Singer, J. David, "Man and World Politics: The Psycho-Cultural Interface," Journal of Social Issues, 24 (July 1968), 127-156.

Smelser, Neil J. Theory of Collective Behavior. New York: The Free Press, 1963.

Smith, M. Brewster, "Personality in Politics: A Conceptual Map, with Application to the Problem of Political Rationality," in Garceau, Oliver, Ed. Political Research and Political Theory. Cambridge: Harvard University Press, 1968.

————, et al. Opinions & Personality. New York: Wiley, 1956.

Stein, M. R. et al., Eds. Identity and Anxiety. New York: The Free Press, 1960.

Stevenson, Leslie. Seven Theories of Human Nature. London: Oxford University Press, 1974.

Stone, William F. The Psychology of Politics. New York: The Free Press, 1974.

Toch, Hans. The Social Psychology of Social Movements. Indianapolis: Bobbs-Merrill, 1965.

Wann, T. W., Ed. Behaviorism and Phenomenology: Contrasting Bases for Modern Psychology. Chicago: University of Chicago Press, 1964.

Wheeler, Harvey, Ed. Beyond the Punitive Society. London: Wildwood House, 1974.

White, Ralph K., and Ronald O. Lippitt. Autocracy and Democracy: An Experimental Inquiry. New York: Harper, 1960.

*Moral psychology*

Bosanquet, Bernard. Psychology of the Moral Self. London: Macmillan, 1897.

Casey, John, "Human Virtue and Human Nature," in Benthall, Jonathan, Ed. The Limits of Human Nature. London: Allen Lane, 1973.

————, Ed. Morality and Moral Reasoning: Five Essays in Ethics. London: Methuen, 1971.

Dahrendorf, Ralf. Homo Sociologicus. London: Routledge & Kegan Paul, 1973.

Freid, Charles: An Anatomy of Values: Problems of Personal and Social Choice. Cambridge: Harvard University Press, 1970.

Fromm, Erich. Man For Himself: An Inquiry into the Psychology of Ethics. New York: Rinehart, 1947.

Gallie, W. B., "Liberal Morality and Socialist Morality," in Laslett, Peter, Ed. Philosophy, Politics and Society. New York: Macmillan, 1956.

Hampshire, Stuart. Morality and Pessimism. Cambridge: Cambridge University Press, 1972.

Hare, R. M. Freedom and Reason. Oxford: Clarendon Press, 1962.

Kaufmann, Walter. Without Guilt and Justice: From Decidophobia to Autonomy. New York: Wyden, 1973.

Kelly, George Armstrong, "A Note on Alienation," Political Theory, 1 (February 1973), 46-50.

Kerner, George C. The Revolution in Ethical Theory. Oxford: Clarendon Press, 1966.

Lukes, Steven, "Alienation and Anomie," in Laslett, Peter, and W. G. Runciman, Eds. Philosophy, Politics and Society: Third Series. Oxford: Basil Blackwell, 1967.

MacIntyre, Alasdair, "Existentialism," in O'Connor, D. J., Ed. A Critical History of Western Philosophy. New York: The Free Press, 1964.

Mandelbaum, Maurice. The Phenomenology of Moral Experience. Glencoe, Ill.: The Free Press, 1955.

Maslow, Abraham H., Ed. New Knowledge in Human Values. New York: Harper & Row, 1959.

Nagel, Thomas. The Possibility of Altruism. Oxford: Clarendon Press, 1970.

Olafson, Frederick A. Principles and Persons: An Ethical Interpretation of Existentialism. Baltimore: The Johns Hopkins Press, 1967.

Pitkin, Hanna Fenichel. Wittgenstein and Justice: On the Significance of Ludwig Wittgenstein for Social and Political Thought. Berkeley: University of California Press, 1972.

Plamenatz, John, "Responsibility, Blame and Punishment," in Laslett, Peter, and W. G. Runciman, Eds. Philosophy, Politics and Society: Third Series. Oxford: Basil Blackwell, 1967.

Quinton, Anthony. Utilitarian Ethics. London: Macmillan, 1973.

Rokeach, Milton. Beliefs, Attitudes and Values. San Francisco: Jossey-Bass, 1968.

Spiegelberg, Herbert, " 'Accident of Birth': A Non-Utilitarian Motif in Mill's Philosophy," Journal of the History of Ideas, 22 (Oct.-Dec. 1961), 475-492.

Urmson, J. O. The Emotive Theory of Ethics. London: Hutchinson, 1970.

Warnock, G. J. The Object of Morality. London: Methuen, 1971.

Warnock, Mary. Existentialism. London: Oxford University Press, 1970.

*Political psychology and political ethics*

Acton, H. B. The Morals of Markets: An Ethical Exploration. London: Longman, 1971.

Apter, David E. Choice and the Politics of Allocation: A Developmental Theory. New Haven: Yale University Press, 1971.

Arrow, Kenneth J., "Gifts and Exchanges," Philosophy & Public Affairs, 1 (Summer 1972), 343-362.

Barry, Brian, "The Public Interest," in Quinton, Anthony, Ed. Political Philosophy. London: Oxford University Press, 1967.

Bay, Christian, "Needs, Wants, and Political Legitimacy," Canadian Journal of Political Science, 1 (September 1968), 241-260.

Benditt, Theodore M., "The Public Interest," Philosophy & Public Affairs, 2 (Spring 1973), 291-311.

Bluhm, William T., "Metaphysics, Ethics, and Political Science," The Review of Politics, 31 (January 1969), 66-87.

Dallmayr, Fred R., "Empirical Political Theory & the Image of Man," Polity, 2 (1970), 443-478.

De Crespigny, Anthony, and Alan Wertheimer, Eds. Contemporary Political Theory. New York: Atherton, 1970.

De George, Richard T. Soviet Ethics and Morality. Ann Arbor: University of Michigan Press, 1969.

———, Ed. Ethics and Society: Original Essays on Contemporary Moral Problems. Garden City, N.Y.: Doubleday, 1966.

Downie, R. S. Government Action and Morality: Some Principles and Concepts of Liberal-Democracy. London: Macmillan, 1964.

Feinberg, Joel, "The Forms and Limits of Utilitarianism," Philosophical Review, 76 (July 1967), 368-381.

Flathman, Richard E. The Public Interest: An Essay Concerning the Normative Discourse of Politics. New York: Wiley, 1966.

Ginsberg, Morris, "Moral Progress: A Reappraisal," in Ayer, A. J., Ed. The Humanist Outlook. London: Pemberton, 1968.

———. The Idea of Progress: A Reevaluation. London: Methuen, 1953.

Haring, Philip S. Political Morality: A General Theory of Politics. Cambridge: Schenkman, 1970.

Hart, H. L. A. Punishment and Responsibility: Essays in the Philosophy of Law. New York: Oxford University Press, 1968.

———. Law, Liberty and Morality. London: Oxford University Press, 1963.

Hayek, F. A. Law, Legislation and Liberty. Chicago: University of Chicago Press, 1973.

Hodgson, D. H. Consequences of Utilitarianism: A Study in Normative Ethics and Legal Theory. Oxford: Clarendon Press, 1967.

de Jouvenel, Bertrand. Sovereignty: An Inquiry into the Political Good. Trans. J. F. Huntington. Cambridge: Cambridge University Press, 1957.

Kamenka, Eugene. Marxism and Ethics. London: Macmillan, 1969.

Lasswell, Harold D., and Harlan Cleveland, Eds. The Ethic of Power:

The Interplay of Religion, Philosophy, and Politics. New York: Harper & Brothers, 1962.

Lukes, Steven. Individualism. Oxford: Basil Blackwell, 1973.

Lyons, David. Forms and Limits of Utilitarianism. Oxford: Clarendon Press, 1965.

MacIntyre, Alasdair. A Short History of Ethics: A History of Moral Philosophy from the Homeric Age to the Twentieth Century. New York: Macmillan, 1966.

Macpherson, C. B., "The Deceptive Task of Political Theory," The Cambridge Journal, 7 (June 1954), 560-568.

O'Malley, Joseph J., "History and Man's 'Nature' in Marx," in Avineri, Shlomo, Ed. Marx's Socialism. New York: Lieber-Atherton, 1973.

Oppenheim, Felix E. Moral Principles in Political Philosophy. New York: Random House, 1968.

Pennock, J. Roland, and John W. Chapman, Eds. Political and Legal Obligation: Nomos XII. New York: Atherton, 1970.

Rogow, Arnold A., "Psychiatry and Political Science: Some Reflections and Prospects," in Lipset, Seymour Martin, Ed. Politics and the Social Sciences. New York: Oxford University Press, 1969.

Sigmund, Paul E. Natural Law in Political Thought. Cambridge: Winthrop, 1971.

Smart, J. C., and Bernard Williams. Utilitarianism: For and Against. Cambridge: Cambridge University Press, 1973.

Sorel, Georges. Reflections on Violence. Trans. T. E. Hulme. London: Macmillan, 1961.

Strawson, P. F., "Social Morality and Individual Ideal," Philosophy, 36 (January 1961), 1-17.

Tucker, Robert C., "Stalin and the Uses of Psychology," in The Soviet Political Mind: Studies in Stalinism and Post-Stalin Change. New York: Frederick A. Praeger, 1963.

Walsh, W. H. Hegelian Ethics. London: Macmillan, 1969.

Walzer, Michael, "Political Action: The Problem of Dirty Hands," Philosophy & Public Affairs, 2 (Winter 1973), 160-180.

Weinstein, Michael. Philosophy, Theory, and Method in Contemporary Political Thought. Glenview, Ill.: Scott, Foresman, 1971.

Wilson, Bryan R. Ed. Rationality. Oxford: Basil Blackwell, 1970.


*Political ethics: liberty*

Ayer, A. J. Philosophy and Politics. Liverpool: Liverpool University Press, 1967.

Bay, Christian. The Structure of Freedom. Stanford: Stanford University Press, 1958.

Cranston, Maurice. Freedom: A New Analysis. London: Longmans, Green, 1953.

Dahrendorf, Ralf, "Liberty and Equality," in Essays on the Theory of Society. Stanford: Stanford University Press, 1968.

Friedman, Richard B., "A New Exploration of Mill's Essay 'On Liberty,' " Political Studies, 14 (October 1966), 281-304.

MacCallum, Jr., Gerald C., "Negative and Positive Freedom," in Laslett, Peter, and W. G. Runciman, Eds. Philosophy, Politics and Society: Fourth Series. Oxford: Basil Blackwell, 1972.

Milne, A. J. Freedom and Rights. London: Allen and Unwin, 1968.

Oppenheim, Felix E. Dimensions of Freedom: An Analysis. New York: St. Martin's Press, 1961.

Pennock, J. R., "Hobbes's Confusing 'Clarity'—The Case of 'Liberty,'" in Brown, K. C., Ed. Hobbes Studies. Oxford: Basil Blackwell, 1965.

Plamenatz, John, "In What Sense is Freedom a Western Idea?" in Current Law and Social Problems. Toronto: University of Toronto Press, 1960.

Polin, Raymond, "John Locke's Conception of Freedom," in Yolton, John W., Ed. John Locke: Problems and Perspectives: A Collection of New Essays. Cambridge: Cambridge University Press, 1969.

Weinstein, W. L., "The Concept of Liberty in Nineteenth Century English Political Thought," Political Studies, 13 (June 1965), 145-162.

*Political ethics: equality*

Bell, Daniel, "Meritocracy and Equality," The Public Interest, 29 (Fall 1972), 29-68.

Benn, Stanley I., "Egalitarianism and the Equal Consideration of Interests," in Pennock, J. Roland, and John W. Chapman, Eds. Equality: Nomos IX. New York: Atherton Press, 1967.

Dallmayr, Fred R., "Functionalism, Justice, and Equality," Ethics, 78 (October 1967), 1-16.

Lakoff, Sanford A. Equality in Political Philosophy. Cambridge: Harvard University Press, 1964.

Oppenheim, Felix E., "Egalitarianism as a Descriptive Concept," American Philosophical Quarterly, 7 (April 1970), 143-152.

Pennock, J. Roland, and John W. Chapman, Eds. Equality: Nomos IX. New York: Atherton Press, 1967.

Plamenatz, John P., "Equality of Opportunity," in Bryson, Lyman et al., Eds. Aspects of Human Equality. New York: Harper & Brothers, 1957.

Sen, Amartya. On Economic Inequality. Oxford: Clarendon Press, 1973.

Tawney, R. H. Equality. 4th Rev. Ed. London: Allen & Unwin, 1952.

Thompson, David. Equality. Cambridge: Cambridge University Press, 1949.

Williams, Bernard, "The Idea of Equality," in Problems of the Self: Philosophical Papers, 1956-1972. Cambridge: Cambridge University Press, 1973.

*Political ethics: justice*

Arrow, Kenneth J., "Rawls' Principle of Just Saving," The Swedish

Journal of Economics, 75 (December 1973).

Barry, Brian. The Liberal Theory of Justice. Oxford: Clarendon Press, 1973.

Bedau, Hugo A. Ed. Justice and Equality. Englewood Cliffs, N.J.: Prentice-Hall, 1971.

Brandt, Richard B., Ed. Social Justice. Englewood Cliffs, N.J.: Prentice-Hall, 1962.

Cahn, Edmund N. The Sense of Injustice: An Anthropocentric View of Law. New York: New York University Press, 1949.

Feinberg, Joel, "Justice, Fairness and Rationality," The Yale Law Journal, 81 (April 1972), 1004-1031.

Friedrich, Carl J., and John W. Chapman, Eds. Justice: Nomos VI. New York: Atherton Press, 1963.

Gewirth, Alan "Political Justice," in Brandt, Richard B., Ed. Social Justice. Englewood Cliffs, N.J.: Prentice-Hall, 1962.

Ginsberg, Morris. On Justice in Society. London: Heineman, 1965.

Hampshire, Stuart, "A New Philosophy of the Just Society," The New York Review (24 February 1972), 34-39.

Hobhouse, L. T. The Elements of Social Justice. London: Allen & Unwin, 1922.

Honoré, A. M., "Social Justice," in Summers, Robert S., Ed. Essays in Legal Philosophy. Oxford: Basil Blackwell, 1968.

Kelsen, Hans. What is Justice? Justice, Law, and Politics in the Mirror of Science. Berkeley: University of California Press, 1960.

Lessnoff, Michael, "John Rawls' Theory of Justice," Political Studies, 19 (March 1971), 63-80.

Nathan, N. M. L. The Concept of Justice. London: Macmillan, 1971.

Nozick, Robert, "Distributive Justice," Philosophy & Public Affairs, 3 (Fall 1973), 45-126.

———. Anarchy, State and Utopia. New York: Basic Books, 1974.

Olafson, Frederick A., Ed. Justice and Social Policy: A Collection of Essays. Englewood Cliffs, N.J.: Prentice-Hall, 1961.

Perelman, Ch. The Idea of Justice and the Problem of Argument. Trans. John Petrie. London: Routledge & Kegan Paul, 1963.

Raphael, D. D., "Justice," in Problems of Political Philosophy. London: Macmillan, 1970.

Rescher, Nicholas. Distributive Justice: A Constructive Critique of the Utilitarian Theory of Distribution. New York: Bobbs-Merrill, 1966.

Ross, Alf. On Law and Justice. Berkeley: University of California Press, 1959.

Runciman, W. G. Relative Deprivation and Social Justice: A Study of Attitudes to Social Inequality in Twentieth-century England. Berkeley: University of California Press, 1966.

Slote, Michael A., "Desert, Consent, and Justice," Philosophy & Public Affairs, 2 (Summer 1973), 323-347.

Stone, Julius. Human Law and Human Justice. Stanford: Stanford University Press, 1965.

Wood, Allen W., "The Marxian Critique of Justice," Philosophy &

Public Affairs, 1 (Spring 1972), 244-282.

*Marxian perspectives on political psychology and ethics*

Althusser, Louis, "Ideology and Ideological State Apparatuses," in Lenin and Philosophy: And Other Essays. Trans. Ben Brewster. London: NLB, 1971.

————. Pour Marx. Paris: Francois Maspero, 1966.

Fromm, Erich, Ed. Socialist Humanism: An International Symposium. Garden City, N.Y.: Doubleday, 1966.

Kolakowski, Leszek. The Alienation of Reason: A History of Positivist Thought. Trans. Norbert Guterman. Garden City, N.Y.: Doubleday, 1968.

Lukacs, Georges. Existentialisme ou Marxisme? Paris: Nagel, 1961.

Markovic, Mihailo. From Affluence to Praxis: Philosophy and Social Criticism. Ann Arbor: University of Michigan Press, 1974.

Mészáros, István. Ed. Aspects of History and Class Consciousness. London: Routledge & Kegan Paul, 1971.

————. Marx's Theory of Alienation. London: Merlin Press, 1970.

Petrović, Gajo. Marx in the Mid-Twentieth Century: A Yugoslav Philosopher Considers Karl Marx's Writings. Garden City, N.Y.: Doubleday, 1967.

Schaff, Adam, "Alienation and Social Action," Diogenes, 57 (Spring 1967), 64-82.

Sebag, Lucien. Marxisme et Structuralisme. Paris: Payot, 1964.

Stojanović, Svetozar. Between Ideals and Reality: A Critique of Socialism and its Future. Trans. Gerson S. Sher. New York: Oxford University Press, 1973.

*Political socialization*

Dawson, Richard E., and Kenneth Prewitt. Political Socialization. Boston: Little, Brown, 1969.

Di Palma, Giuseppe, and Herbert McClosky, "Personality and Comformity: The Learning of Political Attitudes," The American Political Science Review, 64 (December 1970), 1054-1073.

Greenstein, Fred I. Children and Politics. New Haven: Yale University Press, 1965.

Hess, R. O., and J. V. Torney. The Development of Political Attitudes in Children. Chicago: Aldine, 1967.

Hyman, H. Political Socialization. Glencoe, Ill.: The Free Press, 1959.

Langton, K. P. Political Socialization. New York: Oxford University Press, 1969.

*Anthropological and biological perspectives*

Ardrey, Robert. The Social Contract. New York: Atheneum, 1970.

Bailey, F. G., Ed. Gifts and Poison: The Politics of Reputation. New York: Schocken Books, 1971.

————. Stratagems and Spoils: A Social Anthropology of Politics. Oxford: Basil Blackwell, 1969.

Banton, Michael. Political Systems and the Distribution of Power. London: Tavistock, 1965.

Bidney, David, Ed. The Concept of Freedom in Anthropology. The Hague: Mouton, 1963.

Corning, Peter A., "The Biological Bases of Behavior and Some Implications for Political Science," World Politics, 23 (April 1971), 321-370.

Dobzhansky, Theodosius. Genetic Diversity and Human Equality. New York: Basic Books, 1973.

Geertz, Clifford, "The Impact of the Concept of Culture on the Concept of Man," in The Interpretation of Cultures. New York: Basic Books, 1973.

————, "Person, Time, and Conduct in Bali," in The Interpretation of Cultures. New York: Basic Books, 1973.

Golding, Martin P., "Ethical Issues in Biological Engineering," UCLA Law Review, 5 (February 1968), 443-479.

Leach, E. R. Political Systems of Highland Burma: A Study of Kachin Social Structure. Boston: Beacon Press, 1965.

————, "The Legitimacy of Solomon: Some Structural Aspects of Old Testament History," in Lane, Michael, Ed. Structuralism: A Reader. London: Jonathan Cape, 1970.

Lévi-Strauss, Claude. Structural Anthropology. Trans. Claire Jacobson and Brooke Grundfest Schoepf. Garden City, N.Y.: Doubleday, 1967.

————. The Savage Mind. Chicago: University of Chicago Press, 1966.

Lorenz, Konrad. On Aggression. New York: Harcourt, Brace and World, 1966.

Pfeiffer, John E. The Emergence of Man. New York: Harper & Row, 1969.

Tiger, Lionel, and Robin Fox. The Imperial Animal. New York: Dell, 1971.

Worsley, Peter M. The Trumpet Shall Sound: A Study of "Cargo Cults" in Melanesia. London: MacGibbon and Kee, 1957.

*Addendum*

Berlin, Isaiah. Vico and Herder: Two Studies in the History of Ideas. London: Hogarth Press, 1975.

Cooper, John. Reason and Human Good in Aristotle. Cambridge: Harvard University Press, 1975.

de Crespigny, Anthony, and Jeremy Cronin, Eds. Ideologies of Politics. London: Oxford University Press, 1975.

George, Alexander L., "Assessing Presidential Character," World Politics, 26 (January 1974), 234-282.

Grundy, Kenneth W., and Michael Weinstein. The Ideologies of Violence. Columbus: Charles E. Merrill, 1974.

Horton, Robin, and Ruth Finnegan, Eds. Modes of Thought. London: Faber & Faber, 1973.

Milgram, Stanley. Obedience to Authority: An Experimental View. New York: Harper & Row, 1974.

Oakeshott, Michael. On Human Conduct. Oxford: Clarendon Press, 1975.

Peters, R. S., Ed. Nature and Conduct. London: Macmillan, 1976.

Plamenatz, John. Karl Marx's Philosophy of Man. Oxford: Clarendon Press, 1975.

Pocock, J. G. A. The Machiavellian Moment: Florentine Political Thought and the Atlantic Republican Tradition. Princeton: Princeton University Press, 1975.

Renshon, Stanley Allen. Psychological Needs and Political Behavior: A Theory of Personality and Political Efficacy. New York: The Free Press, 1974.

Rubin, Vitaly A. Individual and State in Ancient China: Essays on Four Chinese Philosophers. Trans. Steven I. Levine. New York: Columbia University Press, 1976.

Shklar, Judith N. Freedom and Independence: A Study of the Political Ideas of Hegel's "Phenomenology of Mind." Cambridge: Cambridge University Press, 1976.

Taylor, Charles. Hegel. Cambridge: Cambridge University Press, 1976.

Unger, Roberto Mangabeira. Knowledge and Politics. New York: The Free Press, 1975.

Wilson, Bryan R. The Noble Savage: The Primitive Origins of Charisma and Its Contemporary Survival. Berkeley: University of California Press, 1976.

# INDEX

343